THE
ADMINISTRATIVE STATE
BEFORE
THE SUPREME COURT

Perspectives on the Nondelegation Doctrine

Edited by Peter J. Wallison and John Yoo

THE AEI PRESS

Publisher for the American Enterprise Institute
Washington, DC

Distributed by arrangement with the Rowman & Littlefield Publishing Group, 4501 Forbes Boulevard, Suite 200, Lanham, Maryland 20706. To order, call toll-free 1-800-462-6420 or 1-717-794-3800. For all other inquiries, please contact AEI Press, 1789 Massachusetts Avenue, NW, Washington, DC 20036, or call 1-202-862-5800.

ISNB-13: 978-0-8447-5042-2   Hardback
ISNB-13: 978-0-8447-5043-9   Paperback
ISNB-13: 978-0-8447-5044-6   eBook

American Enterprise Institute
1789 Massachusetts Avenue, NW
Washington, DC 20036
www.aei.org

Printed in the United States of America

Content

Introduction

PETER J. WALLISON

The separation of powers is a distinguishing feature of the US Constitution. Designed by the framers in 1787, it vests all legislative power in Congress, all executive and law enforcement power in the president and the executive branch, and all judicial power in the Supreme Court and inferior courts.

The framers chose this structure because they had seen, in other countries, that the people's liberties are in jeopardy if the same person or group can both make the laws and enforce them. In *Federalist* 47, for example, James Madison wrote, "There can be no liberty where the legislative and executive powers are united in the same person, or body of magistrates."[1]

The framers placed particular faith in the judiciary to intercede if one of the branches overstepped its bounds. In *Federalist* 78, Alexander Hamilton referred to the judiciary as the "Guardian of the Constitution" and noted that judges were given lifetime tenure in office so they would have the "fortitude" to take on the elected branches if one or both sought to exceed their constitutional authority.[2]

This idea, that the judiciary bears some responsibility for protecting and preserving the Constitution and its separation of powers, is what gave rise to the nondelegation doctrine (NDD), the focus of this book—a judge-made rule that is intended to prevent Congress from delegating or transferring its legislative responsibilities to the president or the agencies of the executive branch.

The Supreme Court last invoked the NDD in 1935, and many legal scholars have considered it outdated or defunct. Yet, in the recent decision in *Gundy v. United States*, all eight members of the Court participating in the case, including the four liberal members, made clear that the NDD is still a viable principle of constitutional jurisprudence. Indeed, a majority of the Court have since signaled that they are willing at least to consider a case in which the NDD would be fully revitalized and updated. If the Court formally moves in this direction, it could strengthen the separation of powers and fundamentally change the way the three branches of the US government function.

The chapters in this book—authored by legal scholars and students of the Constitution—offer ideas for how the Court might restore the NDD's role in the constitutional system or apply it appropriately in the future. A brief summary of each chapter is included at the end of the introduction.

The New Deal and the Change in the Role of Congress

The framers' constitutional design, which vested all legislative power in Congress, worked as intended for about 150 years, through the Civil War and World War I. During this period, control of Congress and the presidency passed from one party to the other, but Congress remained the most powerful of the three branches, retaining—and fully exercising—the sole power to make the laws.

Much changed, however, with the Great Depression and President Franklin D. Roosevelt's New Deal. As the economy failed to respond to his initial policies, Roosevelt asked for additional powers from Congress, most of which were to be exercised by executive branch agencies—not only the familiar cabinet agencies such as the Departments of Labor, Treasury, and Commerce but also many new independent agencies such as the National Labor Relations Board and the Federal Communications Commission (FCC). These agencies and the traditional cabinet departments were often given a new kind of wide-ranging authority—to act in the "public interest" or make sure that prices were "fair and reasonable."

Open-ended powers like these, in the hands of unelected officials, raised questions about whether Congress was actually making the laws or simply delegating its legislative authority to unelected officials in the executive branch. If so, it would amount to a major change in the structure of the constitutional system by placing in the same hands the power to both make and enforce the laws.

Although the framers were concerned that one of the elected branches would reach for excessive power, they did not foresee that the most troubling problem—arising first in the New Deal—would be the willingness of Congress to hand over to the president and the executive branch a great deal of its discretionary authority, much of which looked to be the legislative authority that the Constitution had vested solely in Congress. Congress would do this for many reasons—often when the same political party controlled both the presidency and Congress and to avoid difficult and controversial policy decisions that could jeopardize their chances for reelection.

Instead of passing laws that embodied these controversial decisions, members of Congress found it easier simply to create goals for the agencies. If the public demanded cleaner air, for example, it was far easier for Congress to authorize the Environmental Protection Agency (EPA) to meet that goal rather than to set rules that required the plant closings or expensive technical retrofits that might be necessary. By merely stating a goal for the agency, Congress could pass these difficult decisions to the EPA. If constituents complained about the loss of jobs because of a power plant's closing, members of Congress could easily deflect responsibility by blaming the EPA, over which they had no control.

In other words, Congress has been willing to sell its own birthright—its unique constitutional power to make the laws—to avoid the controversies associated with its responsibilities. As John Hart Ely wrote in 1981, "By refusing to legislate our legislators are escaping the sort of accountability that is crucial to the intelligible functioning of a democratic republic."[3]

One of the principal reasons for revitalizing the NDD is that it would force Congress to do its job—to make the difficult policy decisions for the country that a legislature is supposed to make, instead of passing these decisions to the administrative agencies of the executive branch.

Chevron and Its Relation to the NDD

No discussion of the prospects for the NDD and its potential role in limiting the authority of administrative agencies would be complete without considering the Supreme Court's evolving view of the 1984 case *Chevron U.S.A. v. Natural Resources Defense Council.*[4] In *Chevron*, the Court directed lower courts, where a statute's terms were ambiguous, to defer to the administrative agency's views about the scope of its powers—if the agency's view was "reasonable." While *Chevron* was not a case about the delegation of legislative authority, it had the same effect as a delegation—expanding the authority that Congress had already given to administrative agencies.

Chevron removed the courts even further from a role in assessing what authority Congress had given to the agencies, empowered agencies to move beyond their specific statutory authorities, and seemed to ignore the language of the 1946 Administrative Procedure Act (APA), which stated that "the reviewing court shall . . . interpret constitutional and statutory provisions, and determine the meaning or applicability of the terms of any agency action."[5] In other words, *Chevron*—along with delegations of legislative authority—enhanced the power of administrative agencies by allowing them to expand their authority beyond what Congress might have intended.

Chevron, then, rapidly became one of the most frequently cited Supreme Court decisions. As more and more regulations emerged from a growing number of administrative agencies, it was becoming clear that the agencies presented a threat not only to the separation of powers but also to democracy itself. One study showed that at least as early as 1993, executive branch agencies were issuing more than 3,000 rules and regulations *every year*, and they issued more than 101,000 between 1993 and 2018.[6] The sheer number of these rules dwarfed the number of laws that Congress might pass; in 2017, for example, the agencies issued 3,281 rules, but Congress enacted only 97 laws.[7] Clearly, *Chevron* had made it even easier for executive branch agencies—now often called the "administrative state"—to make the rules that should, in the US constitutional system, be made by the legislature and not unelected officials.

Thus, the constitutional problems associated with Congress delegating significant open-ended powers to the executive branch were compounded by the willingness of the Supreme Court and lower courts—in and after *Chevron*—to allow administrative agencies to interpret their authorities broadly.

The Supreme Court's restoration of the NDD, if it occurs, would not directly affect *Chevron* jurisprudence. The NDD applies only to Congress and whether Congress is delegating its legislative authority to the executive branch. *Chevron*, on the other hand, is a judge-made rule and will not be modified in any way if the Supreme Court ultimately restores the NDD. Accordingly, to make the NDD's restoration fully effective, the additional authority granted to administrative agencies under *Chevron* would have to be substantially modified or withdrawn by the Supreme Court through a change in how *Chevron* is applied.

None of the chapters in this book deal with the *Chevron* issue. However, a change in the Court's composition over recent years, as discussed below, offers the possibility that the Court is moving to limit *Chevron*'s scope.

What Is Legislative Authority?

Returning, then, to the NDD, the key question for the judiciary is how to define the legislative authority that may be exercised only by Congress, based solely on what the framers intended when they wrote in Article I of the Constitution: "All legislative powers herein granted shall be vested in a Congress of the United States." All the chapters in this volume address, in one way or another, this issue.

The Supreme Court first confronted the problem of defining legislative authority in 1825. In a case that year, *Wayman v. Southard*,[8] the Court was asked whether Congress could delegate to the judiciary the authority to adopt rules for processing certain cases. Chief Justice John Marshall concluded that the Constitution required only that Congress make the "important decisions" and could delegate to others those decisions that were minor or "of lesser interest."

> The line has not been exactly drawn which separates *those important subjects* which must be *entirely regulated by the legislature itself* from those of *less interest* in which a general provision may be made and power given to those who are to act under such general provisions to fill up the details.[9] (Emphasis added.)

Thus, Chief Justice Marshall laid out a viable—if difficult—standard for determining the difference between legislation, which is the exclusive province of Congress, and matters of "less interest," which can be handled by another branch in filling in the details. As Marshall suggested, this is not a solution; it is a guideline. It moves the inquiry from what is "legislation" to what is an "important" decision implicit in congressional legislation—something a court can decide.

Following Marshall's *Wayman* decision, several cases that reached the Supreme Court raised the issue of whether Congress had delegated its legislative authority to the president or some lesser officer or agency of the executive branch. In each case, the Court concluded that an unconstitutional delegation had not occurred.

In 1928, in *J. W. Hampton Jr. & Co. v. United States*,[10] the Court articulated a standard that differed from Marshall's but was so inherently ambiguous that it lent itself to dismissing challenges based on alleged delegations of legislative authority. *J. W. Hampton* was a tariff case, in which the president was authorized to increase an existing tariff rate to "equalize the . . . costs of production in the United States and the principal competing country."[11] In finding that no delegation had occurred, the Court relied on the idea that the law had established a guideline that limited the scope of the president's action: "If Congress shall lay down by legislative act an *intelligible principle* to which the person or body authorized to fix such rates is directed to conform, such legislative action is not a forbidden delegation of legislative power."[12] (Emphasis added.)

At first, *J. W. Hampton* had no effect on the Supreme Court's view of the NDD. Seven years later, for example, in 1935, two cases arose out of Depression-era legislation that seemed to delegate legislative power, and a unanimous Supreme Court struck them down. In neither case did the Court cite *J. W. Hampton*. The first was *Panama Refining Company v. Ryan*,[13] in which the president had been authorized under the National Industrial Recovery Act (NIRA) to prohibit the interstate transportation of petroleum products in certain circumstances. An opinion written by Chief Justice Charles Evans Hughes—speaking for a unanimous Court (which included other distinguished jurists such as Benjamin Cardozo and Louis Brandeis)—began its analysis by pointing out the lack of standards in the power Congress had given to the president.

> [It] does not state whether or in what circumstances or under
> what conditions the President is to prohibit the transportation
> of the amount of petroleum or petroleum products produced

in excess of the state's permission. It establishes no criteria to govern the President's course. It does not require any finding by the President as a condition of his action. The Congress . . . thus declares no *policy* as to the transportation of the excess production. So far as this section is concerned, it gives to the President an unlimited authority to determine the policy and to lay down the prohibition, or not to lay it down, as he may see fit.[14] (Emphasis added.)

Then the Court concluded with this:

From the beginning of the government, the Congress has conferred upon executive officers the power to make regulations. . . . Such regulations become, indeed, binding rules of conduct, but they are valid only as subordinate rules and when found to be within the framework of the *policy* which the Legislature has sufficiently defined.[15] (Emphasis added.)

This was an analysis very much in the mold initially established by Chief Justice Marshall in *Wayman*. To avoid a finding of delegation, Congress must make a *policy* decision that directs and *limits* the range of action of the president or an administrative agency in the executive branch; a policy decision would be an *important* decision in Marshall's terms and thus one that Congress had to make.

The second case is the much more famous *A. L. A. Schechter Poultry Corp. v. United States*.[16] In this case, also arising under the NIRA, Congress had authorized private industry groups to establish rules of "fair competition" for commercial activities. These would then be binding on the entire industry by operation of law after the president's approval. Again, in another opinion by Chief Justice Hughes, the Court unanimously struck down the NIRA as an unconstitutional delegation of legislative power, because Congress had enacted no standards and made no policy decisions that were intended to guide the president's decisions.

Section 3 of the Recovery Act is without precedent. It supplies no standards for any trade, industry or activity. It does not undertake to prescribe rules of conduct to be applied to particular states of fact determined by appropriate administrative procedure. Instead of prescribing rules of conduct, it authorizes the making of codes to prescribe them. *For that legislative undertaking, § 3 sets up no standards,* aside from the statement of the general aims of rehabilitation, correction and expansion described in section one. In view of the scope of that broad declaration, and of the nature of the few restrictions that are imposed, *the discretion of the President in approving or prescribing codes, and thus enacting laws for the government of trade and industry throughout the country, is virtually unfettered.* We think that the code-making authority thus conferred is an unconstitutional delegation of legislative power.[17] (Emphasis added.)

As noted earlier, Hamilton clearly recognized that the judiciary would be on treacherous ground if—as the "Guardian of the Constitution"—it challenged one of the elected branches. That's why, he argued in *Federalist* 78, the framers provided that judges would have appointments for life, giving them the "fortitude" to stand up to the more powerful president and Congress.

Hamilton was remarkably prescient. In the 1936 election, President Roosevelt and the Democratic Party won a huge victory at the polls, with Democratic supermajorities in both the House and Senate. When Congress reconvened in 1937, Roosevelt retaliated against the Court, proposing that it be expanded to 16 members and giving him the opportunity to appoint seven new justices who would be more in sympathy with the New Deal.

Because the Constitution does not specify the number of Supreme Court justices and Congress was likely to comply with Roosevelt's demand, this was a very real threat to the Court's independence—a threat the framers had not anticipated. Although public opposition to what was called "court-packing" ultimately defeated the plan, the Supreme Court recognized the gravity of the threat. On March 29, 1937, in two cases in which the chief justice again wrote the majority opinions, the Court upheld two statutes that would likely have been challenged as unconstitutional under the Court's previous jurisprudence. As former Chief Justice William Rehnquist described it,

In the case of *Jones & Laughlin v. NLRB*, which upheld the constitutionality of the Wagner Act, the Court markedly expanded
upon its previous definitions of the scope of congressional
authority to regulate commerce among the states. In *West Coast
Hotel v. Parrish*, which upheld the state minimum-wage law, the
Court all but abandoned its previous insistence that freedom of
contract was protected by the Due Process Clause.[18]

In other words, after the threat of court-packing, the Court changed its
policy direction. Also, the nine justices of the 1935 Court began to retire
and were gradually replaced by President Roosevelt between 1937 and 1941.
The new Court was made up of men who had come of age during what has
become known as the Progressive Era between 1880 and 1920 and were
willing to support the development of a powerful executive branch. Most
of Roosevelt's new agencies were approved by this Court, and even after
the New Deal, precedents such as *Chevron* were set in place that assured
the continued growth in the power of administrative agencies.

J. W. Hampton's Intelligible Principle Returns

In addition, between 1935 and 2018, the Court dismissed all claims that
Congress had violated the NDD by using the language of *J. W. Hampton*,
which held that a delegation of legislative authority would not be found
if Congress had laid down an adequate "intelligible principle" to guide
the agency involved. This enabled the Court to avoid the difficulty of
defining what the framers meant by vesting "legislative powers" solely
in Congress.

For example, in 2001, the Supreme Court decided *Whitman v. American Trucking Associations*, a case that challenged the Clean Air Act as an
unconstitutional delegation of legislative authority. Justice Antonin Scalia, writing for the Court, stated that Congress had provided an adequate
"intelligible principle" when it directed the EPA to "set air quality standards
at a level that is 'requisite'—that is, not lower or higher than is necessary—
to protect the public health with an adequate margin of safety."[19] In effect,
the "intelligible principle" in this case was the single word "requisite." It is

hard to see how a court could see this as a restriction on the power Congress had granted to the EPA.

The Supreme Court's use of the intelligible principle in the *Whitman* decision seemed to signal the end of its interest in protecting the separation of powers by preventing Congress' delegation of legislative authority. However, *Whitman* drew a concurring opinion from Justice Clarence Thomas, who expressed doubt that the intelligible-principle test effectively addressed the delegation of legislative authority. Thomas wrote:

> I am not convinced that the intelligible principle doctrine serves to prevent all cessions of legislative power. I believe that there are cases in which the principle is intelligible and yet the significance of the delegated decision is simply too great for the decision to be called anything other than "legislative."
>
> As it is, none of the parties to this case has examined the text of the Constitution or asked us to reconsider our precedents on cessions of legislative power. On a future day, however, I would be willing to address the question whether our delegation jurisprudence has strayed too far from our Founders' understanding of separation of powers.[20]

Changes in the Composition of the Court Revive Interest in Limiting Administrative Power

That future day was a long time in coming, as the members of the Supreme Court bar recognized the seeming futility of arguing that a statute or an administrative overreach was the result of an unconstitutional delegation of legislative authority. However, by 2013, it was becoming apparent that some members of the Supreme Court were concerned that *Chevron* was reducing the judiciary's role in determining how much authority Congress had provided to administrative agencies.

The case that brought this dispute to a head was *City of Arlington v. FCC*. Justice Scalia, always a strong supporter of *Chevron*, wrote the majority opinion supporting the FCC's decision on *Chevron* grounds, but Chief Justice John Roberts filed a dissent in which Justices Anthony Kennedy and

Samuel Alito joined. The Roberts dissent began with a reference to Madison's famous statement that "the 'accumulation of all powers, legislative, executive, and judiciary, in the same hands, . . . may justly be pronounced the very definition of tyranny.'"[21] Roberts then stated that before a court can give *Chevron* deference to an agency's interpretation of its own statutory authority, it must decide whether Congress "has in fact delegated to the agency lawmaking power over the ambiguity [in the agency's statutory authority] at issue,"[22] and, the chief justice continued, "We do not leave it to the agency to decide when it is in charge."[23]

This was a direct challenge to the idea that courts should defer to the agency's view of its own statutory authority, and it prefigures a more aggressive view on the Court about the NDD. If the Court were to find that Congress had not delegated "lawmaking authority" to the agency, *Chevron* would be unavailable, and whether Congress had delegated lawmaking authority to the agency was precisely the question the NDD raised.

Significantly, the chief justice seemed to go beyond *Chevron* to Hamilton's concept that the judiciary is the "guardian of the Constitution" and responsible for protecting the separation of powers itself.

> *Chevron* importantly guards against the Judiciary arrogating to itself policymaking properly left, under the separation of powers, to the Executive. But there is another concern at play, no less firmly rooted in our constitutional structure. *That is the obligation of the Judiciary not only to confine itself to its proper role, but to ensure that the other branches do so as well.*[24] (Emphasis added.)

The breach between Scalia and Roberts on the scope of *Chevron* was closed in 2015, when Scalia joined a unanimous decision in *Perez v. Mortgage Bankers Association*. In a remarkable turnabout, given his history of strong support for *Chevron*, Scalia agreed that the APA had been consistently ignored in the Court's *Chevron* jurisprudence.

> Heedless of the original design of the APA, we have developed an elaborate law of deference to agencies' interpretations of statutes and regulations. Never mentioning [the APA's] directive that the "reviewing court . . . interpret . . . statutory provisions,"

we have held that *agencies* may authoritatively resolve ambiguities in statutes [citing *Chevron*].[25] (Emphasis in original.)

The future of *Chevron* now looks uncertain. Indeed, since 2015, two new justices who have expressed doubt about *Chevron*—Neil Gorsuch and Brett Kavanaugh—have joined the Court. They join the three justices who dissented in *City of Arlington* on the question of *Chevron*'s scope. A third new justice, Amy Coney Barrett, with an originalist and textualist background, has also joined the Court since *City of Arlington* was decided.

With Chief Justice Roberts and Justices Alito and Thomas already expressing doubt about *Chevron*, it looks likely to be seriously challenged when an appropriate case reaches the Court. If so, that is one of the two props supporting enhanced administrative power—the other being the somewhat profligate use of the intelligible-principle test to address questions about the delegation of legislative authority, discussed below.

Gundy v. United States—a Missed Opportunity

On March 5, 2018, the Court issued a writ of certiorari to the Second Circuit Court of Appeals, seeking to review the nondelegation claim—and *only* the nondelegation claim—of Herman Gundy in *Gundy v. United States*. Gundy had been convicted as a sex offender under state law and could be required by the attorney general (AG) under the new federal Sex Offender Registration and Notification Act (SORNA) to register as a sex offender with the Department of Justice. Gundy argued that SORNA gave the AG the discretionary authority to require the registration of some, but not all, previous state law offenders. This discretion, he argued, was legislative in nature—in effect, the AG had been delegated the authority to write the law and who would be subject to it—and thus had violated the NDD.

Oral argument before the Supreme Court occurred on October 2, 2018, before a bench of eight justices. Justice Kavanaugh, who had not yet been confirmed by the Senate, could not participate. He had been nominated by President Donald Trump on July 9, 2018, and after a lengthy set of hearings, he was confirmed on October 6.

The Court's decision came down on June 20, 2019. Justice Elena Kagan wrote the plurality opinion (i.e., a non-majority opinion) for Justices Ruth Bader Ginsburg, Stephen Breyer, and Sonia Sotomayor, which held that no violation of the NDD had occurred because the AG did not have sufficient discretion under SORNA to make his *Gundy* decision a legislative act. However, and importantly, Justice Kagan did not question whether the NDD was still viable constitutional law. The first sentence of her plurality opinion is: "The nondelegation doctrine bars Congress from transferring its legislative power to another branch of Government."[26] Thereafter, she noted it was an "easy" case because the Court plurality found there was no delegation of legislative authority where Congress lays down an intelligible principle for the administrative agency to follow, which had occurred in *Gundy*. As Justice Kagan read the statute, the AG had not been given the discretionary authority Gundy had alleged.

Chief Justice Roberts and Justice Thomas joined in a dissenting opinion by Justice Gorsuch, discussed below. Justice Alito concurred with the plurality without joining the Kagan opinion but stated, "If a majority of this Court were willing to reconsider the approach we have taken for the past 84 years [that is, since 1935 and the decisions in *Panama Refining* and *A. L. A. Schechter Poultry*], I would support that effort,"[27] indicating he was willing to consider applying the NDD without using the highly flexible intelligible-principle test.

Several months later, in a different case, Justice Kavanaugh stated that he also believed the Court should reconsider the NDD in an appropriate case. Because the delay in confirming Kavanaugh had deprived the Court of a full bench of nine justices to hear *Gundy*, an opportunity to restore the NDD was missed, but five justices had now expressed interest in considering a revival of the NDD.

Nevertheless, those on the Court who want to consider the NDD's applicability will now have to wait for an appropriate case to appear in the federal court system. Oddly, despite five justices' interest in the subject, two cases raising the NDD issue after *Gundy* were denied certiorari by the Court, both without comment.

Still, we can learn a lot from the Gorsuch dissent in *Gundy*, which argued for the restoration of the NDD in light of the *Gundy* facts. The principal issue in the case was whether Congress had given the AG discretion on how to handle the cases of those sex offenders who, like Gundy, had been convicted under state law and now could be required by the AG to register under the new federal statute. If so, this fact would have strengthened the case for invoking the NDD. The AG, in effect, would have had the power, with respect to each state offender, to both create a law and apply it.

Despite evidence that the AG had been given—and indeed used—such power, the plurality opinion by Justice Kagan argued, to the satisfaction of the three other liberal justices, that SORNA did not confer sufficient discretion on the AG to create a delegation of legislative authority.

Justice Gorsuch's dissent went well beyond the basic question of the AG's discretion, beginning his argument with Madison's key point in *Federalist* 47: "There can be no liberty where the legislative and executive powers are united in the same person, or body of magistrates." Gorsuch then continued:

> The framers knew, too, that the job of keeping the legislative power confined to the legislative branch couldn't be trusted to self-policing by Congress; often enough, legislators will face rational incentives to pass problems to the executive branch. . . . So when a case or controversy comes within the judicial competence, the Constitution does not permit judges to look the other way; we must call foul when the constitutional lines are crossed. Indeed, the framers afforded us independence from the political branches in large part to encourage exactly this kind of "fortitude . . . to do [our] duty as faithful guardians of the Constitution."
>
> Accepting, then, that we have an obligation to decide whether Congress has unconstitutionally divested itself of its legislative responsibilities, the question follows: What's the test?[28]

Importantly, Gorsuch's answer to this question was *not* the intelligible-principle test.

We sometimes chide people for treating judicial opinions as if they were statutes, divorcing a passing comment from its context, ignoring all that came before and after, and treating an isolated phrase as if it were controlling. But that seems to be exactly what happened here. For two decades, no one thought to invoke the "intelligible principle" comment as a basis to uphold a statute that would have failed more traditional separation-of-powers tests. In fact, the phrase sat more or less silently entombed until the late 1940s. Only then did lawyers begin digging it up in earnest and arguing to this Court that it had somehow displaced (*sub silentio* of course) all prior teachings in this area.

This mutated version of the "intelligible principle" remark has no basis in the original meaning of the Constitution, in history, or even in the decision from which it was plucked. . . . It has been abused to permit delegations of legislative power that on any other conceivable account should be held unconstitutional.[29]

In the end, Justice Gorsuch agrees that the intelligible principle might be adequate to determine whether a statute has conformed to constitutional requirements, but only if it meets the same standards as the Court used in 1935.

Does the statute assign to the executive only the responsibility to make factual findings? Does it set forth the facts that the executive must consider and the criteria against which to measure them? And most importantly, did Congress, and not the Executive Branch, make the policy judgments? Only then can we fairly say that a statute contains the kind of intelligible principle the Constitution demands.[30]

Essays by Our Scholars on the NDD

The chapters in this volume address a number of questions associated with the NDD. They outline how the Court could make a solid case for the NDD, where Chief Justice Marshall derived his distinction between "important matters" and "matters of less interest," how the states have handled nondelegation issues under state constitutions, and what issues and government decisions may be outside the ambit of the NDD. As editors, John Yoo and I simply asked a distinguished group of legal scholars to discuss how the NDD should be interpreted or implemented. What we got is a diverse and thought-provoking collection of essays, which we hope will be useful for the judiciary, the bar, Congress, and the public.

Judge Douglas H. Ginsburg, senior United States circuit judge of the US Court of Appeals for the District of Columbia Circuit and professor of law at the Antonin Scalia Law School, George Mason University, argues that reviving the NDD is likely to require Congress to take more responsibility for policy decisions in legislation, and both Congress and administrative agencies have the ability to adjust to the change. There are many reasons to believe that the NDD, if restored, will not seriously endanger existing regulations.

Todd Gaziano and Ethan Blevins of the Pacific Legal Foundation note that vague statutes and overly broad delegation are similar and should be similarly treated by the courts. The Supreme Court's development of an effective void-for-vagueness standard in criminal cases shows that the Court will not have difficulty formulating and applying the NDD in a similar case-by-case setting.

Mark Chenoweth and Richard Samp of the New Civil Liberties Alliance believe the Supreme Court's 1944 decision in *Yakus v. United States* demonstrates how the judiciary can establish and enforce standards for determining whether Congress has delegated its exclusive legislative power. Under *Yakus*, a statute would be valid only if it provides standards by which the *judiciary* can determine "whether the will of Congress has been obeyed."

Gary Lawson, Phillip S. Beck Professor of Law at Boston University School of Law, believes that Marshall's 1825 decision in *Wayman*, which laid the foundation for determining what must be done by Congress ("an important subject") and what can be left to an administrative agency (a matter of "lesser interest"), was based on how private agency contracts were interpreted under common law. Accordingly, the contours of a workable and legally grounded constitutional NDD can be drawn from a careful study of this private-law background.

Jonathan H. Adler, Johan Verheij Memorial Professor of Law at the Case Western Reserve University School of Law, writes that to enhance democratic governance, an NDD must assure that authority granted to an administrative agency is not interpreted to extend beyond subjects that Congress could have had in mind at the time the authorizing legislation was enacted.

Michael B. Rappaport, Hugh and Hazel Darling Foundation Professor of Law at the University of San Diego School of Law, argues that in implementing the NDD, an originalist court should recognize two tiers—a lenient and a strict tier. In the strict tier, which encompasses legislation affecting private rights, the courts should invalidate any legislation that authorizes an administrative agency to make policy decisions. Agencies should be permitted only to determine the meaning of the law they are administering and find the facts necessary to carry it out. In the lenient tier, which would apply to such things as foreign and military affairs and the management of government property, Congress can delegate policy authority to the executive.

John Harrison, James Madison Distinguished Professor of Law at the University of Virginia School of Law, notes that where the government owns the property and licenses its use by the public—as is true for navigable rivers, air, water, and the airwaves—the executive is acting as an owner of the property on behalf of the public. In these cases, Congress may give the executive broader discretion than is true when the government is affecting private rights. An intelligible principle may be a safe harbor in these cases.

Saikrishna Bangalore Prakash, James Monroe Distinguished Professor of Law at the University of Virginia School of Law, contends that while the Supreme Court's restoration of the NDD will be unsettling for the legal system, it is unlikely to be disruptive; each branch has tools that will help it manage the transition and prevent a fundamental derangement of existing administrative rules and regulations.

Joseph Postell, associate professor of political science at Hillsdale College, examines state court interpretations of the NDD under state constitutions, which also have a constitutional separation of powers.

Finally, *David Schoenbrod,* Trustee Professor of Law at the New York Law School, contends that the intelligible-principle test is not judicially manageable. Instead, the Supreme Court should specifically approve all new agency regulations deemed "significant" by the Office of Management and Budget's Office of Information and Regulatory Affairs.

Notes

1. *Federalist,* no. 47 (James Madison).

2. This and other issues associated with the separation of powers and the growth of the administrative state are covered in detail in Peter J. Wallison, *Judicial Fortitude: The Last Chance to Rein in the Administrative State* (New York: Encounter Books, 2018).

3. John Hart Ely, *Democracy and Distrust: A Theory of Judicial Review* (Cambridge, MA: Harvard University Press, 1980): 132.

4. *Chevron U.S.A. v. Natural Resources Defense Council,* 467 US 837, 843 (1984).

5. Administrative Procedure Act, Pub. L. No. 79-404, § 10(e).

6. Clyde Wayne Crews Jr., *Ten Thousand Commandments: An Annual Snapshot of the Federal Regulatory State: 2018 Edition,* Competitive Enterprise Institute, April 18, 2018, https://cei.org/sites/default/files/Ten_Thousand_Commandments_2018.pdf.

7. Crews Jr., *Ten Thousand Commandments,* 4.

8. *Wayman v. Southard,* 23 US (10 Wheat.) 1, 45 (1825).

9. *Wayman,* 23 US at 42–45.

10. *J. W. Hampton Jr. & Co. v. United States,* 276 US 394 (1928).

11. *J. W. Hampton,* 276 US at 401.

12. *J. W. Hampton,* 276 US at 409.

13. *Panama Refining Company v. Ryan,* 293 US 388 (1935).

14. *Panama Refining,* 293 US at 415.

15. *Panama Refining,* 293 US at 428–29.

16. *A. L. A. Schechter Poultry Corp. v. United States,* 295 US 495 (1935).

17. *A. L. A. Schechter Poultry,* 295 US at 541–42.

18. William H. Rehnquist, *The Supreme Court: How It Was, How It Is* (New York: William Morrow & Co., 1987), 229.

19. *Whitman v. American Trucking Associations,* 531 US 457 (2001).

20. *Whitman,* 531 US at 487.

21. *City of Arlington v. FCC,* 569 US 312 (2013).

22. *City of Arlington,* 569 US at 317.

23. *City of Arlington,* 569 US at 327.

24. *City of Arlington*, 569 US at 290.

25. *Perez v. Mortgage Bankers Association*, 575 US 92 (2014).

26. *Gundy v. United States*, 139 S. Ct. 2116 (2019) (slip op.).

27. *Gundy*, 139 S. Ct. 2116.

28. *Gundy*, 139 S. Ct. 2116 (Gorsuch, J., dissenting).

29. *Gundy*, 139 S. Ct. 2116 (Gorsuch, J., dissenting).

30. *Gundy*, 139 S. Ct. 2116 (Gorsuch, J., dissenting).

Reviving the Nondelegation Principle in the US Constitution

DOUGLAS H. GINSBURG

The separation of powers was among the most important features of the Framers' Constitution. Whereas the political theorists of the past had extolled the separation of the legislative and executive branches, lest too much power be wielded by one at the inevitable expense of the other, the Framers went further and separated the judicial function from the legislative. An independent judiciary would be able to administer justice, as the oath says, "without respect to persons"[1] and to check the two political branches should they exceed their respective powers.

The importance of this design is reflected in the first words of Articles I, II, and III, which "vest" the legislative, executive, and judicial "powers," respectively, in the Congress, the President, and the Supreme Court (and such inferior courts as the Congress may establish).

From the outset of the Republic, it was apparent to all that the Executive, charged with enforcing the laws enacted by the Congress, would require a degree of discretion in going about that task. The Congress simply could not anticipate and resolve all the questions the Executive would have to address in order faithfully to execute the laws the Congress had enacted. If the Congress left too much discretion to the Executive, however, then it might plausibly be claimed that it had delegated its legislative power to the other branch, in contravention of the separation of powers generally and of the vesting clauses in particular.

This was the claim that came before the Supreme Court in *Wayman v. Southard* in 1825, which concerned a provision of the law establishing the federal courts that authorized the Supreme Court to regulate "matters of practice" before the courts.[2] Chief Justice John Marshall began his analysis by noting, "It will not be contended that Congress can delegate to the courts or to any other tribunals powers which are strictly and exclusively legislative."[3] As for powers less clearly vested in the Congress, he noted,

> The line has not been exactly drawn which separates those important subjects which must be entirely regulated by the legislature itself from those of less interest in which a general provision may be made and power given to those who are to act under such general provisions to fill up the details.[4]

Others in this volume trace Chief Justice Marshall's distinction through the many subsequent cases challenging a congressional delegation up to the current standard applied by the Court—namely, whether the Congress has given the Executive (or the Judiciary, as the case may be) an "intelligible principle" to guide its discretion.[5] For the present purpose, it is enough to point out that the Court drained all meaning from this phrase when it held an agency's mandate to regulate in the "public interest" was sufficient guidance.[6] Indeed, it has been 85 years since the Court held a congressional delegation unconstitutional,[7] during which time the Congress has gotten into the habit of delegating vast powers to executive agencies, specifying only a list of general goals, such as providing for outdoor recreation and preserving nature, to which they should be put.[8] The Congress rarely specifies how the Executive is to resolve tension among the goals it sets out.

Legislators have clear incentives for delegating to others what Chief Justice Marshall called "important subjects."[9] Addressing them in legislation could require many hours of tedious work and might require compromises that would be difficult to explain to constituents or to interest groups that contributed to a member's election campaign. Better to enshrine a list of worthy goals in legislation and leave it to executive agency officials to make the decisions that impose burdens upon regulated parties.

These incentives are very strong; they will be mitigated, but they will not go away altogether merely because the Court reinvigorates the nondelegation doctrine and holds some delegations unconstitutional. That is not to say that nothing would change in the operation of the administrative state. The Congress likely will start to assume more responsibility for making policy decisions in its statutes, if only to avoid the opprobrium of the courts repeatedly saying it violated the Constitution. More certainly, a great deal will change in the relationships among the executive agencies and their congressional masters as the polity shifts away from bureaucratic back toward representative government. Because increased regulation is often responsive to public demand, however, do not expect a significant diminution in the scale or scope of the federal government.

What's the Test?

In recent years, several members of the Supreme Court have expressed misgivings about the demise of the nondelegation doctrine. Aggregating sentiments expressed by different justices in different cases, a majority now appears willing to reconsider the edentulous standard for upholding a delegation in a case that cleanly and unavoidably presents the issue. In *Gundy v. United States*, decided in 2019 by a Court of eight (for Justice Brett Kavanaugh did not participate), a plurality of four justices was willing to interpret a statutory delegation to the point of substantially revising it in such a way that it could be upheld.[10] Indeed, the statute as revised by the plurality was so highly prescriptive that Justice Elena Kagan could say with some justification that "if [this statute's] delegation is unconstitutional, then most of Government is unconstitutional."[11] Justice Samuel Alito concurred in the judgment but not the opinion, observing that the statute contains "a discernable standard that is adequate under the approach this Court has taken for many years."[12] More important, however, he also said, "If a majority of this Court were willing to reconsider the approach we have taken for the past 84 years, I would support that effort."[13] Because three justices dissented, through an opinion by Justice Neil Gorsuch, and Justice Kavanaugh has since expressed his openness to reconsidering the Court's prevailing approach, there appears to be a majority of at least five to do so.[14]

Justice Gorsuch's 33-page dissenting opinion, joined by Chief Justice John Roberts and Justice Clarence Thomas, lays out in detail an alternative approach to delegations that is grounded squarely upon the separation of powers and the reasons that underlay the Framers' design for government. Here are some key excerpts on that subject.

When it came to the legislative power, the framers understood it to mean the power to adopt generally applicable rules of conduct governing future actions by private persons . . .[15]

The framers understood, too, that it would frustrate "the system of government ordained by the Constitution" if Congress could merely announce vague aspirations and then assign others the responsibility of adopting legislation to realize its goals. Through the Constitution, after all, the people had vested the power to prescribe rules limiting their liberties in Congress alone. No one, not even Congress, had the right to alter that arrangement. As Chief Justice Marshall explained, Congress may not "delegate . . . powers which are strictly and exclusively legislative. . . ."[16]

Nor was the point only to limit the government's capacity to restrict the people's freedoms. Article I's detailed processes for new laws were also designed to promote deliberation. . . .[17]

. . . Restricting the task of legislating to one branch characterized by difficult and deliberative processes was also designed to promote fair notice and the rule of law, ensuring the people would be subject to a relatively stable and predictable set of rules. And by directing that legislating be done only by elected representatives in a public process, the Constitution sought to ensure that the lines of accountability would be clear: The sovereign people would know, without ambiguity, whom to hold accountable for the laws they would have to follow.[18]

If Congress could pass off its legislative power to the executive branch, the "[v]esting [c]lauses, and indeed the entire structure of the Constitution," would "make no sense."[19] Without the involvement of representatives from across the country or the demands of bicameralism and presentment, legislation would risk becoming nothing more than the will of the current President. . . . Accountability would suffer too. Legislators might seek to take credit for addressing a pressing social problem by sending it to the executive for resolution, while at the same time blaming the executive for the problems that attend whatever measures he chooses to pursue. . . .[20]

The framers warned us against permitting consequences like these. As Madison explained, "'[t]here can be no liberty where the legislative and executive powers are united in the same person, or body of magistrates.'"[21]

Having thus laid out the problem, Justice Gorsuch set out to find the solution.[22] Accepting, then, that we have an obligation to decide whether Congress has unconstitutionally divested itself of its legislative responsibilities, the question follows: What's the test?[23]

Some commentators seem to treat that question as one for them to answer. But read in context, I think it is purely rhetorical. Indeed, Justice Gorsuch spends the next three pages answering it.

Here is his answer, in brief.

> First, we know that as long as Congress makes the policy decisions when regulating private conduct, it may authorize another branch to "fill up the details."[24] . . .
> . . . Through all [the later] cases, small or large, runs the theme that Congress must set forth standards "sufficiently definite and precise to enable Congress, the courts, and the public to ascertain" whether Congress's guidance has been followed.[25]

Here the Justice is quoting a 1944 case challenging a law that delegated to the president the power to set maximum prices and made it a crime to sell goods at a higher price. The Court upheld the law (and the defendants' convictions), on the ground that Congress made policy decisions "sufficiently definite and precise" to be responsible for the results.[26]

This is, no doubt, the most important aspect of the answer to the question, "What's the test," if only because it will most often be dispositive. Justice Gorsuch goes on, however, to identify two less frequently arising situations in which the Court has repeatedly and correctly upheld delegations to the other branches.

> Second, once Congress prescribes the rule governing private conduct, it may make the application of that rule depend on executive fact-finding.[27] . . .

Third, Congress may assign the executive and judicial branches certain non-legislative responsibilities. While the Constitution vests all federal legislative power in Congress alone, Congress's legislative authority sometimes overlaps with authority the Constitution separately vests in another branch. So, for example, when a congressional statute confers wide discretion to the executive, no separation-of-powers problem may arise if "the discretion is to be exercised over matters already within the scope of executive power."[28]

Summing up, the Justice explains:

> To determine whether a statute provides an intelligible principle, we must ask: Does the statute assign to the executive only the responsibility to make factual findings? Does it set forth the facts that the executive must consider and the criteria against which to measure them? And most importantly, did Congress, and not the Executive Branch, make the policy judgments? Only then can we fairly say that a statute contains the kind of intelligible principle the Constitution demands.[29]

This three-part answer to the question, "What's the test," if adopted by the Court, should prove fully adequate for determining whether a statute delegates the legislative power of the Congress to the Executive or the Judicial Branch. Perhaps some weird delegation thus far unimagined will prove vexing. There should be no doubt, however, that Justice Gorsuch has offered up a principled and judicially manageable test.

Again, as the Justice noted, the key inquiry is whether the Congress has made "the policy decisions," even if it left it to the agency "to fill up the details" that arise in implementing that decision. Distinguishing between "policy decisions" and implementation is a judicially manageable task,[30] given the common law process by which particular instances evolve into a discernable doctrine or standard by which later courts are guided. The key to applying this distinction lies in understanding what constitutes a policy decision. Policy decisions require making a choice between conflicting values, such as human health versus economic growth.[31] The Congress may resolve the trade-off—that is, decide on the policy—and it may give the Executive discretion as to how best to implement that policy, but it may not allow the Executive to make the policy decision by deciding which value is more important.

Take as an example *Industrial Union Department, AFL-CIO v. American Petroleum Institute*, in which the Court considered a delegation of authority to the Occupational Safety and Health Administration (OSHA) to set a permissible level of workplace exposure to benzene.[32] Congress had instructed OSHA to "set the standard which most adequately assures, to the extent feasible, on the basis of the best available evidence, that no employee will suffer material impairment of health."[33] In his opinion concurring in the judgment, Justice William Rehnquist noted that setting this standard required OSHA to choose between conflicting values, specifically, "whether the statistical possibility of future deaths should ever be disregarded in light of the economic costs of preventing those deaths."[34] As he explained:

> It is difficult to imagine a more obvious example of Congress simply avoiding a choice which was both fundamental for purposes of the statute and yet politically so divisive that the necessary decision or compromise was difficult, if not impossible, to hammer out in the legislative forge.[35]

It is unsurprising, indeed altogether understandable, that our most representative branch should want to cede to others what Justice Rehnquist called "one of the most difficult issues that could confront a decisionmaker."[36] But it is not consistent with the allocation of "all legislative Powers" to the Congress, for with power comes responsibility. In practice, the Congress' abdication has meant this critical judgment concerning the value of human life has been made scores of times—in as many regulations—by unaccountable officials in the executive, rather than by our elected representatives.[37] The result has been a profusion of inconsistent outcomes among and even within executive agencies.[38]

Although the nondelegation doctrine is a necessary implication from the structure of the federal government, some judges and scholars have doubted a judicially manageable test for nondelegation could be found.[39] Although the Supreme Court has never spelled out precisely what makes a constitutional rule "manageable," Professor Richard Fallon has gleaned some guidance from the Court's decisions: "For a standard to count as judicially manageable, the most basic requirement is intelligibility, or 'capability of being understood.'"[40] If "lower courts likely would apply a proposed standard unpredictably or inconsistently, the standard is likely to be deemed judicially unmanageable."[41] Not surprisingly, therefore, the Court has found manageable some very difficult questions regarding the border separating the Executive and Legislative Branches. To do so, it has used "familiar principles of constitutional interpretation," such as the careful examination of "textual, structural, and historical evidence.... This is what courts do."[42]

The experience of state courts shows that enforcing a robust nondelegation doctrine is quite manageable indeed.[43] Florida is a leading example.[44] Its courts have taken a measured and nuanced approach. The Supreme Court of Florida scrutinizes delegations most closely when an agency is given the power to define criminal conduct.[45] By contrast, it has required less when the legislature is addressing a complex subject, such as determining the "prudently incurred" upfront costs a provider of nuclear power should be able to recover from its ratepayers.[46] Because the legislature had "made the fundamental and primary policy decision to 'promote utility investment . . . and allow for the recovery in rates of all prudently incurred costs,'"[47] and recognizing "the arcane complexities of utility rate-making,"[48] the court would not disturb the legislature's decision to delegate the particulars of cost recovery to an executive agency. Florida's intermediate courts of appeals have likewise shown how applying the usual rules of statutory analysis—as federal courts regularly do—can save an otherwise impermissible delegation.[49] Florida's experience suggests the nondelegation doctrine can be operationalized in a predictable and reasoned way. There is no reason to think the federal courts could not do the same.

What's the Effect?

Would restoring representative government really, as Justice Kagan suggested in *Gundy*, mean that "most of Government is unconstitutional" now? She is surely correct in implying that executive departments and agencies are now the principal source of the laws that govern us. Administrative agencies are issuing about 3,000 regulations with the force of law each year, roughly 28 times the number of public laws enacted annually by the Congress.[50]

To be sure, many—probably most—of those regulations do not adopt a policy decision; they implement a policy decision made by the peoples' representatives in the Congress, assembled and expressed in a statute. The nondelegation doctrine is concerned only with regulations that adopt a policy that cannot be traced back to a constitutionally adequate statutory delegation; these regulations state the agency's policy, not that of the Congress.

How important and how numerous are such illegitimate regulations? Some can be very consequential; we have already referred to regulations that implicitly attach a certain monetary value to each human life—the quintessential policy that should be determined by our elected representatives.

Still, even if only a modest percentage of regulations are unmoored to a policy decision made by the Congress, they must be quite numerous. An agency tasked with regulating an industry or, more narrowly, addressing a particular problem will not stand idle simply because the Congress has failed to provide policymaking guidance. Furthermore, administrative agencies sometimes wander away from their statutory role in search of new ground to occupy. And they may feel compelled to make a policy decision because a new problem has arisen in their general area of responsibility that no statute addresses. In addition, as seen in three high-profile examples, an agency may be pressed by the president or the Supreme Court to make a bold policy decision it would rather have avoided.

Consider: Nothing in the Communications Act of 1934, even as amended by the Telecommunications Act of 1996, tells the Federal Communications Commission (FCC) what, if anything, to do about the internet. By 2014, the agency was under strong public pressure to lay down *some* rules governing internet service providers.[51] The agency favored a light touch and proposed rules that stopped short of burdening internet service providers with the obligations of common carriers.[52] In a YouTube video, President Barack Obama urged the FCC to reverse course and enact strict regulations under Title II of the Act.[53] The President's input helped drive public interest in the rulemaking, regarding which the agency received nearly four million comments.[54] In the end, the FCC classified internet service providers as common carriers.[55] The FCC revoked this classification a few years later, finding regulation of common carriers would discourage investment by internet service providers, among other ill effects.[56]

Similarly, the Food and Drug Administration (FDA) claimed for decades that it lacked authority under the Federal Food, Drug, and Cosmetic Act (FDCA) to regulate cigarettes.[57] Despite doubts about the agency's legal authority,[58] President Bill Clinton instructed the FDA to take action.[59] Underscoring the political salience, tobacco became a key campaign issue in the 1996 election,[60] and the FDA's regulation was trumpeted as a promise kept.[61] The Court found it "evident that Congress' tobacco-specific statutes [had] effectively ratified the FDA's long-held position that it lacks jurisdiction under the FDCA to regulate tobacco products."[62]

Relatedly, when the Environmental Protection Agency (EPA) was confronted in 1999 with a petition filed by several states questioning whether the Clean Air Act of 1970 authorized it to issue mandatory regulations to address global climate change,[63] the agency said it thought not. It took a Supreme Court decision to force the EPA into this uncharted territory.[64]

New developments, like the internet, are sure to arise over the many decades in the life of an executive agency. The Congress does update statutes from time to time, but there will always be situations that are too important for the agency to ignore yet too new, or just too controversial, for the Congress to have addressed.

In many instances, of course, the agency has willingly, even enthusiastically, forged ahead, resolving major policy issues as it sees fit.[65] As long as the nondelegation doctrine remains dormant, expect more of the same.

If the Court revisits the doctrine, however, and reinvigorates it even roughly along the lines Justice Gorsuch has proposed, then just forging ahead will become quite risky. Agencies will predictably be more circumspect, more wary of judicial reversal. The Congress will likewise be more hesitant to enact delegations of doubtful constitutionality. We will consider their responses and those of others to the new environment later in the chapter.

Initially, however, we should distinguish between regulations already on the books and those promulgated after the revival of the nondelegation doctrine. Naturally, a firm burdened by some agency's self-determined policy will want to challenge the implementing regulation as an unconstitutional delegation of legislative authority. There are significant limits to the ability of a firm to do so, however.

First, the Congress has limited pre-enforcement review of many agency actions.[66] For example, orders to which the Hobbs Act applies are subject to pre-enforcement challenge for only 60 days after the order was issued.[67] After that the firm would first have to violate the regulation and be sanctioned by the agency in order to challenge it.[68] Under some statutes, the validity of a regulation may not be raised as a defense to an action for enforcement; the limited period for pre-enforcement review is an aggrieved party's one and only shot.[69] These limitations will substantially retard the flow of nondelegation cases progressing through the courts. As a practical matter, the revived doctrine will be raised primarily in challenges to future regulations.[70]

Second, nondelegation decisions will be limited by courts' obligation to resolve a constitutional issue only as a last resort. Able counsel challenging a regulation make every colorable argument, and should they prevail on one of them, the decision of the court will end there. The sequence typically involves arguments based upon the agency's interpretation of the statute purportedly authorizing the regulation, its interpretation of the regulation itself, procedural errors in promulgating the regulation, the substantive arbitrariness of the regulation, and, finally, any constitutional arguments. Success on any nonconstitutional ground precludes reaching any constitutional argument.[71]

Still, in light of the views hitherto expressed by a majority of the justices, many more cases challenging a regulation will now include a nondelegation argument. Some are sure to reach that issue. If the lower courts reject the nondelegation argument, the proponents will seek review by the Supreme Court. The Court will choose carefully and grant review only when it sees a case in which the issue is clearly presented; indeed, it may limit review to the nondelegation question, as it did in *Gundy*, when it denied review of three of the four questions presented by the defendant.[72]

Even then, the Court may adopt and apply a newly reinvigorated nondelegation doctrine and yet determine that the statute invoked by the agency is not an unconstitutional delegation. That would put the Congress on notice of what it is expected to do in future legislation, the agencies on notice to refrain from making policy decisions in future regulations, and the bar on notice of what are likely to be successful challenges in the future.

If this scenario plays out in the wake of *Gundy*, it will not be the first time the Court has announced a major development in the law but held it did not affect the outcome in that case. The tactic is most familiar from the Court's assertion in *Marbury v. Madison* of its right to hold a law unconstitutional, only to determine the present case gave it no occasion (or, indeed, jurisdiction) to do so.[73] In this way, the potentially affected institutions are deprived of a cause to protest while the larger legal community debates, digests, and ultimately assimilates the idea.[74]

What Responses?

With the nondelegation doctrine revived, agencies, courts, the Congress, and the president all will have changed incentives and different options. Consider first the agencies' perspective.

Agency Options. With respect to regulations already promulgated, even if they are not grandfathered by the Supreme Court making the nondelegation doctrine nonretroactive, agencies will not likely take any action. Seeking a legislative ratification would be bootless. Congressmen would certainly not take up a controversial issue and risk offending constituents and donors only to protect a regulation that might survive a constitutional challenge; there will be time enough for that if the regulation does not survive.

Concerned that it lacks the delegated authority to deal with a new situation requiring a new regulation—as in the example of the internet—the agency may have a better chance of obtaining legislation resolving the policy decisions it faces. The agency can approach its House and Senate authorizing committees, with which it has ongoing relationships (at the staff and principals level), to lay out the issues for decision and volunteer to draft legislation delegating the authority it needs. If the committee members are unreceptive, the agency will have to decide whether to devote resources to a project of doubtful validity or to do nothing until such time as the Congress is willing to take up the matter.

If the agency does go forward, any regulation it devises will have to be submitted to the Office of Information and Regulatory Affairs (OIRA) to be reviewed for consistency with Administration policy. If the lack of delegated authority elicits a veto at this point, the agency will have invested its resources for naught—a prospect sufficiently unattractive that it may dissuade the agency from acting at all. Alternatively, the agency may seek an opinion from OIRA before investing its resources. Then OIRA will have to assess the risk of going forward without statutory authority.

Court Options. Suppose an agency has issued a regulation for which it has no warrant from the Congress and a court is likely to hold it invalid for want of delegated authority. As the agency would point out to the court, particularly if the regulation is long-standing rather than newly issued, private parties may have made large investments or otherwise relied upon it. In such a case, it would be unfair to them and a disservice to public policy for the regulation (or perhaps the agency's entire regulatory regime) to be vacated.[75] Courts, being practical institutions, try to avoid such untoward consequences whenever possible.

Consider the courts' experience with redistricting cases. If the electoral districts that a state proposes do not pass muster under the one-person, one-vote standard and the leeway it allows, then the court would likely give the state a deadline by which to bring in a conforming proposal. Failing to do so would lead the court to draw its own electoral map.[76] That situation is materially affected by the pendency of an election. There may be no similar hammer with which to force action by a date certain if a court were to defer entering its judgment vacating an agency's regulation.

Where there is not an action-forcing event, courts have not hesitated to impose a seemingly arbitrary deadline for the legislature to act in the wake of the court's judgment holding a law unconstitutional. In *Moore v. Madigan*, for instance, the court held a gun control law unconstitutional but stayed its judgment for 180 days to enable the state legislature to devise a constitutional alternative.[77]

A lower federal court would surely stay its judgment in a nondelegation case for the United States to seek review in the Supreme Court. The Supreme Court could, in turn, stay its judgment for a time to enable Congress to decide the policy question.[78] How long the stay should last is a nice question.

It would have to be answered in each case with an eye to the congressional calendar. And, of course, even if it is given time to do so, the Congress may still fail to supply the missing policy decision for all the usual reasons.

Congress' Options. As we have seen so far, a nondelegation problem may reach Congress through either of two routes. The agency, recognizing it lacks authority to deal with a new issue, may seek authorizing legislation before taking administrative action. Alternatively, a court may refer a problem to the Congress after determining that an agency's action involved making a policy decision that had to be made, if at all, by the legislature.

If the problem comes to the Congress because a court has sent it there, then the Congress will be in an unaccustomed relation to the agency that issued the unconstitutional regulation. In the ordinary sequence of things leading to a nondelegation problem, the Congress created an agency and delegated some authority to it, which the agency then used to make a policy decision that the Congress did not address and will probably never revisit.

With a reinvigorated nondelegation doctrine, however, the problem will come back to the Congress to make the missing policy decision. Decisions that were not made because they were controversial must now be made, one way or another, whether by action or inaction. It is reasonable to expect that some members will not be happy with the agency's policy for the usual reason that it is contrary to the interests of constituents or of campaign donors. Those members now can try to shape the policy decision to their own liking, thereby triggering a process of negotiation with other members and perhaps with the agency itself. In other words, the restoration of representative government will also be the revival of ordinary politics in lieu of technocratic, administrative policymaking.

But wait! The Congress could enact legislation without waiting for a policy problem to come to it through either of the aforementioned routes. It might, for example, ratify all outstanding regulations, or all the regulations of a particular agency, in an omnibus statute simply stating that it approves and adopts as its own all the policy decisions embodied, implicitly or explicitly, in those regulations.[79] That would preserve the status quo by mooting any nondelegation doctrine challenge to extant regulations but leave any new regulation open to the possibility of being held unconstitutional if the Congress does not first make the requisite policy decision. Of course, the Congress could make clear that its ratification for constitutional purposes does not cure any defects the regulations may have under the Administrative Procedure Act. Then, presumably, any statutory challenges to the regulations would be unaffected.

An omnibus statute might seem unappealing because it would bring pressure from lobbyists on each side of every affected issue. Some interests are benefited and some harmed by the regulatory status quo; with ratification of the status quo, those harmed would lose their chance to make a nondelegation challenge to the regulation(s) burdening them, while those benefited would avoid the risk of the regulation being invalidated by a court. All the drawbacks of a legislative fight over a particular regulation would be magnified manyfold by a fight over wholesale ratification.

On the other hand, wholesale ratification of existing regulations may be more appealing than resolving (or confronting by not resolving) individual delegation problems seriatim as they arise year after year. Members could justify wholesale ratification of agency policies on the ground that failure to do so could prove disastrous to those who have justifiably relied upon an agency's policy decisions.[80]

The relative appeal of wholesale versus case-by-case handling of the problems generated by revival and retroactive application of the nondelegation doctrine would depend upon the breadth of the Supreme Court's first few decisions. A narrowly written decision deeply rooted in the particular facts of the case would not raise the specter of a long series of nondelegation cases, each with the potential of presenting the Congress with a legislative fight over whether to supply the missing policy decision. Alternatively, a broadly written decision or a series of decisions might at some point make the Congress more inclined to have one big donnybrook rather than years of distracting and divisive conflicts over particular regulatory policies.

Putting aside the unlikely possibility of a veto-proof majority, any legislative response to revival of the nondelegation doctrine, whether as a bill or a joint resolution, would require the concurrence of the president. As generally happens, the interests that lose their battle on the Hill will promptly decamp to the White House for a last-ditch effort to defeat the bill by persuading the president not to sign the measure. The president's decision will depend upon two sometimes conflicting considerations—namely, politics and ideology.

The politics of both the interest group and the interbranch sort differ somewhat with each issue, whereas ideology is a constant. A president skeptical of regulation, such as Ronald Reagan or Donald Trump, will be less inclined to sign a measure that insulates a regulation, much less a host of regulations, against potential invalidation in the courts. At the same time, the Administration may have a variety of issues on which it is dealing with a particular congressional committee or with the leadership and may see no choice but to acquiesce. Again, reviving the nondelegation doctrine will restore a measure of ordinary politics and political horse trading.

Opportunities for Gamesmanship or Resistance. A revitalized nondelegation doctrine would offer participants in the regulatory process new opportunities for political—that is, policy-related—maneuvering. Consider the Administrator of the OIRA, who properly acts as a guardian of the president's policies and priorities.

An agency proposing to issue a new regulation under a suspect delegation would present the Administrator with a choice. If, on behalf of the president, he favors the rule and wants the Administration to get credit for it, he could allow it to go forward and let the agency take its chances in court; the president may well be out of office by the time the courts make a final decision. Alternatively, if the regulation is too unlikely to survive a challenge, he might advise the agency to seek legislation adopting the policy entailed in the proposed regulation. On the other hand, if he disfavors the regulation, he could hold it up (indefinitely) under the banner of constitutional fidelity or, if he is confident Congress will not adopt the policy, send the agency on a futile mission to seek authorizing legislation.

An agency head, though further removed from the president, would have similar opportunities. A recalcitrant EPA Administrator, for example, could invoke the lack of a congressional policy decision in defense of the agency's inaction. Meanwhile, agency staff will have an incentive not to invest in a regulation likely to be challenged successfully on nondelegation grounds. This may lead them to rely more upon case-by-case adjudication; they could better protect their underlying policy position by simultaneously evading OIRA review and limiting the number of parties with standing to mount a challenge.[81]

All this assumes the normal rules of governmental infighting apply. A president with strong views about over- or under-regulation may ignore the Marquis of Queensberry rules and take the gloves off. A president bent on defeating regulatory efforts from within could direct the Attorney General not to defend them against a nondelegation challenge in court.[82] Whereas in the past a president may have selected judicial nominees based in part upon their general attitudes toward regulation, a future president might be more interested in a prospective justice's or judge's views on the nondelegation doctrine. The Senate could respond in kind when considering judicial nominations. Indeed, the Congress could limit the lower courts' use of the nondelegation doctrine by narrowing judicial review.[83]

The Bottom Line

Reinvigorating the nondelegation doctrine will change the Congress' incentive to avoid making controversial policy decisions. To be sure, deferring a controversial issue will still buy time; why do today what you might never have to do and at worst will have to do in a few, perhaps many, years? But after two or at most three cases holding a particular delegation unconstitutional, continuing to enact new laws that are likely to be overturned will seem both irresponsible and a poor use of the legislators' time.

If Justice Kagan is correct in anticipating a plethora of successful nondelegation decisions directed at the vast stock of extant regulations—which I have shown is unlikely—then the Congress' incentives would change even more significantly. The Congress then might want to adopt omnibus legislation ratifying all the agency policies theretofore issued. It would then face only the prospect of some new situation arising and inducing an agency to act beyond its remit so the issue comes back by referral from the Supreme Court to the Congress. Those situations do arise and by their nature cannot be anticipated by the legislature or by the agency. At least to that modest extent, though one can hope for a good deal more, the nondelegation doctrine will do the work the Framers began by so carefully making the separation of powers the foundation of our Constitution.

Acknowledgments

I am grateful to Christopher DeMuth, C. Boyden Gray, Kristin Hickman, and Jeffrey Sutton for insightful comments on an earlier version of this chapter and to Cerin Lindgrensavage, Jacob Philipoom, and Edward Stein for research assistance.

Notes

1. 28 USC § 453.
2. *Wayman v. Southard*, 23 U.S. (10 Wheat.) 1, 42 (1825).
3. *Id.* at 42.
4. *Id.* at 43.
5. *See Whitman v. American Trucking Associations*, 531 U.S. 457, 472 (2001) (quoting *J.W. Hampton, Jr., & Co. v. United States*, 276 U.S. 394, 409 (1928)).
6. *See, e.g., National Broadcasting Co. v. United States*, 319 U.S. 190 (1943) (upholding regulations by the Federal Communications Commission enacted under the authority of a statute that authorized the Commission to enact regulations in "the public interest").
7. *See A.L.A. Schechter Poultry Corp. v. United States*, 295 U.S. 495 (1935); *Panama Refining Co. v. Ryan*, 293 U.S. 388 (1935).
8. *See, e.g.*, section 102 of the Federal Land Policy and Management Act of 1976, 43 U.S.C. § 1701(a)(8) (mandating that "the public lands be managed in a manner that will protect the quality of scientific, scenic, historical, ecological, environmental, air and atmospheric, water resource, and archeological values; that, where appropriate, will preserve and protect certain public lands in their natural condition; that will provide food and habitat for fish and wildlife and domestic animals; and that will provide for outdoor recreation and human occupancy and use.").
9. *Wayman*, 23 U.S. at 43.
10. *Gundy v. United States*, 139 S. Ct. 2116 (2019).
11. *Id.* at 2130. Justice Kagan completed the thought with the explanation, "dependent as Congress is on the need to give discretion to executive officials to implement its programs." As will be shown, the problem at which the nondelegation doctrine is directed is not the discretion to implement programs but rather the discretion to make policy decisions.
12. *Id.* at 2131.
13. *Gundy*, 139 S. Ct. at 2131.
14. In a later case, Justice Kavanaugh wrote that "Justice Gorsuch's scholarly analysis of the Constitution's nondelegation doctrine in his *Gundy* dissent may warrant further consideration in future cases." *Paul v. United States*, 140 S. Ct. 342 (2019) (concurring in denial of certiorari). Justice Amy Coney Barrett has not spoken to the issue, but she has committed to following the "original public meaning" of the Constitution, which

suggests she may be sympathetic to reviving the nondelegation doctrine. *See Nomination of the Honorable Amy Coney Barrett to Be an Associate Justice of the Supreme Court of the United States, Hearing Before the Senate Commission on the Judiciary, Day 2*, 116th Cong. (Oct. 13, 2020), https://www.judiciary.senate.gov/meetings/nomination-of-the-honorable-amy-coney-barrett-to-be-an-associate-justice-of-the-supreme-court-of-the-united-states-day-2 (quotation appears at 02:53:57).

15. *Id.* at 2133. In the excerpts that follow, Justice Gorsuch's footnotes have been renumbered or omitted.

16. *Id.* (quoting *Marshall Field & Co. v. Clark*, 143 U.S. 649, 692 (1892) and *Wayman*, 23 U.S. at 42).

17. *Id.* at 2134.

18. *Id.* (citing David Schoenbrod, Power Without Responsibility 99 (1993); The Federalist No. 50, at 316; The Federalist No. 62, at 378-80).

19. *Id.* at 2134-35 (quoting Gary Lawson, *Delegation and Original Meaning*, 88 Va. L. Rev. 327, 340 (2002)).

20. *Id.* at 2135.

21. *Id.* (quoting The Federalist No. 47, at 302).

22. I say find, and not craft, the solution because the Justice sought no further than the Court's own precedents.

23. *Gundy*, 139 S. Ct. at 2135.

24. *Id.* at 2136 (quoting *Wayman*, 23 U.S. at 43).

25. *Id.* (quoting *Yakus v. United States*, 321 U.S. 414, 426 (1944)).

26. *Yakus*, 321 U.S. at 426. As others have detailed, the standards at issue in *Yakus* were in fact neither definite nor precise. James R. Conde and Michael S. Greve, *Yakus and the Administrative State*, 42 Harv. J.L. & Pub. Pol'y 807, 861 (2019) (noting the law at issue "was a full-blown embodiment of a constitutionally unconstrained administrative state."). This was the view of Justice Owen Roberts in his dissenting opinion in *Yakus*, *see* 321 US at 448–53. That the *Yakus* Court failed to practice what it preached does not, of course, undercut the logical force of the principle it articulated.

27. *Gundy*, 139 S. Ct. at 2136. Justice Gorsuch gives as an example the construction of the Brooklyn Bridge, which the Congress made dependent upon "a finding by the Secretary of War that the bridge wouldn't interfere with navigation of the East River." *Id.* The Supreme Court upheld this delegation in *Miller v. Mayor of New York*, 109 U.S. 385 (1883).

28. *Gundy*, 139 S. Ct. at 2137 (quoting David Schoenbrod, *The Delegation Doctrine: Could the Court Give It Substance?*, 83 Mich. L. Rev. 1223, 1260 (1985)). The Justice here instances *Wayman*, 23 U.S. at 43, where the Congress delegated power to the Court to prescribe its own rules of procedure. As the Justice explains, "Even in the absence of any statute, courts have the power under Article III 'to regulate their practice.'" *Gundy*, 139 S. Ct. at 2137 (quoting *id.*).

29. *Id.* at 2141. In using the phrase "intelligible principle" here, Justice Gorsuch does not endorse what he calls the "mutated version" of the intelligible-principle test that has prevailed for the past several decades. *See id.* at 2139. His point is that under a revitalized nondelegation doctrine, the Congress must clearly (i.e., intelligibly) set forth its decision on each matter of policy.

30. *Cf. Zivotofsky ex rel. Zivotofsky v. Clinton*, 566 U.S. 189, 197–201 (2012) (holding it is manageable for a court to decide a difficult separation-of-powers question through "careful examination of . . . textual, structural, and historical evidence.").

31. For example, in *Michigan v. EPA*, 576 U.S. 743 (2015), the Supreme Court held the Environmental Protection Agency acted unreasonably in failing to consider cost when determining whether regulation of mercury emissions was "appropriate and necessary."

32. *Industrial Union Department, AFL-CIO v. American Petroleum Institute*, 448 U.S. 607 (1980).

33. 29 U.S.C. § 655(b)(5).

34. *Industrial Union Department*, 448 U.S. at 672.

35. *Id.* at 687 (1980).

36. *Id.* at 672 (1980).

37. *See* Jack Thorlin, Statistical Life, Political Liberties, and the Pursuit of Policy Happiness: The Need for a Standard and Transparent Value of a Statistical Life in Federal Rulemaking, 23 Tex. Rev. L. & Pol'y 53 (2018).

38. *See id.* at 76-80. For example, in 2009 one agency in the Department of Transportation determined a human life was worth $6 million. *See* Department of Transportation, Positive Train Control Systems, 74 Fed. Reg. 35,950, 36,002. Five years later, a different agency in the same Department determined a life was worth $9.1 million. *See* Federal Aviation Administration, Fuel Tank Vent Fire Protection, 79 Fed. Reg. 48,098, 48,102. The EPA has used valuations ranging (in 1997 dollars) from $2.4 million to $12.6 million per life in the same proposed rule. *See* Environmental Protection Agency, Effluent Limitations Guidelines, Pretreatment Standards, and New Source Performance Standards for the Iron and Steel Manufacturing Point Source Category," 65 Fed. Reg. 81,964, 82,007 (2000).

39. See, *e.g., Mistretta v. United States*, 488 U.S. 361, 415–16 (1989) (Scalia, J., dissenting) ("[W]hile the doctrine of unconstitutional delegation is unquestionably a fundamental element of our constitutional system, it is not an element readily enforceable by the courts."); Gillian E. Metzger, *1930s Redux: The Administrative State Under Siege*, Harv. L. Rev. 1, 88 (2017). ("Justice Thomas's effort to prohibit any delegation of policymaking authority in setting general rules is practically infeasible and at odds with longstanding practice. But more functionalist assessments, focused on determining when a delegation goes too far, are similarly unworkable."); *cf.* Gary Lawson, *Delegation and Original Meaning*, 88 Va. L. Rev. 327, 361 (2002) ("Surely, one might think, the constitutionality of legislative authorizations cannot turn on something as ephemeral and ultimately circular, as a distinction between 'important subjects' and matters of 'less interest.' Perhaps the search for a manageable nondelegation principle must continue.").

40. Richard H. Fallon, Jr., *Judicially Manageable Standards and Constitutional Meaning*, 119 Harv. L. Rev. 1274, 1285 (2006); *see also id.* at 1281–97 (synthesizing principles from the Supreme Court's cases).

41. *Id.* at 1290; *see also Vieth v. Jubelirer*, 541 U.S. 267, 278 (2004) (plurality op.) (explaining "law pronounced by the court must be principled, rational, and based upon reasoned distinctions.").

42. *Zivotofsky v. Clinton*, 566 U.S. 189, 201 (2012). *Zivotofsky* concerned the

constitutionality of a statute that gave a United States citizen born in Jerusalem the option to list "Jerusalem, Israel" as his place of birth on his passport. The State Department refused to honor one such request on the ground that the statute unconstitutionally interfered with the President's exclusive power to recognize a foreign sovereign. The lower courts dismissed the case as one presenting a political question. The Supreme Court, however, held the courts were competent to consider the parties' "detailed legal arguments regarding whether [the statute] is constitutional in light of powers committed to the Executive, and whether Congress's own powers with respect to passports must be weighed in analyzing this question." *Id.* at 197–98.

43. *See* James Rossi, *Institutional Design and the Lingering Legacy of Antifederalist Separation of Powers Ideas in the States*, 52 Vand. L. Rev. 1167, 1201 (1999) (finding that of the 43 states with some form of nondelegation doctrine, 20 enforce a "strong" version similar to that envisioned by Justice Gorsuch).

44. *See generally* A. J. Kritikos, *Resuscitating the Non-Delegation Doctrine: A Compromise and an Experiment*, 82 Mo. L. Rev. 441 (2017) (discussing Florida's application of the doctrine).

45. *See B.H. v. State*, 645 So. 2d 987, 993 (Fla. 1994) ("The delegation of authority to define a crime . . . is of such a different magnitude from noncriminal cases that more stringent rules and greater scrutiny certainly is required.").

46. *See S. All. for Clean Energy v. Graham*, 113 So. 3d 742, 748–51 (Fla. 2013).

47. *Id.* at 748 (quotation omitted).

48. *Id.* at 750 (cleaned up).

49. *See Imhotep-Nguzo Saba Charter Sch. v. Dep't of Educ.*, 947 So. 2d 1279, 1284 (Fla. Dist. Ct. App. 2007) ("In our opinion, the 'Guiding Principles; Purpose' section of the statute, when coupled with the mandatory application requirements, save the legislative delegation from separation of powers problems.").

50. *See* Clyde Wayne Crews Jr., *Ten Thousand Commandments: An Annual Snapshot of the Federal Regulatory State*, Competitive Enterprise Institute, 2020, Edition 6, p. 5, https://cei.org/sites/default/files/Ten_Thousand_Commandments_2020.pdf (calculating that in 2019, "agencies issued 28 rules for every law passed by Congress and signed by the president," and noting that "the average ratio for the past decade has also been 28.").

51. *See* Edward Wyatt, *Obama Asks F.C.C. to Adopt Tough Net Neutrality Rules*, New York Times (Nov. 10, 2014), https://www.nytimes.com/2014/11/11/technology/obama-net-neutrality-fcc.html.

52. Federal Communications Commission, Protecting and Promoting the Open Internet —NPRM, 76 Fed. Reg. 37,447 (July 1, 2014).

53. Obama White House, *President Obama's Statement on Keeping the Internet Open and Free*, YouTube (Nov. 10, 2014), https://www.youtube.com/watch?v=uKcjQPVwfDk.

54. Federal Communications Commission, Protecting and Promoting the Open Internet—Final Rule, 80 Fed. Reg. 19,738 (April 13, 2015). *See* Brooks Boliek et al., *The FCC Chair's Internet Pivot*, Politico (Feb. 2, 2015), https://www.politico.com/story/2015/02/tom-wheeler-net-neutrality-114785. ("It was clear Obama's comments had been a major force in shaping the FCC rules.").

55. Boliek et al., *The FCC Chair's Internet Pivot*, Politico (Feb. 2, 2015), https://www.

politico.com/story/2015/02/tom-wheeler-net-neutrality-114785.

56. Federal Communications Commission, "Restoring Internet Freedom," *Federal Register* 83 (Feb. 22, 2018): 7852, https://www.federalregister.gov/documents/2018/02/22/2018-03464/restoring-internet-freedom.

57. *See FDA v. Brown & Williamson Tobacco Corp.*, 529 U.S. 120, 145–46 (2000).

58. Philip J. Hilts, *Clinton to Seek New Restrictions on Young Smokers*, NY Times (Aug. 10, 1995), https://www.nytimes.com/1995/08/10/us/clinton-to-seek-new-restrictions-on-young-smokers.html; Ann Devroy & John Schwartz, *Clinton Moves to Limit Teenage Smoking*, Washington Post (Aug. 11. 1995), https://www.washingtonpost.com/archive/politics/1995/08/11/clinton-moves-to-limit-teenage-smoking/d3c357d7-5dd8-4d6f-b245-17fdaf919dd2.

59. *See* William J. Clinton, Press Conference, *Protect Our Children from Tobacco* (Aug. 10, 1995), https://clintonwhitehouse4.archives.gov/WH/New/other/smoke.html (announcing the FDA would regulate tobacco, leading to the regulations at issue in *Brown & Williamson*).

60. William Neikirk, *Clinton Readies Tobacco Crackdown*, Chicago Tribune (Aug. 22, 1996), https://www.chicagotribune.com/news/ct-xpm-1996-08-22-9608220218-story.html.

61. White House, "A Record of Achievement" (Accessed Sept. 15, 2021), https://clintonwhitehouse2.archives.gov/WH/New/html/tobaccorec.html.

62. *Brown & Williamson*, 529 U.S. at 1306–07.

63. *Massachusetts v. EPA*, 549 U.S. 497, 510 (2007).

64. *Id.* at 528–32.

65. Consider the Federal Trade Commission's (FTC) abuse of its originally vague authority to prohibit "unfair" business practices. *See* 15 U.S.C. § 45. In the 1970s, the FTC claimed this delegation gave it the power to proscribe acts it viewed as "immoral, unethical, oppressive, . . . unscrupulous," or otherwise against "public policy." *See* J. Howard Beales, *The FTC's Use of Unfairness Authority: Its Rise, Fall, and Resurrection*, Fed. Trade Comm'n (May 30, 2003), https://www.ftc.gov/public-statements/2003/05/ftcs-use-unfairness-authority-its-rise-fall-and-resurrection. Most controversially, the agency proposed regulations that would have deemed all advertising directed to children "unfair." This provoked a stiff backlash from the public and Congress. *Id.* The FTC thereafter issued a policy statement defining (and limiting) its unfairness authority, which Congress ratified by statute. *Id.*; FTC Act Amendments of 1994, Pub. L. 103-312, § 9, 108 Stat. 1691, 1695 (codified at 15 U.S.C. § 45(n)).

66. *See PDR Network, LLC v. Carlton & Harris Chiropractic, Inc.*, 139 S. Ct. 2051, 2059–60 (2019) (Kavanaugh, J., concurring in the judgment) (summarizing the statutory landscape).

67. 28 U.S.C. §2344 (providing that many orders of agencies including the Federal Communications Commission and the Departments of Agriculture and Transportation may be challenged "within 60 days of [their] entry."). Other similar statutes apply to review of specified orders or regulations from many other agencies. *See, e.g.*, 5 U.S.C. § 7123(a)(2) (Federal Labor Relations Authority); 15 U.S.C. § 78y(a)(1) (Securities & Exchange Commission).

68. *See PDR Network*, 139 S. Ct. at 2059 (Kavanaugh, J., concurring in the judgment). ("If no one files a facial, pre-enforcement challenge to an agency order, or if a court of

appeals upholds the agency's interpretation, then a party who later wants to engage in proscribed activity and disagrees with the agency's interpretation faces a difficult decision. The party must take the risk of engaging in the activity and then arguing against the agency's legal interpretation as a defendant in an enforcement action.") In *Gundy*, when the sanction was criminal, the defendant raised his nondelegation challenge as a defense to an indictment.

69. *See id.* (listing the Clean Air Act, the Clean Water Act, and the Comprehensive Environmental Response, Compensation, and Liability Act as examples).

70. Indeed, it will be applied exclusively to future regulations in the unlikely event that the Court decides the new, more rigorous standard should not be applied retroactively. For a time, the Supreme Court limited the retroactive effect of certain decisions in civil cases. *See Chevron Oil Co. v. Huson*, 404 U.S. 97, 106–07 (1971) (announcing standards for making a decision non-retroactive). For the past few decades, however, the doctrine of non-retroactivity has seen no application outside of criminal procedure. *Harper v. Va. Dep't of Taxation*, 509 U.S. 86, 90 (1993) ("[T]his Court's application of a rule of federal law to the parties before the Court requires every court to give retroactive effect to that decision."). There are now signs of renewed interest in the doctrine, however. *See Barr v. American Association of Political Consultants*, 140 S. Ct. 2335, 2355 n.12 (2020) (Kavanaugh, J., for a plurality of three) (invalidating an exception to liability for debt collectors but announcing "no one should be penalized" for relying on the exception prior to the Court's decision); *see generally* Samuel Beswick, *Retroactive Adjudication*, 130 Yale L. J. 276 (2020).

71. In *Gundy* itself, the defendant initially prevailed in district court on his statutory interpretation argument; only after the court of appeals reversed that judgment did the district court go on to the nondelegation issue. *See United States v. Gundy*, 2013 WL 2247147 at *13 (S.D.N.Y. 2013). ("Because the Court has granted his motion on statutory grounds, it need not reach his constitutional claims."); *United States v. Gundy*, 695 F. App'x 639, 641 n.2 (2d Cir. 2017) (rejecting Gundy's nondelegation challenge after the defendant was convicted on remand).

72. *Gundy v. United States*, 138 S. Ct. 1260 (2018) (granting certiorari).

73. *Marbury v. Madison*, 5 U.S. (1 Cranch) 137 (1803). *See* Susan Low Bloch, *The Marbury Mystery: Why Did William Marbury Sue in the Supreme Court*, 18 Const. Comment 607, 621–23, 626–27 (2001).

74. The *Marbury* maneuver has been widely emulated. *See* Steven Arrigg Koh, *Marbury Moments*, 54 Colum. J. Transnat'l L. 116, 118 (2015) (*"every court has its* Marbury *moment.* Rigorous review of domestic and international courts reveals numerous seminal decision points in which a court (1) in its early history (2) rules on the nature of its own authority or an axiomatic principle of law (3) in a manner that is not textually transparent. Such *Marbury* moments invariably create controversy, but those that succeed do so when the judicial and political actors within the relevant jurisdiction ultimately accept the court's decision.").

75. *See, e.g.,* Brief for the United States, Gundy v. United States, 139 S. Ct. 2116 (2019), (No. 17-6086), 2018 WL 3727086 at *54–55 ("Holding Section 20913(d) unconstitutional would mean that pre-Act offenders would have no federal obligation to register unless and until Congress intervenes, potentially enabling many offenders to travel or relocate

to new jurisdictions without registering and without facing federal criminal sanctions for failing to register.").

76. *See Brown v. Kentucky Legislative Research Comm'n*, 966 F. Supp. 2d 709, 724, 726 (E.D. Ky. 2013); *Prince v. Kramer*, No. CIV. NO. 9668, 1972 WL 123242, at *2 (W.D. Wash. Apr. 21, 1972).

77. *Moore v. Madigan*, 702 F.3d 933, 942 (7th Cir. 2012).

78. In an analogous context, Judge Guido Calebresi has suggested that, in order to break a legislative logjam, a court announces its intention to strike down an anachronistic common law rule, rather than actually doing so: Thus, the court "'stays' its action . . . while the legislature has time to act." Guido Calebresi, *A Common Law for the Age of Statutes* (Cambridge, MA: Harvard University Press, 1982): 159–60. Following this approach would be prudent here.

79. I doubt the Supreme Court would require anything more specific; it is more appropriately deferential to assume Congress knew what policies it was adopting as its own. *See Hall v. United States*, 566 U.S. 506, 516–19 (2012) ("We assume that Congress is aware of existing law when it passes legislation); *id.* at 519 ("Absent any indication that Congress intended a conflict between two closely related chapters, we decline to create one."); *FAA v. Cooper*, 566 U.S. 284, 292 (2012) ("When Congress employs a term of art, it presumably knows and adopts the cluster of ideas that were attached to each borrowed word in the body of learning from which it was taken") (cleaned up); *Lorillard v. Pons*, 434 U.S. 575, 580 (1978) ("Congress is presumed to be aware of an administrative or judicial interpretation of a statute and to adopt that interpretation when it re-enacts a statute without change.").

80. This rationale is akin to Judge Robert Bork's rationale for saying at his confirmation hearing that some Supreme Court "decisions have been made around which too much has been built, and around which too many expectations have clustered, for them to be overruled." *Nomination of Robert H. Bork to be Associate Justice of the Supreme Court of the United States: Hearings before the Senate Comm. on the Judiciary*, 100th Cong. 260 (1987). *See also* Robert H. Bork, The Tempting of America: The Political Seduction of the Law, New York: Simon & Schuster, 158 (1990) ("The previous decision on the subject may be clearly incorrect but nevertheless have become so embedded in the life of the nation, so accepted by the society, so fundamental to the private and public expectations of individuals and institutions, that the result should not be changed now. This is a judgment addressed to the prudence of a court, but it is not the less valid for that.").

81. For a discussion of agencies' incentives to avoid rulemaking, see Stuart Shapiro, *Agency Oversight as 'Whac-A-Mole': The Challenge of Restricting Agency Use of Nonlegislative Rules*, 37 Harv. J.L. & Pub. Pol'y 523 (2014). For some advantages of rulemaking over adjudication, see Charlotte Garden, *Towards Politically Stable NLRB Lawmaking: Rulemaking vs. Adjudication*, 64 Emory L.J. 1469, 1473–77 (2015).

82. Doing so would be controversial, although not unprecedented. *See* Aziz Huq, *Enforcing (but Not Defending) Unconstitutional Laws*, 98 Va. L. Rev. 1001, 1008 (2012) (describing the Obama Administration's approach to the Defense of Marriage Act). Some scholars argue a president who refuses to defend a law he believes to be unconstitutional neglects his duty to "take Care that the Laws be faithfully executed." *Id.* Others argue the president has a duty to make an independent judgment on the

constitutionality of the laws, which requires that he not defend an invalid statute. *Id.*

83. The Fifth Amendment, however, may limit the Congress's ability to preclude judicial review where fundamental rights are concerned, as they might be in a particular delegation case. *See Battaglia v. General Motors Corp.*, 169 F.2d 254, 257 (2d Cir. 1948) ("While Congress has the undoubted power to give, withhold, and restrict the jurisdiction of courts other than the Supreme Court, it must not so exercise that power as to deprive any person of life, liberty, or property without due process of law.").

The Nondelegation Test Hiding in Plain Sight: The Void-for-Vagueness Standard Gets the Job Done

TODD GAZIANO AND ETHAN BLEVINS

When a customary antibiotic is no longer effective against a harmful bacterium, researchers don't rush to invent a new antibiotic. Developing a new drug is daunting, and many have unintended impacts. Instead, doctors survey existing medicines for their effectiveness against the new strain.

The analogy is imperfect, but developing a completely new nondelegation test that works effectively to stop excessive delegations is also filled with unknown difficulties and potential unintended consequences. Luckily, there is a legal standard that has already proved workable and effective against a similar separation-of-powers violation.

In this chapter, we show that the void-for-vagueness standard is a workable test judges have been using for over 100 years to address both the notice and separation-of-powers problems inherent in vague criminal law delegations.[1] Criminal laws must: (1) be clear enough to provide fair notice and (2) be enacted by elected legislators to ensure democratic legitimacy. Fair notice satisfies constitutional due process; legislative action alone satisfies the constitutional separation of powers. The nondelegation doctrine serves the same purposes and functions. And thus, we argue that the successful use of the void-for-vagueness test for criminal statutes demonstrates that the courts can use it effectively to police noncriminal delegations as well.

Of the two constitutional defects the void-for-vagueness test addresses, the notice problem is the one most familiar to lawyers, and its classic expressions are laws or ordinances that authorize police to arrest people for ill-defined acts of "loitering" or "vagrancy."[2] Yet legal clarity at some point is not enough. The Supreme Court has stressed in recent decades that legislatures themselves must supply the required fair notice and that it cannot be supplied by later law enforcers or court rulings. In the classic example, an ordinance that expressly authorized the police to write and post a detailed vagrancy code might satisfy the notice problem, but it wouldn't cure the separation-of-powers problem.[3]

It's this second, structural component in the void-for-vagueness cases that maps almost seamlessly onto the nondelegation context. Scores of Supreme Court cases and hundreds of lower court decisions have developed a jurisprudence defining when a criminal statute is void under this standard. When the void-for-vagueness test was first developed, however, significant penalties for violating civil rules were limited. The coercive effect of civil regulations is now common, increasing the need to police those as well.

As we explain below, it's time the courts apply the same test to strike down all vague delegations of power to administrators who write coercive rules that bind the general public, whether they be labeled civil or criminal. If anything, the need for clear legislative definition is greater for coercive civil statutes because there are far fewer procedural protections against erroneous civil liability determinations than there are for criminal convictions.

This chapter first discusses the historical and practical challenges in enforcing the nondelegation doctrine. It then addresses how the void-for-vagueness doctrine can resolve many of these challenges, and it concludes with a recommendation that the courts revise another doctrine that improperly limits judicial review and hinders nondelegation enforcement.

Part I:
Historical and Practical Challenges
to Nondelegation Enforcement

Before we discuss the void-for-vagueness standard and how it provides a proven and workable test for the courts to employ on nondelegation challenges, it is important to discuss some common arguments against nondelegation policing. We also address what's changed in recent years to make it more likely that courts will overcome these arguments and challenges.

The Courts' Unavoidable Role in Policing Congressional Delegations.
Every current member of the Supreme Court has agreed that the legislative nondelegation rule is crucial to the Constitution's separation of powers.[4] The sticking point during the past 80 or more years has been how to properly enforce it. What standard should the courts use to judge congressional delegations, and how searching or deferential should judges be in applying it? Justice Antonin Scalia famously argued in 1989 that the nondelegation rule was "fundamental" to our system of government but not "readily enforceable" by judicial means.[5] Many commenters have since chimed in that active judicial enforcement would be virtually impossible or calamitous.[6]

We wonder if some commenters' concern about more robust judicial review is colored by their preference for the agency regulations that broad delegations allow.[7] We also think that Justice Scalia's mature thinking on democratic accountability is in line with the approach we suggest in this chapter, even if he resisted a more activist approach to delegation policing earlier in his career.[8]

Regardless of how difficult the judicial task may be, it's no harder than some other line-drawing exercises the courts regularly undertake.[9] More importantly, no current justice disputes that the judiciary must police the legislative nondelegation line.

For example, Justice Elena Kagan conceded in her majority opinion in *Gundy v. United States* that the delegation to the attorney general in the Sex Offender Registration and Notification Act (SORNA), which allowed the attorney general to decide whether and how registration requirements applied to pre-act offenders, would present a nondelegation problem if it were as open-ended as the petitioner read it.[10] Justice Kagan also conceded—and no justice who joined her opinion disagreed—that the judiciary must carefully examine problematic legislative delegations to determine if they cross the constitutional line. In *Gundy*, the majority interpreted the problem away by reading SORNA to cabin the attorney general's discretion based on his or her factual determination of the feasibility in retroactively applying registration requirements. Yet Justice Kagan's statement of the nondelegation principle itself is quite conventional:

Article I of the Constitution provides that "[a]ll legislative Powers herein granted shall be vested in a Congress of the United States." Accompanying that assignment of power to Congress is a bar on its further delegation. Congress, this Court explained early on, may not transfer to another branch "powers which are strictly and exclusively legislative."[11]

The majority in *Gundy* embraced the weak or "mutated" version (as the dissent labeled it) of the Court's "intelligible principle" test,[12] but that is where the reform focus should be, not with common academic arguments that the Constitution allows Congress to re-delegate its lawmaking power to executive officials as long as it retains the power to reverse those grants of power.

Although an unlikely majority in *Gundy* upheld the SORNA delegation, Justice Neil Gorsuch's scholarly dissent (joined in full by Chief Justice John Roberts and Justice Clarence Thomas) expressed an eagerness to reconsider decades of cases to revive a more active judicial review of congressional delegations. Justice Samuel Alito's brief concurrence expressed an openness to such reexamination in a future case if a majority of the Court were interested.[13] And six months later, Justice Brett Kavanaugh's short statement respecting the denial of certiorari in a later SORNA case supplied that important fifth vote for reconsideration in a future case,[14] adding a hint as to how he might approach the issue through the lens of the major questions doctrine.[15]

What's Different Now? The fact that five justices might reinvigorate the policing of the nondelegation doctrine (in more than name only) has inspired renewed scholarship opposing and supporting that result. One recent article attempted to show that the historical argument for the nondelegation doctrine in our Constitution is weak.[16] Forceful arguments have already been published in response,[17] and both the originalist arguments for the legislative nondelegation rule remain strong.[18]

Yet we believe the academic debate about framing-era understandings and early congressional delegations is unlikely to have much, if any, practical effect. The fact that no member of the Supreme Court disputes the constitutional rule against re-delegations or divestments of lawmaking power from Congress to others is unlikely to change after 195 years of unbroken precedent.

In contrast, Justice Gorsuch's dissent in *Gundy*[19] has advanced the project of reinvigorating nondelegation enforcement in two important ways. The first is to explain in convincing detail, certainly more and to better effect than in any previous Supreme Court opinion, why the legislative nondelegation principle is essential to our Constitution's separation-of-powers framework. Although Gorsuch touched on the framers' historical understanding of legislative delegations,[20] his principal argument is that the American separation-of-powers design in the US Constitution is fundamentally incompatible with legislative delegations. That doesn't directly address how the judiciary should police the nondelegation rule, but it ought to stiffen the spine of some judges who neglect their duty[21] and encourage other judges who are already attuned to separation-of-powers deficiencies that delegation policing is a priority.[22]

Gorsuch reminds us that "the framers went to great lengths to make lawmaking difficult," including fracturing the legislative task among two houses of Congress and a president, each with different constituencies, lengths of office, and modes of election.[23] The constitutional gauntlet required to make law was a conscious feature of the charter's longest article, not a bug. The fact that legislative power was considered the most serious threat to liberty supplies the motive, but the design is unmistakable: Legislation requires carefully proscribed and coordinated action compared to executive or judicial action. This tricky, public dance by our most democratically accountable representatives ensures that the resulting laws will benefit from compromise, consensus, and sensitivity to different interests, all of which were designed to lessen "the danger of those errors which flow from want of due deliberation, or . . . which proceed from the contagion of some common passion or interest."[24]

From a design standpoint alone, it is inconceivable that the framers would have taken such great care in whom they vested the people's lawmaking power, how those lawmakers were elected, and how they must cooperate to make laws but didn't care a whit if this "most dangerous" power was later re-delegated to the executive or unelected administrators. If the re-delegation of lawmaking power were permitted, Gorsuch concluded, "the '[v]esting [c]lauses, and indeed the entire structure of the Constitution,' would 'make no sense.'"[25]

Gorsuch's second significant contribution in his *Gundy* dissent is the subject of this chapter—namely, to pose the question "What is the test?"[26] and discuss how earlier practice and the existing case law might shape that test.

As we later elaborate, the answer to Justice Gorsuch's question is hiding in plain sight (if it is hiding at all), and Gorsuch comes close to explicitly embracing it twice in his dissent. It is applying the void-for-vagueness doctrine more broadly, not just to laws that delegate vague yet coercive criminal law powers but to all vague laws that coercively bind the general public.

Two Common Challenges to All Judicial Nondelegation Standards. Before exploring the void-for-vagueness doctrine and how it could supply the principal nondelegation test, it's worth addressing two common challenges to developing any manageable judicial standard. The first has a reasonable premise but contains an erroneous leap of logic: Because no statute can ever be complete or perfectly clear in its meaning and application, it's not possible to distinguish between permissible and impermissible gap-filling exercises. The second challenge is that a single nondelegation standard that works for all cases and circumstances must be adopted.

The Inevitability of Statutory Gap Filling Is No Reason for Despair. No statute can be perfectly clear in all its applications, and thus, some gap filling is almost always necessary—whether by administrative rulemaking, executive enforcement, or judicial construction. Yet there is a wide continuum between unavoidable and interstitial (i.e., small) gap-filling enterprises and wholescale delegations of rulemaking authority for different subject matters to particular regulatory agencies—what Justice Scalia described as "junior varsity Congress[es]"[27]—for those agencies to define completely new rights, duties, and obligations only vaguely hinted at by the authorizing statutes.

Outside law, the word "interstitial" refers to extremely tiny spaces, such as the gap between individual grains of sand or between cells of an organism. Interstitial gap filling in legal parlance involves small matters Congress could not have reasonably foreseen or truly administrative (non-substantive) details such as the required electronic form and address that an agency specifies for a statutory filing. Executive or judicial gap filling of this type presents no constitutional problem, as both the majority and dissent in *Gundy* explain in different ways. Gorsuch's dissent quotes Chief Justice John Marshall, who distinguished

> those "important subjects, which must be entirely regulated by the legislature itself," and "those of less interest, in which the general provision may be made, and power given to those who are to act . . . to fill up the details."[28]

But without meaningful judicial enforcement of that distinction or something like it, Congress is encouraged to delegate huge swaths of legislative power over different subject matters, with the merest instruction that an entire policy area be regulated "in the public interest."[29] Consider the organic statute of the Occupational Safety and Health Administration (OSHA), which authorizes OSHA to set numerous "workplace standards" (i.e., workplace mandates) that are "reasonably necessary *or appropriate* to provide safe or healthful employment and places of employment."[30] (Emphasis added.) Under this capacious power, a workplace mandate need not be "reasonably necessary" as long as it is "reasonably appropriate," whatever that means. Such broad and vague grants of legislative power to set national policy allow Congress to evade electoral responsibility for the resulting substantive rules, which are created by civil service staff instead.[31]

That some enforcement discretion may be necessary is no excuse for extreme judicial deference when confronted with alleged abuses. Some government searches are necessary in enforcing criminal laws, too, but that doesn't mean anything goes. A search's reasonableness is almost entirely defined by judicial precedent, and based on that body of precedent, we now know that some searches are reasonable and others are clearly unreasonable. And still others continue to present difficult line-drawing problems.

The courts will never be free from making the final calls in hard cases. But the resolution of these hard cases is a special blessing to the legal system and the rule of law because it helps define the line that divides the two extremes, all of which has a salutary effect in guiding officials to enforce order without abusing individual rights.

Returning to the lawfulness of congressional delegations: That some statutory gap filling is inherently, implicitly, or expressly authorized is no ground to conclude that the courts could never develop a body of law that distinguishes the permissible from the impermissible. Unlike a legislature writing a comprehensive statute or code, courts need to decide only one application or problem at a time and can reconsider their prior distinctions relatively easily. It's called jurisprudence.

More Than One Unvaried Test May Be Required. It is not skirting the key question posed by Justice Gorsuch to suggest that the Supreme Court should not try to adopt one universal test without variation for all nondelegation questions. The Court applies different tests in several areas of constitutional law—and wisely so. The void-for-vagueness standard would work almost seamlessly for the large set of coercive regulatory delegations that are analogous to criminal laws and bind individuals, even though a single test might not be appropriate for all nondelegation questions.

In Justice Gorsuch's discussion of past cases, he listed areas where broad delegations to the executive branch may be fine or at least don't pose the same separation-of-powers problems as in other contexts. Those include delegations conditioned on specific executive fact findings and those involving shared powers with the president or the courts, and Gorsuch implied the same may be true of laws that don't regulate private conduct.[32] This last category includes government benefits or other spending programs that have no coercive or binding effect on individuals. Whether all such delegations should be exempt from constitutional scrutiny—and we think not[33]—it's certainly plausible the Court might want to apply a different test, or a variation, to them.

Delegations of nonlegislative or shared powers merit special consideration. For example, if Congress provides that the president may meet and negotiate treaties with any foreign minister the president chooses for any reason, that is certainly open-ended, but that power already is constitutionally vested in the president.[34] Thus, the void-for-vagueness test might not get the job done in shared-power situations, but that's because there is often no separation-of-powers job to do.

The same or similar analysis may apply even if shared power laws implicate private rights. The military justice system has been increasingly codified in recent decades, but the president possesses power in the absence of congressional laws to enforce military discipline as the commander in chief.[35] Laws that grant the president and military officers broad discretion in military justice proceedings affect soldiers' liberty and salary (and might implicate other constitutional rights), but they don't raise the same separation-of-powers issues as regulatory programs that are wholly creatures of congressional law; in these cases, Congress is arguably confirming constitutional authority and discretion the president already was granted. That is likewise true of many laws regarding foreign trade, foreign policy, and other powers shared among Congress, the president, and the courts.

So how would it work if the Supreme Court didn't apply the same nondelegation standard to all challenges? Exactly like it does in other areas of law. Consider the various standards the courts use to enforce First Amendment speech rights in different settings. Is the restriction on speech in a public forum? If so, is it a reasonable time, place, and manner restriction, unconnected to the speech's content? Genuine government speech is unregulated, although some government-funded speech falls in a gray area. A content-based restriction on private speech in a public forum is reviewed under the most exacting standard, and prior restraints on such speech are even more difficult to justify. With First Amendment defenses to defamation, it depends on whether the plaintiff is a public figure, whether the challenged statement was one of fact or opinion, and sometimes whether the challenged remarks were satire, the defendant is a media entity, and the statement was on a matter of public concern.

Each of those First Amendment tests can present difficult line-drawing issues, and half the battle may be over which test is proper. Significantly, the Court didn't devise all these tests at once. No one could have foreseen the need for so many variations, but perhaps that was fortunate. Otherwise, the Supreme Court might not have issued landmark rulings after World War I and then proceeded along that course to *West Virginia State Board of Education v. Barnette* in 1943 and the more speech-protective rulings in the 1960s and beyond. The more speech-protective trend, including subjecting more categories of speech to strict scrutiny, could be a function of the justices' evolving views of the underlying constitutional right. But it probably also reflects an increased comfort with judicial policing of—and the heightened scrutiny needed to protect—the same right.

Likewise, the high court need not worry about identifying one test in its next decision that will govern every future case involving the re-delegation of lawmaking power. It is enough for the courts to operate as they always have, slowly illuminating the line through case-by-case determinations.[36]

Part II:
The Void-for-Vagueness Standard Gets the Job Done for Statutes That Bind the Public with Coercive Sanctions

We noted earlier that Justice Scalia's commitment to democratic accountability and the separation of powers, particularly in the latter years of his tenure, drove him to question whether Congress really had made the political or policy decision attributed to it. If not, he often urged that the issue be returned to Congress rather than let courts or regulatory agencies decide it.[37] Although that's routine for vague criminal laws, the same practice should be adopted for any statute that binds the public through coercive sanctions.

Although Justice Scalia may have been comfortable with our modest expansion of legislative policing to include coercive civil laws, the Supreme Court still must confront the judicial reticence to directly enforce the nondelegation rule in Scalia's *Mistretta v. United States* dissent, which he reiterated for eight members of the Court in 2001: "We have 'almost never felt qualified to second-guess Congress regarding the permissible degree of policy judgment that can be left to those executing or applying the law.'"[38]

That reluctance resonated with both ideological sides of the bench during the last three decades of the 20th century. Liberal appointees had a strong faith in the competence of administrative experts to write binding rules for a complex world, and conservative appointees were still reacting against what they deemed "judicial activism," unmoored from neutral principles and grounded in personal preferences. Even though many academics retain their faith in broad policy delegations to the administrative state,[39] a growing number of legal scholars, political commentators, and judges in the past decade question practices that violate the separation of powers.[40]

Regardless of such historical influences, however, the past judicial reluctance to enforce the legislative delegation line due to its *difficulty* is misguided. The Supreme Court has shown through its void-for-vagueness jurisprudence that it is fully capable of finding and enforcing a line that separates permissible discretion from lawmaking in the enforcement of a law.

The Void-for-Vagueness and Nondelegation Doctrines Serve the Same Separation-of-Powers Purpose. In his *Gundy* dissent, Justice Gorsuch described a unifying foundation in the Supreme Court's nondelegation jurisprudence: "Through all these cases [involving different delegations], small or large, runs the theme that Congress must set forth standards 'sufficiently definite and precise to enable Congress, the courts, and the public to ascertain' whether Congress's guidance has been followed."[41] That theme echoes the dominant theme in void-for-vagueness cases. Indeed, Justice Gorsuch also noted that "most any challenge to a legislative delegation can be reframed as a vagueness complaint."[42] His previous expression of that valuable insight partially inspired the amicus brief the Pacific Legal Foundation filed in *Gundy*.[43] We build on that brief here.

Void for vagueness sounds in both due process and separation of powers, though early courts were slow to recognize its structural component. Courts first recognized vagueness as a due process problem more than 200 years ago. One colorful historical example arose with a law forbidding seamen from "making a revolt."[44] Four sailors aboard the *Vixen* had imprisoned their captain in his cabin after the captain had allegedly gone mad and threatened to blow up the ship with a keg of gunpowder.[45] A Pennsylvania judge dismissed the charge because the word "revolt" had so many "multifarious" definitions that selecting one definition "may fix a crime upon these men, and that of a capital nature; when, by making a different selection, it would be no crime at all."[46]

The Supreme Court has raised two due process rationales for invalidating laws with "multifarious" meanings: fair notice and arbitrary enforcement. Due process requires that the law be understandable so the public can "steer between lawful and unlawful conduct."[47] Courts "insist that laws give the person of ordinary intelligence a reasonable opportunity to know what is prohibited, so that he may act accordingly."[48]

For our purposes, however, the second rationale is more relevant: A law must not allow those enforcing it to essentially make it up as they go along.

As the Supreme Court has put it, "A vague law impermissibly delegates basic policy matters to policemen, judges, and juries for resolution on an *ad hoc* and subjective basis."[49] As far back as 1875, the Supreme Court recognized that "if the legislature could set a net large enough to catch all possible offenders and leave it to the courts to step inside and say who could be rightfully detained, and who should be set at large," the effect would "to some extent substitute the judicial for the legislative department of the government."[50] Of course, as Justice Gorsuch recently recognized, the problem is not just "allowing judges to assume legislative power" but also transferring "legislative power to police and prosecutors, leaving to them the job of shaping a vague statute's contours through their enforcement decisions."[51] At least since the 1980s, the Supreme Court has stated that this structural rationale is the more important of the two principles driving the void-for-vagueness doctrine.[52]

This concern for transferred legislative power evokes the animating principle behind the nondelegation doctrine. The void-for-vagueness doctrine's anti-delegation rationale "is a corollary of the separation of powers—requiring that Congress, rather than the executive or judicial branch, define what conduct is sanctionable and what is not."[53] And just like the nondelegation doctrine, this aspect of the void-for-vagueness doctrine is necessitated by the Constitution's vesting of lawmaking power solely in the legislative branch. Where a law is too vague to guide enforcement actions, such actions by logical necessity become acts of lawmaking. Thus, "vague statutes have the effect of delegating lawmaking authority to the executive," thereby making it "likely that any individual enforcement decision will be based on a construction of the statute that accords with the executive's unstated policy goals."[54]

The History of Void-for-Vagueness Cases Shows That Courts Can Competently Identify Unconstitutional Delegations. While the Supreme Court has not invalidated a single statute under the nondelegation doctrine itself since 1935, it has regularly applied the void-for-vagueness doctrine to strike down improper delegations. Although analogous rulings go back much further, in the past century alone the Court has successfully applied the void-for-vagueness test to separate statutes that grant the normal discretion inherent in executing a law from statutes that grant the unbounded discretion that amounts to creating a law. By working to find and draw this line, the Court has successfully enforced the principle that the legislative branch may not delegate lawmaking power through overly vague laws. The following discussion of these cases demonstrates that the courts are capable of drawing this line.[55]

One of the first statutes struck down by the Supreme Court in 1921 as expressly "void for vagueness" forbade grocers from making "any unjust or unreasonable rate or charge in handling or dealing in or with any necessaries."[56] This language delegated lawmaking power to juries because Congress had failed to come up with "an ascertainable standard of guilt."[57] The undefined terms "unjust and unreasonable" were so vague that

> to attempt to enforce the section would be the exact equivalent of an effort to carry out a statute which in terms merely penalized and punished all acts detrimental to the public interest when unjust and unreasonable in the estimation of the court and jury.[58]

Sixteen years later, the Supreme Court invalidated a Georgia statute prohibiting "any attempt, by persuasion or otherwise, to induce others to join in any combined resistance to the lawful authority of the State."[59] This broad language embraced anyone who "ought to have foreseen that his utterances might contribute in any measure to some future forcible resistance to the existing government."[60] No limiting principle was established as to how long a time frame could be imagined when determining that resistance might eventually be induced. "If a jury returned a special verdict saying twenty years, or even fifty years, the verdict could not be shown to be wrong."[61] For that reason, the law "license[d] the jury to create its own standard in each case."[62] In other words, the Court felt confident in determining when a lawmaker delegated lawmaking power to a jury.

Likewise, the Supreme Court struck down a statute that made it illegal "for any person to stand or loiter upon any street or sidewalk of the city after having been requested by any police officer to move on."[63] The Court explained that such a broad law "'does not provide for government by clearly defined laws, but rather for government by the moment-to-moment opinions of a policeman on his beat.'"[64] The Court did not hesitate to divide the line between a law that guided a police officer's enforcement actions and one that left the work of lawmaking to an officer's ad hoc judgment.

A few years later, the Court struck down an obscenity ordinance that forbade movie theater owners from admitting minors to movies judged "not suitable for young persons" by the city's Motion Picture Classification Board.[65] The board itself was instructed to find "not suitable for young persons" any film containing a violent scene "likely to incite or encourage crime or delinquency on the part of young persons" or any sexual scenes "likely to incite or encourage delinquency or sexual promiscuity on the part of young persons or to appeal to their prurient interest."[66] The Court explained that because these standards left such wide discretion to the individual board members, the result would be "'regulation in accordance with the beliefs of the individual censor, rather than regulation by law.'"[67] Note that only the structural, or separation-of-powers, concern with vagueness was present here; fair notice was still provided because the Motion Picture Classification Board established in advance what movies would be unsuitable for youth. The Court expressed no trepidation about marking the moment when a law became an abdication of lawmaking responsibility.

The next statute to fall was a Jacksonville, Florida, vagrancy ordinance that criminalized, among other activities, "persons wandering or strolling around from place to place without any lawful purpose or object."[68] The law was an invalid delegation because of the "unfettered discretion it place[d] in the hands of the Jacksonville police."[69] The true "law" would have effectively been created by the police, because there were "no standards governing the exercise of the discretion granted by the ordinance."[70] Rather than conforming to the requirements of written law passed by a legislature, Jacksonville citizens were in effect "required to comport themselves according to the lifestyle deemed appropriate by the Jacksonville police and the courts."[71]

Two years later, the Supreme Court put to rest a Massachusetts statute that prohibited "treat[ing] contemptuously the flag of the United States."[72] Because the term "contemptuously" went undefined, the statute granted "unfettered latitude" to "law enforcement officials and triers of fact."[73] The statute had "a standard so indefinite that police, court, and jury were free to react to nothing more than their own preferences for treatment of the flag."[74] The statute thus failed the constitutional "requirement that a legislature establish minimal guidelines to govern law enforcement."[75] The Court found once again that discretion crossed a line such that the legislature had delegated away its lawmaking power: "Statutory language of such a standardless sweep allows policemen, prosecutors, and juries to pursue their personal predilections. Legislatures may not so abdicate their responsibilities for setting the standards of the criminal law."[76]

The Supreme Court also struck down a statute that required persons validly stopped by the police "to provide a 'credible and reliable' identification and to account for their presence."[77] Fatally, the statute "contain[ed] no standard for determining what a suspect has to do in order to satisfy the requirement to provide a 'credible and reliable' identification."[78] Thus, the Court recognized that "the statute vest[ed] virtually complete discretion in the hands of the police to determine whether the suspect ha[d] satisfied the statute." Even though many valid statutes vest *some* discretion in police, the Court was up to the task of determining that this level of discretion crossed the line such that police, not legislators, were the ones truly creating law.

More recently, the Supreme Court struck down a Chicago ordinance that prohibited failing to disperse after being instructed by a police officer, whenever that officer reasonably believed that at least one of the persons in a group was a gang member and that the group was "loitering."[79] The ordinance defined "loitering" as simply "remain[ing] in anyone place with no apparent purpose."[80] Once again, the Supreme Court determined that "the broad sweep of the ordinance" violated "'the requirement that a legislature establish minimal guidelines to govern law enforcement.'"[81] The Court found that the statute impermissibly conferred "vast discretion" on the police, because the statute's text "'provide[d] absolute discretion to police officers to decide what activities constitute loitering.'"[82] Just like each of the previous cases, the ordinance fell on separation-of-power grounds, independent of any notice problem.

In each of these cases, the statutory prescriptions were so standardless that they effectively re-delegated lawmaking power away from the legislature and to some other actor down the road. Although some discretion and inconsistency in application of written law is inevitable, the Court consistently confronted the necessary task of determining whether the discretion exceeded the limits of mere law *application* and crossed the line into law *creation*. The

Court has proved capable of meeting this sometimes-difficult line-drawing challenge, just as it has in many other areas of constitutional law.

The fact that the enquiry in either type of case is the same has a crucial practical consequence: The courts have *already* been drawing the line between permissible and impermissible grants of discretion for more than a century through an extensive body of void-for-vagueness cases. Those cases serve as both an illustration that the judiciary is up to the line-drawing task and a robust set of precedents that can aid judges in drawing the same line in nondelegation cases.

Similarity Between the Doctrines. The void-for-vagueness and nondelegation doctrines are closely related variants of the same fundamental principle: that legislative power may not be re-delegated from the legislature to any other government actor or third party. The void-for-vagueness doctrine is frequently used to police delegations in criminal laws, but not exclusively; it applies to noncriminal speech restrictions and deportation statutes, so the criminal context is not a meaningful distinction. The void-for-vagueness and nondelegation doctrines differ in only three respects: (1) the *recipients* of the re-delegated power, (2) the scope of the doctrines' applications, and (3) saving constructions. These differences, however, should not dissuade the courts from using the void-for-vagueness doctrine in addressing nondelegation cases, especially those involving private rights.

Sufficient Deliberation Does Not Cure Excessive Delegations. The void-for-vagueness doctrine requires "that a statute provide standards to govern the actions of police officers, prosecutors, juries, and judges."[83] The nondelegation doctrine requires that a statute provide the same (or quite similar) standards to govern the actions of executive branch rule makers or other agency officials. In either case, the fundamental inquiry is the same: whether a statute grants so much discretion that legislative power has effectively been re-delegated from the legislature to another entity. That entity's identity does not matter, since the federal legislative power is vested exclusively in Congress.

Indeed, the vague laws discussed above could easily be reimagined as vesting precisely the same level of discretion in an executive *rule maker* rather than in police, judges, or juries, and in each case the Supreme Court's reasoning would have required the same result. Suppose, for example, that the provision at issue in the flag case, instead of vesting *juries* with the unguided choice as to when flag treatment was "contemptuous," vested that choice in the state attorney general to establish a regulation that would govern all future trials. Just as the Supreme Court determined for individual juries, the hypothetical regulation would have resulted in the attorney general making a decision based on his or her own notion of what the law should be. The extent of abdication by the legislature would have been identical, and thus the violation of separation of powers would have been the same.

Some vagueness decisions express concern about the ad hoc or non-deliberative nature of decisions made by police or other actors enforcing vague statutes, and that certainly makes the decisions more problematic. The Supreme Court has rightly condemned allowing snap judgments to govern as opposed to deliberative policymaking: "Recognizing that the ordinance does reach a substantial amount of innocent conduct, we turn, then, to its language to determine if it 'necessarily entrusts lawmaking to the moment-to-moment judgment of the policeman on his beat.'"[84] Those statements relate as much, if not more, to the notice problem in legislative delegations.

Such statements should not be read, however, as implying that vague or overly broad delegations are fine so long as nonlegislative bodies exercising delegated authority engage in a deliberative process like rulemaking. After all, in the obscene movie case cited above, the Motion Picture Classification Board had plenty of opportunity to deliberate in determining what movies were unsuitable for youth.[85] And in *United States v. Reese*, the Court's concern was with courts deciding who was guilty among those caught in an expansive dragnet,[86] and judges would certainly deliberate over that. Or to return to the flag hypothetical, an attorney general's considered choice of rule would be just as unguided as the choices of police and juries, and the resulting regulation would have been "nothing more than their own preferences for treatment of the flag."[87] Because the result in the flag case was based on separation-of-powers concerns, the hypothetical statute would be invalid for precisely the same reasons.

While rulemaking may involve more deliberation than the on-the-spot decisions of an arresting officer or even the relatively short deliberative opportunities of a jury, the essential problem remains the same: unelected officers making policy decisions outside the many safeguards imposed by Article I. The framers vested lawmaking in a legislature in part to forestall "the danger of those errors which flow from want of due deliberation."[88] But "*due* deliberation" is the form of deliberation established by the constitutional framework, requiring different elected officials with different tenures and constituencies to develop a democratic consensus on important policy questions. No amount of agency deliberation, even after public comment,[89] can transform the institutional incentives that guide agency behavior to approximate the incentives and safeguards imposed by the constitutional structure of Article I.[90]

The Void-for-Vagueness Test Should Be Applied to All Vague Criminal and Civil Laws. Courts have sometimes employed an enfeebled form of the void-for-vagueness test outside the criminal context. A meaningful distinction between civil and criminal laws is becoming less apt in any context, but it should certainly play no role in the relative strength of the nondelegation doctrine.

In vagueness cases, the Supreme Court has held that "the degree of vagueness that the Constitution allows depends in part on the nature of the enactment," offering "greater tolerance of enactments with civil rather than criminal penalties because the consequences of imprecision are qualitatively less severe."[91] The Supreme Court has made some narrow exceptions to that position, such as in removal cases due to "the grave nature of deportation."[92]

No courts have made a similar distinction with nondelegation, nor should they. For one, as Justice Gorsuch noted in a recent concurrence, the distinction between civil and criminal penalties in today's legal landscape makes little sense, given that "so many civil laws today impose so many similarly severe sanctions,"[93] such as civil commitment, revocation of a business license, confiscation of a home, or ruinous fines. That distinction grows even more flimsy in light of the many statutes with both civil and criminal penalties for the same offenses.[94] Additionally, recall that nondelegation preserves the structural integrity of constitutional governance;

the soundness of that structure does not turn on formalistic distinctions between civil and criminal.

Courts Should Avoid Saving Constructions That Undermine Nondelegation Principles. When resolving vagueness claims, courts often employ saving constructions to preserve an otherwise unconstitutional statute. Such an approach must be adapted to the nondelegation context with caution.

It is well accepted that if a law is readily susceptible to two interpretations, one constitutional and one not, courts should adopt the constitutional interpretation. In the vagueness context, however, courts have sometimes read limits into a statute that don't exist, slipping from interpretation into invention.[95]

A limiting construction that isn't genuinely grounded in the statutory text does not hand back the scepter of lawmaking authority to its rightful bearer; instead it steals the scepter with the left hand instead of the right. Rather than the executive exercising improper delegated authority, the court exercises it instead.[96] Thus, aggressive limiting constructions pose a special threat in the nondelegation context by simply ratifying an unlawful delegation and "wielding a power [the Supreme Court] long ago abjured: the power to define new federal crimes."[97]

Even more problematic is the ill-considered Burger Court holding that agency regulations can provide a saving construction for an otherwise unconstitutionally vague statute. In *Village of Hoffman Estates v. The Flipside, Hoffman Estates*, the Supreme Court rejected a vagueness challenge that prohibited the unlicensed sale of items "designed or marketed for" illegal drug use.[98] The Court upheld the law in part because regulations had clarified "a standard with an otherwise uncertain scope."[99]

More recently, the Supreme Court has rejected the notion that regulations can cure a nondelegation problem.

> The idea that an agency can cure an unconstitutionally standardless delegation of power by declining to exercise some of that power seems to us internally contradictory. The very choice of which portion of the power to exercise—that is to say, the prescription of the standard that Congress had omitted—would *itself* be an exercise of the forbidden legislative authority.[100]

If the vagueness and nondelegation tests are harmonized, as they should be, the Court's more recent pronouncement quoted above should prevail.

A willingness to let either courts or agencies rewrite a statute as a means of curing vagueness may come from a previous focus on the fair-notice component of the void-for-vagueness rationale. For the purpose of fair notice, it doesn't matter as much which branch of government fills in the details of a vague law, so long as someone does. But the Supreme Court has repeatedly held that the separation-of-powers rationale behind the vagueness doctrine is the dominant one. And in the nondelegation context, that rationale is everything. Thus, agencies cannot cure a nondelegation problem through regulatory clarification.

Part III:
Ending Abuses of the "No Law to Apply" Doctrine
to Permit Nondelegation Review

Some arguments agencies have made to limit judicial review of their actions overlap in perverse ways with those not to enforce the nondelegation rule. In addition to exceptions to judicial review that existed in common law, agencies have argued that certain statutory powers are impliedly committed to their sole discretion because the statute has no criteria by which to measure the agency's conduct.[101] These statutes have been said to have "no law to apply," meaning *judges* have no law to apply in evaluating agency conduct. While recent Supreme Court decisions interpreting the Administrative Procedure Act (APA) have limited these agency attempts to foreclose judicial review,[102] some courts continue to accept the "no law to apply" argument to deny judicial review.[103]

A "no law to apply" exception to judicial review that is broader than traditional common-law limits on judicial review collides headlong with the nondelegation doctrine. After all, a statute that has "no meaningful standard against which to judge the agency's exercise of discretion," which is the language in one early case that has been applied more broadly than intended,[104] also contains no meaningful law that limits agency discretion in any manner. That's a serious problem if it infringes private rights. Such a law would not satisfy the void-for-vagueness test. And since these laws would fail *any* meaningful nondelegation test, the Court should create a categorical nondelegation rule against statutes that fit this category and infringe private rights.

The EPA's authority to veto permits under the Clean Water Act is a prime example of how the "no law to apply" doctrine clashes with the nondelegation doctrine. Under the Clean Water Act, the EPA can rescind or limit permits issued by the Army Corps of Engineers that allow permittees to engage in otherwise unlawful discharges into navigable waters. The EPA can exercise that authority either before or after a permit is granted if the EPA deems that the permit "will have an *unacceptable* adverse effect" on the environment.[105] (Emphasis added.) The EPA wielded this authority to sweep a valid permit out from under a multimillion-dollar mining operation after the project had begun and well after the mine had spent several million dollars on regulatory compliance.[106]

Yet some courts have held that the EPA's exercise of this authority is committed to agency discretion and therefore unreviewable.[107] These courts have noted that the EPA's authority to decide whether an "unacceptable adverse effect" exists (and whether to do anything about it) vests "unfettered discretion" in the agency as to whether to veto a permit.[108] In the mining example, the EPA declared environmental costs "unacceptable" while ignoring the permittees' reliance on the permit and other economic costs.[109]

An authorization for an agency to decide what constitutes an "unacceptable adverse effect" would raise serious nondelegation concerns. It is impossible for permittees to know what the EPA might deem "unacceptable." The term may or may not require or allow consideration of economic impact, and even then the EPA has claimed absolute discretion in balancing costs and benefits. The term thus vests the EPA with the normative judgment calls that typically characterize legislation. Thus, what makes the unlimited EPA's veto authority vulnerable under a nondelegation theory has been wrongly held to make it unreviewable under the APA.

Judicial Review Under the APA and the "No Law to Apply" Variant. In an important set of cases that implicate private rights, the APA offers a right to judicial review for those "suffering legal wrong because of agency action, or adversely affected or aggrieved by agency action within the meaning of a relevant statute."[110] Two statutory exceptions exist: statutes that expressly preclude judicial review[111] and agency actions "committed to agency discretion by law."[112]

An express preclusion is relatively clear, but what fits the second category? The Supreme Court recently summarized four areas that traditionally were not subject to judicial review at common law and were incorporated in the "committed to agency discretion by law" exemption: (1) a decision not to enforce, (2) a decision to terminate an employee, (3) a decision not to reconsider agency action, and (4) distributions of funding.[113]

If the second category were limited to such common-law exceptions, it would not raise many nondelegation issues, in part because some of the traditionally exempt actions don't directly affect private rights.[114] Yet many statutory actions that agencies have argued in recent decades are committed to their discretion do not fit one of the traditional areas. Instead, the agencies argue that since they have been given such broad discretion in the statute to take action, there is "no law to apply" in reviewing their exercise of such discretion.

There are two key observations about the contested "no law to apply" argument against judicial review: First, it sharply conflicts with an oft-cited justification for a flaccid approach to nondelegation enforcement. Courts have excused their timidity in voiding vague statutes that grant open-ended discretion to regulators by noting that at least judicial review of the final agency action under that statute provides a backstop to ensure that an agency's broad exercise of discretion is not arbitrary or capricious.[115] Aside from the fact that judicial review cannot be an adequate substitute for divesting legislative power from Congress,[116] the "no law to apply" doctrine effectively ensures that unlawful delegations in fact are not subject to even the ersatz offer of judicial review.

Second, the "no law to apply" doctrine obstructs nondelegation challenges in the cases most likely to present a serious nondelegation problem. A law that is likely to fail under any nondelegation standard is among those most likely to also constitute a law without a "meaningful standard" by which to judge agency actions. Hence, meritorious nondelegation challenges trip on the courthouse steps.[117]

A striking irony here is that the government frequently asked courts in recent decades to rule that there was no manageable standard in a statute by which to evaluate the final agency action, and the courts readily engaged in that analysis. (At least they did before the Supreme Court's recent rulings limiting the practice.) And yet, the government has also maintained that courts can't make nearly identical determinations of whether a statute is too standardless to satisfy nondelegation.[118]

The older "no law to apply" cases, regardless of how problematic or viable that exception to judicial review is today, still indicate that resolving nondelegation questions may not be as difficult as academics and some justices have long claimed. Since courts appear more willing to decide that there is "no law to apply" than to decide that no "intelligible principle" exists, perhaps the real hesitation has not been the lack of a manageable test, but rather a lack of judicial fortitude to invalidate unlawful delegations.[119]

If a wrongful application of the "no law to apply" doctrine prevents judicial review of a pre-enforcement challenge, opportunities to bring a nondelegation challenge might still arise as a defense to agency enforcement actions, when federal courts come upon the scene in a deferential posture. Judges should consider nondelegation questions with the full strength of *de novo* review, but an existing administrative adjudication may tip the scale. More importantly, forcing regulated parties to await enforcement puts them in the untenable position of having to avoid lawful conduct or risk liability before seeking to uphold their constitutional rights against overreaching agency action.

Solutions to the "No Law to Apply" Problem. Given the inherent tension between Article I's vesting clause and the APA's reviewability standards, courts should construe the APA's "committed to agency discretion" exception as narrowly as possible. Thankfully, the Supreme Court is already moving in that direction.

In *Weyerhaeuser Company v. US Fish and Wildlife Service*, the Court held that the US Fish and Wildlife Service's decision not to exclude certain areas from a critical habitat designation was reviewable.[120] The service had designated private land as critical habitat for an endangered frog, including areas where the frog did not and could not live. The service enjoys statutory authority to exclude certain areas from a critical habitat designation, and property owners in the affected area challenged the service's decision not to exclude their land.

At the agency's urging, the US Court of Appeals for the Fifth Circuit held that the decision not to exclude uninhabitable land was unreviewable because "the section establishes a discretionary process by which the Service *may* exclude areas from designation, but it does not articulate any standard governing when the Service *must* exclude an area from designation."[121] The Supreme Court's reversal on the reviewability question imposed a vital limit on the APA exception to judicial review. According to the Court, the exception should apply only to "agency decisions that courts have traditionally regarded as unreviewable."[122] These circumstances include "the allocation of funds from a lump-sum appropriation or a decision not to reconsider a final action."[123]

The Supreme Court reiterated the strong presumption in favor of judicial review in *Department of Commerce v. New York*, the dispute over reinstating a citizenship question in the 2020 Census.[124] The government insisted that adding the citizenship question was unreviewable agency action, based on the broad discretion the statute granted the Commerce secretary.

> The Secretary shall . . . take a decennial census of population . . . *in such form and content as he may determine.* . . . In connection with any such census, the Secretary is authorized to obtain such other census information as necessary.[125] (Emphasis added.)

Despite the seeming breadth of the secretary's discretion, the Supreme Court held that including the citizenship question was reviewable. The Court noted once again that the exception applies primarily to agency decisions "that courts traditionally have regarded as 'committed to agency discretion.'"[126] The Court provided two examples: decisions not to initiate enforcement against a particular party and an intelligence agency's termination of an employee based on national security interests.[127] The Court also found that the standards in the census statute, while weak, still offered some foothold by which to judge the secretary's action.[128]

Weyerhaeuser and *Department of Commerce* represent a narrowing of the "committed to agency discretion" exception to judicial review, especially the argument that review is unavailable when there supposedly is "no law [for the court] to apply." And the high court seems reluctant to expand areas of traditional non-reviewability beyond the narrow set of cases in which the Court has already held agency action to be unreviewable. Indeed, Justice Alito argued in his dissent in *Department of Commerce* that there was no established history of reviewability of census-related decisions before adoption of the APA, and the Court still held that such decisions weren't traditionally *un*reviewable. The traditional non-reviewable agency decisions are limited to the four categories mentioned above.

Both cases also declined to mention another factor that had appeared in prior implied "committed to agency discretion" cases, which is whether the agency action displays "general unsuitability" for judicial review because the action is based on a "complicated balancing of a number of factors which are peculiarly within its expertise."[129]

In the short time since *Weyerhaeuser* and *Department of Commerce*, at least one circuit court appears to have read both cases as imposing a higher presumption of reviewability than existed previously.[130] Even so, other lower courts continue to cite and apply the "no law to apply" doctrine.[131] While maimed, the doctrine limps on.

Part of any strategy to reinvigorate the nondelegation doctrine should include continuing to roll back the "no law to apply" barrier to judicial review. Courts should decline APA review only where the agency action is expressly precluded from review or fits one of the four areas traditionally committed to agency discretion. And instead of denying judicial review in other instances when the statute provides no judicial guide to evaluate the final agency action and truly contains "no [discrete] law [for the courts] to apply," the courts should apply a categorical rule that it violates the nondelegation principle.

And even when an APA claim is precluded (under either exception), the Court should remain open to a nondelegation challenge to the underlying statute in a coercive enforcement or other action against a private party.[132] There is a nondelegation violation whenever Congress punts on the basic policy decisions and re-delegates vague legislative authority that infringes private rights, whether the APA is a vehicle to resolve it or not.

Conclusion

In the next few years, we believe the Supreme Court will reconsider its approach to enforcing the nondelegation rule and answer the question Justice Gorsuch posed in *Gundy*—what should the proper test be. The Court has a rich history of decisions in a closely related area of law that can illuminate that path forward. Its void-for-vagueness jurisprudence should bolster the Court's confidence in the judiciary's competence to police the nondelegation line, at least for the most important category of statutes: those that bind the public through coercive sanctions. With that tool and a direction to act, the courts can begin to prune back the most excessive delegations of legislative power and restore one of the most significant, if not the most important, structural protections of liberty in the Constitution.

Acknowledgments

The authors are grateful for helpful comments and other assistance from Tawnda Dyer, Sheldon Gilbert, William Haun, Damien Schiff, Elizabeth Slattery, Alison Somin, and Jonathan Wood.

Notes

1. The Supreme Court first used the term "void for vagueness" in *United States v. L. Cohen Grocery Company*, 255 US 81 (1921), but it first struck down a law as unconstitutionally vague in *International Harvester Company of America v. Kentucky*, 234 US 216 (1914). And courts have dismissed criminal indictments on vagueness-like grounds for almost 200 years. The common-law rule of lenity helps on the margin as well. As between two interpretations of an ambiguous criminal law, the rule of lenity applies a presumption in favor of the criminal defendant, but it works as a clear statement rule only and not a bar on legislative delegations.

2. See *Shuttlesworth v. City of Birmingham*, 382 US 87, 90 (1965) (loitering); *Papachristou v. City of Jacksonville*, 405 US 156, 156 n.1 (1972) (vagrancy); and *City of Chicago v. Morales*, 527 US 41, 47 (1999) (loitering). See also the discussion of these and other cases later in this chapter.

3. See the discussion in the second part of this chapter. Fittingly, the Supreme Court also has held that a genuine nondelegation problem can't be cured by subsequent

agency statements that narrow an overbroad or vague congressional delegation. *Whitman v. American Trucking Associations*, 531 US 457, 472 (2001).

4. See the discussion below of the majority and dissenting opinions in *Gundy v. United States*, 139 S. Ct. 2116 (2019) and Justice Kavanaugh's opinion in response to a subsequent petition challenging the same statute at issue in *Gundy*. Justice Amy Coney Barrett's views remain less clear, but some of her general thoughts can be gleaned from her academic writing, including Amy Coney Barrett, "Suspension and Delegation," *Cornell Law Review* 99, no. 2 (January 2014): 251, https://scholarship.law.cornell.edu/cgi/viewcontent.cgi?article=4618&context=clr .

5. See *Mistretta v. United States*, 488 US 361, 415 (1989) (Scalia, J., dissenting). "While the doctrine of unconstitutional delegation is unquestionably a fundamental element of our constitutional system, it is not an element readily enforceable by the courts."

6. See, for example, Gillian E. Metzger, "1930s Redux: The Administrative State Under Siege," *Harvard Law Review* 131, no. 1 (November 10, 2017): 88, https://harvardlawreview.org/wp-content/uploads/2017/11/001-095_Online.pdf ("An additional reason for skepticism is the difficulty anti-administrativists face in constructing a plausible test for constitutionally permissible delegations."); Peter H. Schuck, "Delegation and Democracy: Comments on David Schoenbrod," *Cardozo Law Review* 20 (1999): 775, 791, https://digitalcommons.law.yale.edu/cgi/viewcontent.cgi?article=2687&context=fss_papers ("The line-drawing problems are simply insuperable, which is why the Supreme Court . . . has resisted any robust nondelegation doctrine."); and Steven F. Huefner, "The Supreme Court's Avoidance of the Nondelegation Doctrine in *Clinton v. City of New York*: More Than 'a Dime's Worth of Difference,'" *Catholic University Law Review* 49 (2000): 337, 415, https://scholarship.law.edu/lawreview/vol49/iss2/3/ (noting the Supreme Court's refusal to "tackle the line-drawing problem of how to invest new life in the nondelegation doctrine without unleashing a parade of horribles").

7. See, for example, Metzger, "1930s Redux," 91 ("the phenomenon of delegation represents such a fundamental and necessary feature of contemporary government that it is mandatory in practice"); Schuck, "Delegation and Democracy," 778; and Julian Davis Mortenson and Nicholas Bagley, "Delegation at the Founding," University of Michigan, 18–19, 2019, https://papers.ssrn.com/sol3/papers.cfm?abstract_id=3512154 (arguing that stronger nondelegation review would implicate health and safety regulations Americans have "come to rely on").

8. One example of Justice Antonin Scalia's shift in thinking was his embrace of the major questions doctrine, which, like the nondelegation doctrine, is designed to make sure Congress decides major policy questions rather than regulatory agencies. See, for example, *Utility Air Regulatory Group v. EPA*, 573 US 302, 324 (2014). Scalia writing for the majority requires "Congress to speak clearly if it wishes to assign to an agency decisions of vast 'economic and political significance'" and rejects the EPA's belated discovery of power to do so in the Clean Air Act. See also *Paul v. United States*, 140 S. Ct. 178 (2019). In his last five years, Scalia directly invoked his concerns about democratic accountability to justify returning matters to Congress if the lawmakers had not spoken clearly enough. In another portion of his majority opinion in *Utility Air Regulatory Group*, 573 US at 328 n.8, Justice Scalia noted that the principle of "democratic governance" prevented agencies from exercising greater discretion than Congress granted

even if that was necessary to provide "a 'sensible regulatory line.'" Justice Scalia's forceful dissent in *King v. Burwell*, 135 S. Ct. 2480, 2506 (2015) (Scalia, J., dissenting), is probably the best statement of his position, and it came in a case in which the majority invoked the major questions doctrine and then, in Scalia's view, judicially decided the policy matter:

> The Court should have left it to Congress to decide what to do about the Act's limitation of tax credits to state Exchanges. If Congress values above everything else the Act's applicability across the country, it could make tax credits available in every Exchange. If it prizes state involvement in the Act's implementation, it could continue to limit tax credits to state Exchanges while taking other steps to mitigate the economic consequences predicted by the Court. If Congress wants to accommodate both goals, it could make tax credits available everywhere while offering new incentives for States to set up their own Exchanges. And if Congress thinks that the present design of the Act works well enough, it could do nothing. Congress could also do something else altogether, entirely abandoning the structure of the Affordable Care Act. The Court's insistence on making a choice that should be made by Congress both aggrandizes judicial power and encourages congressional lassitude.

An application of the void-for-vagueness standard to judge both criminal and civil law delegations is exactly the approach a historically minded champion of the separation of powers like Justice Scalia would embrace.

9. Consider the difficult First and Fourth Amendment issues discussed later in this section and especially the application of the "no law to apply" doctrine discussed in the third section of this chapter.

10. *Gundy*, 139 S. Ct. at 2123.

11. *Gundy*, 139 S. Ct. at 2123 (quoting *Wayman v. Southard*, 23 US (10 Wheat.) 1, 42–43 (1825)) (internal citation omitted).

12. Justice Neil Gorsuch convincingly explained why the intelligible-principle test, especially its weak and mutated version, is inadequate and has no textual foundation. See *Gundy*, 139 S. Ct. at 2137–43. In keeping with the premise of this book, we don't devote further space to discussing why that is so here.

13. Justice Samuel Alito's interest in reform may seem incongruous with his vote in *Gundy*, but he removed further doubt about his willingness to stop legislative delegations when he joined a dissent by Justice Clarence Thomas a year later that identified an immigration statute they would strike down as an unlawful delegation of lawmaking power if it authorized the DACA program at issue. *Department of Homeland Security v. Regents of the University of California*, 140 S. Ct. 1891 (2020) (Thomas, J., dissenting) ("In my view, even if DACA were permitted under the federal immigration laws and had complied with the APA, it would still violate the Constitution as an impermissible delegation of legislative power.").

14. *Paul*, 140 S. Ct. at 178 (Kavanaugh, J., statement respecting the denial of certiorari).

15. Pursuant to the *Chevron* doctrine, courts generally defer to agency interpretations of statutes they administer based on an assumption that statutory silence or

ambiguity is an implicit delegation by Congress to agencies to fill in the details. Under the "major questions" exception, courts will not presume that statutory silence on major questions "of economic and political significance" is a delegation to agencies to decide the matter. See, for example, *FDA v. Brown & Williamson Tobacco Corp.*, 529 US 120, 159 (2000). See also Nathan Richardson, "Keeping Big Cases from Making Bad Law: The Resurgent 'Major Questions' Doctrine," *Connecticut Law Review* 49 (2016): 355, https://scholarcommons.sc.edu/law_facpub/296/. Some have described the major questions doctrine as a substitute for nondelegation policing. See, for example, Jacob Loshin and Aaron Nielson, "Hiding Nondelegation in Mouseholes," *Administrative Law Review* 62, no. 1 (Winter 2010): 19, https://www.jstor.org/stable/41805937. It may have been to a small degree, but it doesn't do the same job. For one, Congress is forbidden from delegating its lawmaking power over more than just major questions of economic and political significance, unless "major" is expanded to include almost all substantive policy decisions. Second, the major questions determination only triggers more careful analysis of a particular statutory construction, not whether the statute as a whole impermissibly delegates lawmaking power over a policy area to another branch of government. And finally, as we discuss, it's no better for courts to decide major policy questions than for regulatory agencies to do so. Justice Scalia's dissent in *King v. Burwell* is as sound an argument as any for this last point.

16. Mortenson and Bagley, "Delegation at the Founding."

17. See Ilan Wurman, "Nondelegation at the Founding," *Yale Law Journal* 130 (2020), https://papers.ssrn.com/sol3/papers.cfm?abstract_id=3559867 (making four arguments against the Mortenson and Bagley paper); and Philip Hamburger, "Delegating or Divesting?," *Northwestern University Law Review* (September 2020), https://northwesternlawreview.org/articles/delegating-or-divesting/ (arguing that the framers spoke of "vesting" and "divesting" constitutional powers, instead of terms such as "delegation" and "nondelegation," and that they agreed Congress could not divest its sole power of legislating and vest it with any other entity).

18. See, for example, Gary Lawson, "Delegation and Original Meaning," *Virginia Law Review* 88, no. 2 (April 2002): 327–404, https://www.jstor.org/stable/1074001; and Michael B. Rappaport, "The Selective Nondelegation Doctrine and the Line Item Veto: A New Approach to the Nondelegation Doctrine and Its Implication for *Clinton v. City New York*," *Tulane Law Review* 76, no. 2 (2001): 265, https://www.tulanelawreview.org/pub/volume76/issue2/the-selective-nondelegation-doctrine-and-the-line-item-veto.

19. *Gundy*, 139 S. Ct. at 2131 (Gorsuch, J., dissenting).

20. For example, Justice Gorsuch quoted John Locke, whose arguments against the permanent *or temporary* divestment of the legislative power from legislators were familiar to the framers:

> The legislative cannot transfer the power of making laws to any other hands; for it being but a delegated power from the people, they who have it cannot pass it over to others. The people alone can appoint the form of the commonwealth, which is by constituting the legislative, and appointing in whose hands that shall be. And when the people have said we will submit to rules, and be governed by laws made by such men, and in such form, *nobody else can say other men shall make laws for them; nor can the people be*

bound by any laws but such as are enacted by those whom they have chosen and authorised to make laws for them.

Gundy, 139 S. Ct. at 21 (quoting John Locke, *Second Treatise* § 141, at 71). (Emphasis added.) Note Locke's particular concern is directed at laws that bind the public.

21. On the need to do so, see Peter Wallison, *Judicial Fortitude: The Last Chance to Rein in the Administrative State* (New York: Encounter Books, 2018), 109–36. The reference to judicial fortitude is taken from Alexander Hamilton's argument in *Federalist* 78 about why life tenure was necessary: to encourage "the bulwarks of a limited Constitution" to do their duty, specifically to enforce the separation of powers. *Federalist*, no. 78 (Alexander Hamilton).

22. Before their appointment to the Supreme Court, then–circuit judges Gorsuch and Kavanaugh were among a growing number of lower-court judges questioning doctrines that helped shift policy decisions from Congress to executive agencies. See, for example, *US Telecom Association v. FCC*, 855 F.3d 381, 426 (Mem.) (DC Cir. 2017) (rejecting deference to the FCC's adoption of the net neutrality rule because "congressional inaction does not license the Executive Branch to take matters into its own hands") (Kavanaugh, J., dissenting from the denial of rehearing en banc); and *Gutierrez-Brizuela v. Lynch*, 834 F.3d 1142, 1149 (10th Cir. 2016) (expressing concern that judicial deference doctrines "permit executive bureaucracies to swallow huge amounts of core judicial and legislative power and concentrate federal power in a way that seems more than a little difficult to square with the Constitution of the framers' design") (Gorsuch, J., concurring).

23. *Gundy*, 139 S. Ct. at 2133–36.

24. *Gundy*, 139 S. Ct. at 2134 (quoting *Federalist* 73). Although Gorsuch didn't mention it, the framers also inserted an origination clause that requires all tax legislation to originate in the House. US Const. art. I, § 7, cl. 1.

25. *Gundy*, 139 S. Ct. at 2134–35 (quoting Lawson).

26. *Gundy*, 139 S. Ct. at 2136.

27. *Mistretta*, 488 US at 427 (Scalia, J., dissenting).

28. *Mistretta*, 488 US at 2136 (quoting *Wayman*, 23 US at 16). See also *Gundy*, 139 S. Ct. at 2136–37.

29. See, for example, *National Broadcasting Co. v. United States*, 319 US 190, 225–26 (1943). Although the delegation at issue was upheld based on additional direction from the statute's purpose and context, administrative state supporters concede that "over the ensuing eight decades the scope of delegations has expanded significantly further." Metzger, "1930s Redux," 88.

30. 29 USC § 652(8). See also Cass R. Sunstein, "Is OSHA Unconstitutional?," *Virginia Law Review* 94, no. 6 (2013): 1407, https://www.virginialawreview.org/articles/osha-unconstitutional/. Sunstein's suggestion to construe the OSHA statute to require cost-benefit balancing to save it from nondelegation infirmity acknowledges two serious hurdles. First, the Court held in *Whitman*, 531 US at 472, that agency rules that narrow a broad delegation (that the DC Circuit had previously credited as addressing a nondelegation problem) cannot cure a legislative delegation violation. And second, Sunstein admits that allowing a court to engage in legislative policymaking and statutory rewriting in the guise of a constitutionally saving construction is equally problematic. Since

his article appeared, there is a third problem with his preferred saving construction of the OSHA statute—besides that it seems implausible to us. For instance, the Court in *Michigan v. EPA*, 135 S. Ct. 2699, 2707 (2015) held for other purposes that "'appropriate' is 'the classic broad and all-encompassing term that naturally and traditionally includes consideration of all the relevant factors."

31. See *Gundy*, 139 S. Ct. at 2133–36 (Gorsuch, J., dissenting). See, more generally, David Schoenbrod, *Power Without Responsibility: How Congress Abuses the People Through Delegation* (New Haven, CT: Yale University Press, 1995).

32. *Gundy*, 139 S. Ct. at 2136 (Gorsuch, J., dissenting).

33. We think some scrutiny is appropriate for spending delegations. Consider the hypothetical act that permanently appropriates such sums as the president may draw from the Treasury for any purpose. Even if individual members of Congress would lack standing to sue, an entire House of Congress might have a justiciable claim. Even so, the rationale of the void-for-vagueness test does not apply with the same force to noncoercive acts.

34. US Const. art. II, § 2, cl. 2 and § 3.

35. The scope of the commander-in-chief power is not defined in the Constitution. See US Const. art. II, § 2, cl. 1. But the inherent duty of commanders to regulate military discipline has existed since time immemorial. In America, that inherent constitutional power can be largely displaced by Congress' express authority to enact "Rules for the Government and Regulation of the land and naval Forces" in US Const. art. I, § 8, cl. 14.

36. See, for example, *National Federation of Independent Business v. Sebelius*, 132 S. Ct. 2566, 2606 (2012) ("We have no need to fix a line. . . . It is enough for today that wherever that line may be, this statute is surely beyond it.").

37. See note 8.

38. *Whitman*, 531 US at 474–75 (quoting *Mistretta*, 488 US at 416 (Scalia, J., dissenting)).

39. See Metzger, "1930s Redux"; and Adrian Vermeule, *Law's Abnegation: From Law's Empire to the Administrative State* (Cambridge, MA: Harvard University Press, 2016). Both double down on such delegations—not only as essential to modern government but as the supposed inevitable working of the rule of law itself.

40. Philip Hamburger, *Is Administrative Law Unlawful?* (Chicago: University of Chicago Press, 2014). Hamburger's book was particularly important in energizing scholarly debate on both sides of the "administrativist" divide, and Justice Gorsuch's confirmation hearings were instrumental in introducing the broader public to concerns about *Chevron* deference and related separation-of-powers problems. Cataloging the scholarly papers and articles is beyond the scope of this chapter, but other notable books include Joseph Postell, *Bureaucracy in America: The Administrative State's Challenge to Constitutional Government* (Columbia, MO: University of Missouri Press, 2017); and Wallison, *Judicial Fortitude*. More significantly, the Supreme Court's separation-of-powers rulings in recent years are a departure from the pro-administrativist bent of preceding decades. See, for example, *Seila Law v. Consumer Financial Protection Bureau*, 591 US ___ (2020) (holding that the single director of the Consumer Financial Protection Bureau must be removable at will by the president); *Kisor v. Wilkie*, 138 S. Ct. 2400 (2019) (limiting deference to agency interpretations of administrative rules); *Lucia v. Securities and Exchange Commission*, 138 S. Ct. 2044 (2018) (holding that the administrative law judge

appointment violated the appointments clause); *Department of Transportation v. Association of American Railroads*, 575 US 43 (2015) (holding that Amtrak is a governmental entity for separation-of-powers analysis); and *National Labor Relations Board v. Noel Canning*, 573 US 513 (2014) (invalidating the president's recess appointments to the National Labor Relations Board during a three-day interval between the Senate's pro forma sessions).

41. *Gundy*, 139 S. Ct. at 2136 (Gorsuch, J., dissenting) (quoting *Yakus v. United States*, 321 US 414, 426 (1944)).

42. *Gundy*, 139 S. Ct. at 2142.

43. Brief Amicus Curiae of Pacific Legal Foundation in Support of Reversal, *Gundy*, 2018 WL 2684377 (May 2018).

44. *United States v. Sharp*, 27 F. Cas. 1041, 1043 (1815).

45. *Sharp*, 27 F. Cas. at 1043.

46. *Sharp*, 27 F. Cas. at 1043.

47. *Grayned v. City of Rockford*, 408 US 104, 108 (1972). Justice Thomas has questioned whether the due process clause in fact supports a void-for-vagueness principle. See *Johnson v. United States*, 135 S. Ct. 2551, 2572 (2015) (Thomas, J., concurring). To the extent that readers share that concern, we think this chapter demonstrates that void for vagueness may at least find a home in Article I's vesting clause and nondelegation doctrine.

48. *Grayned*, 408 US at 109.

49. *Grayned*, 408 US at 108–9.

50. *United States v. Reese*, 92 US (2 Otto) 214, 221 (1875). Although the 1875 Court didn't expressly note the resulting loss in democratic accountability, the framers and modern-day scholars agree that democratic governance is seriously impaired if voters are prevented from holding legislators responsible for ultimate policy results. See Schoenbrod, *Power Without Responsibility*, 99–106; and Hamburger, *Is Administrative Law Unlawful?*, 355–76, 420–23.

51. *Sessions v. Dimaya*, 138 S. Ct. 1204, 1227–28 (2018) (Gorsuch, J., concurring in part and concurring in the judgment).

52. *Kolender v. Lawson*, 461 US 352, 358 (1983). See, most recently, *United States v. Davis*, 139 S. Ct. 2319, 2325 (2019). (Gorsuch writing for the majority noted that the separation of powers was a "pillar" of the vagueness doctrine.) See also Guyora Binder and Brenner M. Fissell, "A Political Interpretation of the Vagueness Doctrine," *University of Illinois Law Review* (November 2019): 1527, 1548–51 (discussing the importance of the separation-of-powers rationale for the vagueness doctrine and its relation to nondelegation principles).

53. *Sessions*, 138 S. Ct. at 1212 (plurality op.).

54. Nathan S. Chapman and Michael W. McConnell, "Due Process as Separation of Powers," *Yale Law Journal* 121 (2012): 1672, 1806, https://www.yalelawjournal.org/pdf/1080_y4sioof3.pdf.

55. While the Supreme Court has struck down many more laws under the void-for-vagueness doctrine than will be listed here, this survey will be limited to those in which the Court explicitly invoked separation-of-powers concerns as a reason for invalidating the statute.

56. *L. Cohen Grocery*, 255 US at 86.

57. *L. Cohen Grocery*, 255 US at 89.

58. *L. Cohen Grocery*, 255 US at 89.

59. *Herndon v. Lowry*, 301 US 242, 246 n.2 (1937).

60. *Herndon*, 301 US at 262.

61. *Herndon*, 301 US at 263.

62. *Herndon*, 301 US at 263.

63. *Shuttlesworth*, 382 US at 90.

64. *Shuttlesworth*, 382 US at 87 (quoting *Cox v. Louisiana*, 379 US 536, 579 (1965) (Black, J., concurring in part and dissenting in part)).

65. *Interstate Circuit v. City of Dallas*, 390 US 676, 680 (1968).

66. *Interstate Circuit*, 390 US at 681.

67. *Interstate Circuit*, 390 US at 685 (quoting *Kingsley International Pictures Corp. v. Regents of the University of the State of New York*, 360 US 684, 701 (1959) (Clark, J., concurring in result)).

68. *Papachristou*, 405 US at 156 n.1.

69. *Papachristou*, 405 US at 168.

70. *Papachristou*, 405 US at 170.

71. *Papachristou*, 405 US at 170.

72. *Smith v. Goguen*, 415 US 566, 568–69 (1974).

73. *Smith*, 415 US at 578.

74. *Smith*, 415 US at 578.

75. *Smith*, 415 US at 574.

76. *Smith*, 415 US at 575.

77. *Kolender*, 461 US at 353.

78. *Kolender*, 461 US at 358.

79. *Morales*, 527 US at 47.

80. *Morales*, 527 US at 47 (alterations in original).

81. *Morales*, 527 US at 60 (quoting *Kolender*, 461 US at 358).

82. *Morales*, 527 US at 61 (quoting *City of Chicago v. Morales*, 687 N.E.2d 53, 63 (Ill. 1997)).

83. *Sessions*, 138 S. Ct. at 1212 (plurality op.).

84. *Morales*, 527 US at 60 (quoting *Kolender*, 461 US at 360).

85. *Interstate Circuit*, 390 US at 680.

86. *Reese*, 92 US at 221.

87. *Smith*, 415 US at 578.

88. *Federalist*, no. 73 (Alexander Hamilton).

89. There's good reason to be skeptical of the influence of public comment procedures on agency deliberations, procedures that Justice Kagan during her academic career called a "charade." Elena Kagan, "Chevron's Nondelegation Doctrine," *Supreme Court Review* 2001 (2001): 201, 231, https://www.scotusblog.com/wp-content/uploads/2010/03/Chevrons-Nondelegation-Doctrine.pdf.

90. For an analysis of how the void-for-vagueness doctrine results in better substantive law by channeling policymaking through the legislature, see Binder and Fissell, "A Political Interpretation of the Vagueness Doctrine," 1547–54.

91. *Sessions*, 137 S. Ct. at 1212 (cleaned up).

92. *Sessions*, 137 S. Ct. at 1213.

93. *Sessions*, 137 S. Ct. at 1231 (Gorsuch, J., concurring).

94. See *Carter v. Welles-Bowen Realty*, 736 F.3d 722,730 (6th Cir. 2013) (noting that deference to agency interpretations and the rule of lenity, which resolves ambiguity in a defendant's favor, clash where hybrid statutes are concerned because "a statute is not a chameleon. Its meaning does not change from case to case.") (Sutton, J., concurring).

95. *Skilling v. United States*, 561 US 358, 422 (2010) (Scalia, J., concurring).

96. Cass Sunstein acknowledged this problem in his defense of OSHA's broad delegation: "The problem is that if . . . agencies cannot rescue open-ended delegations through subsidiary policymaking in the guise of interpretation, courts should not be able to do so either." Sunstein, "Is OSHA Unconstitutional?"

97. *Skilling*, 561 US at 415 (Scalia, J., dissenting).

98. *Village of Hoffman Estates v. The Flipside, Hoffman Estates*, 455 US 489, 491 (1982).

99. *Village of Hoffman Estates*, 455 US at 504.

100. *Whitman*, 531 US at 472–73.

101. See, for example, *Markle Interests v. US Fish and Wildlife Service*, 827 F.3d 452 (5th Cir. 2016) (agency decision not to exclude property from critical habitat designation was unreviewable because Congress had failed to articulate judicially manageable standards for review of the agency decision), judgment vacated by *Markle Interests v. US Fish and Wildlife*, 139 S. Ct. 590 (2018); and *Bristol Bay Economic Development Corp. v. Hladick*, No. 3:19-cv-00265-SLG (Consolidated), 2020 WL 1905290 (D. Alaska Apr. 17, 2020) (EPA rescission of Clean Water Act permit was unreviewable because there was "no law to apply" to the determination that the permit would have an "unacceptable adverse effect" on the environment).

102. See *Weyerhaeuser Company v. US Fish and Wildlife Service*, 139 S. Ct. 361 (2018); and *Department of Commerce v. New York*, 139 S. Ct. 2551 (2019).

103. For example, *Trout Unlimited v. Pirzadeh*, 1 F.4th 738, 752–53 (9th Cir. 2021).

104. The language is from *Heckler v. Chaney*, 470 US 821, 830 (1985). Like the "intelligible principle" passage in *J. W. Hampton*, it was not intended to create a freestanding test. The Supreme Court explained that the claim in *Heckler* fit a traditional exception to judicial review—namely, the common-law presumption of non-reviewability of agency decisions not to bring an enforcement action. In defending the traditional exception, the Court explained there was no "meaningful standard against which to judge the agency's exercise of [nonenforcement] discretion." But the high court has since refused to expand the exception based on that condition alone. See the section "Judicial Review Under the APA and the 'No Law to Apply' Variant."

105. 33 USC § 1344(c).

106. See *Mingo Logan Coal v. EPA*, 829 F.3d 710 (DC Cir. 2016).

107. See, for example, *Trout Unlimited*, 1 F.4th at 752–53; *City of Olmsted Falls v. Environmental Protection Agency*, 266 F. Supp. 2d 718, 722–23 (N.D. Ohio 2003); *Cascade Conservation League v. M.A. Segale*, 921 F. Supp. 692, 698–99 (W.D. Wash. 1996); and *Preserve Endangered Areas of Cobb's History v. US Army Corps of Engineers*, 915 Supp. 378, 381 (N.D. Ga. 1995). But see *Alliance to Save Mattaponi v. US Army Corps of Engineers*, 515 F. Supp. 2d 1, 8 (D.D.C. 2007).

108. *Trout Unlimited*, 1 F.4th at 752–53.

109. See *Mingo Logan*, 839 F.3d at 733 (Kavanaugh, J., dissenting).

110. 5 USC § 702.

111. 5 USC § 701(a)(1).

112. 5 USC § 701(a)(2).

113. See *Weyerhaeuser*, 139 S. Ct. at 361; and *Department of Commerce v. New York*, 139 S. Ct. 2551 (2019).

114. An agency decision not to bring an enforcement action, which was at issue in *Heckler*, 470 US at 830, generally does not directly violate the rights of private parties.

115. See Thomas W. Merrill, "Delegation and Judicial Review," *Harvard Journal of Law and Public Policy* 33 (2010): 73.

116. Judicial review of agency action is already enfeebled by deference doctrines such as *Chevron* and the APA's forgiving standards of review, especially as misinterpreted and made more deferential by the courts. But even so, generalized APA review ensures only that agencies do not act in an arbitrary and capricious manner or directly contrary to the law presumed to be valid; it cannot serve as a surrogate for nondelegation analysis, which is meant to ensure "that important choices of social policy are made by Congress, the branch of our Government most responsive to the popular will." *Industrial Union Department, AFL-CIO v. American Petroleum Institute*, 448 US 607, 685 (1980) (Rehnquist, J., concurring in the judgment). Agencies making key policy decisions pursuant to vague laws can still operate in otherwise nonarbitrary ways.

117. At least one commentator has argued that constitutional challenges, including nondelegation challenges, would not be barred by the "committed to agency discretion" exception to judicial review, but the courts have not made such a sweeping declaration. See Amee B. Bergin, "Does Application of the APA's 'Committed to Agency Discretion' Exception Violate the Nondelegation Doctrine?," *Boston College Environmental Affairs Law Review* 28 (2004): 363, 395, https://lawdigitalcommons.bc.edu/ealr/vol28/iss2/3/.

118. See, for example, *Mistretta*, 488 US at 361, Brief for the United States, 1988 WL 1026050 *23 ("In deciding whether [the nondelegation] standard has been satisfied, the Court has been most reluctant to conclude that Congress has unconstitutionally yielded its power to another Branch.").

119. See Wallison, *Judicial Fortitude*, 109–36 (discussing the nondelegation doctrine).

120. *Weyerhaeuser*, 139 S. Ct. 361 (2018).

121. *Markle Interests v. US Fish and Wildlife Service*, 827 F.3d 432, 474 (5th Cir. 2016).

122. *Weyerhaeuser*, 139 S. Ct. at 370.

123. *Weyerhaeuser*, 139 S. Ct. at 370 (internal citation omitted).

124. *Department of Commerce*, 139 S. Ct. at 2551.

125. 13 USC § 141.

126. *Department of Commerce*, 139 S. Ct. at 2568.

127. *Department of Commerce*, 139 S. Ct. at 2568.

128. *Department of Commerce*, 139 S. Ct. at 2568. The majority noted, for instance, that mandating a population count for the purpose of apportioning representation gave rise to a duty of accuracy and that the secretary's power to gather information through direct inquiry is limited where administrative records can suffice.

129. *Heckler*, 470 US at 831.

130. See *Union of Concerned Scientists v. Wheeler*, 954 F.3d 11 (1st Cir. 2020).

131. See, for example, *Trout Unlimited*, 1 F.4th at 752–53 (denying review where EPA's discretionary veto authority over Clean Water Act permits left no law to apply); *Eads v. Federal Bureau of Prisons*, No. 19-18394, 2021 WL 1085459 *2-3 (D. New Jersey 2021) (holding that Federal Bureau of Prisons' statutory duty to "provide for the safekeeping, care, and subsistence" did not contain sufficient standards for courts to review the bureau's medical care of inmates); *Chicago Teachers Union v. DeVos*, 468 F. Supp. 3d 974, 987–88 (N.D. Ill. 2020) ("Because of the extremely general wording" of CARES Act grant of authority to Department of Education to waive certain statutory requirements, the statute does not provide "sufficient guidance for the Court to assess the Secretary's exercise of discretion."); *Freedom Watch v. McAleenan*, No. 19-cv-1374, 2020 WL 922909, at *10-12 (D.D.C. Feb. 26, 2020) (declining to review Department of Homeland Security action because no substantive standards guided its discretion); and *Wood v. US Department of Agriculture Rural Housing Service*, No. 2:19-cv-00897, 2020 WL 1521801, at *3 (S.D. W. Va. Mar. 30, 2020) (citing the "no law to apply" standard as good law).

132. See *Webster v. Doe*, 486 US 592 (1988) (holding that at least some constitutional claims may be heard even if statutory claims are precluded by APA § 701(a)(2)). See also *Webster*, 486 US at 617–18 (Scalia, J., dissenting) (disagreeing with that distinction but arguing strongly against the "no law to apply" rationale).

Reinvigorating Nondelegation with Core Legislative Power

MARK CHENOWETH AND RICHARD SAMP

The nondelegation doctrine—which "bars Congress from transferring its legislative power to another branch of Government"[1]—holds a unique liminal status in constitutional law. Throughout our nation's history, the Supreme Court has strongly endorsed the doctrine as an important mechanism enforcing the separation of powers.[2] Yet that strong endorsement in theory turns into lip service in practice, as the Court has consistently rejected nondelegation-based challenges. Since the mid-1940s, it has applied a vacuous test for determining whether a statute delegates legislative authority in violation of Article I, § 1 of the US Constitution.[3] No statute has ever flunked that test.

The problem is not (just) that justices are easy graders; the test itself is flawed. It directs courts to determine merely whether "Congress has supplied an intelligible principle to guide the deleg[at]ee's use of discretion."[4] If a statute supplies such a principle, the test deems Congress not to have delegated *legislative* power, and any nondelegation doctrine claim is rejected. The Court has also construed the term "intelligible principle" extremely broadly, encompassing virtually any statement by Congress regarding how an agency should exercise its delegated powers. Thus, for example, the Supreme Court upheld a delegation to the Occupational Safety and Health Administration to establish workplace safety standards "reasonably necessary or appropriate to provide safe or healthful employment and places of employment."[5] If courts are to return to the business of providing meaningful review of whether a statute delegating power to a federal agency complies with the Vesting Clause (as we believe they should), the toothless intelligible-principle test will need to be replaced, or at least supplemented, by one(s) with more bite.

Judicial nonenforcement of the Vesting Clause might be more constitutionally palatable if there were some method by which Congress could easily reclaim any delegated legislative power. But there is not. Recent congressional deadlock demonstrates that repealing statutes that have delegated power to the executive branch requires overcoming Senate filibusters, gaining majority approval in both houses of Congress, and garnering the president's approval—a task not entirely in Congress' hands.

For this reason, the term "delegation" misleads. It suggests a revocable assignment of legislative authority to an agent of a kind that can be reclaimed unilaterally. Yet when Congress adopts legislation that grants lawmaking power to a federal department or agency, reversing that grant is a Herculean labor. Absent presidential consent, recovery of even small amounts of delegated legislative power requires obtaining veto-proof, two-thirds majorities in both houses of Congress.

This chapter proposes some alternative tests focused on the concept of "core legislative power." The first section reviews the various concerns about the nondelegation doctrine that likely have led the Supreme Court to shy away from enforcing the Vesting Clause—even as the justices continue to articulate the important role the nondelegation doctrine plays in upholding separation-of-powers principles. The second section proposes three new standards that will enable more meaningful judicial review of whether federal statutes delegate legislative power. The final section explains how these new standards account for the Supreme Court's legitimate concerns that have led it to adopt limits on the nondelegation doctrine.

Causes of Judicial Abdication of Vesting Clause Enforcement

The Supreme Court has not invoked the nondelegation doctrine to strike down a federal statute since 1935, before the vacuous version of the intelligible-principle test now in use took its current form.[6] In *Panama Refining Company v. Ryan,* the Court struck down a statute that authorized the president to prohibit interstate transportation of certain petroleum products but that provided "no definition of circumstances and conditions in which the transportation is to be allowed or prohibited."[7] And in

A. L. A. Schechter Poultry Corp. v. United States,[8] the Court held that federal legislation authorizing the president to establish "codes of fair competition" for a wide variety of industries failed to establish any meaningful guidance regarding the content of those codes—and thereby transferred legislative power to the executive branch in violation of the Vesting Clause.

But in later years, the Court has rejected nondelegation challenges to statutes that delegated sweeping powers to federal agencies and that were not meaningfully distinguishable from the statutes at issue in *Panama Refining* and *A. L. A. Schechter Poultry.* We have identified three concerns that may have led the Supreme Court to eschew enforcement of the nondelegation doctrine in the decades following *Panama Refining* and *A. L. A. Schechter Poultry.*

Incompatibility with the Modern Administrative State. Numerous commentators have alleged that the nondelegation concept is anachronistic in today's complex society. It may have been workable in 1787, they argue, when the federal government had a limited role and Congress could realistically write all the rules governing executive branch conduct. But modern America could not continue to operate without an extensive administrative state with the authority to write rules governing new and complex issues that arise on a daily basis.[9]

There is considerable reason to question the assertion that modern government could not function if major policy decisions were made by Congress, not administrative agencies. For example, Congress (through its adoption of the lengthy Internal Revenue Code) has established all major policies governing taxation of income. Yet the income-tax system continues to run smoothly. Although the IRS is authorized to write regulations that "fill up the details,"[10] it must do so in compliance with the policies Congress established.

In addition, one could imagine a system under which any major regulations promulgated by the executive branch returned to Congress for a vote before going into effect. Or, major regulations could include a provision automatically sunsetting them after two or three years unless Congress voted to maintain them. Indeed, such ideas have been proposed in this volume as a means to restore congressional control over executive policymaking. These schemes would grant federal agencies considerable leeway to respond to new and complex problems while obviating any perceived need for Congress to adopt laws granting agencies open-ended legislative power.[11]

Nonetheless, the Supreme Court has on occasion explicitly cited inability-to-function concerns to justify its rejection of nondelegation doctrine claims. In a 1946 decision upholding Section 11(b) of the Public Utility Holding Company Act of 1935 (which authorized the Securities and Exchange Commission to act to ensure that the corporate structure of holding companies did not "unduly or unnecessarily complicate the structure"), the Court said:

> The judicial approval accorded these "broad" standards for administrative action is a reflection of the necessities of modern legislation dealing with complex economic and social problems. The legislative process would frequently bog down if Congress were constitutionally required to appraise beforehand the myriad situations to which it wishes a particular policy to be applied.[12]

The Court cited similar concerns in a decision upholding a statute that delegated policymaking responsibilities to the judiciary: "Our jurisprudence has been driven by a practical understanding that, in our increasingly complex society, replete with ever-changing and more technical problems, Congress simply cannot do its job absent an ability to delegate power under broad general directives."[13]

So, one can reasonably conclude that the Supreme Court will be reluctant to adopt any new nondelegation doctrine test that the Court fears may interfere with efficient government operations—regardless of whether the Court believes the Constitution mandates its results.

Fear of Results-Oriented Judicial Overreach. The Supreme Court's reluctance to adopt an enforceable test for judging nondelegation claims may also arise from a suspicion that some judges would use such authority to strike down statutes they find objectionable for policy reasons. Indeed, the Court's 1935 decisions in *Panama Refining* and (to a lesser extent) *A. L. A. Schechter Poultry* have been unfairly criticized by some commentators as results-oriented decisions written by justices ideologically opposed to President Franklin D. Roosevelt's New Deal policies.[14] But *Panama Refining* was an 8–1 decision, and *A. L. A. Schechter Poultry* was unanimous. These were not ideologically riven decisions.

Both *Panama Refining* and *A. L. A. Schechter Poultry* remain good law, they continue to be cited favorably by the Court, and (as noted above) the nondelegation doctrine continues to be touted by the Court as important to maintaining the constitutionally mandated separation of powers. In a 1980 opinion, then–Associate Justice William Rehnquist opined that *Panama Refining* and similar nondelegation doctrine cases had unfairly fallen "under a cloud" because they were issued at the same time as decisions that invoked substantive due process to strike down other New Deal programs.[15] While many of those substantive due process decisions were later overruled and are now widely viewed as having been driven at least in part by policy disagreements with New Deal programs, Rehnquist opined that *Panama Refining* and *A. L. A. Schechter Poultry* "suffer from none of the excesses of judicial policymaking that plagued some of the other decisions of that era."[16]

Nonetheless, lawsuits raising nondelegation claims in most instances seek to prevent regulation (or challenge enforcement) by executive branch agencies, so any judicial decrees validating those claims will tend to reduce government regulation of the private sector. Thus, the Supreme Court may fear that a substantial revitalization of the nondelegation doctrine would grant judges with policy-based objections to government regulation (e.g., of business practices) too much leeway to issue rulings designed to hamper those agencies' operations.

There is considerable reason to doubt that revitalizing the nondelegation doctrine would lead to increased instances of results-oriented judicial overreach. For one thing, courts predisposed to hamper an agency's operations already possess a powerful tool for doing so: They can rule that the agency is acting in excess of its statutory authority.[17] Moreover, there are sound separation-of-powers reasons to prefer judicial focus on nondelegation doctrine claims rather than on excess-of-statutory authority claims. When courts increase enforcement of the nondelegation doctrine, they are not simply enhancing their own power; they are also enhancing Congress' power by ensuring that Congress plays its constitutionally mandated role in deciding important policy issues.[18]

Difficulty Sorting Legislative from Executive Action. The Supreme Court recognizes that *any* delegation of legislative power violates the Vesting Clause.[19] It has nonetheless been reluctant to strictly enforce the nondelegation doctrine in light of the inherent difficulty in distinguishing between a federal agency's unconstitutional exercise of delegated legislative power and an agency's customary exercise of permissible discretion in executing the law.

The Court's many attempts to distinguish verboten legislative power from proper executive power have not succeeded in overcoming that difficulty. For example, it stated in *Marshall Field & Co. v. Clark*:

> The true distinction . . . is between the delegation of power to make law, which necessarily involves a discretion as to what it shall be, and conferring authority or discretion as to its execution, to be exercised under and in pursuance of the law. The first cannot be done; to the latter no valid objection can be made. . . . Half the statutes on our books are in the alternative, depending on the discretion of some person or persons to whom is confided the duty of determining whether the proper occasion exists for executing them. But it cannot be said that the exercise of such discretion is the making of the law.[20]

Such statements fail to establish a clear rule for distinguishing between a statute that delegates "power to make law" and one that merely confers "discretion as to its execution." In some instances, the discretion conferred by the statute consists of nothing more than the authority to engage in fact-finding, and the statute then directs an agency to act in a specified manner depending on its finding.[21] But more frequently, an administrator tasked with enforcing a statute is faced with a factual situation not expressly contemplated by Congress. Has Congress then merely granted the administrator discretion to determine his or her course of action based on policies set out in the statute, or has Congress violated the Vesting Clause by delegating to the administrator the power to draft the policy on his or her own?

The Founders recognized that often there is no easy answer to that question. James Madison stated in *Federalist 37*:

Experience has instructed us that no skill in the science of government has yet been able to discriminate and define, with sufficient certainty, its three great provinces—the legislative, executive, and judiciary. . . . Questions daily occur in the course of practice, which prove the obscurity which reigns in these subjects, and which puzzle the greatest adepts in political science.[22]

Chief Justice John Marshall recognized, in *Wayman v. Southard*, that the Vesting Clause did not prohibit Congress from delegating the task of "fill[ing] up the details" of legislation,[23] but he made no effort to clarify how significant those "details" could be before the delegated discretion transforms into an unconstitutional delegation of legislative power.

The Supreme Court has cited this line-drawing difficulty as a reason for throwing up its hands and declining to second-guess a congressional decision to delegate authority to the executive branch. Justice Antonin Scalia succinctly explained that rationale as follows:

While the doctrine of unconstitutional delegation is unquestionably a fundamental element of our constitutional system, it is not an element readily enforceable by the courts. Once it is conceded, as it must be, that no statute can be entirely precise, and that some judgments, even some judgments involving policy considerations, must be left to the officers executing the law and to the judges applying it, the debate over unconstitutional delegation becomes a debate not over a point of principle, but over a question of degree. . . . Since Congress is no less endowed with common sense than we are, and better equipped to inform itself of the "necessities" of government . . . it is small wonder that we have almost never felt qualified to second-guess Congress regarding the permissible degree of policy judgment that can be left to those executing or applying the law.[24]

But such reticence is in considerable tension with the Founders' vision of the courts as "faithful guardians of the Constitution."[25] Alexander Hamilton argued that courts have a "duty" to "declare all acts contrary to the manifest tenor of the Constitution void" and that judicial review of legislation is "essential" to preserving the Constitution's limits on "legislative authority."[26]

Moreover, while the line-drawing difficulty articulated by Justice Scalia may justify courts exercising great caution before striking down a federal statute under the nondelegation doctrine, it has no relevance when the challenged statute delegates—or divests—*all* nontrivial policymaking responsibilities to the executive branch. Under those circumstances, no line drawing is necessary; the federal courts should not quail at classifying such divested authority as "legislative power[ ]" within the meaning of the Vesting Clause—and rule it out accordingly.

Replacing the Intelligible-Principle Test

The Court currently adjudges nondelegation doctrine claims under the intelligible-principle test: It rejects such claims so long as "Congress has supplied an intelligible principle to guide the deleg[at]ee's use of discretion."[27]

The Court first employed the phrase "intelligible principle" in 1928 in *J. W. Hampton Jr. & Co. v. United States*.[28] In rejecting a nondelegation doctrine challenge to the Tariff Act of 1922, Chief Justice William Howard Taft explained for the Court, "If Congress shall lay down by legislative act an intelligible principle to which the person or body authorized to fix such rates is directed to conform, such legislative action is not a forbidden delegation of legislative power."[29]

That statement broke no new ground; it made clear, in compliance with prior case law, that the requisite intelligible principle had to spell out rules to which the administrator must "conform." And the tariff statute upheld by *J. W. Hampton* imposed strict limits on the Tariff Commission's authority to impose supplemental tariffs. It permitted such tariffs only if the commission made a factual finding that costs of producing the article in the United States were greater than in the exporting country, provided guidance on how to determine costs of production, and permitted supplemental tariffs only in an amount necessary to compensate for the difference in production costs (and in no event greater than 50 percent of the tariffs already imposed by the statute).[30] Chief Justice Taft's reference to an "intelligible principle" was "just another way to describe the traditional rule that Congress may leave the executive the responsibility to find facts and fill up details."[31]

Starting in the late 1940s, however, as "intelligible principle" became the Court's principal standard governing nondelegation doctrine challenges, that phrase became unmoored from the traditional rule.[32] Moreover, the phrase's meaning gradually expanded with repeated use—like a worn-out elastic band—so that "intelligible principle" has come to be understood as encompassing virtually any statutory language that directs administrators to consider one or more factors when determining how to carry out their duties, even when administrators are afforded unconstrained discretion to determine what role those factors should play in their ultimate decisions.[33] Indeed, the Court's discussion of the intelligible-principle test often consists of little more than reciting rote assertions: that the Court has not invalidated a statute under the nondelegation doctrine since 1935; that since then it has upheld, "without deviation, Congress' ability to delegate power under broad standards"; and that the challenged statute provides at least as much guidance regarding how it is to be implemented as did statutes previously deemed to provide the requisite intelligible principles.[34]

Under recent case law, it is fair to conclude that a statute supplies the requisite intelligible principle even if it merely states policy goals and imposes no material constraints on an agency's authority to establish rules governing the regulated community. Commentators agree that if the nondelegation doctrine is to play any meaningful role in ensuring compliance with the Vesting Clause, the intelligible-principle test must be replaced by a more exacting standard.[35] But there is little likelihood that the Court will adopt a new standard unless the standard is responsive to the concerns—described above—that have led the Court over the past 75 years to shrink from enforcing the Vesting Clause. To this end, the next few sections propose a series of viable replacements for the intelligible-principle test that together provide a more exacting standard to police compliance with the nondelegation doctrine—tests that, we submit, would be administrable by the federal courts.

First, we propose that all statutes challenged under the nondelegation doctrine be subjected to a somewhat enhanced—but still relatively lenient—review standard. Under this initial cut, which we refer to as the "absence of standards" test, a statute granting powers to an administrative agency violates the Vesting Clause if it imposes *no* meaningful or judicially administrable limits on the scope of agency authority.

Second, as a more robust alternative or supplement to the absence-of-standards test, we suggest a review standard with more teeth: A statute is valid only if it provides standards by which the judiciary may adjudge whether the executive is complying with restrictions Congress enumerated in the legislation.

Third, we propose that courts should apply far closer Vesting Clause scrutiny when challenged legislation authorizes federal agencies to perform one of five "core" legislative functions that we identify. Because performing any one of those functions ordinarily constitutes exercising legislative power, closer scrutiny of such legislation is warranted. Legislation that divests core legislative power is not commonplace, but the dire threat it poses to separation-of-powers principles requires vigorous and unapologetic judicial gatekeeping.

A Minimum Prerequisite for Judges to Enforce: Does the Statute Establish *Any* Ascertainable Standards? As noted above, it is often difficult to distinguish between statutes that delegate power to make law (prohibited by the Vesting Clause) and statutes that merely confer discretion as to their execution (constitutionally permissible). But that difficulty should not dissuade the Court from invalidating statutes that unquestionably fall into the former category. And, as a first cut, when a statute fails to include *any* binding standards that limit an agency's rulemaking authority—but rather lists some goals to which the agency should aspire—Congress should be deemed to have improperly delegated its legislative authority.

The Court articulated a viable review standard along those lines in a 1944 decision, *Yakus v. United States*.[36] That case held that nondelegation doctrine claims should be evaluated based on whether, in the challenged statute, "there is an *absence of standards* for the guidance of the Administrator's action, so that it would be impossible in a proper proceeding to ascertain whether the will of Congress has been obeyed."[37] (Emphasis added.)

A relatively undemanding version of this test, which should serve as a minimum prerequisite, is satisfied by most statutes that have come before the Court. If the government can point to at least *some* potential regulations that would be barred by the statute in question—even though those regulations are otherwise consistent with the agency's general mission—then there is not a complete "absence of standards." That would remain true even if the challenger could point to regulations whose adoption entails some degree of policymaking by the adopting agency.

The statute at issue in *Yakus*—a wartime price-control statute—serves to illustrate the point. Congress could not realistically set the price of every product sold in the United States. Instead, the Emergency Price Control Act of 1942[38] established rules for how the administrator was to establish those prices. As amended, the act set out general policies governing prices and then directed the administrator "to give due consideration, as far as practical, to prevailing pricing during the designated base period [September 1942] with prescribed administrative adjustments to compensate for enumerated disturbing factors affecting prices."[39]

No doubt the act could have been more specific regarding the extent to which price ceilings were required to be tied to prices that prevailed in September 1942; it was left to the administrator's discretion to determine just how close the tie should be. But the Court rejected a nondelegation doctrine challenge because the act unquestionably adopted *some* standards that limited the administrator's price-setting authority.[40] He was not permitted, for example, to designate September 1941 (instead of September 1942) as the "base period" from which to compute price ceilings.

In contrast, federal statutes fail to establish *any* "standards" (thereby improperly delegating legislative authority) if they merely state vacuous aspirational goals or recite factors that federal agencies should take into account—without providing guidance on *how* those factors should be taken into account. When a statute instructs an agency to adopt "reasonable" regulations or regulate "in the public interest," it imposes *no* meaningful or judicially administrable limits on the scope of regulations.[41]

The absence-of-standards test suggested by *Yakus* would permit at least some meaningful review of nondelegation doctrine claims yet would likely not trigger the concerns that have led the Supreme Court to largely abandon enforcement of the Vesting Clause. The absence-of-standards test would not bring the administrative state to a halt. Congress could continue to grant agencies considerable discretion in executing their assigned statutes; it would simply need to ensure that each such grant of discretion includes at least one discernible limit on agency action. Because application of the absence-of-standards test is relatively straightforward (can the government identify at least one nontrivial regulatory action that is germane to the agency's mission but nonetheless explicitly prohibited by the statute?), courts would no longer be asked to draw fine lines between permissible uses of customary executive discretion and unconstitutional delegations of legislative power.

A recent nondelegation challenge to legislation governing imports illustrates the absence-of-standards test's bite. In *American Institute for International Steel v. United States*,[42] a group of steel importers challenged a federal statute under which President Donald Trump imposed supplemental tariffs on steel imports.[43] The statute authorizes the imposition of tariffs on imports to the extent necessary to ensure, in the president's judgment, "that such imports will not threaten to impair the national security."[44] The statute provides a lengthy list of factors that the president should consider in deciding whether imports impair national security—and thus arguably satisfies the current intelligible-principle test. But it cannot survive scrutiny under the absence-of-standards test because it grants the president unbounded discretion in determining how to apply the listed factors. Indeed, government attorneys defending against *American Institute for International Steel*'s nondelegation doctrine challenge could not point to any tariffs that the president would not be authorized to impose under the impair-the-national-security standard.

The absence-of-standards test will not ferret out every impermissible delegation of legislative power. But it has the advantage of being an administrable standard that establishes a bright-line, easily enforceable rule. The absence-of-standards test would enable courts to step in and enforce the Vesting Clause when legislation grants agencies unbridled authority to establish policy.

Courts applying this test must be careful not to assume that if a statute satisfies the absence-of-standards test, any regulatory action under that statute is allowed that is not explicitly prohibited. That assumption would run contrary to a government of limited powers.[45] Rather, the point of the test is merely to serve as a first hurdle; it can be failed, but clearing it does not mean that a challenged statute complies with the Vesting Clause or that any regulatory action undertaken pursuant to the statute is allowed.

A Clear-Statement Principle for Judges to Enforce: Does the Statute Demarcate Limits Judges Can Police? A second, more stringent test can be derived from *Yakus* and applied alternatively or in conjunction with the absence-of-standards test described above. This stricter "sufficient-judicial-standards" test would adjudge a statute valid only if it provides standards by which the judiciary may discern whether the executive is complying with restrictions demarcated in the legislation—that is, can *judges* tell "whether the will of Congress has been obeyed"[46]? So conceived, such a clear-statement principle would shift the focus from whether Congress has given an "intelligible principle" *to the executive* (which judges may be ill-equipped to ascertain) to ask instead whether Congress has provided sufficient standards *to the judiciary* to enable judges to police the delegation line (which every judge ought to be able to discern and which Hamilton deemed it "essential" for them to do to preserve limits on legislative authority).

Under this stricter version of *Yakus*, if a statute lacks sufficient guideposts for courts to discern its limits or ascertain the legislative will of Congress, the answer would not be for the court to throw up its hands and give up on deciding whether a delegation of legislative power occurred—nor, contra *City of Arlington v. FCC*,[47] to defer to the agency's reasonable interpretation of the scope of its own jurisdiction.[48] Instead, the very lack of sufficient judicially administrable standards to adjudicate the limits of any permissible delegation of executive discretion would itself be deemed to violate the Vesting Clause by delegating open-ended legislative power (somewhat akin to the overbreadth doctrine in the First Amendment context).

A clearer statement from the legislature, better specifying the limits of the contemplated delegation, would be required in the future to uphold it. Congress, in other words, *must* delineate the boundaries in which agencies may work. It "must set forth standards 'sufficiently definite and precise to enable Congress, *the courts*, and the public to ascertain' whether Congress's guidance has been followed."[49] (Emphasis added.) Or, in the words of *Yakus* itself, the nondelegation inquiry must focus on whether the challenged statute "sufficiently marks the field within which the Administrator is to act so that it may be known whether he has kept within it in compliance with the legislative will."[50]

Without such limits, the delegation could not reasonably be categorized as being confined to the customary exercise of discretion in executing the law. In a Constitution of limited powers, in which legislative power is not only carefully circumscribed but also assigned exclusively to the legislative branch, it makes sense not to permit broad delegations that the judicial branch is incapable of policing. Otherwise, there is no way to prevent impermissible delegations whenever the legislative and executive branches are complicit in attempting to transfer core legislative power.

Moreover, given that Congress cannot easily or unilaterally reclaim any divested legislative power once it gives up that power, it makes sense for courts to be sure that Congress has carefully delineated the scope of the legislative policy across which executive discretion may be exercised before upholding it. Otherwise, even a permissible delegation could be exploited or expanded by executive officials and turned into a delegation of legislative power that Congress did not authorize—and one it could not then unilaterally unwind.

Judicial error in the direction of not approving a delegation encompassing executive discretion that Congress meant to happen is much easier to correct (primarily because the president will agree to the fix) than judicial error in the direction of approving impermissible delegations of legislative power by Congress (whether or not the current Congress meant to surrender them). The latter may never get corrected because the president has no incentive to give up legislative power that a federal agency under him has arrogated to itself—even if improperly—let alone legislative power that has been delegated to him directly. Because over-enforcement of the Vesting Clause is thus more readily remediable (and the attendant consequences less dire) than is under-enforcement of it, the sufficient-judicial-standards version of the *Yakus* test would counsel courts to err on the side of forcing Congress to articulate clear limits on any questionable delegation.

A "judicially administrable standards" test would be relatively easy for judges to enforce as well. It recognizes the limits of judicial competence to reliably distinguish, in close cases, between a statute that improperly delegates legislative power and one that merely confers discretion as to its execution. If a party with standing challenged the statute in question as deficient (or, perhaps more likely, challenged a regulation based on the flawed statute as an impermissible delegation due to the lack of judicially administrable standards in the statute), the question for the Court would be simple: Does the challenged law or regulation provide adequate standards for the Court to ascertain whether the executive is complying with any restrictions demarcated in the legislation?

At the same time, recall that, if no restrictions are enumerated in the law, then it fails even the lax absence-of-standards test derived from *Yakus* and is an impermissible delegation of legislative power for that reason. To have standing, such a plaintiff would need to show injury-in-fact. For this reason, it generally would not be possible to challenge a statute or regulation on "insufficient standards" grounds until an administrative agency begins to enforce or apply the statute. A facial challenge to a statute would have to allege direct injury from the overbreadth of the statute itself—if, say, it confers both permissible discretion *and* impermissible core legislative power.

The price controls at issue in *Yakus* and the tariffs litigated in *American Institute for International Steel* are both forms of financial regulation. When dealing with money, Congress should have no difficulty setting parameters that constrain an agency's policy choices and thereby avoid delegating legislative power. It may be more difficult for Congress to fashion judicially administrable fetters that confine agency conduct when not dealing with dollars and cents, but the Vesting Clause does not permit Congress to delegate nonfinancial legislative power any more than it permits Congress to delegate any other legislative power. And just because the job may be hard does not free Congress from the obligation to do it.

At the same time, it is not for the courts to devise the constraints that any particular legislative act puts on an administrative agency to ensure that the policies that agency pursues do not exceed the boundaries Congress has demarcated. It is Congress' job to articulate the strictures. A court's role is confined to ensuring that Congress (1) has established those limits in a way that precludes the delegation of legislative power and (2) has supplied feasible standards that enable courts to tell whether an agency has exceeded the applicable limits. If Congress has done those two things, then a court ought to be able to enforce those congressionally demarcated limits on agency action—and must do so.

A Constitutional Prohibition for Judges to Enforce: Congress May Never Delegate Core Legislative Power. Once a judge is satisfied that Congress has spoken clearly enough to effectuate a delegation encompassing executive discretion and carefully enough to specify the lawful limits of that delegation, there are still substantive constraints on how much power, what kind of power, and how irrevocably Congress may delegate any power to the executive branch. The Vesting Clause vests "all legislative Powers" in Congress. In other words, through the Constitution, the people have already delegated the legislative power to Congress, so Congress is not free to subdelegate that power to anyone else. Or, as Chief Justice Taft put the point in J. W. Hampton, *"delegata potestas non potest delegari."*[51] Although some amount of delegation of executive discretion may be unavoidable to effectuate Congress' legislative agenda, constitutional limits subject to judicial enforcement persist.

Some commentators have suggested that the nondelegation doctrine should focus on preventing delegation of legislative powers for major national policies. Justice Rehnquist argued that an "important function" of the nondelegation doctrine is that it "ensures . . . that important choices of social policy are made by Congress, the branch of our Government most responsive to the popular will."[52] Justice Brett Kavanaugh recently cited that argument in connection with his observation that this opinion by Justice Rehnquist, as well as that by Justice Neil Gorsuch (in *Gundy v. United States*), "may warrant further consideration in future cases."[53]

The chief difficulty with adopting a major-national-policy approach to enforcing the nondelegation doctrine is that there are no objective means of determining a "major" issue. Measuring "major" based on financial cost would eliminate consideration of social issues (e.g., abortion and tolerance of religious objectors) that many citizens would classify as "major." Nor does the Vesting Clause distinguish between major and minor policy decisions; it bans *all* delegation of legislative power. Most people, for example, would not classify regulations governing shoe design as "major," but a statute that delegated unconstrained authority to a federal agency to adopt such regulations would be just as objectionable as a statute delegating similarly unconstrained authority to regulate health care nationwide.[54]

Rather than asking courts to discern the subjective importance of the *issue* addressed by a disputed statute, a more appropriate focus of nondelegation doctrine attention would be for courts to assess the particular *function* that Congress is transferring when it adopts a piece of legislation. We submit that the nondelegation doctrine is implicated when the disputed statute involves delegating the exercise of any core congressional functions. The delegation of legislative power in connection with one of these core functions is particularly likely to wreak havoc on separation-of-powers principles and thus calls for closer judicial scrutiny of challenges to delegated authority.

We have identified five Article I powers that can properly be labeled "core" components of Congress' irreducible legislative power, although there are undoubtedly others.

First comes the power to impose taxes, a power carefully circumscribed by the Constitution.

Second is the power to expend federal funds and otherwise dispose of federal property. While Congress could not possibly exert legislative control over the details of every federal expenditure, it has historically used its spending powers to direct how much money each federal agency can spend, adopt general policies regarding spending priorities, and supervise—and conduct oversight review of—agency spending.

Third, enacting criminal statutes is a core congressional function, because the alternative (delegating legislative power to the executive branch) has an untenable result—placing the lawmaking and the law-enforcing powers in a single branch of government.

Fourth, a core function of Congress is to resolve policy disputes that surface during the legislative process. Congress may pass legislation adopting its preferred policy, it may delegate conditional fact-finding to an agency on which to base resolution of the dispute, or it may choose to do nothing. What the Vesting Clause prohibits it from doing is dodging the requirements of bicameralism, indirectly binding a future Congress through executive action, or otherwise delegating this core policy conflict-resolution function to a federal agency or other executive branch entity.

Finally, Congress may not surrender its ability to act as a check on the executive branch. Any statute that more than marginally dilutes Congress' core power to hold the executive accountable and counterbalance executive power would be subject to heightened scrutiny and ultimately nonenforcement under the nondelegation doctrine.

If challenged, a statute adopted by Congress that shares or transfers one of these five core functions should undergo close judicial scrutiny to determine whether the authority that the statute assigns to a federal department or agency effects an unconstitutional delegation of legislative power. That close scrutiny should not be limited to cases involving controls on private conduct. The Vesting Clause prohibits *all* delegation of legislative power.

The Founders adopted the clause to restrict lawmaking authority, both to discourage new laws imposing restrictions on personal liberty and prevent the deliberative process from being short-circuited.[55] If Congress were permitted to delegate its legislative authority to others, Article I's detailed and intentionally cumbersome processes for new laws (designed to promote deliberation) could easily be circumvented.[56] Thus, for example, spending legislation is not exempted from nondelegation doctrine scrutiny simply because it often does not give rise to controls on private conduct.[57]

The Taxing Power. Article I, § 8 of the Constitution enumerates the powers of Congress. First in place among these enumerated powers is the "Power to lay and collect taxes." The taxing power is extremely broad in scope. Indeed, the Supreme Court recently recognized that "the breadth of Congress's power to tax is greater than its power to regulate commerce."[58]

Because of its breadth, the taxing power can be highly dangerous if abused. Chief Justice Marshall famously noted that "the power to tax involves the power to destroy."[59] In recognition of those dangers, the Founders placed special controls on the enactment of federal taxes.

In addition to the usual hurdles that proposed legislation must overcome before becoming law—approval by both Houses of Congress plus either the president's approval or an override of a presidential veto by both Houses—tax bills must also comply with the Origination Clause, which provides that "all bills for raising Revenue [must] originate in the House of Representatives."[60] The Direct Tax Clause imposes an additional limit on federal taxing authority: "No Capitation, or other direct, Tax shall be laid, unless in Proportion to the Census or Enumeration."[61]

If Congress were permitted to delegate its taxing power to a federal administrative agency, the Constitution's controls on tax legislation would be bypassed. The dangers thereby created are such that careful judicial review of any alleged delegation of taxing power is warranted.

The issue of delegated taxing authority arises most frequently in the context of legislation authorizing administrative agencies to impose fees on recipients of their services (e.g., entry fees at national parks). It is well accepted that Congress may delegate to an administrative agency the authority to assess fees on these recipients, provided that the fees imposed do not exceed the value of those services. But fees are normally categorized as "taxes" if the fees exceed that value, and the Supreme Court recognized in 1974 that Congress' delegation of its taxing power raises serious constitutional questions under the Vesting Clause.[62]

The Court appeared to backtrack from that position in a 1989 decision involving "user fees" imposed on pipeline companies by the Department of Transportation (DOT).[63] The Court held that legislation authorizing DOT to impose user fees did not violate the nondelegation doctrine; it also stated that suits alleging unconstitutional delegation of taxing power were not subject to closer scrutiny than other types of nondelegation doctrine claims.[64] The Court's rejection of heightened scrutiny for taxing power claims was likely *dicta*, however, given that the challenged statute included numerous standards that constrained DOT's authority to assess user fees.

As the Supreme Court recognized, Congress has "wisely" chosen "to be more circumspect in delegating authority under the Taxing Clause than under other of its enumerated powers."[65] That circumspection reflects the "core" nature of the taxing power and justifies imposing more exacting scrutiny to claims involving delegation of discretionary authority under the taxing power. The test outlined in *National Cable Television Association v. United States* provides a sound basis for evaluating claims that Congress has improperly delegated the legislative power to tax: Courts should find that Congress has violated the Constitution by delegating its taxing power if challenged legislation delegates authority to impose fees that exceed the value of an agency's services. No intelligible principle, however specified, can save such an unlawful delegation of core legislative power.

The Spending Power. Another core function of Congress is the power to fund government operations ("the power of the purse") and authorize expenditure of federal funds. It is well established that the expenditure of federal funds is contingent on congressional approval—as demonstrated by periodic shutdowns of the federal government when Congress fails to approve a budget on time. Congress' spending power derives from several constitutional provisions, including the Vesting Clause, the Appropriations Clause,[66] and Article IV's Property Clause—which grants Congress power to "dispose of and make all needful Rules and Regulations respecting . . . Property belonging to the United States."[67]

Given the scope of federal expenditures, Congress cannot plausibly make every granular decision regarding who is to receive money expended by the federal government. But Congress routinely adopts spending bills that specify how much money each federal agency is to spend and the nature of the projects on which the money is to be spent. Congress jealously guards its "power of the purse" and regularly seeks to rein in agencies it determines are not complying with its appropriations mandates.

The congressional check on executive branch spending would be lost if Congress were to delegate its legislative power to authorize spending or to authorize spending from sources of funding outside Congress' control. Because that annual check on spending is a core tool Congress uses to ensure the balance of powers among the three branches of government, courts should carefully scrutinize any delegated (or surrendered) spending authority that could upset that balance.

One unprecedented delegation of the spending power is the subject of a pending challenge in federal court. The Consumer Financial Protection Act, adopted by Congress in 2010, established the Consumer Financial Protection Bureau (CFPB) as an "independent bureau" in the Federal Reserve System.[68] The act seeks to maintain CFPB's independence from both the president and Congress by, among other things, removing CFPB from the normal congressional budgeting process. Instead, CFPB funds come from the Federal Reserve Board of Governors, which gives CFPB a portion of the earnings of the Federal Reserve System.[69] Nor does the Board of Governors determine CFPB's budget; the act specifies that the CFPB director unilaterally determines the CFPB budget, and the Board of Governors must comply with the director's funding requests.[70]

A lawsuit challenging the act's funding mechanism alleges that the act violates the Vesting Clause and the Appropriations Clause by delegating Congress' legislative power of the purse to the CFPB director and the

Federal Reserve Board of Governors.[71] That claim may well prevail even if evaluated solely under the lax absence-of-standards test described above. The act provides *no* standards that limit the funding the CFPB director is authorized to demand from the Federal Reserve Board of Governors— other than that the demand may not exceed 12 percent of the total annual expenses of the Federal Reserve System.[72] But given that Congress' spending power plays such a major role in reining in executive branch excesses, Congress' decision to abjure all control and oversight as to CFPB's funding and expenditures should be subject to a more exacting scrutiny under the nondelegation doctrine, a scrutiny it is highly unlikely to withstand.

If anything, the Supreme Court's recent decision in *Seila Law v. Consumer Financial Protection Bureau*[73] makes the constitutional problem with CFPB's funding mechanism even worse.[74] Post–*Seila Law*, the CFPB director is removable at will by the president, which puts the agency's self-funding authority under the president's direct control.[75] For now, such complete surrender of Congress' spending function to the executive branch enables the president to spend CFPB money without any congressional oversight or input whatsoever. That freewheeling funding regime is inimical to the plan for government spending spelled out in Article I of the Constitution.

Another kind of end run around congressional spending power occurred in the Department of Justice (DOJ) during the Obama administration. As part of its agreements with major banks, settling lawsuits stemming from the financial collapse of 2008–09, DOJ reduced settlement amounts owed to the US Treasury in exchange for defendants making "voluntary" contributions to third-party groups favored by the administration. For example, one settlement with Bank of America in August 2014 required the bank to pay hundreds of millions of dollars to a variety of nonprofit groups, ranging from activist legal services groups to providers of low-income housing.[76] Any statute purporting to authorize DOJ to engage in such third-party settlement activity, under which funds are effectively appropriated outside Congress' appropriations process, should be subject to enhanced judicial scrutiny under a nondelegation theory.[77] Under our proposed enhanced review standard, a statute authorizing an agency to accumulate, direct, or expend such federal funds (other than limited fees) is unconstitutional.

Drafting Criminal Statutes. Writing criminal laws is another core area of legislative power. Congress cannot delegate this responsibility outside the legislative branch because, by definition, the federal government is one of the parties to a federal criminal proceeding. Even where application of a statute with dual civil and criminal applications is being challenged, the federal government will be a party to the case. Hence, tolerating any delegation of legislative power to create criminal law from Congress to the executive branch would place the lawmaking and the law-enforcing powers in a single branch of government—a result antithetical to constitutional norms.

A key liberty-enhancing feature of the US Constitution is that no citizen can be imprisoned without the concurrence of all three branches of government and a jury of that citizen's peers. Congress has to write the criminal law and establish the appropriate penalty range, the executive branch has to file suitable charges and prosecute the case, and a judge (or jury, if a defendant prefers) has to determine whether the person is guilty of the crime charged. If Congress could delegate its criminal law-drafting function, it would collapse the division of the government's potent criminal power built into the Constitution. That would violate not only the separation of powers but also a criminal defendant's right to due process of law.

The Supreme Court's recent *Gundy* decision starkly illustrates these dangers.[78] The petitioner was convicted of failing to register as a sex offender, as he was required to do under 2010 regulations issued by the attorney general. A 2006 statute[79] authorized the attorney general to determine whether pre-2006 sex offenders (a category that included the petitioner) should be required to register. The Supreme Court rejected the petitioner's nondelegation doctrine challenge to the statute, construing the statute to apply retroactively to pre-2006 offenders and holding that the statute therefore provided an "intelligible principle."[80]

Nonetheless, it was only as a result of the regulations adopted by the attorney general, not the provisions of a statute, that hundreds of thousands of pre-2006 sex offenders became subject to registration requirements and substantial criminal penalties for noncompliance (up to 10 years in prison, which in some cases is greater than the sentence for the underlying sex offense). In other words, the Justice Department both drafted the law that created the criminal offense and prosecuted the petitioner for violating the law. Permitting the attorney general to wear both hats at once does not square with separation-of-powers principles.

As Justice Gorsuch charged in his dissenting opinion:

> Nor is it hard to imagine how the power at issue in this case—the power of a prosecutor to require a group to register with the government on pain of weighty criminal penalties—could be abused in other settings. To allow the nation's chief law enforcement officer to write the criminal laws he is charged with enforcing—to "unit[e]" the "legislative and executive powers . . . in the same person"—would be to mark the end of any meaningful enforcement of our separation of powers and invite the tyranny of the majority that follows when lawmaking and law enforcement responsibilities are united in the same hands.[81]

In a 1991 case, the Supreme Court considered a claim that it should apply a standard of review more stringent than the intelligible-principle test to nondelegation doctrine claims arising under criminal statutes.[82] The Court ultimately declined to resolve the issue because it determined that the challenged criminal statute "passes muster even if greater congressional specificity is required in the criminal context."[83] But the question raised there deserves to be answered in some future decision.

Justice Gorsuch's dissenting opinion in *Gundy*, joined by Chief Justice John Roberts and Justice Clarence Thomas, combined with the concurring opinion of Justice Samuel Alito (who expressed willingness to reconsider the "extraordinarily capacious standards" the Court applies in nondelegation doctrine cases)[84] and a recent statement by Justice Kavanaugh,[85] suggest that a majority of the justices may be willing to adopt stricter review standards in future nondelegation doctrine challenges, particularly in a challenge to a criminal statute.

Resolving Identified Policy Disputes. The Supreme Court has explained that "necessity" dictates its deferential approach to congressional decisions to delegate authority. It has concluded that "Congress simply cannot do its job absent an ability to delegate power under broad general directives."[86] According to the Court, a certain amount of delegation is required so that administrative officials will have the flexibility to address the many factual scenarios that Congress could not have contemplated when it adopted the legislation.[87] The Court has also suggested that delegation permits Congress to draw on the expertise of specialists who can address complex "technical problems" that Congress may feel ill-equipped to address.[88]

But even if flexibility and expertise justifications were arguably relevant in other contexts, they are irrelevant when members of Congress have directly confronted an issue during the legislative process, the issue does not require complex fact-finding, or the only impediment to congressional resolution of the issue is the inability of a majority in both Houses to agree on a policy solution. Under those circumstances, it is not "necessity" that drives the decision to delegate authority; it is expedience.

Hence, a statute will survive nondelegation doctrine scrutiny involving this core legislative power only if: (1) Congress resolves all explicit policy conflicts that arise during consideration of the statutory scheme (either by answering them in the statute, specifying an answer depending on subsequent agency fact-finding, or leaving them for future legislative resolution) and (2) Congress has not delegated policymaking to the executive branch that evades the legislative process.

When members of Congress delegate authority to administrative agencies to decide well-defined and well-understood issues left unresolved by Congress, they are doing so either to avoid political accountability for controversial decisions or because they hope administrators will be able to resolve the issues in the manner the members sought (but failed) to amass a legislative majority to achieve through legislation.[89] Neither of those rationales justifies disregarding the Vesting Clause's ban on delegating legislative power. Congressional statutes enjoy a presumption of constitutionality, but that does not mean Congress may dodge a constitutional requirement such as bicameralism.

Two recent Supreme Court cases involved statutes whereby Congress avoided resolving well-recognized, contentious issues by punting them to an administrative agency for resolution. *Little Sisters of the Poor Saints Peter and Paul Home v. Pennsylvania*[90] arose in the aftermath of adoption of the Affordable Care Act (ACA).[91] Members of Congress could not agree on whether group health plans should be required to offer contraceptive coverage to plan participants. Some key pro-life members of the Democratic caucus indicated they would vote against a bill that explicitly forced employers to cover contraceptives.

The compromise solution was an ACA provision that gave members plausible deniability, requiring the US Department of Health and Human Services (HHS) to compile a list of "additional preventive care" that would be available to women at no cost.[92] The provision quite deliberately provided no guidance to HHS regarding whether contraceptives should be included on the list or whether exceptions should be made for employers with religious objections to paying for certain contraceptives.

During the Obama administration, HHS adopted a "contraceptive mandate" in its ACA implementing regulations and created a conscience exception for a limited set of religious objectors. During the Trump administration, HHS kept the contraceptive mandate but expanded the conscience exception considerably. The scores of lawsuits filed by groups objecting to one or the other of the HHS rules have resulted to date in three Supreme Court decisions, the latest being the July 8, 2020, decision in *Little Sisters of the Poor*. One can reasonably expect a new round of lawsuits if the Biden administration revises the HHS rule yet again.

The real problem here is that Congress drafted the contested ACA provision to avoid having to decide a controversial issue involving paying for birth control (an issue of which it was well aware), and it delegated to HHS authority to resolve the issue without providing any guidelines regarding how HHS should go about doing so (because guidelines would have been contentious too). The Constitution puts Congress in charge of deciding such questions. When Congress instead delegates decision-making to an administrative agency solely because it is unable or unwilling to decide the issue itself, and not because the "necessities" of governance required it to do so, courts reviewing a nondelegation doctrine challenge to the statute should apply a more exacting standard of review.[93]

Gundy[94] arose from similar compromise legislation. Congress adopted the Sex Offender Registration and Notification Act (SORNA)[95] in 2006 to tighten the requirements of sex-offender registration schemes. Congress inserted in SORNA a provision that delegated to the attorney general authority to decide whether SORNA should apply to pre-2006 offenders.[96]

Considerable evidence indicates that Congress adopted that provision because the House and Senate bills disagreed on whether the new requirements should apply retroactively to those offenders. Applying the law retrospectively threatened to create substantial problems for some state registration statutes already on the books.

Nonetheless, the Supreme Court rejected a convicted sex offender's nondelegation doctrine challenge to SORNA. The plurality cited legislative history to conclude—despite the absence of any statutory language providing guidance to the attorney general on how he should resolve the issue—that Congress really did intend SORNA to apply to pre-2006 offenders "as soon as feasible."[97]

But only four justices adopted that strained interpretation of SORNA. A far more plausible interpretation—the one adopted by three dissenting justices—is that Congress was well aware of the retroactive-application issue and nonetheless delegated to the attorney general authority to decide the issue at his complete discretion.[98] In Justice Gorsuch's telling:

> Because Congress could not achieve the consensus necessary to resolve the hard problems associated with SORNA's application to pre-Act offenders, it passed the potato to the Attorney General. . . . Then, too, there is the question of accountability. In passing this statute, Congress was able to claim credit for "comprehensively" addressing the problem of the entire existing population of sex offenders (who can object to that?), while in fact leaving the Attorney General to sort it out.[99]

Whether or not Justice Gorsuch's account of Congress' motivation is correct in this instance, such an example would raise a serious constitutional concern. Legislation that delegates policymaking authority to the executive branch, solely because the two Houses of Congress cannot agree on a policy, defeats the Constitution's bicameralism requirement.[100] As the *Gundy* example demonstrates, the intelligible-principle test is far too deferential to check Congress when it passes legislation that passes the buck. When evidence demonstrates that Congress has delegated authority to decide an identifiable policy dispute because it is unable or unwilling to resolve the issue itself, that attempted delegation of core legislative power must be subject to legal challenge and then judicial review as an impermissible transfer of Congress' legislative function to "achieve the consensus necessary to resolve" policy conflicts.

As the *Little Sisters of the Poor* and SORNA examples should demonstrate, the core legislative power to resolve policy conflicts being discussed here is not implicated routinely. Most statutes do not blatantly punt issues to the executive branch for resolution the way the ACA did with the contraceptive mandate. Nor do many statutes kick an issue to a federal agency for resolution when the House and Senate were not able to agree, as happened in SORNA. These kinds of legislative process breakdowns are exceptional. But, when they occur, the federal courts must uphold the Vesting Clause and force *Congress* to make the relevant policy decisions.

The Legislative Check on Executive Power. It may sound obvious to say so, but Congress may not surrender its ability to check the power of the executive branch. As discussed above, giving up the power of the purse would be one way for Congress to surrender its ability to check executive power, but it does not take much imagination to devise other impermissible ways that Congress could turn over core oversight, accountability, or other leverage. The Constitution bestowed these forms of legislative power to Congress to not only separate government power but also enable the legislature to serve as a check on the executive (and the judiciary). Any statute that delegates power to the executive to such an extent that it disables the legislature's ability to carry out its checking function should be subject to judicial challenge under the nondelegation doctrine.

Perhaps the easiest way to both envision what a surrender of legislative checking power might look like and understand how this situation might come about is to consider a recent example from the Commonwealth of Pennsylvania. The state constitution there features a clause quite similar to the Vesting Clause in the US Constitution. It states: "The legislative power of this Commonwealth shall be vested in a General Assembly, which shall consist of a Senate and a House of Representatives."[101] So it vests the legislative power in the legislature—*not* in the governor.

Yet in response to the recent novel coronavirus pandemic, Gov. Tom Wolf issued a Proclamation of Disaster Emergency under the Emergency Code, a 1978 statute that allows the governor to initiate an emergency unilaterally. He then issued multiple executive orders that had binding legal effect without any legislative action.

These ostensibly temporary powers met with resistance, especially to the extent they forced businesses to shut down entirely. But matters really came to a head when the governor extended the emergency after the first 90-day declaration expired. The legislature, in the control of the opposite political party from the governor, voted on a concurrent resolution in both houses of the General Assembly to end the state of emergency. By a bipartisan vote of 121–81 in the House and 31–19 in the Senate, the legislature passed the resolution. The 1978 Emergency Code provides that the legislature may end the emergency declaration "at any time" by concurrent resolution. Rather than accept that outcome from 60 percent of his legislature, however, Gov. Wolf sued the legislature, arguing that any concurrent resolution had to be presented for his signature to be valid.

Pointing to a different constitutional provision, Gov. Wolf claimed that concurrent resolutions have to be presented to him, as would be the case with a piece of legislation.[102] But, of course, if the governor can veto the concurrent resolution, the state of emergency cannot be ended without his permission unless the General Assembly can secure a two-thirds vote in both houses to override the veto. Nonetheless, the state supreme court agreed with the governor's argument. In a 4–1–2 vote in *Wolf v. Scarnati*,[103] the state supreme court upheld the portion of the state emergency code that allowed a unilateral declaration of emergency by the governor but struck down the portion saying that a concurrent resolution of the legislature could end it "at any time."

Gov. Wolf was thus allowed to arrogate several core legislative functions mentioned above, including the spending power and the drafting of criminal laws. So, it might seem that identifying this fifth core function (checking the power of the executive) is superfluous. However, the greater problem in Pennsylvania now is that the legislature's ability to counterbalance the governor has been completely stripped for the duration of the emergency—that is, until the governor himself declares that the emergency is over (or the legislature can secure a two-thirds vote in both houses of the General Assembly).

It would be hard to find a more blatant violation of the nondelegation doctrine than Pennsylvania's 1978 Emergency Code (as interpreted by the state supreme court). The statute not only disenfranchises the elected legislature but also effectively enables single-branch lawmaking by the governor. The state constitution does not even permit the governor to initiate lawmaking ordinarily. In theory, it might permit single-branch lawmaking by the legislature—but only with a supermajority two-thirds vote of both houses of the General Assembly following a gubernatorial veto.

But as interpreted by the court, the 1978 Emergency Code inverts the usual checks and balances. Instead of making single-branch lawmaking difficult, the court construed the Emergency Code to require two-thirds votes in both houses of the General Assembly to *stop* the governor's single-branch lawmaking. That construction places the Emergency Code in direct conflict with the Pennsylvania Constitution's vesting clause, a core constitutional constraint on lawmaking. As a result of that construction, a statute passed by a simple majority vote in a former legislative session effectively delegated *vast* legislative authority to the governor and eliminated the General Assembly's ability to check the power of the executive.

Pennsylvania's situation provides an object lesson on the importance of the nondelegation doctrine. Its Supreme Court held that

> The General Assembly itself decided to delegate power to the Governor under Section 7301(c). Current members of the General Assembly may regret that decision, but they cannot use an unconstitutional means [*i.e.*, the concurrent resolution] to give that regret legal effect.[104]

But this obtuse ruling misses the point that the legislature was never free to transfer this much lawmaking power to the governor in the first place. Even if the legislature of 1978 genuinely meant to design an emergency regime like this—where a lopsided power arrangement would result in the governor's taking the legislative power upon unilaterally declaring an emergency and keeping that power until he declares the emergency over—the vesting clause of that state's constitution, like its counterpart in the US Constitution, forbids it.

Any similar surrender of power by Congress would raise distinct nondelegation doctrine concerns even if the president did not go on a spending spree, write new criminal penalties, or purport to resolve any policy disputes. The US Constitution vests legislative power solely in Congress, in part to check executive power; any statute that purports to surrender that checking power—even in an emergency—must be subject to heightened judicial review under any nondelegation doctrine worth its salt. Otherwise, it might become too easy for a governor (or president) to sideline the legislature completely in a crisis.

Youngstown Sheet & Tube Co. v. Sawyer, known as the Steel Seizure Case, supports the principle that the president should not be permitted to cite "emergency" conditions as justification for unilateral executive branch lawmaking.[105] In that case, the Supreme Court struck down President Harry Truman's executive order taking possession of the nation's steel mills; he justified the action by claiming that a potential strike at the mills created a national emergency because it threatened production of steel needed for the Korean War effort. The Court held that the Constitution vests all lawmaking authority in Congress, that Congress had adopted no legislation authorizing President Truman's actions, and that a domestic emergency does not authorize the president to exercise legislative powers.[106]

The case differs from *Wolf* in one important respect: Gov. Wolf relied on a decades-old statute that purportedly delegated unfettered emergency powers to the executive (a proposition the legislature disputed), while President Truman relied solely on inherent executive branch authority to legislate during emergencies. But both cases implicate the same underlying constitutional principle: The power to establish policy belongs to the legislature alone.

There may be times when a legislature might not be in session when an emergency arises, or else it might not be able to convene immediately as a crisis is unfolding when crucial decisions have to be made—like quarantining people with a communicable disease. Thus, legislation authorizing limited executive branch policymaking during pandemics, or some even more debilitating cataclysm, might make sense. But once a legislature reassembles, that signals its readiness to resume its proper constitutional lawmaking role. Expansive delegation (or assumption) of discretionary authority is then no longer justified. Even in an emergency then, courts should not be willing to relax their scrutiny of nondelegation doctrine claims in the absence of very strong evidentiary support for any such "necessity" claims.

Limitations on the Nondelegation Doctrine

The executive branch's need for discretionary powers is greatest in foreign affairs. The president's ability to respond to fast-developing foreign crises would be severely hampered if he were required to seek congressional approval before responding. So, there is substantial reason to apply less exacting judicial review to statutes that arguably grant the president legislative power over foreign policy issues (other than the ability to declare war). Such deference is consistent with the view (expressed both in court decisions and by leading commentators) that executive power inherently includes significant discretionary authority over foreign affairs.[107]

Application of the nondelegation doctrine is also inappropriate for governmental practices that were deemed in late 18th-century and early 19th-century America not to constitute exercises of delegated *legislative* power. A partial list of such practices includes:

- Determinations of facts (including tax assessments, customs determinations, and presidential determinations about acts of state under conditional statutes);

- Executive inspection and seizure (notably by customs officers);[108]

- The selection of locations (for post offices, post roads, and district boundaries);

- Regulatory licensing and other delegated legislation in federal enclaves where Congress enjoyed local power (such as the District of Columbia and US territories); and

- Executive rulemaking regarding the distribution of various benefits and other privileges (ranging from pensions to patents).[109]

Each of these practices was, and still is, considered an ordinary exercise of discretion by officials when executing the law. Executive branch officials who engage in these practices are simply "fill[ing] up the details" of the statutes they are charged with administering.[110] The Vesting

Clause does not require that all power be maintained in Congress, only all legislative power.

We have outlined five core functions that, by their nature, constitute the exercise of legislative power and that call for stricter judicial scrutiny whenever challengers allege that legislation has improperly delegated those functions. When other governmental functions are implicated, courts should be guided by historical practice in determining whether an agency exercising those functions is doing nothing more than exercising ordinary discretion to administer the law.

Conclusion

The intelligible-principle test anticipated in *J. W. Hampton* has long outlived its usefulness. Although the concept initially proved stringent enough to rein in unconstitutional delegations of legislative power in cases like *Panama Refining* and *A. L. A. Schechter Poultry* (whose holdings were fully consistent with *J. W. Hampton*), something had gone awry by the time *Lichter v. United States* specified a toothless version of the test 20 years after *J. W. Hampton*.

Drawing inspiration from the intervening 1944 case of *Yakus*, this chapter has outlined two tests that can work together to supplant the intelligible-principle test with something more robust and more susceptible of judicial administration. In addition, by fleshing out the concept of "core legislative power" as a third constraint on delegation rooted in the Vesting Clause of Article I, this chapter has supplied guardrails the judiciary can use to enforce the nondelegation doctrine.

Three principal considerations underlie the Supreme Court's unwillingness to vigorously enforce the nondelegation doctrine: (1) a concern that the modern American government could not operate effectively if Congress were not permitted to delegate significant policymaking responsibilities to administrative agencies; (2) a concern that results-oriented judges with objections to government regulation of the business community would use the nondelegation doctrine to strike down the regulations of disfavored agencies; and (3) a concern that there are no clear rules by which courts can easily distinguish between the delegation of legislative powers (impermissible) and the conferring of discretion as to the law's execution (permissible). The revised enforcement standards we propose would reinvigorate the nondelegation doctrine while paying heed to each of those three concerns.

Most importantly, our proposed enforcement standards provide courts with relatively straightforward rules that will facilitate predictable answers regarding whether a federal statute violates the Vesting Clause. As a first-cut minimum, every federal statute that delegates power to the executive branch is subject to a nondelegation doctrine challenge if it fails to articulate *some* ascertainable standard that unequivocally limits an agency's rulemaking authority. Applying this absence-of-standards test should be relatively straightforward. If the government can point to at least *some* potential regulations that would be barred by the statute, then there is not an absence of standards. Most existing statutes satisfy that test; others—such as statutes that direct an agency to regulate in the "public interest" or adopt "reasonable" regulations—do not. Courts should have little difficulty distinguishing the two categories.

More stringently, every federal statute that delegates power to the executive branch is subject to nondelegation doctrine challenge if it fails to supply sufficient judicial standards whereby a *court* can ascertain whether the agency is conducting itself consistently with the will of Congress. If the statute does not contain enough specificity to enable the courts to determine whether the executive is complying with statutory restrictions, then that should in itself be deemed a Vesting Clause violation.

We also propose that statutes that implicate one of five "core" legislative powers be subject to heightened nondelegation doctrine scrutiny. This functional approach will rarely require judges to draw fine lines between delegations of legislative power and delegations of discretion in executing a statute. Line-drawing problems will arise less frequently when looking at the *function* Congress is delegating rather than the *issue* it is addressing. Most federal statutes do not implicate impermissible delegation of core functions of Congress. We are not suggesting, for example, that a routine appropriations bill implicates the "core" spending power, but closer scrutiny is warranted when Congress divests its authority to set funding levels or establish spending policy for an agency.

Because this approach focuses on core legislative power, judges will not be able to use insignificant incursions on legislative power or minor delegations to refuse to enforce otherwise valid statutes. History suggests that Congress is less likely to delegate legislative power when exercising its core functions. For example, except in rare instances (e.g., CFPB funding), Congress jealously guards its spending power, and federal tax statutes generally include extremely detailed policy guidance.

Our third "core" function (writing criminal laws) may have the greatest immediate effect. Criminal defendants will certainly have standing to challenge any criminal penalties created outside of Congress. And, unfortunately, some reports indicate that federal administrative agencies have been quite promiscuous about generating criminal penalties on their own, rather than merely implementing penalties passed by Congress. If this proves to be true, then defendants who have been subjected to administrative criminal penalties will have a new—or at least no longer disregarded—avenue of potential relief.

Our fourth "core" function (resolving identified policy disputes) is likewise apt to affect only a limited number of cases. Its application is limited because the burden will be on the party challenging federal legislation to establish that Congress faced a policy conflict, eschewed resolving that dispute, yet nonetheless delegated resolution of the policy controversy to an administrative agency without specific instructions.

The fifth "core" function (maintaining a check on executive power) is similarly limited. It comes into play only when statutes purport to grant the executive the authority to cut the (current or future) legislature out of the policymaking process. A statute violates this prohibition if it grants (e.g., to Pennsylvania's governor) authority to issue "emergency" policies even as the legislature is in session and objects. A statute is unobjectionable if it grants the executive authority to exercise discretion in carrying out its statutory duties or grants very short-term emergency policymaking authority until the legislature can come back into session—and so long as the legislature then does not have to secure veto-proof majorities to unwind the policies the executive adopted on an ostensibly emergency basis.

Our proposed enforcement standards also are unlikely to facilitate results-oriented judicial overreach. Because the proposed standards establish relatively clear rules regarding what the Vesting Clause requires, judges seeking to overturn a statute based on policy concerns would have a difficult time concocting a nondelegation-doctrine basis for doing so. They would be far more likely to rely on other existing, more malleable tools—including striking down a regulatory action because they deem it to exceed statutory authority or violate the Administrative Procedure Act's arbitrary-or-capricious standard.

Finally, our proposed enforcement standards are unlikely to interfere with government effectiveness. The Supreme Court's nondelegation doctrine case law has repeatedly stressed "necessity": Congress must be permitted to delegate at least some discretionary power to the executive branch if the federal government is to operate effectively in the modern world. But as noted above, the area in which broad presidential discretion is most necessary—foreign affairs—is largely exempt from nondelegation claims because the Constitution itself grants the president significant discretionary authority over foreign affairs. There is simply no need for Congress to delegate additional legislative power over such matters to the executive branch.

Nor will our proposed enforcement standards interfere with well-crafted legislation designed to delegate discretionary authority in situations in which Congress cannot realistically establish all rules (e.g., implementing a broad-ranging price-control program as in *Yakus* by establishing price ceilings for every product offered for sale). So long as Congress enacts judicially ascertainable and administrable standards that unequivocally limit an agency's rulemaking authority to at least some extent, Congress need not fear that its legislation will be struck down as a Vesting Clause violation.

At the very least, the Supreme Court needs to acknowledge that the intelligible-principle standard is toothless as currently applied and does nothing to ensure compliance with the Vesting Clause's demand that "Congress cannot delegate legislative power to the President"—"a principle universally recognized as vital to the integrity and maintenance of the system of government ordained by the Constitution."[111] A new, reinvigorated standard along the lines of the tests proposed here is required if the "vital" constitutional principle enshrined in the Vesting Clause is to be given effect.

However, the Supreme Court need not adopt this entire concept in one case. Rather, the Court may recognize each of the core legislative powers discussed herein and protect them going forward in separate nondelegation challenges over time. Such a piecemeal approach can gradually reestablish a series of forbidden delegation red lines that Congress may not cross as it legislates. Proceeding in this fashion will prevent Congress from divesting the legislative power that the Constitution vests in it while providing the legislative branch and executive branch time to gradually adjust to the reinvigoration of the nondelegation doctrine.

Notes

1. *Gundy v. United States*, 139 S. Ct. 2116, 2121 (2019) (plurality).

2. See, for example, *Wayman v. Southard*, 23 US (10 Wheat.) 1, 42 (1825); *Marshall Field & Co. v. Clark*, 143 US 649, 692 (1892) ("That Congress cannot delegate legislative power to the President is a principle universally recognized as vital to the integrity and maintenance of the system of government ordained by the Constitution."); *J. W. Hampton Jr. & Co. v. United States*, 276 US 394, 406 (1928) ("It is a breach of the national fundamental law if Congress gives up its legislative power and transfers it to the President, . . . or if by law it attempts to invest itself or its members with . . . executive power."); *Mistretta v. United States*, 488 US 361, 371–72 (1989); and *Gundy*, 139 S. Ct. at 2123 (plurality).

3. Article I, § 1 (hereinafter, the "Vesting Clause") states, "All legislative Powers herein granted shall be vested in a Congress of the United States." In light of Article I's use of the word "vested," it is more accurate to speak of the ban on "divestment" or "divestiture" of legislative power rather than a ban on "delegation" of power. Further, the phrase "nondelegation *doctrine*" misleadingly implies that the limitations on executive branch lawmaking are rooted in a court-created doctrine rather than the text of the Constitution. We nonetheless use the term "nondelegation doctrine" throughout this chapter to conform to the terminology generally employed by the editors of this volume.

4. *Gundy*, 139 S. Ct. at 2123 (plurality).

5. *Industrial Union Department, AFL-CIO v. American Petroleum Institute*, 448 US 607, 642–46 (1980) (plurality).

6. The vacuous version of the intelligible-principle test was fully in force by the time of *Lichter v. United States*, 334 US 742, 785 (1948).

7. *Panama Refining Company v. Ryan*, 293 US 388, 430 (1935).

8. *A. L. A. Schechter Poultry Corp. v. United States*, 295 US 495 (1935).

9. See, for example, Richard B. Stewart, "The Reformation of American Administrative Law," *Harvard Law Review* 88, no. 8 (1975): 1667.

10. *Wayman*, 23 US at 42–43.

11. See, for example, Regulations from the Executive in Need of Scrutiny Act of 2017, H.R. 26, 115th Cong. The Regulations from the Executive in Need of Scrutiny (REINS) Act would require Congress to approve all major regulations before they could take effect. The US House of Representatives has passed the REINS Act on several occasions, most recently in January 2017, but the US Senate has not approved the legislation.

12. *American Power & Light Co. v. SEC*, 329 US 90, 105 (1946).

13. *Mistretta*, 488 US at 372.

14. See, for example, Cary Coglianese, "Dimensions of Delegation," *University of Pennsylvania Law Review* 167 (2019): 1849, 1877–78.

15. *Industrial Union Department, AFL-CIO v. American Petroleum Institute*, 448 US 607, 674 (1980) (Rehnquist, J., concurring).

16. *Industrial Union Department, AFL-CIO*, 448 US at 675. See also *Bond v. United States*, 564 US 211 (2011), citing *A. L. A. Schechter Poultry* as precedent.

17. See, for example, *Louisiana Public Service Commission v. FCC*, 476 US 355 (1986) (stating that "an agency literally has no power to act . . . unless and until Congress confers power upon it.").

18. For example, whether federal law should prohibit the sale or possession of "bump stocks" is just one of many issues over which a federal agency has arrogated policymaking authority. A bump stock is a device that, when attached to a semi-automatic rifle, increases the rate at which that rifle can be fired. Federal statutes do not address the legality of bump stocks, but they do prohibit "machine guns." Following a highly publicized mass shooting in Las Vegas in which the shooter used bump stocks, the Bureau of Alcohol, Tobacco, Firearms, and Explosives (ATF) adopted a regulation reclassifying bump stocks as "machine guns" and prohibiting their possession. The nondelegation doctrine might have been a more appropriate focus of the Court's attention. As interpreted by ATF, the relevant statute grants the agency unchecked legislative authority to choose which weapons and devices are to be prohibited—in violation of the Vesting Clause. A decision rejecting ATF's statutory interpretation on nondelegation grounds would ensure that Congress (not a federal agency) is the body that establishes gun-control policy. Further, it would force Congress to cease its practice of passing along to others the resolution of controversial issues.

19. *Whitman v. American Trucking Associations*, 531 US 457, 472 (2001).

20. *Marshall Field*, 143 US at 693–94 (citations omitted).

21. See, for example, *Miller v. Mayor of New York*, 109 US 385, 393 (1883) (upholding legislation making construction of the Brooklyn Bridge dependent on a finding by the secretary of war that the bridge would not interfere with East River navigation).

22. *Federalist*, no. 37 (James Madison), 228 (C. Rossiter ed. 1961).

23. *Wayman*, 23 US at 42–43.

24. *Mistretta*, 488 US at 415–16 (Scalia, J., dissenting).

25. *Federalist*, no. 78 (Alexander Hamilton), 470.

26. *Federalist*, no. 78 (Alexander Hamilton), 470.

27. *Gundy*, 139 S. Ct. at 2123 (plurality).

28. *J. W. Hampton*, 276 US at 409.

29. *J. W. Hampton*, 276 US at 409.

30. *J. W. Hampton*, 276 US at 401.

31. *Gundy*, 139 S. Ct. at 2139 (Gorsuch, J., dissenting).

32. See, for example, *Lichter*, 334 US at 785.

33. See, for example, *Federal Energy Administration v. Algonquin SNG*, 426 US 548, 559 (1976); and David Schoenbrod, "The Delegation Doctrine: Could the Court Give It Substance?," *Michigan Law Review* 83, no. 5 (1985): 1223, 1231 ("The [intelligible-principle] test has become so ephemeral and elastic as to lose its meaning").

34. *Mistretta*, 488 US at 373. As examples of statutes previously found to provide "intelligible principles" sufficient to survive constitutional challenge, *Mistretta* cited *Federal Power Commission v. Hope Natural Gas Co.*, 320 US 591, 600 (1944) (upholding delegation to Federal Power Commission to determine just and reasonable rates); and *National Broadcasting Co. v. United States*, 319 US 190, 225–26 (1943) (upholding delegation to the Federal Communications Commission to regulate broadcast licensing as "public interest, convenience, or necessity" requires).

35. See, for example, Schoenbrod, "The Delegation Doctrine."

36. *Yakus v. United States*, 321 US 414 (1944).

37. *Yakus*, 321 US at 426.

38. 56 Stat. 23 (1942).

39. 56 Stat. 23 (1942) at 423.

40. 56 Stat. 23 (1942) at 423.

41. Critics of the nondelegation doctrine often point to the Administrative Procedure Act (adopted in 1946) as offering an alternative means by which courts can provide an adequate check on administrative action. But the Administrative Procedure Act's principal review standard—whether agency action is "arbitrary, capricious, an abuse of discretion, or otherwise not in accordance with law" (5 USC § 706(2)(A))—is no more easily applied than the nondelegation doctrine and often results in unpredictable, one-off court decisions. See, for example, *Department of Homeland Security v. Regents of the University of California*, 140 S. Ct. 1891 (2020).

42. 806 Fed. App'x 982 (Fed. Cir.), *cert. denied*, 141 S. Ct. 133 (2020).

43. Section 232 of the Trade Expansion Act of 1962, 19 USC § 1862.

44. Section 232(c)(1)(A).

45. "An administrative agency's power to regulate . . . must always be grounded in a valid grant of authority from Congress." *FDA v. Brown & Williamson Tobacco Corp.*, 529 US 120, 161 (2000). Courts have repeatedly rejected the notion that an agency is authorized to act "any time a statute does not expressly negate the existence of a claimed administrative power." *Chamber of Commerce v. NLRB*, 721 F.3d 152, 169 (4th Cir. 2013). In rejecting claims that whenever a statute neither authorizes nor prohibits a regulatory activity, it should be deemed to contain a "gap" that an agency is authorized to fill, under *Chevron U.S.A. v. Natural Resources Defense Council*, 467 US 837 (1984), Judge Diarmuid O'Scannlain has explained: "A statute's deliberate non-interference with a class of activity is not a 'gap' at all; it simply marks the point where Congress decided to stop authorization to regulate. . . . The Department [of Labor, in acting to fill a supposed gap,] is in reality legislating, yet that is a power the Constitution does not permit executive agencies to exercise." *Oregon Restaurant and Lodging Association v. Perez*, 843 F.3d 355, 360 (9th Cir. 2016) (O'Scannlain, J., dissenting from denial of rehearing en banc in an opinion joined by nine other circuit court judges).

46. *Yakus*, 321 US at 425 ("Nor does the doctrine of separation of powers deny to Congress power to direct that an administrative officer . . . ascertain the conditions which Congress has made prerequisite to the operations of its legislative command. . . . The only concern of courts is to ascertain whether the will of Congress has been obeyed.").

47. *City of Arlington v. FCC*, 569 US 290 (2013).

48. See also *Wayman*, 23 US at 45 ("The power given [by Congress] to the court to vary the mode of proceeding in this particular is a power to vary minor regulations which are within the great outlines marked out by the legislature in directing the execution.").

49. *Gundy*, 139 S. Ct. at 2136 (Gorsuch, J., dissenting) (quoting *Yakus*, 321 US at 426) (emphasis added).

50. *Yakus*, 321 US at 425.

51. *J. W. Hampton*, 276 US at 405.

52. *Industrial Union Department*, 448 US at 685 (Rehnquist, J., concurring).

53. *Paul v. United States*, 140 S. Ct. 342 (2019) (statement of Kavanaugh, J., respecting the denial of *cert.*) ("Justice Rehnquist opined that major national policy decisions must be made by Congress and the President in the legislative process, not delegated by Congress to the Executive Branch.").

54. The Supreme Court has on occasion imposed a "clear statement" requirement when deciding whether a statute authorizes an administrative agency to exercise regulatory authority over a major policy question of great economic and political importance. The theory behind that canon of statutory interpretation is that Congress does not hide elephants in mouseholes; if it really wants to grant an agency sweeping new authority to act, it will say so expressly. See, for example, *FDA v. Brown & Williamson*, 529 US at 120 (declining to interpret the Food, Drug, and Cosmetic Act as authorizing the Food and Drug Administration to ban cigarette sales, in the absence of a clear statement in the act to that effect). But the nondelegation doctrine is not a canon of statutory interpretation; rather, it is a constitutionally based prohibition against delegation of legislative powers, regardless of whether the delegation involves a "major" policy question. Nor, as some have suggested, does *Wayman v. Southard* support a Vesting Clause rule that distinguishes between major and minor policy decisions. *Wayman* rejected a nondelegation challenge to a federal statute that prescribed basic rules governing execution of federal court judgments (e.g., property seized from the judgment debtor should be sold publicly on a cash-only basis), but that also delegated to court-appointed officials some discretion on how to execute those rules (e.g., the extent of notice provided for the sale and whether the debtor should be permitted to retain the property pending the sale). *Wayman*, 23 US at 43–46. Chief Justice Marshall held that this delegation of discretion did not violate the Vesting Clause because it was "within the great outlines marked out by the legislature in directing the execution" and permitted court officials merely to "fill up the details." *Wayman*, 23 US at 45, 43. The Court declined to recognize any exception from the nondelegation doctrine based on a claim that the matter at issue was minor, stating unequivocally that the Vesting Clause prohibits delegation of all "powers which are strictly and exclusively legislative." *Wayman*, 23 US at 43.

55. *Gundy*, 139 S. Ct. at 2134 (Gorsuch, J., dissenting).

56. *Gundy*, 139 S. Ct. at 2134 (Gorsuch, J., dissenting).

57. Of course, a plaintiff raising claims under the Vesting Clause is subject to the Article III standing requirements imposed on all other federal-court litigants. As Supreme Court case law makes clear, sometimes a spending decision is not susceptible to judicial challenge because no one has suffered the injury-in-fact necessary to establish Article III standing. See, for example, *Valley Forge Christian College v. Americans United for Separation of Church and State*, 454 US 464 (1982). But once standing is established, a Vesting Clause claimant is not limited to challenging only certain types of legislation.

58. *National Federation of Independent Business v. Sebelius*, 567 US 519, 573 (2012).

59. *McCulloch v. Maryland*, 17 US (4 Wheat.) 316, 431 (1819).

60. US Const. art. I, § 7.

61. US Const. art. I, § 9, cl. 4.

62. *National Cable Television Association v. United States*, 415 US 336, 342 (1974). To avoid constitutional problems, the Court narrowly construed the relevant statute so as to limit the fees that the Federal Communications Commission (FCC) was authorized to impose on cable television operators to no more than the value of the FCC's services. *National Cable Television Association*, 415 US at 343.

63. *Skinner v. Mid-America Pipeline Co.*, 490 US 212 (1989).

64. *Skinner*, 490 US at 223–24.

65. *Skinner*, 490 US at 223.

66. US Const. art. I, § 9, cl. 7 ("No money shall be drawn from the Treasury, but in consequence of Appropriations made by Law.").

67. US Const. art. IV, § 3, cl. 2.

68. 12 USC § 5491(a).

69. 12 USC § 5497(a)(1).

70. 12 USC § 5497(a)(1).

71. *Law Offices of Crystal Moroney, P.C. v. Bureau of Consumer Financial Protection*, No. 7:19-cv-11594-KMK (S.D.N.Y.). These same claims are also being raised as defenses to an enforcement action in *Bureau of Consumer Financial Protection v. Law Offices of Crystal Moroney, P.C.*, No. 20-3471 (2d Cir.) (appeal from order enforcing CID).

72. 12 USC § 5497(a)(2)(A)(iii). That percentage is subject to increase after 2012. 12 USC § 5497(a)(2)(B).

73. *Seila Law v. Consumer Financial Protection Bureau*, 140 S. Ct. 2183 (2020).

74. See Markham S. Chenoweth and Michael P. DeGrandis, "Out of the Separation-of-Powers Frying Pan and into the Nondelegation Fire: How the Court's Decision in *Seila Law* Makes CFPB's Unlawful Structure Even Worse," University of Chicago Law Review Online, August 27, 2020, https://lawreviewblog.uchicago.edu/2020/08/27/seila-chenoweth-degrandis/. The plaintiffs in *Seila Law* did not raise a nondelegation challenge to CFPB's structure, and thus the Court did not address the issue. But as explained in the text, Congress' decision to divest itself of all control over CFPB spending raises serious Vesting Clause issues.

75. *Seila Law*, 140 S. Ct. at 2207–11 (plurality); and *Seila Law*, 140 S. Ct. at 2224–45 (Kagan, J., concurring in the judgment as to severability and dissenting in part).

76. Attorney General Jeff Sessions put a stop to this unconstitutional practice in 2017. See US Department of Justice, Office of Public Affairs, "Bank of America to Pay

$16.65 Billion in Historic Justice Department Settlement for Financial Fraud Leading up to and During the Financial Crisis," press release, August 21, 2014, https://www.justice.gov/opa/pr/bank-america-pay-1665-billion-historic-justice-department-settlement-financial-fraud-leading.

77. See US Department of Justice, "9-16.325—Prohibition on Settlement Payments to Third Parties," in *The Justice Manual*, January 2020, https://www.justice.gov/jm/jm-9-16000-pleas-federal-rule-criminal-procedure-11; Office of the Attorney General, "Prohibition on Settlement Payments to Third Parties," June 5, 2017, https://www.justice.gov/opa/press-release/file/971826/download; and "Prohibition on Settlement Payments to Non-Governmental Third Parties," *Federal Register* 85, no. 242 (December 16, 2020): 81409–11.

78. *Gundy*, 139 S. Ct. 2116 (2019).

79. 34 USC § 20913(d).

80. *Gundy*, 139 S. Ct. at 2129 (plurality); and *Gundy*, 139 S. Ct. at 2131 (Alito, J., concurring in the judgment).

81. *Gundy*, 139 S. Ct. at 2144–45 (Gorsuch, J., dissenting) (quoting *Federalist*, no. 47 (James Madison), 302).

82. *Touby v. United States*, 500 US 160 (1991).

83. *Touby*, 500 US at 166.

84. *Gundy*, 139 S. Ct. at 2131 (Alito, J., concurring in the judgment).

85. *Paul*, 140 S. Ct. at 342 (statement of Kavanaugh, J., respecting the denial of *cert.*).

86. *Gundy*, 139 S. Ct. at 2123 (plurality).

87. *Mistretta*, 488 US at 372.

88. *Mistretta*, 488 US at 372. The "expertise" rationale for permitting delegation of legislative authority is open to serious question. Nothing in the Vesting Clause prevents Congress from delegating fact-finding authority to experts employed by administrative agencies. All that the Constitution requires is that Congress itself establish the policies that flow from factual findings—whether those findings are made by Congress itself or by third parties. Moreover, Congress has access to expertise through conducting hearings and thus does not have to rely on agency expertise.

89. *Gundy*, 139 S. Ct. at 2135, 2144 (Gorsuch, J., dissenting).

90. *Little Sisters of the Poor Saints Peter and Paul Home v. Pennsylvania*, 140 S. Ct. 2367 (2020).

91. Pub. L. 111-148 (2010).

92. 42 USC § 300gg-13(a)(4).

93. Justice Thomas' opinion for the Court in *Little Sisters of the Poor* noted, "No party has pressed a constitutional challenge to the breadth of the delegation involved here." *Little Sisters of the Poor*, 140 S. Ct. at 2382. Hence, the Court did not address whether the ACA's "additional preventive care" provision violated the nondelegation doctrine. Even under the existing intelligible-principle review standard, that provision might not pass constitutional muster; it would be even less likely to survive review under the more exacting replacement tests outlined here.

94. *Gundy*, 139 S. Ct. at 2116.

95. 34 USC § 20901 *et seq.*

96. 34 USC § 20913(d) (stating that "the Attorney General shall have the authority

to specify the applicability of the requirements of this subchapter to sex offenders convicted before the enactment of this chapter").

97. *Gundy*, 139 S. Ct. at 2123–24 (plurality).

98. *Gundy*, 139 S. Ct. at 2143–44 (Gorsuch, J., dissenting).

99. *Gundy*, 139 S. Ct. at 2144.

100. Note that such legislation enables evasion of the constitutional requirement of presentment as well. US Const. art. I, § 7, cl. 2. Although President George W. Bush signed SORNA, the text he signed did not explicitly require retroactive application. The legislative punt to the attorney general simultaneously empowered the executive branch while enabling the president who signed the law to avoid responsibility for the law's later effects (brought about by adoption of subsequent administrative regulations under President Barack Obama).

101. Pa. Const. art. II, § 1.

102. Pa. Const. art. III, § 9.

103. 233 A.3d 679 (Pa. 2020).

104. *Wolf*, 233 A.3d at 706.

105. *Youngstown Sheet & Tube Co. v. Sawyer*, 343 US 579 (1952).

106. *Youngstown Sheet & Tube*, 343 US at 587–89 (stating that "the Founders of this Nation entrusted the lawmaking power to the Congress alone in both good and bad times").

107. See, for example, *United States v. Curtiss-Wright Export Corp.*, 299 US 304, 324 (1934); and Schoenbrod, "The Delegation Doctrine," 1260–65.

108. Notably, early inspection was not an open-ended inspection of private business records, but rather an inspection of goods or buildings (e.g., distilleries) for compliance with congressionally established requirements. Contemporary inspections of private business records are vastly different.

109. See Philip Hamburger, "Delegating or Divesting?," Northwestern University Law Review Online, September 30, 2020, https://northwesternlawreview.org/articles/delegating-or-divesting/.

110. *Wayman*, 23 US at 42–43.

111. *Marshall Field*, 143 US at 692.

A Private-Law Framework for Subdelegation

GARY LAWSON

In 1825, Chief Justice John Marshall confidently proclaimed, "It will not be contended that Congress can delegate to the Courts, or to any other tribunal, powers which are strictly and exclusively legislative."[1] He explained, "The difference between the departments undoubtedly is that the legislature makes, the executive executes, and the judiciary construes the law."[2] One might term this the "civics book" model of government: Each federal institution has its constitutionally assigned role, and the legislature's assigned role is to make the law, which the other departments will then execute and/or interpret.

One potential problem with the "civics book" model is that it assumes that one can distinguish the making of a law from its execution or interpretation. Sometimes that distinction seems straightforward. If Congress enacted into the United States Code a literal inkblot,[3] it would functionally, and constitutionally, be an act of lawmaking—rather than execution or interpretation—for the executive or judiciary to purport to apply that contentless "law." (For someone who doubts the existence of any kind of constitutional subdelegation[4] rule, this example is a good test case.) But at other times the lines among those government functions and departments become blurred. If the executive "executes" and the judiciary "construes" the Clean Air Act[5] or Section 10(b) of the Securities Exchange Act,[6] are they performing a legislative function? Do those statutes, and countless others like them, subdelegate to other actors "powers which are strictly and exclusively legislative" and hence are not subdelegable?

Two centuries ago, Chief Justice Marshall was aware of this potential line-drawing problem. Right after laying out the "civics book" model, he added, "but the maker of the law may commit something to the discretion of the other departments, and the precise boundary of this power is a subject of delicate and difficult inquiry."[7] That sounds ominous to persons who worry about constraints on judges.[8] How would one conduct such a "delicate and difficult inquiry," in a judicially administrable fashion, to determine when and whether congressional grants of discretion to other actors cross a constitutional line?

Chief Justice Marshall had an answer:

> The line has not been exactly drawn which separates those *important subjects* which must be entirely regulated by the legislature itself from those of *less interest* in which a general provision may be made and power given to those who are to act under such general provisions to fill up the details.[9] (Emphasis added.)

That's it? That's all that America's most famous chief justice could come up with? It's OK for executives and courts to handle matters of "less interest," but Congress has to resolve the "important subjects"?

Yes, actually, that's it. That is the best Marshall could do in 1825. It is also the best I could do in 1994 when I first tried to formulate an originalist account of the Constitution's non-subdelegation principle and came up with: "Congress must make whatever policy decisions are sufficiently important to the statutory scheme at issue so that Congress must make them."[10] Eight years later, I still could do no better:

> Chief Justice Marshall's circular formulation was right all along, and rather than wind our way back to it indirectly, we might as well take the freeway. The line between legislative and executive power (or between legislative and judicial power) must be drawn in the context of each particular statutory scheme. In every case, Congress must make the central, fundamental decisions, but Congress can leave ancillary matters to the President or the courts. One can try to find alternative ways to express the distinction between fundamental and ancillary matters, such as focusing on case-resolving power or demonstration of political commitment or choices among salient alternatives, but in the end, one cannot really get behind or beneath the fact that law execution and application involve discretion in matters of "less

interest" but turn into legislation when that discretion extends to "important subjects." That is the line that the Constitution draws, and there is no escape from it.[11]

The seeming vagueness of these formulations is surely what gives pause to some judges, including most notably the irreplaceable Justice Antonin Scalia,[12] about whether a constitutional non-subdelegation doctrine can provide enough guidance to judges so that decisions applying that doctrine are grounded in something derived from the Constitution rather than from the judges' own personal policy preferences.

There is some reason to think that Justice Neil Gorsuch shares these concerns about finding judicially manageable standards for a non-subdelegation doctrine—not enough to abandon the non-subdelegation principle altogether but enough to lead him to search for an alternative account of the principle. In *Gundy v. United States*,[13] Justice Gorsuch called for resurrection of the non-subdelegation doctrine after more than 80 years of dormancy.[14] He managed to get not only Justice Clarence Thomas but also Chief Justice John Roberts to join his opinion, and Justice Samuel Alito indicated he would be willing to reconsider the Court's subdelegation jurisprudence if four other votes for reconsideration could be found.[15] Shortly thereafter, Justice Brett Kavanaugh, who did not participate in *Gundy*, wrote in a concurrence to a denial of certiorari, "Justice Gorsuch's thoughtful *Gundy* opinion raised important points that may warrant further consideration in future cases."[16]

That sounds a lot like five justices at least willing to think carefully about reviving some kind of non-subdelegation doctrine. The question is: What kind of doctrine are they prepared to revive? Would five justices today be willing to agree with Chief Justice Marshall that courts need to distinguish "important subjects" from "matters of less interest"?

Justice Gorsuch evidently had these concerns much on his mind in *Gundy*. He is well aware of both Chief Justice Marshall's account of subdelegation and my belief that Chief Justice Marshall was essentially right as a matter of original meaning; Justice Gorsuch's dissenting opinion in *Gundy* cites—on more than one occasion—both *Wayman v. Southard*[17] and me.[18] But those multiple citations conspicuously avoid emphasizing the test for subdelegations that Chief Justice Marshall endorsed.[19]

Justice Gorsuch had something else to offer in response to his own question: "What's the test?"[20]

After noting Marshall's and James Madison's observations about the difficulty of the inquiry, Justice Gorsuch found three principles that he believes can and should guide an inquiry into the boundaries of the legislative power to vest discretion in executive or judicial actors.

> First, we know that as long as Congress makes the policy decisions when regulating private conduct, it may authorize another branch to "fill up the details." . . .
>
> Second, once Congress prescribes the rule governing private conduct, it may make the application of that rule depend on executive fact-finding. . . .
>
> Third, Congress may assign the executive and judicial branches certain non-legislative responsibilities. . . . So, for example, when a congressional statute confers wide discretion to the executive, no separation-of-powers problem may arise if "the discretion is to be exercised over matters already within the scope of executive power."[21]

Talking about "important subjects" and matters of "less interest" was pretty clearly off the table for Justice Gorsuch. It shouldn't be—not for Justice Gorsuch nor for any other justice who knows the Constitution forbids subdelegation of legislative authority but who worries about giving judges seemingly open-ended power.

There is far more to Chief Justice Marshall's test than meets the eye. When Marshall wrote his seemingly cryptic comments in 1825, he was doing so as a lawyer trained in the law of agency. His reference to matters of "less interest" was shorthand for the agency-law notion of *incidental* powers, meaning powers that, naturally and by implication, go along with powers expressly granted to agents or subagents. Under founding-era agency-law principles, agents could authorize subagents to "fill up the details" of powers granted to the agents, but *only* with respect to incidental matters, and under founding-era principles of government, federal executive and judicial officials applying congressional laws were subagents subject to these background rules of agency law. Thus, for Marshall, the power of federal executive or judicial subagents to "fill up the details" of federal statutes was not a freestanding power but simply an alternative formulation for the power of agents to employ subagents to address matters of "less interest." That power, in turn, is cabined and defined by agency-law principles that set forth the circumstances under which agents, such as Congress, can rely on subagents to help carry out their functions.

The bottom line is that the Constitution permits a measure of subdelegation of legislative power, but the contours of permissible subdelegation do not correspond precisely to Gorsuch's formulation. The private law of agency defines the public-law limits of subdelegation. Once one fully understands that Chief Justice Marshall was drawing on those private-law norms in 1825, his approach reveals itself as far more structured and grounded in background legal understandings than might have been suggested by his simple reference to "important subjects" and matters of "less interest." Thus, Justice Gorsuch does not need to run away from Chief Justice Marshall's inquiry; he simply needs to flesh out its private-law background, which—unlike the standard he articulated in *Gundy*—does not leave judges free to roam through their personal preferences.

In the context of private-law agency arrangements, lawyers and courts had faced subdelegation questions for centuries before the Constitution was ratified. In cases when a principal delegated authority to an agent, there was always a question about subdelegation—whether the agent was authorized to subdelegate some of his or her authority to others. The same question arose under the Constitution. Because the founders conceived that the people had delegated their lawmaking authority to Congress when they adopted the Constitution, there was always a question of how much Congress could sub-delegate that authority.

There are good reasons to think that the Constitution draws on private-law background norms for much of its meaning, and the subdelegation problem is an excellent candidate for elaboration in private-law terms. Thus, a distinction between "important subjects" and "matters of less interest"—properly understood, as Chief Justice Marshall surely understood it, as a shorthand reference to principles of founding-era agency law—is a theoretically and practically sound test for identifying unconstitutional legislative subdelegations.

The first section of this chapter fleshes out the real meaning of Chief Justice Marshall's cryptic-at-first-glance comments in *Wayman*, suggesting how the Constitution's original meaning, which was aptly if tersely reflected in *Wayman*, lends itself to a legally rigorous reconstruction of the subdelegation doctrine. The second section compares that original meaning to Justice Gorsuch's alternative formulation, suggesting some similarities and a few potential differences. The last section ruminates about one possible way to frame the subdelegation problem in a fashion that will not spook justices who have absorbed the mindset that the normative principle of "judicial restraint" trumps constitutional meaning in a large set of real-world cases.

In sum, the Supreme Court does not need to create a non-subdelegation doctrine. It needs only to rediscover it.

The Agency-Law Origins of the Subdelegation Principle[22]

To determine, as a matter of original meaning,[23] whether a congressional grant of discretionary authority amounts to a forbidden subdelegation of legislative power, one needs to know the origin of the subdelegation principle. The principle's origin will have much to say about its content. Advocates of a constitutional subdelegation principle have invoked a wide range of arguments to ground such a principle. Many of those arguments—some of which I have made previously—contribute much to an understanding of the Constitution's allocation of authority among governmental institutions, and many of those arguments are "correct," in that they are part of a mosaic of arguments that collectively support the proposition that *some* form of constitutional subdelegation principle must exist. But only one of those arguments, drawn from the character of the Constitution as a fiduciary instrument, ultimately provides the concrete *content* of that subdelegation principle.

First, one could try to derive the subdelegation principle from the "civics book" model of enumerated institutional powers: The president and the judiciary cannot exercise legislative powers because the Constitution grants them none. Nor, the argument continues, does Congress have an enumerated power to subdelegate its legislative powers to others. Hence, the Constitution's basic scheme of enumerated powers implies a principle of non-subdelegation. That is essentially the core of Justice Gorsuch's argument for a non-subdelegation principle in *Gundy*.[24]

Some scholars argue in response that (1) Congress does have the authority under the necessary and proper clause to give other actors as much discretion as Congress wishes[25] and (2) once Congress enacts such a statute granting extensive or even limitless discretion to the president or the courts, the other actors are formally exercising "executive" or "judicial" power when they make the law.[26] For the "civics book" argument to succeed, the Constitution must have some implicit *substantive* principle that would make it not "proper" for Congress to grant too much discretion to other actors or that precludes the executive and judicial powers from exercising that amount or kind of discretion. The "civics book" argument is thus a fine logical structure, and it is among the many arguments that support the conclusion that some form of subdelegation doctrine must exist. But it is incomplete without that substantive principle that helps establish the content of any such doctrine.

A second argument against subdelegation of legislative authority looks to the Constitution's elaborate mechanisms for electoral accountability. Much of the Constitution concerns the procedures for selecting members of Congress and determining the electorate that will perform the selecting. Surely, one might reason, the Constitution would not care so much how members of Congress are selected if they aren't actually supposed to make the key decisions. Martin Redish's "political commitment" principle reflects a variant of this argument,[27] as does David Schoenbrod's accountability-based "consent of the governed" approach.[28]

The counter to this argument is that members of Congress are elected to exercise their constitutional powers. If one of those constitutional powers is the power to grant unlimited discretion to other actors, then that is simply part of the package of powers they were elected to exercise. Again, the real issue is whether there is some underlying *substantive* limitation on Congress' ability to punt away too much of its decision-making responsibility.

The third argument—and the one to which the others eventually must reduce to have concrete content—directly locates a non-subdelegation principle in the very fiber of the Constitution. It took me 20 years plus the indispensable Rob Natelson to grasp this point, but the real ground for the Constitution's non-subdelegation principle is the nature of the Constitution as a particular kind of legal instrument. Chief Justice Marshall grasped this point in 1825, even though he did not expressly articulate it, and his grasp generated the test that he so tersely announced. We must today understand what Chief Justice Marshall took for granted in 1825.

The argument starts with a basic premise: No text can expressly contain all the rules for its own interpretation. Even if it purported to do so, one would need external rules of interpretation to guide the interpretation of the text's internally expressed rules of interpretation—even if only to tell one to treat those internally expressed rules seriously rather than metaphorically, frivolously, or sarcastically. There are background norms of interpretation at work in any act of communication, whether it is a dramatic poetry reading, a conversation between spouses, or a lawyerly study of the United States Constitution. Those background norms will differ depending on what kind of document one is interpreting; the background rules for interpreting poems are not going to be identical to the background rules for interpreting health care proxy designations or end-of-life instructions.[29]

The Constitution is not a poem. Nor is it a chain novel, a diary, or a script for a Monty Python sketch. It is a legal document, written in a dialect of English that one might call "legal English."[30] Background rules of interpretation that would encourage one to look for metaphor, irony, or sarcasm in the constitutional text are unlikely to help the reader discern that text's actual communicative meaning (though such background rules might be helpful in discerning the meaning of certain poems, diaries, or scripts for Monty Python sketches).

The universe of documents known as legal documents is comprised of many different forms, including contracts, wills, and health care proxies. Granting that these are all materially different in some respect from poems, diaries, or Monty Python scripts: Where in this universe of legal documents does the Constitution best fit?

I have cowritten a book on exactly that question,[31] which argues that the Constitution looks most like a power of attorney, with a corporate charter coming in a close second (and a trust instrument running a distant third). My coauthor and I are planning a revised second edition that will focus less on the distinctions among those options than on their similarities. As it happens, that debate matters less to the subdelegation puzzle than it does to some other questions of constitutional meaning, because *all* the plausible characterizations of the Constitution—including the plausible characterization of "sui generis"—locate it somewhere within a family of instruments that one can broadly call "fiduciary" instruments.[32]

The Constitution's grants of power to Congress in Article I (and Articles IV and V) are, in form, the written record of a delegation of authority from a principal, "We the People," to an agent, "a Congress of the United States." It is a delegation that would be familiar to any 18th-century observer who had encountered instruments such as powers of attorney—and that was certainly familiar to the Committee of Detail,[33] consisting of four attorneys and a businessman, all of whom no doubt had a classical education that emphasized a fiduciary account of government.[34] Just as one could delegate to a private agent management authority over a portion of one's affairs, such as running a farm or selling goods abroad, the Constitution represents a delegation to a public agent (or series of agents) of some authority over a portion of We the People's affairs. And 18th-century fiduciary delegations, in any context, carried a principle against subdelegation—the more appropriate term than nondelegation, given the initial constitutional delegation of authority to Congress—in their wake.[35]

Authorities for this proposition about a presumptive lack of authority for agency subdelegation are numerous—and, as far as I can tell, unanimous. Matthew Bacon's enormously influential *A New Abridgement of the Law*,[36] first published in 1730, explained:

> One who has an Authority to do an Act for another, must execute it himself, and cannot transfer it to another; for this being a Trust and Confidence reposed in the Party, cannot be assigned to a Stranger whose Ability and Integrity were not so well thought of by him for whom the Act was done; therefore an (a) Executory having Authority to sell, cannot sell by Attorney.[37]

Note that this maxim is not confined to any specific kind of instrument; it describes a rule applicable to all instances of what today we would call fiduciary authority. Six further editions of the treatise, extending into the middle of the 19th century, repeated the maxim, with examples drawn from contexts as varied as powers of appointment and guardianships.[38]

Early 19th-century treatises on agency law said the same thing. Samuel Livermore, a noted agency-law theorist,[39] wrote in 1818:

> An authority given to one person cannot in general be delegated by him to another; for being a personal trust and confidence it is not in its nature transmissible, and if there be such a power to one person, to exercise his judgment and discretion, he cannot say, that the trust and confidence reposed in him shall be exercised at the discretion of another person.[40]

Livermore's treatise offers examples from case law involving attempts at subdelegation in contexts ranging from powers of appointment in wills, in which the holder of the power tries to designate another person to exercise it,[41] to the lack of privity between merchants and subdelegees in the absence of express authority on the part of the agents to subdelegate power,[42] to the lack of authority of factors and supercargoes to entrust the sale of goods to subagents without the express consent of their principals.[43] Joseph Story's even more famous treatise on agency law similarly explained:

> One, who has a bare power or authority from another to do an act, must execute it himself, and cannot delegate his authority to another; for this being a trust or confidence reposed in him personally, it cannot be assigned to a stranger, whose ability and integrity might not be known to the principal or who, if known, might not be selected by him for such a purpose.[44]

Story cites as examples many of the same cases that appear in Livermore's treatise. James Kent piled on:

> An agent, ordinarily, and without express authority, has not power to employ a sub-agent to do the business, without the knowledge or consent of his principal. The maxim is, that *delegatus non potest delegare* [one to whom power is delegated

is not able further to delegate that power], and the agency is generally a personal trust and confidence which cannot be delegated.[45]

I am not aware of any 18th- or 19th-century source that contradicts these authors on the basic agency law of subdelegation. "The founding-era rule against subdelegation of delegated agency authority is as clearly established as any proposition of law can be established."[46] Founding-era private-law lawyers understood very well the problem of subdelegation of authority.

Once the Constitution is seen in agency-law terms, the rule against subdelegation follows as a matter of course, as it would for any document in the family of fiduciary instruments. The Constitution's text and structure confirms and reinforces this fundamental fiduciary principle. Text- and structure-based arguments against subdelegation—such as the ones that I made for 20 years before meeting Natelson and that Justice Gorsuch was making in *Gundy*—are not *wrong*. Far from it. They are simply incomplete. The same is true of arguments from the dictates of representative government.

The substantive content of the subdelegation principle, which every textual and structural feature of the Constitution confirms and reconfirms, comes from the nature of the Constitution as a particular kind of legal instrument, for which a rule against subdelegation is the background presumption. The Constitution contains a principle against subdelegation because it is the kind of document that contains a principle against subdelegation. That is why Chief Justice Marshall could say with such assurance, "It will not be contended that Congress can delegate to the courts or to any other tribunals powers which are strictly and exclusively legislative."[47] To anyone who sees the Constitution as a kind of fiduciary instrument, the conclusion is obvious.

But identifying a basic principle against subdelegation of legislative authority is only the beginning. Just as well established in the founding era as the principle against agency subdelegation were the *exceptions* to this general rule. The rule against subdelegation of agency authority was a presumptive rule, not an absolute one. Three key principles carved out a space for permissible subdelegation by agents.

First, parties could expressly authorize any kind or degree of subdelegation that they wished in the agency instruments themselves: "An authority may be delegated to another, where the attorney has an express authority for that purpose."[48] The crucial term is "express." Given the strong background interpretative rule against subdelegation, "when it is intended, that an agent shall have a power to delegate his authority, it should be given to him by express terms of substitution."[49] This exception has no application to the United States Constitution, which does not contain an express authority to subdelegate. The only linguistically plausible source of a power to subdelegate would be the necessary and proper clause, and that does not even come close to constituting an express authorization for subdelegation.[50] Indeed, if anything, the necessary and proper clause affirmatively negates any such inference, though that is a tale for another time and a different scholarly life.[51]

Second, the normal background rule against subdelegation might not hold in specific contexts where there is a clear custom or tradition of allowing subdelegation, so that a particular instrument in such a setting most likely contemplates an arrangement outside the usual expectations of fiduciary law. An 1814 English case (cited by both Livermore and Story), while finding no privity of contract between a merchant and a subagent when the agent had no express authorization to subdelegate authority, said in dictum that the answer might have been different if there had been a "usage of trade such as to authorize one broker to put the goods of his employer into the hands of a sub-broker to sell."[52]

Other cases also refer to customs and practices permitting subdelegation, such as a custom of subdelegating the collection of notes to local banks when the debtor is at a distance.[53] Again, this will not work as a blanket validation of subdelegation of congressional legislative authority, if only because there could not possibly be a custom or tradition of subdelegation in a regime of separated powers such as that created by the Constitution when there was no established history of such separation-of-powers regimes from which to induce a custom or tradition.[54] The American separation-of-powers structure, embodied in the Constitution and in the state constitutions that preceded it, was unique in human history, so references to other traditions are of limited value for understanding that structure. Conceivably, there could be specific customs or traditions that could allow broader scope for subdelegation of legislative authority in certain areas. This is the thrust of much of Michael Rappaport's work in this area,[55] and the common-law framework might be able to accommodate many of his conclusions as customary exceptions to the usual presumptive rule against subdelegation.

The third principle, which is closely related to the first two principles, concerns the *kinds* of tasks that were, and were not, subject to the background presumption against subdelegation. If you hire a factor and supercargo to sell your goods overseas, is the supercargo expected personally to pilot the boat, swab the decks, and cook the fish cakes on the journey? Must the factor personally deliver any necessary title documents to the local recorder? The agency instrument can, if the parties so choose, specifically address these questions—and can give any answer they please, including making the supercargo swab the decks—but what if the instrument is silent?

The background rule was that subdelegation was presumptively forbidden for those *discretionary* aspects of the tasks at hand that involve a significant element of judgment but was presumptively allowed for *ministerial* or minor aspects of the tasks. What counted as discretionary or ministerial would vary with the particular circumstances. A collection agent can allow a subdelegee to deliver an eviction notice,[56] a general shipping agent can let subdelegees sign bills of lading,[57] and insurance agents can let clerks sign policies.[58] These are all ministerial, or lesser, tasks that can be subdelegated without specific reference in the agency agreement.

The assumption, subject always to clarification or alteration by the terms of the instrument, is that the parties intend to allow a measure of subdelegation on less important matters to facilitate the efficient accomplishment of the chief ends of the instrument. In the words of an early 20th-century article on agency law written by a notable treatise writer,

> There are many cases wherein from the nature of the duty, or the circumstances under which it is to be performed, the employment of subagents is imperatively necessary, and the principal's interests will suffer if they are not so employed. In such cases, the power to employ the necessary subagents will be implied.[59]

As Story summarized it:

> But there are cases, in which the authority [to subdelegate] may
> be implied; as where it is indispensable by the laws, in order to
> accomplish the end; or it is the ordinary custom of trade; or it
> is understood by the parties to be the mode, in which the par-
> ticular business would or might be done. . . . In short, the true
> doctrine, which is to be deduced from the decisions, is, (and it
> is entirely coincident with the dictates of natural justice,) that
> the authority is exclusively personal, unless, from the express
> language used, or from the fair presumptions, growing out of
> the particular transaction, or of the usage of trade, a broader
> power was intended to be conferred on the agent.[60]

If any of this sounds vaguely familiar, it is because one good way to
express the principle expounded by Story is to say that power to subdelegate, absent express authorization or custom to the contrary, is strictly forbidden for *important matters* but will be implied for matters of *less interest*.
Chief Justice Marshall, in *Wayman v. Southard*, was faithfully translating
the private law of agency into the Constitution. He had done the same six
years earlier in *McCulloch v. Maryland*, when he construed the necessary
and proper clause as a standard agency-law incidental powers clause familiar from numerous private-law contexts.[61] As a matter of original meaning,
that was exactly the right move, to the extent that the Constitution's character as a fiduciary instrument draws into play the basic rules for interpreting fiduciary instruments.

So, how would a Marshallian determine what counts as a matter of "less
interest"? Private law cannot always provide a definitive answer, if only
because the inquiry of what is more and less important depends heavily on
context. The ultimate inquiry is to figure out what is either so incidental
or so absolutely essential to a decision that one must reasonably presume
that the principal intends for the agent to do all those minor things necessary to fulfill his or her obligation.

Notice that the inference of authority to subdelegate occurs at both tails
of the distribution: Intent to authorize some measure of subdelegation is
implied when the task at hand seems to require it and when the task is so

routine that it cannot possibly matter who performs it. The agent must personally perform those tasks that fall in the middle of the spectrum. The shape of the distribution varies with the context; what is permissible in one setting may well be flatly forbidden in another.

While crisp, Scalia-like rules are therefore not likely to emerge from the common law of agency, some examples from the 18th- and early 19th-century cases may be instructive. One can start with some easy cases that illustrate clear instances of permissible and impermissible subdelegation and then move toward some harder cases.

For an example of readily permissible subdelegation, one can look to *Goswill v. Dunkley*,[62] decided sometime before 1748.[63] The plaintiff gave the defendant custody of a watch and a sword to sell in Porto Bello, Panama, thus making the defendant the selling agent for the plaintiff. The defendant agent claimed that to keep the sword and watch safe, "he put them into the warehouse of the South-Sea Company."[64] There was a break-in at the warehouse, the goods were stolen, and the plaintiff sued the defendant. The plaintiff argued that

> these goods were delivered to the defendant under a special and particular trust; and that he could not defend himself against the plaintiff's demand, by shewing that he had lodged them in a warehouse, which was a committing them to the care of a third person.[65]

The court disagreed and ruled for the defendant. That has to be right. It seems obvious that the parties did not contemplate that the sword and watch would never leave the agent's direct physical custody until the instant of sale (though one can imagine contracts, and perhaps contexts such as a valuable ring, that so require). The defendant surely could not subdelegate the task of finding an appropriate buyer, negotiating the price, and so forth, but storing the goods in a warehouse does not pass off the agent's responsibility to the principal any more than does hiring a captain to pilot the ship to Panama. The defendant would certainly be responsible for exercising due care in the selection of a subdelegee,[66] but this seems clearly to be the kind of function that all parties could reasonably expect other agents to handle. In Chief Justice Marshall's terms, in an agency arrangement for selling goods overseas, the actual physical storage of the goods is a matter of "less interest"—though selecting the appropriate place may well be an "important subject" that the agent must personally perform.

For an example of clearly forbidden subdelegation, look no further than the 1740 decision in *Ingram v. Ingram*.[67] Ingram had been given

> a power of disposing of a reversionary interest in copyhold land ... in such shares and proportions as he should think fit among the issue of the marriage, and for want of such appointment by the husband, to his right heirs.[68]

He could execute the power by deed or will. In his will, Ingram, "reciting the power under the articles and settlement, delegates it to his wife, that she may, in such shares and proportions as she shall think proper, dispose of it between his son and daughter."[69] The court invalidated the purported subdelegation: "This must be considered as a power of attorney which could be executed only by the husband, to whom it is solely confined, and is not in its nature transmissible or delegatory to a third person."[70]

These are polar cases, to be sure, but they have analogues in the Constitution. Consider the grant to Congress of the power "to coin Money, [and] regulate the Value thereof."[71] Does the first part of the grant mean that members of Congress must personally work in the mint stamping coins?[72] Obviously not. The "important subject" in that grant of power is the authorization to produce coins, the specification of the metals to be employed, the denominations to be issued, and so forth. The actual coining or minting is, in this context, a ministerial task, or at least a matter of "less interest," and Congress would be within its authority to subdelegate to executive agents the power to "fill up the details" of the actual minting process. On the other hand, a subdelegation to executive agents of the power to fix the value of the coins goes to the heart of what the provision is all about—namely, to "regulate the Value thereof." Subdelegating that primary authority to executive agents would be like subdelegating the authority to distribute the reversion in *Ingram v. Ingram*.

Thus, there are easy cases to be found in the Constitution and the common law of agency. For some problems, one needs only, as Justice Story put it, "the dictates of natural justice," sprinkled with a modicum of common sense and some attention to the terms and purposes of the agency arrangement. But some cases are not so easy. Two early 19th-century cases are especially instructive.

In *Catlin v. Bell*, the plaintiff entrusted the defendant shipper with some hats to be sold in the West Indies.

> It was then stated, that the defendant not being able to sell the goods in the island to which they were destined, had sent them to the Caraccas, in search of a market, where they had been destroyed by an earthquake.[73]

If the earthquake had happened in the assigned port of destination while the hats were in the shipper's control, presumably the shipper would not have been liable for that act of God (unless the contract made the agent strictly liable, which seems unlikely). It was held, however, "that there being a special confidence reposed in the defendant with respect to the sale of the goods, he had no right to hand them over to another person, and to give them a new destination."[74] Thus, even though the agent may have sincerely thought he was serving the principal's best interests by trying to get the best price, that alone would not justify entrusting the items to someone else to perform the central task of selling the goods. Here, the "important subjects" were both shipping and selling the goods, and neither of those elements could be subdelegated without express permission or custom to support it. A matter of "less interest" would surely be storing the goods pending sale; had the defendant responsibly chosen a warehouse in the West Indies and the goods been stolen from that warehouse, the defendant presumably would not have been liable absent a showing of negligence in the choice of warehouseman.

Now consider *Bromley v. Coxwell*.[75] William Bromley entrusted James Coxwell with "one hundred engravings from his plate of His Majesty on horseback"[76] to sell in India, hoping to get at least a guinea for each. Bromley significantly overestimated either his artistic talent[77] or His Majesty's overseas popularity, or perhaps both, because Coxwell in Calcutta was able to sell only one engraving for just three shillings and five pence—about one-sixth of a guinea.[78] Coxwell then tried selling them in

Madras "but with no better success."[79] At that point, Coxwell "left the residue in the hands of an agent at Madras to be disposed of by him."[80]

Upon Coxwell's return to England, Bromley sued him for conversion. Bromley won at trial but lost on appeal. To some extent, the case turned on the appropriateness of conversion as a remedy, but all three appellate judges at least doubted whether there was any liability. The authorizing language in the agency instrument was as follows:

> William Bromley agrees to send out by James Coxwell one hundred engravings from his plate of His Majesty on horse-back under these conditions, that provided James Coxwell can dispose of any one or all of them at above one guinea each, he the said James Coxwell is to be accountable to William Bromley on his return to England, for as many as he may dispose of at one guinea each; and William Bromley agrees to take all or as many as may be returned by the said James Coxwell, provided he the said James Coxwell cannot sell them in India or at any other port he may touch at, without expecting any sum from James Coxwell, or making any charge; and William Bromley further agrees to and authorizes to sell them for whatever they may fetch, if not more than one guinea may be offered for them separately.[81]

Judge Heath remarked, "I do not see why he [Coxwell] was not at liberty to leave them with an agent to be sold." Judge Rooke thought it was fine that "the Defendant left them in India judging for the best," and Judge Chambre said that "the agreement does not express the Defendant shall sell the goods himself; it seems therefore that the delivery to his agent was within the terms of the agreement."[82]

There is obviously much we do not know about the context of the arrangement from the brief case report that could easily bear on the most reasonable background assumptions to make regarding subdelegation. Was Coxwell known to be a factor, with extensive contacts in India? Was Coxwell just a random traveler taking the goods to India? Did Coxwell run an import-export business with multiple locations, so the use of subagents would be taken for granted?

While none of the following information appears in the case report, my extraordinary research assistant, Ross Chapman, uncovered that from April 2, 1799, to July 8, 1800, Coxwell was the fourth mate aboard the *Marquis of Lansdown*, a 647-ton ship, on a voyage between England and India under the East India Company.[83] Officers on those ships were paid little; they made their money as private traders who were allowed to bring and sell their own goods on the voyage, provided their goods did not compete with anything the East India Company sold.[84]

All this was surely known to Bromwell (and probably the court as well). If Bromwell knew his consignee was a sailor hoping to make some money on the side, rather than a professional art dealer, then some kind of subdelegation was likely contemplated; Coxwell was probably not chosen for his unique expertise in selling engravings—or even for his extensive contacts in India, since this appears to have been his first voyage as a mate on an East India Company vessel.

Thus, it makes sense that the court was willing to infer a power to subdelegate the sale of the items from the *absence* of any specification that Coxwell was to perform the task. The "important subject" was apparently getting the goods to India for sale; how and where they were sold was evidently a matter of "less interest." The language of the instrument lends itself to this construction: The essence of the agreement is "get these engravings to India and see if you can sell them—for anything at all—however and wherever you can manage to do it." In that context, subdelegation to effectuate the sales seems a natural consequence of the arrangement.

Do these cases yield a crisp line that can always be drawn between what is important and what is of less interest? Of course not. Relatively few constitutional doctrines have lines so crisp and clear that some element of judgment is never necessary. The point is only that courts have been exercising judgment about subdelegation of agency authority for a long time. This is not a novel inquiry or one without guideposts or analogies on which to draw. It is a distinctively legal inquiry.

In light of the cases, here is one tentative thought about the application of these principles to one particular Article I power. The power to subdelegate has often been found in the context of debt collection in distant locations—which was obviously a major issue in earlier times, without instantaneous money transfers and communication and when debt collection, and even the negotiation of notes and bills of exchange, had to be done in person. Authorizing an agent to collect a debt or transfer a note would normally, as a matter of custom and practice, carry with it power to designate an appropriate subagent in the debtor's or transferee's jurisdiction.[85]

There are circumstances, in short, in which a local subagent is likely to have knowledge and access that is not readily available to the prime agent. If that is an expected state of affairs, one might reasonably presume that the parties to the agreement would anticipate some measure of subdelegation to local agents to take advantage of that specialized local knowledge. Where the task depends on general skill and knowledge, however, rather than localized skill or knowledge, the baseline presumption against subdelegation would hold.

All this is potentially relevant to the Constitution because some of Congress' enumerated powers require uniform, nationwide application and some do not, which may help establish which (if any) congressional powers might implicitly authorize some measure of subdelegation by analogy to the common-law cases discussed. In some instances, the requirement of uniformity is express: With respect to the taxing power, "all Duties, Imposts and Excises shall be uniform throughout the United States";[86] Congress has power "to establish an uniform Rule of Naturalization, and uniform Laws on the subject of Bankruptcies throughout the United States";[87] and Congress can implement the Constitution's full faith and credit requirement by "general Laws."[88] For other powers, a uniformity requirement seems implicit: Could there really be a different value for federal coin in one state rather than another or different federal patent laws for Texas and Wisconsin?

Other powers, however, do not seem to require the same degree of uniformity. The power to "establish Post Offices and post Roads"[89] surely does not force Congress to have the same number, or even proportion, of post roads and post offices in each state. More fundamentally, the power to "regulate Commerce . . . among the several States"[90] does not contain an express uniformity requirement, and it is not obvious that it contains an implicit one.

Indeed, the Constitution by implication denies any such general uniformity requirement by singling out one kind of commercial regulation—port regulations—for uniformity: "No Preference shall be given to any

Regulation of Commerce or Revenue to the Ports of one State over those of another."[91] Thus, regulation of commerce may be a field in which local knowledge and variation might be invaluable; the regulations appropriate to New York may not be appropriate for Wyoming. Does that provide a ground for applying the subdelegation doctrine less rigidly with regulation of commerce than with some other congressional powers? More specifically, could different air pollution rules be appropriate in New York than in Wyoming, with those different rules ascertained by subagents with local knowledge? Without answering these questions, suffice it to say that if one is looking for limiting principles to shield key elements of the modern regulatory state from a reinvigorated subdelegation doctrine, this is a possible avenue to explore.

This body of private-law agency doctrine helps give content to Chief Justice Marshall's distinction between the "important subjects" that the legislature must decide and those matters of "less interest" that can be subdelegated to others; indeed, the Marshallian formulation can be seen as a shorthand reference to this private-law doctrine. In an agency instrument, the principal described with particularity what the agent was authorized to do. The agent presumptively had to perform those tasks, unless the nature of the instrument, the task, or both counseled otherwise. Unless it was a general power of attorney, agents did not have unlimited authority to act—and agents certainly did not have unlimited authority to allow others to act on the principal's behalf. The nature of the initial delegation limits, in legally defined ways, the nature of permissible subdelegations.

In the context of the Constitution, this cuts in two directions. On the one hand, all substantive executive rulemaking is probably not per se a forbidden subdelegation; it will depend very much on the context. On the other hand, congressional grants of discretionary authority, whether rulemaking or adjudicatory, to other actors cannot be unlimited or so ill-defined in scope that no one—including the agency, the courts, or Congress—could determine where they began or ended. Nor can those grants of authority go beyond what a sensible understanding of the tasks conferred on Congress permits. Reasonable people could perhaps disagree about hard cases, as reasonable judges and lawyers have disagreed about hard cases in the private-law context for centuries. But these are disagreements about law, not policy or theories of government.

As Justice Marshall recognized, the important matters were what Congress, as any agent under common law, was required to perform; "matters of less interest" were those items that Congress could pass to others, because they were not central to the delegation involved, and with respect to those matters of less interest, subdelegees could fill up the details. In sum, there was plenty of law on subdelegation in 1788 when the Constitution was ratified and in 1825 when the Supreme Court decided *Wayman*. One just needs to know where to look for it. The key elements of that law are in the founding-era common law of agency.

"Fill up the Details": Gorsuch vs. Marshall

In *Gundy*, Justice Gorsuch proposed three alternative principles as an account of the constitutional non-subdelegation rule. It is accordingly useful to see how Justice Gorsuch's principles compare, as a matter of both law and judicial manageability, to Chief Justice Marshall's agency-law doctrine. As it happens, Justice Gorsuch's principles loosely map onto the common-law categories for ascertaining permissible subdelegations, but the common-law categories are better grounded in original meaning and better suited for judicial application.

Justice Gorsuch's third principle—that there is no subdelegation problem when Congress is simply helping execute powers already vested in other actors—loosely corresponds to the common-law category of express authorization. The necessary and proper clause allows Congress to make necessary and proper laws "for carrying into Execution," inter alia, federal executive or judicial powers. If that is all Congress is doing, it is doing something the Constitution expressly permits it to do. That is not truly an express authority to subdelegate, because the powers being executed already exist in the executive and judicial actors, who do not need congressional authorization to do what the Constitution already entitles them to do.[92] Thus, Justice Gorsuch is not really identifying a permissible domain of subdelegation—and the Constitution does not expressly provide one either. He is simply describing a context in which grants of discretion do not raise issues of subdelegation.

Justice Gorsuch's second principle—that Congress can employ executive or judicial agents as fact finders to determine the applicability of laws—roughly corresponds to the agency-law exception for established customs and practices. The application of law often requires findings of fact. If, for example, a statute prescribes a calendar date for its own effectiveness, someone has to determine whether that specific calendar date has arrived and thus whether the law is in effect. If that seems trivial (how hard can it be to read a date off a calendar?), it is precisely the triviality that makes it illustrative. In applying such laws, do executives or courts refer the matter to the legislature to determine whether the specified effective date has arrived? Of course not. They decide the matter for themselves. Isn't that sort of decision exactly what executing and construing laws is all about? Whatever custom or tradition of government action was incorporated into the Constitution's separation-of-powers scheme through the basic definitions of legislative, executive, and judicial power, surely this much at least qualifies: Executing and judging includes ascertaining the factual conditions for application of a law.

Of course, once one moves beyond calendars as measures of a law's effective date, things get a bit cloudier. Suppose the effective date of a law is prescribed in terms of events other than planetary motions, so that a law becomes or stays effective, say, upon the eruption of a volcano or some other country continuing to respect American neutrality or a foreign country not imposing reciprocally unequal or unreasonable tariffs on imported American goods. Someone has to determine whether the conditions for the law's effectiveness have been satisfied. Who does that? Again, executive and judicial agents customarily and traditionally perform that task. This is the category of so-called contingent legislation that Justice Gorsuch's second principle was describing, represented by a large percentage of the pre–New Deal subdelegation cases in the Supreme Court.[93]

The question here is whether the principle, expressed in terms of either fact-finding or custom, contains limits on the kinds of facts that Congress can charge executive or judicial agents with ascertaining. Calendar dates are at one extreme. At the other would be a law that prescribes its effective date to be "whenever the president [or perhaps the attorney general] decides it should apply." Can an executive or judicial actor's will be the triggering contingency for a statute's effectiveness? And if the answer is no, are there other "facts" that are so open-ended or policy laden that committing their determination to executive or judicial agents effectively makes those actors legislators?[94]

Justice Gorsuch clearly wants to avoid how-much-is-too-much kinds of questions, but contingent legislation may not lend itself to categorical judgments. No formulation of a test can eliminate the need for judgment, at some point in the process, about whether ascertainment of a contingent "fact" amounts to making the law. That is an issue under current doctrine, it would be an issue under Chief Justice Marshall's test, and it would be an issue under Justice Gorsuch's three principles.[95]

The real action concerns Justice Gorsuch's first principle, which allows Congress to let executive or judicial agents "fill up the details." The quoted phrase comes from the end of a sentence in *Wayman*:

> The line has not been exactly drawn which separates those important subjects which must be entirely regulated by the legislature itself from those of less interest in which a general provision may be made and power given to those who are to act under such general provisions to fill up the details.[96]

The key is to understand what it means to "fill up the details." In *Wayman*, the term applies only to, and indeed simply alternatively describes, *matters of less interest*. It is fine, says Chief Justice Marshall, to let agents "fill up the details" on those less important matters. But that *does not* mean Congress is permitted to let agents "fill up the details" on "important subjects." To the contrary, those "important subjects . . . *must be entirely regulated by the legislature itself.*" (Emphasis added.) The key distinction for Chief Justice Marshall is thus not big pictures versus details. It is important subjects versus matters of less interest. Congress can authorize executive officials to fill in details, in either a large or small number, only for matters of "less interest."

Accordingly, one must be careful if one wants to say, as Justice Gorsuch said in *Gundy*, that even under a robust non-subdelegation principle Congress can "accomplish all it might wish to achieve. It may always authorize executive branch officials to fill in even a large number of details."[97] Whether Congress is free to accomplish all it might wish to achieve depends very much on what Congress wishes to achieve. If Congress wants to transfer authority over important subjects to executive or judicial agents, then no, Congress cannot accomplish that end. With matters of less interest, however, Congress is certainly free to either resolve those matters on its own or instruct agents to "fill up the details."

Thus, Justice Gorsuch's first principle is correct if, but only if, the detail-filling capacity of subagents that he has in mind is not freestanding but is limited only to subjects that by their nature, as matters of "less interest," can permissibly be charged to the discretion of subagents. Put another way, for Chief Justice Marshall and the agency-law view he represents, "fill up the details" is somewhat of a throwaway embellishment on the true inquiry, which looks to the nature of the agent's tasks in the context of the obvious purposes of the instrument in question. One must be wary not to allow a phrase such as "fill up the details" to become itself the central object of inquiry. It matters very much precisely what is being filled up.

Starting and Ending Points

As outlined above, the Constitution's original meaning includes a vigorous subdelegation doctrine. That does not mean, however, that a judge, as opposed to a scholar, must run the subdelegation doctrine to its ultimate conclusion, even if the judge considers the Constitution's original meaning to be its actual meaning. The law in the world, as opposed to the law in the academy, is full of circumstances in which principle gives way to practice. A major scholar has written a 500-page book illustrating precisely this point.[98]

A perfectly sensible account of real-world adjudication, for example, would be to say:

1. The subdelegation doctrine presupposes some conception of separated powers, so it does not permit any and all arrangements that Congress would like to enact;

2. The proper test for subdelegation is the agency-law test that would have been obvious to any private-law lawyer in 1788; but

3. As a matter of adjudicative precedent, laws that have been upheld or on which significant institutional capital has been constructed will be grandfathered in, whether or not they are consistent with original meaning; but

4. That is as far as things will be allowed to go, so new innovations or laws that are recent enough not to have given rise to significant expectation interests are fair game for serious judicial investigation and possible invalidation.

This set of propositions keeps a measure of faith with the Constitution's original meaning by not allowing past distortions in practice to distort constitutional meaning while recognizing that constitutional meaning is not the only force driving constitutional adjudication.

For an illustration of how past mistakes can effectively become exceptions to constitutional rules, consider an example raised earlier in this chapter: Congress' power to "regulate the Value" of money. Determining the value of money is plainly an important subject—really *the* important subject—in this delegation of power from We the People to Congress, so subdelegation of that power would be flatly forbidden by basic principles of agency law (though the physical minting of coins, in accordance with congressional instructions regarding value, would surely be a matter of less interest that could be entrusted to subagents). For more than a century, however, Congress has subdelegated power over the value of money to the Federal Reserve Board.[99] As a matter of original meaning, this is a flagrant violation of the subdelegation doctrine. Nonetheless, many important institutions and expectations have grown around that subdelegation over the past century. It would shock no one if a judge, however originalist in orientation, chose to leave the Federal Reserve Act in force. By the same token, however, novel *additions* to the existing subdelegation of power to fix the value of money would not have the same pedigree, and an originalist judge who is reluctant to invalidate the 1913 act might not have such qualms about holding the line against extensions of an error that is itself too deeply embedded to be undone.

To be clear: I am not endorsing this approach of balancing deeply embedded precedents against original meaning as an adjudicative theory.

Adjudicative theory is a subspecies of moral and political theory, and I have nothing interesting or useful to contribute to the world as a moral or political theorist. I simply note that for a justice who considers fidelity to original meaning an important part of adjudicative theory but thinks it must be bounded by some measure of extra-constitutional considerations, this method of "this far but no further" is a possible approach.

A full explication of the implications of this approach would require a book-length discussion of adjudicative theory, and that is not on the menu for the moment. For now, I want to make only two points.

First, one must keep clear the difference between ascertaining constitutional *meaning* and engaging in constitutional *decision-making*. They are very different enterprises. The former is an empirical, descriptive enterprise that seeks to answer the question: What is the objective communicative content of a particular expression or set of expressions? The latter is a normative enterprise: How should real-world legal actors choose to deploy the instruments of governmental violence? It is possible to say that constitutional decision-making should be based solely on constitutional meaning, but it is also possible to say that the latter is relevant to the former but not necessarily decisive for it.[100] If we assume five justices think that constitutional meaning contributes more than trivially and rhetorically to constitutional decision-making, there may be some attraction to the idea that vested expectations ought not to be undone, however unconstitutional they may be, but that future expectations need to conform to constitutional meaning.

As a matter of interpretative theory, the key point to emphasize is that precedent is a device for guiding normative decision-making. It is not a device for ascertaining constitutional meaning. Past precedents do not "fix" or "liquidate" (to use the in-vogue Madisonian term[101]) the Constitution's communicative meaning. They might, however, generate vested expectations, and if one treats those expectations as vested *rights*, then there is an adjudicative basis for leaving those vested rights untouched.

Second, private law, this time the law of property rather than the law of agency, provides an apt analogy. Consider the law of adverse possession. If someone adversely possesses an interest, it does not change the communicative meaning of the grant that created the interest. The grant, as a matter of communicative meaning, still conveyed the property to the previous possessor. The law simply chooses to ignore the grant's ordinary legal consequences. And adverse possession has no effect, communicative or legal, on the other interests in the grant. Adverse possession of the present interest has no effect on the future interests. Nor would an objectively faulty judgment allowing adverse possession of the present interest justify later objectively faulty judgments regarding the future interests. The grant's meaning is one thing; its legal effect is another.

Justice Scalia recognized the aptness of the comparison. In *Tyler Pipe Industries v. Washington State Department of Revenue*,[102] he argued for limiting the application of the dormant commerce clause doctrine to cases of interstate discrimination. In resisting the Court's expansion of the doctrine in that case, Justice Scalia remarked: "It is astonishing that we should be expanding our beachhead in this impoverished territory [of the dormant commerce clause], rather than being satisfied with what we have already acquired by a sort of intellectual adverse possession."[103]

When courts choose precedent over constitutional meaning, they are allowing a past wrong to prevail over the formally valid title (with objective communicative meaning playing the role of title), at least partly because of the passage of time and the formation of expectations based on mere possession. Many arguments in favor of precedent—stability, reliance, cost savings, and so forth—are also potential arguments for adverse possession.[104] But precedent in this sense is a tool for decision-making. It is not a tool for interpretation of a text. Rather, it is a reason for choosing to ignore the interpretation of a text. As Christopher Green has brilliantly put it:

> Recognizing the distinction between when to interpret and how to interpret is the key to seeing why recognizing the power to adhere to a possibly-incorrect earlier decision does not entail recognizing a general power to revise the Constitution freely. Deciding that it is more important that some issues are more importantly settled than settled correctly does not alter the criterion for what answers are actually correct. The Constitution still means what it means, and interpreters subject to an adverse-possession rule need neither surrender

their convictions about its meaning through the equivalent of an intellectual lobotomy, nor believe that interpreters are free to shift and morph the meaning of the Constitution without any constraint. Precisely because it is part of constitutional construction, and not constitutional interpretation, an adverse-possession model for adherence to incorrectly-decided precedent would merely limit the power of present interpreters to give effect to their interpretations; it would not affect their interpretations as such.[105]

If one recognizes precedent as akin to adverse possession, it will become clear that allowing the precedent or possession to prevail over the meaning or title in one instance does not affect the validity of surrounding meanings or titles. The effects of adverse possession are confined to the specific possessory interest that has been adversely possessed. There are good reasons to treat precedents the same way, allowing previous interpretative errors to stand when reliance or other interests strongly counsel it but not using that mistake as a justification for future mistakes. Hence: "this far but no further."[106]

One could obviously say much more about how to frame an argument along these lines. That is not my wheelhouse; I am neither an adjudicative theorist nor a litigator. But for those who value both constitutional meaning and settled practice, "this far but no further" has promise as a limiting principle, if a limiting principle one seeks.

* * *

Debate about subdelegation has often placed original meaning in opposition to judicial capacity. Much of the time, concerns about judicial capacity have won out over the claims of original meaning. There is no need for such sharp opposition. Original meaning points us to a vibrant body of founding-era agency law that at least helps us pose the right questions, even if it does not uniformly prescribe crisp answers to all those questions. It is hard to ask more than that of constitutional doctrine. It is not obvious why one would ask more than that of the non-subdelegation doctrine.

Acknowledgments

I am profoundly grateful to Peter Wallison for making so many insightful suggestions and comments that he should probably be listed as a coauthor. I thank Robert G. Natelson for making it all possible, Guy Seidman for helping make the possible a reality, and Ross Chapman for some truly amazing research assistance.

Notes

1. *Wayman v. Southard*, 23 US (10 Wheat.) 1, 42 (1825). In contemplating what will and will not be contended, Chief Justice Marshall evidently anticipated neither the modern legal academy nor modern Supreme Court justices. See Julian Davis Mortenson and Nicholas Bagley, "Delegation at the Founding," *Columbia Law Review* 121, no. 2 (2021): 277–368, https://www.columbialawreview.org/wp-content/uploads/2021/03/Mortenson-Bagley-Delegation_at_the_Founding.pdf; Eric A. Posner and Adrian Vermeule, "Interring the Nondelegation Doctrine," *University of Chicago Law Review* 69 (2002): 1721, https://chicagounbound.uchicago.edu/cgi/viewcontent.cgi?article=2731&-context=journal_articles; and *Whitman v. American Trucking Associations*, 531 US 457, 487 (2001) (Stevens, J., concurring in part and concurring in the judgment). In defense of Chief Justice Marshall: How could anyone in 1825—outside of an asylum—anticipate the modern legal academy or modern Supreme Court justices? In all seriousness, for responses to the recent Mortenson/Bagley article, see Aaron Gordon, "A Rebuttal to 'Delegation at the Founding,'" March 25, 2020, https://papers.ssrn.com/sol3/papers.cfm?abstract_id=3561062; and Ilan Wurman, "Nondelegation at the Founding," *Yale Law Journal* (forthcoming), https://papers.ssrn.com/sol3/papers.cfm?abstract_id=3559867. For responses to the earlier Posner/Vermeule article, see Larry Alexander and Saikrishna Prakash, "Reports of the Nondelegation Doctrine's Death Are Greatly Exaggerated," *University of Chicago Law Review* 70, no. 4 (2003): 1297–329, https://chicagounbound.uchicago.edu/cgi/viewcontent.cgi?article=5230&context=uclrev; and Gary Lawson, "Discretion as Delegation: The 'Proper' Understanding of the Nondelegation Doctrine," *George Washington Law Review* 73, no. 2 (2005): 235–68.

2. *Wayman*, 23 US at 42.

3. See Robert H. Bork, *The Tempting of America: The Political Seduction of the Law* (Washington, DC: Free Press, 1990), 166 (calling the 14th Amendment's privileges or immunities clause an "indecipherable inkblot").

4. It is conventional in constitutional discourse to refer to "nondelegation" or the "nondelegation doctrine" when discussing Congress' ability to vest discretion in executive or judicial officials. Because the subject of this chapter is subdelegation under common law, the proper terms here are "subdelegation" and the "non-subdelegation

doctrine." Power is initially delegated by the people, through the Constitution, to Congress, and the question is whether Congress, pursuant to the instrument of delegation, can then *subdelegate* all or part of its delegated authority to some other actor. See Philip Hamburger, *Is Administrative Law Unlawful?* (Chicago: University of Chicago Press, 2014), 377. Accordingly, while the term "non-subdelegation doctrine" is concededly a bit awkward, this is an instance in which intellectual precision is more important than elegance, and I will accordingly use the terms "subdelegation" and "non-subdelegation doctrine" rather than their more familiar but less accurate substitutes.

5. See 42 USC § 7409(b)(1) (2018) (defining primary air quality standards, to be set by the Environmental Protection Agency administrator, as "ambient air quality standards the attainment and maintenance of which in the judgment of the Administrator, based on such criteria and allowing an adequate margin of safety, are requisite to protect the public health").

6. See 15 USC § 78j(b) (2018) (declaring it unlawful "to use or employ, in connection with the purchase or sale of any security . . . any manipulative or deceptive device or contrivance in contravention of such rules and regulations as the Commission may prescribe as necessary or appropriate in the public interest or for the protection of investors").

7. *Wayman*, 23 US at 42–43. See *Federalist*, no. 37 (James Madison). "Experience has instructed us that no skill in the science of government has yet been able to discriminate and define, with sufficient certainty, its three great provinces—the legislative, executive, and judiciary. . . . Questions daily occur in the course of practice, which prove the obscurity which reigns in these subjects, and which puzzle the greatest adepts in political science."

8. For myself, I worry much less about constraints on judges than I do about getting constitutional meaning right, especially when one is talking about something as basic to the Constitution as its allocation of powers among different institutions. But that is a topic for another day. See, for example, Steven G. Calabresi and Gary Lawson, "The Rule of Law as a Law of Law," *Notre Dame Law Review* 90, no. 2 (2014): 483, https://scholarship.law.nd.edu/ndlr/vol90/iss2/1/. The point of this contribution is to show that, whatever may be true in other contexts, the constitutional rule against subdelegation is *both* interpretatively correct *and* consistent with judicial modesty, to the extent that one considers judicial modesty an important value.

9. *Wayman*, 23 US at 43.

10. Gary Lawson, "The Rise and Rise of the Administrative State," *Harvard Law Review* 107 (1994): 1231, 1239.

11. Gary Lawson, "Delegation and Original Meaning," *Virginia Law Review* 88, no. 2 (April 2002): 327, 376–77, https://www.jstor.org/stable/1074001?seq=1.

12. Professor Antonin Scalia was quite keen on resurrecting the non-subdelegation doctrine. In 1980, he wrote, "Even with all its Frankenstein-like warts, knobs, and (concededly) dangers, the unconstitutional delegation doctrine is worth hewing from the ice." Antonin Scalia, "A Note on the Benzene Case," *Regulation* (July/August 1980): 25, 28. Yet, Justice Antonin Scalia became perhaps the Court's most forceful opponent of policing the breadth of Congress' grants of discretion to executive or judicial agents. See *Whitman*, 531 US at 457; and *Mistretta v. United States*, 488 US 361, 415–16 (1989) (Scalia, J., dissenting). His reasons for declaring the non-subdelegation doctrine effectively

unenforceable were grounded in judicial restraint rather than constitutional meaning: "Once it is conceded, as it must be, that no statute can be entirely precise, and that some judgments, even some judgments involving policy considerations, must be left to the officers executing the law and to the judges applying it, the debate over unconstitutional delegation becomes a debate not over a point of principle, but over a question of degree." For Justice Scalia, anything that was a matter of degree rather than principle was prima facie nonjusticiable. For a critical examination of Justice Scalia's commitment to rules in constitutional adjudication, see Calabresi and Lawson, "The Rule of Law as a Law of Law."

13. *Gundy v. United States*, 139 S. Ct. 2116 (2019).

14. *Gundy*, 139 S. Ct. at 2131 (Gorsuch, J., dissenting).

15. *Gundy*, 139 S. Ct. at 2130 (Alito, J., concurring in the judgment).

16. *Paul v. United States*, 589 US (2019) (statement of Justice Kavanagh respecting the denial of certiorari).

17. See *Gundy*, 139 S. Ct. at 2133, 2135, 2137 (Gorsuch, J, dissenting).

18. See *Gundy*, 139 S. Ct. at 2135, 2140 (Gorsuch, J., dissenting).

19. Chief Justice Marshall's formulation gets cited at one point. See *Gundy*, 139 S. Ct. at 2136 (Gorsuch, J., dissenting). But, as we will shortly see, Justice Gorsuch reframes the test to mean something different from what it actually says. My proposed formulation, understandably enough, ends up somewhere at the bottom of the Marianas Trench.

20. *Gundy*, 139 S. Ct. at 2135 (Gorsuch, J., dissenting).

21. *Gundy*, 139 S. Ct. at 2135–37 (Gorsuch, J., dissenting) (footnotes omitted).

22. With acknowledgment and profound gratitude to Rob Natelson. See Robert G. Natelson, "The Agency Law Origins of the Necessary and Proper Clause," *Case Western Reserve Law Review* 55, no. 2 (2004): 243, https://scholarlycommons.law.case.edu/cgi/viewcontent.cgi?referer=https://www.google.com/&httpsredir=1&article=1581&context=caselrev.

23. There are, of course, a great many versions of "original meaning." The version employed here locates meaning in the hypothetical intentions of the hypothetical author of the Constitution ("We the People"), which operationally is equivalent to the understandings that would have been held by a reasonable intended reader of the document in 1788 (for purposes of the non-subdelegation doctrine). Fleshing out the characteristics of the intended reasonable reader is a task for another life. See Gary Lawson, "Reflections of an Empirical Reader (Or: Could Fleming Be Right This Time?)," *Boston University Law Review* 96 (2016): 1457, https://core.ac.uk/download/pdf/270213613.pdf. Fortunately, I doubt whether the differences among versions of original meaning matter much for purposes of the non-subdelegation doctrine; I suspect all those versions will converge to a common core of meaning in this context.

24. *Gundy*, 139 S. Ct. at 2133 (Gorsuch, J., dissenting). It was also at earlier times the core of my argument. See, for example, Lawson, "Delegation and Original Meaning"; and Lawson, "Discretion as Delegation." The present article reflects a modification of those prior views, which I now see to be incomplete.

25. US Const. art. I, § 8, cl. 18 ("The Congress shall have Power . . . To make all Laws which shall be necessary and proper for carrying into Execution the foregoing Powers, and all other Powers vested by this Constitution in the Government of the United

States, or in any Department or Officer thereof").

26. For the classic statement of this position, see Posner and Vermeule, "Interring the Nondelegation Doctrine."

27. See Martin H. Redish, *The Constitution as Political Structure* (Oxford, UK: Oxford University Press, 1995), 136–37.

28. See David Schoenbrod, "Consent of the Governed: A Constitutional Norm That the Courts Should Substantially Enforce," *Harvard Journal of Law & Public Policy* 43 (2020): 213, https://www.harvard-jlpp.com/wp-content/uploads/sites/21/2020/01/Schoenbrod-FINAL.pdf.

29. For more on this crucial point about the relationship between background interpretative rules and documentary type, see Gary Lawson and Guy Seidman, *"A Great Power of Attorney": Understanding the Fiduciary Constitution* (Lawrence, KS: University Press of Kansas, 2017), 8–11.

30. See John O. McGinnis and Michael B. Rappaport, "The Constitution and the Language of the Law," *William & Mary Law Review* 59 (2018): 1321, https://scholarship.law.wm.edu/wmlr/vol59/iss4/4/.

31. See Lawson and Seidman, *"A Great Power of Attorney."*

32. In a recent article, Professors Sam Bray and Paul Miller argue, with considerable force, that there was no general category of "fiduciary" instruments known to lawyers in the late 18th century. See Samuel L. Bray and Paul B. Miller, "Against Fiduciary Constitutionalism," *Virginia Law Review* 106, no. 7 (November 2020): 1479, https://www.virginialawreview.org/articles/against-fiduciary-constitutionalism/. They claim instead that there were various power-conferring instruments in specific settings, and it was not until considerably after the ratification of the Constitution that those disparate documents were categorized and synthesized with the label "fiduciary." That is all true; no one in 1788 would think to write a treatise on something called "fiduciary law." Indeed, some legal dictionaries of that time did not even contain entries for the term "agent." Nonetheless, the categorization of the Constitution as a fiduciary instrument is descriptively accurate. The reason later writers were able to synthesize these disparate documents into a modern category of "fiduciary instruments" is because there was something there to synthesize. There were certain characteristic features of those documents immanent in the structure of the law, even if there was no established terminology for expressing those features in the form of a general theory. There was no *vocabulary* of fiduciary law in the 18th century, but there was a *substance* of fiduciary law in the 18th century. Robert Natelson has exhaustively cataloged the core features of 18th-century fiduciary law (though they did not call it that at the time). See Robert G. Natelson, "The Legal Origins of the Necessary and Proper Clause," in *The Origins of the Necessary and Proper Clause*, ed. Gary Lawson et al. (Cambridge, UK: Cambridge University Press, 2010): 57–59; and Robert G. Natelson, "Judicial Review of Special Interest Spending: The General Welfare Clause and the Fiduciary Law of the Founders," *Texas Review of Law & Politics* 11 (2007): 239, https://scholarship.law.umt.edu/cgi/viewcontent.cgi?article=1051&context=faculty_lawreviews. Even without the modern vocabulary, a reasonable 18th-century observer could and would see elements in the Constitution that resemble the elements in a power of attorney, a corporate charter, and so forth.

33. The Committee of Detail was a group of five distinguished members of the Constitutional Convention—Oliver Ellsworth, Nathaniel Gorham, Edmund Randolph,

John Rutledge, and James Wilson—who were responsible for shaping the Convention's principles into a concrete draft of the Constitution. See William Ewald, "The Committee of Detail," *Constitutional Commentary* 28 (2012): 1997, https://conservancy.umn.edu/bitstream/handle/11299/163466/1-Ewald-282-TheCommitteeofDetailAccepted.pdf.

34. See Lawson and Seidman, *"A Great Power of Attorney,"* 31–37; and Carl J. Richard, *The Founders and the Classics: Greece, Rome, and the American Enlightenment* (Cambridge, MA: Harvard University Press, 1994).

35. To be clear: No one doubts that legislative authority can be delegated. We the People are fully capable of delegating that authority to Congress or some other body. The legal question is whether the recipient of that delegation can then *subdelegate* the authority to another actor.

36. On the underappreciated significance of Matthew Bacon's *A New Abridgement of the Law*, see Lawson and Seidman, *"A Great Power of Attorney,"* 113.

37. Matthew Bacon, *A New Abridgement of the Law* (1730), 1:203. "Attorney" in this context does not mean a lawyer. It simply means someone who is authorized to act on behalf of another—essentially what today we would call an "agent." See Giles Jacob, *A New Law Dictionary*, 6th ed. (1750) (defining attorneys as "those Persons who take upon them the Business of other Men, by whom they are retained").

38. See Lawson and Seidman, *"A Great Power of Attorney,"* 113–14.

39. Noted enough to be cited by the United States Supreme Court in the 21st century and at least eight times in the 19th century. See *Domino's Pizza Inc. v. McDonald*, 546 US 470, 475 (2006).

40. Samuel Livermore, *A Treatise on the Law of Principal and Agent and of Sales by Auction* (1818), 1:54.

41. See *Ingram v. Ingram*, 26 Eng. Rep. 455 (1740).

42. See *Cockran v. Irlam*, 105 Eng. Rep. 393 (1814).

43. See *Catlin v. Bell*, 171 Eng. Rep. 59 (1815).

44. Joseph Story, *Commentaries on the Law of Agency, as a Branch of Commercial and Maritime Jurisprudence* § 13, at 14 (1844).

45. James Kent, *Commentaries on American Law* (1827), 2:496. Kent and others may have misunderstood the Latin maxim they invoked. See Patrick W. Duff and Horace E. Whiteside, "Delegata Potestas Non Potest Delegari: A Maxim of American Constitutional Law," *Cornell Law Review* 14, no. 2 (1929): 168, https://scholarship.law.cornell.edu/clr/vol14/iss2/4/; and Sean P. Sullivan, "Power, but How Much Power? Game Theory and the Nondelegation Principle," *Virginia Law Review* 104, no. 7 (November 2018): 1229, 1248, virginialawreview.org/articles/powers-how-much-power-game-theory-and-non-delegation-principle/ (relying on the Duff/Whiteside account). That question is important as a matter of legal history but unimportant for interpretive theory. What matters for understanding founding-era agency law is what reasonable founding-era legal actors would have believed about the referents of fiduciary concepts, not whether they would have been historically right to believe it.

46. Lawson and Seidman, *"A Great Power of Attorney,"* 114.

47. *Wayman*, 23 US at 42.

48. Livermore, *A Treatise on the Law of Principal and Agent and of Sales by Auction*, 1:55. Again, see note 35. An "attorney" in this context is simply an agent and not necessarily a lawyer.

49. Story, *Commentaries on the Law of Agency*, 15–16.

50. For an example of what an express authorization for subdelegation would look like, see Floyd R. Mechem, *A Treatise on the Law of Agency* (1914), 299.

51. See, for example, Lawson, "Discretion as Delegation"; and Lawson, "Delegation and Original Meaning."

52. *Cockran v. Irlam*, 103 Eng. Rep. at 394.

53. See, for example, *Dorchester & Milton Bank v. New England Bank*, 5 Mass. 177, 188 (1848).

54. Such a custom or tradition could, of course, evolve over time, and arguably such a custom prevails in the United States today. Indeed, if the fiduciary principles embodied in the Constitution are supposed to track contemporary rather than 18th-century norms, there is a case that much modern subdelegation is not merely permissible but affirmatively *required*. See Restatement (Third) of Trusts § 80 (2007); and John H. Langbein, "Reversing the Nondelegation Rule of Trust-Investment Law," *Missouri Law Review* 59 (1994): 105, https://digitalcommons.law.yale.edu/cgi/viewcontent.cgi?referer=https://www.google.com/&httpsredir=1&article=1486&context=fss_papers. A living constitution may well provide considerable room for subdelegation. My concern, however, is with the actual dead Constitution, not with a fictitious living one. See Gary Lawson, "The Fiduciary Social Contract," *Social Philosophy & Policy* (forthcoming). The circumstances to which constitutional concepts apply change over time, but the criteria for including something within those concepts does not. See Lawson, "Reflections of an Empirical Reader." That fixing of the criteria for inclusion in a concept is precisely the "original" part of "originalism"—a point I will develop further in a forthcoming article. To be sure, non-originalists are unlikely to find persuasive this article's argument, which seeks to ascertain the Constitution's original meaning, but this article is not trying to convince non-originalists of anything.

55. See Michael B. Rappaport, "A Two Tiered and Categorical Approach to the Nondelegation Doctrine" (working paper, University of San Diego School of Law, San Diego, CA, 2020), https://papers.ssrn.com/sol3/papers.cfm?abstract_id=3710048; and Michael B. Rappaport, "The Selective Nondelegation Doctrine and the Line Item Veto: A New Approach to the Nondelegation Doctrine and Its Implications for *Clinton v. City of New York*," *Tulane Law Review* 76 (2001): 265.

56. See, for example, *McCroskey v. Hamilton*, 108 Ga. 640, 34 S.E. 111 (1899).

57. See, for example, *Bennitt v. Guiding Star*, 53 F. 936 (S.D. Ohio 1893).

58. See, for example, *Bodine v. Exchange Fire Ins. Co.*, 51 N.Y. 117 (1872).

59. Floyd R. Mechem, "Delegation of Authority by an Agent," *Michigan Law Review* 5, no. 2 (December 1906): 94, 99. In some circumstances, the end can *only* be accomplished through subdelegation, as where the agent is not a licensed attorney or auctioneer but such a person is necessary to complete the transaction. In those circumstances, the assumption is that the parties contemplated subdelegation to the appropriate professionals. See, for example, *Strong v. West*, 110 Ga. 382, 35 S.E. 693 (1900).

60. Story, *Commentaries on the Law of Agency*, 16–17.

61. For the full story on *McCulloch* and agency law, see Lawson and Seidman, "A Great Power of Attorney," 87–90; and Gary Lawson and David B. Kopel, "Bad News for Professor Koppelman: The Incidental Unconstitutionality of the Individual Mandate," Yale Law Journal Online 121 (2011): 267, 277–79. For the seminal study of the agency-law

character of the necessary and proper clause, see Natelson, "The Agency Law Origins of the Necessary and Proper Clause."

62. *Goswill v. Dunkley*, 93 Eng. Rep. 779.

63. The case report is undated, but the reporter volume covers a period that ends in 1748.

64. *Goswill*, 93 Eng. Rep. 779.

65. *Goswill*, 93 Eng. Rep. 779–80.

66. The court noted: "If the warehouse was not a place of safe custody, that should have been replied." 93 Eng. Rep. 780. I explore in another article some of the difficult issues surrounding selection of appropriate subdelegees when subdelegation is permissible. See Lawson, "The Fiduciary Social Contract."

67. *Ingram*, 26 Eng. Rep. at 455.

68. *Ingram*, 26 Eng. Rep. at 455.

69. *Ingram*, 26 Eng. Rep. at 455.

70. *Ingram*, 26 Eng. Rep. at 455.

71. US Const. art. I, § 8, cl. 5.

72. This example actually came up in the 1791 postal debates in Congress. See 2 Annals of Cong. 230–31 (1791) (statement of Rep. Sedgwick).

73. *Catlin*, 171 Eng. Rep. at 59.

74. *Catlin*, 171 Eng. Rep. at 59.

75. *Bromley v. Coxwell*, 126 Eng. Rep. 1372 (1801).

76. *Bromley*, 126 Eng. Rep. at 1372.

77. I am in awe of my research assistant, Ross Chapman, who managed to track down the engraving. See William Bromley, *King George III*, November 20, 1798, stipple engraving, National Portrait Gallery, https://www.npg.org.uk/collections/search/portrait/mw141942/King-George-III. It's certainly not Louvre material, but it doesn't seem all that bad.

78. Coxwell was fully authorized to take the lower price. See *Bromley*, 126 Eng. Rep. at 1372 ("'William Bromley further agrees to and authorizes to sell them for whatever they may fetch, if not more than one guinea may be offered for them separately.'").

79. *Bromley*, 126 Eng. Rep. at 1372.

80. *Bromley*, 126 Eng. Rep. at 1372.

81. *Bromley*, 126 Eng. Rep. at 1372.

82. *Bromley*, 126 Eng. Rep. at 1373.

83. See Charles Hardy, *A Register of Ships, Employed in the Service of the Honorable the United East India Company, from the Year 1760 to 1819*, 3rd ed. (1820), 195. The case report identified Coxwell as "a mate of an East Indiaman," and the *Marquis of Lansdown*'s 1799 voyage was Coxwell's first as a mate. The *Marquis of Lansdown* sailed port on April 2, 1799, just two months after the agreement between Bromley and Coxwell.

84. See Earl H. Pritchard, "Private Trade Between England and China in the Eighteenth Century (1680–1833)," *Journal of the Economic and Social History of the Orient* 1, no. 1 (1957): 108, https://www.jstor.org/stable/3596041?refreqid=excelsior%3A424a7bb-f1bde429a410d2291b4d8c99e8&seq=1. See also H. V. Bowen, "Privilege and Profit: Commanders of East Indiamen as Private Traders, Entrepreneurs and Smugglers, 1760–1813," *International Journal of Maritime History* 19, no. 2 (2007): 43, https://journals.sagepub.com/doi/abs/10.1177/084387140701900204.

85. See, for example, *Thomas Wilson & Co. v. Smith*, 44 US (3 How.) 763 (1845).

86. US Const. art. I, § 8, cl. 1.

87. US Const. art. I, § 8, cl. 4.

88. US Const. art. IV, § 1.

89. US Const. art. I, § 8, cl. 7.

90. US Const. art. I, § 8, cl. 3.

91. US Const. art. I, § 9, cl. 6.

92. If the congressional laws purport to *limit* rather than *facilitate* the powers vested by the Constitution in the president or the courts, they are not laws "for carrying into Execution" those powers and thus are not authorized by the necessary and proper clause; one does not "carry[] into Execution" a power by prohibiting or limiting its exercise. See David E. Engdahl, "Intrinsic Limits of Congress' Power Regarding the Judicial Branch," *BYU Law Review* 75 (1999): 172–74. Indeed, the most important question in these contexts is not whether Congress has subdelegated legislative power by granting too much discretion but whether congressional attempts to *limit* rather than *facilitate* the discretion of executive or judicial actors improperly intrude on those actors' constitutional prerogatives. Can Congress fix the form of notice for judicial auctions? Determine the payment terms for winning bidders in such auctions? Tell courts what evidence they can and cannot admit into the record in those proceedings? Order courts to rule in favor of one particular party? A similar sequence of questions can be framed about congressional attempts to regulate the exercise of executive power—and the questions are no easier to resolve in that context. I have tentatively explored these issues elsewhere, and we can mercifully pass them over here. See Gary Lawson, "Controlling Precedent: Congressional Regulation of Judicial Decision-Making," *Constitutional Commentary* 18 (2001): 191, https://scholarship.law.umn.edu/cgi/viewcontent.cgi?article=1373&context=concomm.

93. See, for example, *Cargo of the Brig Aurora v. United States*, 11 US (7 Cranch) 382 (1813); *Marshall Field & Co. v. Clark*, 143 US 649 (1892); and *J. W. Hampton Jr. & Co. v. United States*, 276 US 394 (1928). For a discussion of these cases, see Lawson, "Delegation and Original Meaning," 361–69.

94. Two justices in 1892 thought that letting the president determine whether other countries had imposed "reciprocally unequal and unreasonable" trade restrictions on American products "certainly extends to the executive the exercise of those discretionary powers which the Constitution has vested in the law-making department." 143 US at 699–700 (Lamar, J., dissenting).

95. Part of the reason the contingent legislation—or "executive or judicial factfinding"—cases are so difficult is that the distinction between law and fact on which they are based is itself a conventional rather than metaphysical distinction. But pursuing that angle leads inexorably to a book-length discussion. See Gary Lawson, *Evidence of the Law: Proving Legal Claims* (Chicago: University of Chicago Press, 2017).

96. *Wayman*, 23 US at 43.

97. *Gundy v. United States*, 139 S. Ct. 2116 (2019).

98. See Lawrence Lessig, *Fidelity & Constraint: How the Supreme Court Has Read the American Constitution* (Oxford, UK: Oxford University Press, 2019). For a trenchant critique of Professor Lessig's normative suggestions, see Amul R. Thapar and Joe Masterman, "Fidelity and Construction," *Yale Law Journal* 129, no. 3 (January 2020): 774,

https://www.yalelawjournal.org/review/fidelity-and-construction. The review does not take serious issue with Professor Lessig's descriptive claims.

99.   See Pub. L. No. 63-43, ch. 6, 38 Stat. 251 (codified in scattered sections of 12 USC).

100.   Larry Solum has defined the "contribution thesis" as the claim that "the content of constitutional law is constrained by the linguistic meaning of the constitutional text." Lawrence B. Solum, "*District of Columbia v. Heller* and Originalism," *Northwestern University Law Review* 103, no. 2 (2009): 923, 954, https://scholarship.law.georgetown. edu/cgi/viewcontent.cgi?article=1833&context=facpub. The contribution thesis does not specify *to what extent* communicative meaning constrains decision-making. This article assumes that at least five justices consider it at least a significant constraint.

101.   The now somewhat trendy idea of "liquidation" is fuzzy. It can refer to settling contested or uncertain meaning of constitutional language by reference to either precedent in a narrow sense, historical practice in a broader sense, settled expectations, or even evolving values. For a detailed survey of the differing uses of the term, see William Baude, "Constitutional Liquidation," *Stanford Law Review* 71, no. 1 (2019): 1, https:// www.stanfordlawreview.org/print/article/constitutional-liquidation/.

102.   *Tyler Pipe Industries v. Washington State Department of Revenue*, 483 US 232 (1987).

103.   *Tyler Pipe Industries*, 483 US at 265 (Scalia, J., concurring in part and dissenting in part).

104.   For a compendium of arguments in favor of adverse possession, see Jeffrey Evans Stake, "The Uneasy Case for Adverse Possession," *Georgetown Law Journal* 89 (2001): 2419, https://www.repository.law.indiana.edu/cgi/viewcontent.cgi?article=1220& context=facpub. To be clear: I am not endorsing the arguments for either precedent or adverse possession. I am simply pointing out their similarities.

105.   Christopher R. Green, "Constitutional Theory and the Activismometer: How to Think About Indeterminacy, Restraint, Vagueness, Executive Review, and Precedent," *Santa Clara Law Review* 54, no. 2 (2014): 403.

106.   For a critique of this idea, see Daniel A. Farber, "The Rule of Law and the Law of Precedents," *Minnesota Law Review* 90 (2006): 1173, 1182–83.

> Unlike the doctrine of adverse possession in property law, which is peripheral to the system of property ownership, stare decisis in constitutional law changes the nature of the enterprise. Bedrock precedents cannot be quarantined; instead, they inevitably affect the system of constitutional law as a whole.
>
> The originalist impulse regarding these bedrock but allegedly "wrong" precedents is to say "this far, but not an inch farther." Under this view, the court should not overrule key precedents, but it should always return to first principles in considering new issues. But this is an untenable stance in a legal system that seeks some form of coherence.

If one regards coherence with previous decisions, as opposed to coherence with constitutional meaning, as the paramount value, there is something to this argument. But it is obviously circular. And it begs important questions about what a precedent contains and what would constitute an expansion of it.

A "Step Zero" for Delegations

JONATHAN H. ADLER

The nondelegation doctrine is poised for a juridical revival—or so it would seem. It has been over 80 years since a majority of the Supreme Court was willing to conclude that a delegation of legislative power to the executive branch is unconstitutional.[1] Yet the doctrine's proponents see signs of hope.[2] In 2019, five justices expressed a willingness to consider enforcing meaningful limits on Congress' ability to delegate broad authority to administrative agencies to promulgate legislative rules of their own devising.[3]

We have been here before. Indeed, it seems someone catches a glimpse of this elusive phoenix stirring in the ashes every 20 years. The nondelegation doctrine was poised for revival in 1980, after *Industrial Union Department, AFL-CIO v. American Petroleum Institute*, known as the Benzene case.[4] Then-Professor Antonin Scalia noted, "The doctrine has acquired a renewed respectability."[5] And yet nothing happened. Others saw a potential rebirth in 2000, before a unanimous Supreme Court brushed aside nondelegation arguments in *Whitman v. American Trucking Associations*.[6] Professor Scalia may have thought the doctrine was "worth hewing from the ice,"[7] even if only to send a message to Congress, but Justice Scalia would have nothing of it, easily dispatching the nondelegation arguments made against the Clean Air Act (CAA).[8]

A persistent problem for nondelegation doctrine proponents has been how to draw the line between permissible delegations of limited policy discretion and impermissible delegations of legislative authority. Professor Scalia warned in 1980 of "the difficulty of enunciating how much delegation is too much."[9] And in 2000, Justice Scalia noted the Court had "almost never felt qualified to second-guess Congress regarding the permissible degree of policy judgment that can be left to those executing or applying the law."[10] If James Madison could not delineate the boundary between legislative and executive power with any precision,[11] it should be no surprise that nondelegation proponents still ask, "What's the test?"[12]

While the Court has not been willing to invalidate congressional enactments on delegation grounds, it has repeatedly reaffirmed the constitutional prohibition on the delegation of legislative power.[13] Nondelegation concerns have influenced other doctrines and judicial approaches to statutory interpretation.[14] The question is whether the Court can do better.

When delegation runs riot, "democracy suffers."[15] Expansive and pervasive delegation has a corrosive effect on the democratic legitimacy of administrative action. In a representative democracy such as ours, the power to prescribe rules for private conduct with the force of law is most appropriately wielded by the people's representatives, through the constitutionally prescribed legislative process. This ensures a degree of democratic legitimacy in the resulting rules. From this standpoint, forcing Congress to provide more precise instructions to agencies enhances democratic accountability for government policy. Operationalizing this concern for the democratic legitimacy of the laws requires more than limiting the scope or span of delegations, however. It also requires a consideration of time.[16]

The delegation of power in one period may not legitimize the later exercise of such power. Whenever power is delegated, there is a risk that the power will be used in ways that were unforeseeable and depart from the delegating party's intent.[17] The passage of time magnifies this problem. When past delegations are used to address unforeseen problems, it is often impossible to say that any particular course of action has democratic warrant. How can a legislature's decision to delegate power be necessary and proper if it does not specify what type of mischief is to be addressed, let alone what power is being delegated? If the delegation of policymaking authority without an intelligible principle is unconstitutional, then so must be the delegation of authority to decide what has been delegated.

Consideration of time, combined with the Constitution's nondelegation baseline, may provide a means to operationalize and reinforce nondelegation principles. Courts should scrutinize agency claims of delegated power more closely, particularly when agencies draw on older or previously unused sources of authority. Delegation of regulatory authority should not be presumed. Rather, it must be shown. And if no delegation of authority was made, then the nondelegation doctrine cannot be violated.[18] Thus, a "step zero" inquiry into the nature and scope of any asserted delegation may help constrain the sorts of unbounded delegations about which a majority of current justices appear to be concerned.[19]

This chapter outlines the case for just such a "step zero" inquiry to advance nondelegation values. The first part explains how excessive delegation undermines the democratic legitimacy of agency action. It is not only the scope of delegation that matters, however. As the second part explains, the passage of time further attenuates the democratic legitimacy of delegated power. Existing court doctrine does not account for such temporal concerns, as the third part illustrates. Various interpretive canons, including the so-called "major questions" doctrine, have filled the gap, as discussed in the fourth part, but they could do more. The final section argues for a "step zero" inquiry that incorporates a nondelegation baseline to curb the unwarranted exercise of agency authority, and then the chapter concludes.

Delegation and Democracy

Critics of delegation have long been concerned about the administrative state's democratic legitimacy, or lack thereof. Article I vests legislative authority in Congress, and yet administrative agencies lodged in Article II often make and execute important policy questions. This state of affairs challenges the underlying constitutional design.

Article I of the Constitution provides that "all legislative powers herein granted shall be vested in a Congress of the United States."[20] Through this provision, "We the People have entrusted or delegated" legislative authority to Congress and not to any other part of the federal government.[21] For a bill to become law, it must be passed by both houses of Congress and signed by the president.[22]

Article I further ensures that "elected representatives assume personal responsibility for the key decisions on the scope of government"[23] by requiring that both Houses "publish" their proceedings.[24] These features were to ensure that "government may not expand its powers in any controversial way unless voters know just whom to blame if blame there be."[25] As the Court explained in *Loving v. United States*, the Constitution's "precise rules of representation, member qualifications, bicameralism, and voting procedure make Congress the branch most capable of responsive and deliberative lawmaking."[26]

The delegation of broad power to draft, implement, and enforce legislation-like regulations enables legislators to shirk responsibility for the resulting policy measures. This may help their political prospects, but it undermines democratic accountability for lawmaking.[27] Legislators can claim credit for supporting the enactment of broad, nice-sounding measures, such as the Clean Water Act or the Occupational Health and Safety Act (because who could be against clean water or occupational health and safety?) and then deflect blame for how such laws are implemented by pointing the finger at the administrative agencies tasked with making the more difficult policy choices.

The primary problem with broad delegation is not that it necessarily produces worse policy outcomes but that it undermines democratic accountability. As John Hart Ely observed in *Democracy and Distrust*, delegation of legislative authority "is undemocratic, in the quite obvious sense that by refusing to legislate, our legislators are escaping the sort of accountability that is crucial to the intelligible functioning of a democratic republic."[28] Due to pervasive delegation, Ely explained:

> much of the law is . . . effectively left to be made by the legions of unelected administrators whose duty it becomes to give operative meaning to the broad delegations the statutes contain. The point is not that such "faceless bureaucrats" necessarily do a bad job as our effective legislators. It is rather that they are neither elected nor reelected, and are controlled only spasmodically by officials who are.[29]

Democratic accountability is undermined further because delegation alters the incentives that individual legislators face. The ability to delegate undermines the incentive to build coalitions in support of political compromises and augments the incentive to engage in constituent service. As David Schoenbrod observes, this shifts much of legislators' work from public lawmaking to private accommodating.[30]

That voters can still elect representatives who are ideologically compatible with their preferences is little consolation. Democratic accountability is not just about supporting politicians who claim to embrace a given political agenda in the hope they will follow through. It also requires the ability to punish them for unwise votes and failing to fulfill campaign promises. Broad delegation makes this more difficult, as it enables legislators to "distance themselves from much of the blame that results from making decisions on new laws."[31]

While delegation alters individual legislators' incentives and actions, it also alters the role and functioning of the "collective Congress."[32] Delegating authority to craft, shape, and implement rules to administrative agencies shifts and concentrates power within the legislative chamber. Individual legislators, especially those with leadership roles or positions on relevant committees, have the opportunity to cajole and pressure agencies to alter their behavior through legislative oversight and other mechanisms. As then-Professor Neomi Rao explained, such individualized efforts to influence agencies come at the expense of Congress' collective power and responsibility to discipline and direct how agencies behave.[33] And because individual members of Congress benefit from this shift in responsibility, delegation creates further incentives for ever more delegation.[34]

While the primary arguments against broad delegation concern the democratic legitimacy of government action, it is not clear that concerns for democratic legitimacy, by themselves, justify a nondelegation rule focused on the breadth or scope of the power delegated.[35] The breadth of a delegation is a crude and imprecise measure of the extent to which it undermines democratic accountability.

Some broad delegation may go too far, but some amount of broad delegation may also be unavoidable. In any bureaucracy, public or private, power and responsibility will be delegated to others.[36] Just as a corporate board delegates some decision-making authority to management, a legislature may choose to delegate some policymaking to an administrative entity. In either case, those delegating will set parameters, but those to whom power is delegated will inevitably enjoy some discretion on implementation.[37] Thus, even those who are not enamored with the modern administrative state acknowledge "some delegation is needed, no matter how limited the government."[38]

There may also be good reasons for broad delegations of policymaking power to administrative agencies. There are contexts in which it would be perfectly rational to delegate far-reaching (if perhaps also time-limited) authority to the executive branch, such as to deal with severe, rapidly evolving threats or crises. Wars, pandemics, and other urgent matters may justify hierarchical decision-making structures, at least until the threat has passed.[39] The most responsible way to handle such delegations may be to make them time limited, but this has been done with relatively few statutes.[40] A nondelegation doctrine that enhances and facilitates democratic governance must focus on more than the breadth of the delegation.

Delegation and Time

The focus on how excessive delegation can undermine the democratic legitimacy of administrative action tends to overlook how time exacerbates delegation's democratic deficit.[41] Delegations to administrative agencies are often perpetual, lacking any expiration date and only infrequently revisited by Congress.[42] Once a statute is enacted, it will often provide a continuing source of authority to an agency unless and until revisited by a subsequent Congress.[43] This means that delegations of authority become the source of authority for agencies to adopt regulatory or other measures at a later time when such measures could not attract majority support. Agencies often use powers delegated well in the past to address problems and develop solutions that were not even contemplated by the enacting Congress, let alone authorized or endorsed by popular will. Indeed, agencies may first decide what they want to do and only then look for a source of statutory authority to do it.

This time-lag problem is magnified by Congress' increased unwillingness (or inability) to engage in regular lawmaking. Old, obsolete statutes are rarely updated to account for societal, technological, or economic changes.[44] This is not a new problem. In 1963, Judge Henry Friendly lamented that the legislature "has diminished the role of the judge by occupying vast fields and then has failed to keep them ploughed."[45] Yet as technological, economic, and social change has accelerated, legislation has not kept pace.[46] Orthodox lawmaking is a thing of the past.[47]

Legislating was never intended to be easy.[48] The constitutional design ensures that lawmaking will tend to be an arduous and drawn-out process, as it takes more than simple majority support to ensure a legislative proposal can navigate the requirements of bicameralism and presentment. However difficult legislating was meant to be, partisan gridlock and legislative dysfunction appear to have made it worse.[49]

We live in a dynamic world, yet our statutes are static. As the world changes and popular understanding of contemporary problems evolves, statutes remain in place. New problems emerge, preexisting problems metastasize, and our understanding of present and prospective problems improves. Yet statutes are infrequently amended to account for these changes.

Technological change, in particular—and the institutional changes and economic opportunities it facilitates—drives statutory obsolescence. The Telephone Consumer Protection Act (TCPA) was enacted in 1991 to limit the use of automated dialing systems for telemarketing. However well-intentioned, the statute's archaic language, written to address the landline-based communications technology of the time, is sufficiently broad that it has enabled the Federal Communications Commission (FCC) to regulate the use of smartphones, as they are capable of storing and generating phone numbers.[50] The statutory language enacted in 1991 was based on a contemporary understanding of how technology could function. Transposing that language to 2020 produces different results than any legislators could have understood they were enacting.[51] In a real way, the TCPA operates as a different legal regime in 2020 than it did in 1991 as the rules and authorities enacted for one set of technologies are applied to another.

The nation's environmental laws provide a textbook example of statutory obsolescence.[52] The basic statutory architecture of federal environmental law was enacted with a burst of legislative activity in the 1970s, when the nation was focused on environmental problems tied to 20th-century industrialization and urban decay.[53] These statutes helped produce significant environmental gains over the past few decades, but they are woefully out-of-date.[54] Their structure and underlying premises "date back to the era of the phonographic record."[55] The focus on industrial point sources of pollution has given way to an understanding that nonpoint sources more significantly contribute to water pollution. Static assumptions about the natural environment have given way to an appreciation of dynamic ecological systems.[56] And so on. Across the board, Congress has not kept pace.[57] Yet agencies continue to regulate, drawing on broad delegations of the past.

The lack of legislative updating does not prevent agencies from seeking to address new or emerging problems.[58] Where new tools are unavailable, regulatory agencies often turn to preexisting delegations, enacted to address different problems, to fill the gap. The Environmental Protection Agency (EPA) regulates greenhouse gases under the CAA, even though Congress never contemplated such regulation, much less expressly delegated any such power to the EPA.[59] The 1970 CAA delegated to the EPA broad powers to address local and regional air pollution, such as through the creation of federal air quality standards that each metropolitan area must meet. Congress revised the CAA in 1977 and again in 1990 to take into account lessons learned from prior regulatory measures, new scientific information, and the recognition of additional environmental problems justifying a regulatory response. Thus, in 1990, Congress added provisions to the CAA to address stratospheric ozone depletion and acid precipitation, two transboundary problems the 1970 act, as written, had not been designed to address. No provisions targeting greenhouse gases were ever adopted, however.[60]

When the Supreme Court concluded that the CAA had, in fact, delegated to the EPA the authority to regulate greenhouse gases, it based its conclusion on a superficially plausible account of the statute's text, but without any regard for the practical implementation concerns or whether Congress actually delegated such expansive and unprecedented authority to the EPA.[61] Nor did it consider whether the relevant provisions could be plausibly applied to greenhouse gases given how the statute is written.[62] The issue was not whether the EPA should have one sort of authority or another to address climate change, but whether Congress delegated to the EPA any such authority at all.

While environmental law contains many examples of statutes that are simultaneously obsolete and the source of ongoing and evolving regulatory authority, it is hardly alone.[63] Even broad, dynamic statutes that anticipate technological change become stale over time, though their broad grants of authority remain. The FCC regulates telecommunications under the terms of a statute drafted in the 1980s but unrevised since 1996. Given the rate of change in communications technologies and associated industries, even if these laws updated every 10 years, they would remain "woefully outdated."[64] In 1996, there were no iPhones or home Wi-Fi networks, no Myspace or Facebook, no Wikipedia or Google, no Netflix or Amazon Prime Video, no Bluetooth devices or Wi-Fi calling, and no Skype or Zoom. When enacting the 1996 reforms, members of Congress had no idea they were authorizing the regulation of such technologies and business models, much less endorsing a particular regulatory approach on how to ensure adequate internet access for content producers.

Just as Congress did not contemplate EPA regulation of greenhouse gases when it last revised the CAA in 1990, Congress did not anticipate the regulation of technologies, devices, and business models that had not yet even been conceived, let alone deployed, when it last revised the Telecommunications Act. In no sense did Congress consider the regulatory choices the FCC would have to make with new telecommunications and internet technologies. Congress did not even know the nature of the questions the FCC would attempt to answer. How then can it be said that Congress provided the FCC with an "intelligible principle" for how it should address unforeseen problems of an unprecedented nature arising from technologies that were not even conceived?

To say that Congress delegated the authority to the FCC to not only address such problems but remake a whole sector of the economy is to say Congress gave the FCC a blank check to be filled out at a later date. If this sort of broad delegation—delegation of the power to decide which problems require governmental intervention, combined with the power to select what interventions will be adopted—is not a delegation of core legislative authority, it would seem nothing is.[65]

Congress may not have anticipated particular scientific or technological developments, but Congress has anticipated the likelihood of unforeseen developments and the need for agencies to act as new problems emerge. This pragmatic justification for continuing reliance on broad—if stale—delegations does not close the democratic deficit of the resulting agency initiatives. Nor can it be claimed that there was any meaningful democratic endorsement of the particular powers or authorities used. It is one thing to authorize the EPA to tighten emission limits on recognized pollutants. It is quite another to authorize the EPA to identify new sets of pollutants to be regulated or curtailed in unforeseen ways, producing trade-offs that were never before considered. Whatever the practical policy wisdom of the resulting agency actions, they are not the product of democratic deliberation.

Arguably *any* past statutory enactment lacks contemporary democratic legitimacy because statutes are not routinely reauthorized or revisited, and the constitutionally prescribed process for enacting legislation makes changing the law difficult. Legislative minorities that could never see their own preferences enacted are often able to frustrate the efforts of legislative majorities to change the law. Some degree of entrenchment is inherent in the constitutionally prescribed system of bicameralism and presentment, as enacting new laws to modify or repeal old ones is always difficult. Thus, there is always a possibility that, at any given time, people are governed by laws that would no longer command majority support.

Delegation of authority to promulgate new rules governing new policy questions that arise due to changes in technology, demographics, economic conditions, or other factors threatens to magnify any democratic deficit caused by the normal entrenchment of statutory rules. A statute enacted into law will necessarily have had sufficient democratic support at the time of its enactment, even if it no longer commands such support at the present time. Its democratic legitimacy comes from the fact that the requirements of bicameralism and presentment were met at the time of enactment, even if later developments render it obsolete. A rule promulgated pursuant to delegated power, on the other hand, need not have *ever* had such democratic support, particularly if the delegation empowers an agency to adopt rules that address problems or concerns yet to emerge when the authorizing statute was enacted.

Whereas statutory entrenchment merely maintains the status quo, delegation allows the continued evolution and deployment of administrative power without an additional legislative enactment and the democratic legitimacy such authorization provides. If an earlier legislature enacts a law that a later legislature would not have enacted, then the later legislature could repeal that law, but the enacted law still unquestionably represents the will of a legislative coalition that was sufficient to navigate bicameralism and presentment at one time.

The same cannot be said when an agency uses broad, open-ended delegations of regulatory authority to address problems beyond the enacting legislature's vision. There is no question that a Congress authorized the EPA to regulate the causes of acid precipitation, for the 1990 CAA expressly said as much. There is a real question, however, whether *any* Congress at *any* time authorized the EPA to regulate greenhouse gases, however worthwhile or important such regulation may be.[66] The most that can be said is that Congress enacted a law with language that, at some later date, may be interpreted to justify the exercise of agency authority to address a problem that Congress did not know the law could be used to address. That sort of broad authority is tantamount to Congress legislating now the power for an agency to legislate later, which even those skeptical of the nondelegation doctrine might conclude is a step too far.

Doctrinal Inadequacies

As noted earlier, nondelegation concerns are typically expressed in terms of the breadth and scope of the power delegated. If an agency is given too much discretion or the authority to exercise too much power, however measured, Congress has delegated legislative power.[67] To whatever extent this can be said, time only magnifies the problem. And insofar as the problem with delegation is that assertions of authority by administrative agencies lack democratic legitimacy, time exacerbates this problem as well.

Framing the constitutional constraint on delegation in terms of whether there is an "intelligible principle" does little to address the democratic deficit underlying most concerns about delegation. Particularly as interpreted by the Supreme Court, the "intelligible principle" standard offers the most minimal constraint on the legislature's delegation of power to adopt and implement regulatory policies and is blind to temporal concerns.[68]

In practice, an "intelligible principle" requires no more than the articulation of a policy aim or relevant policy concerns against which the agency's action can be measured. In *Whitman*, for instance, the relevant language from the CAA deemed to provide an "intelligible principle" for setting National Ambient Air Quality Standards (NAAQS) did not meaningfully constrain the ultimate level the EPA selected. Under the CAA, the EPA was to set the NAAQS for ground-level ozone at a level "the attainment and maintenance of which" is "requisite to protect the public health" with "an adequate margin of safety."[69] This certainly requires the EPA to focus on the health consequences of different pollution levels in the ambient air, but it does not meaningfully limit the EPA's range of choices.[70]

As the US Court of Appeals for the DC Circuit had noted, the EPA believed there is no "safe" level of exposure to ground-level ozone. That is, there is no level (above zero) below which no adverse effects on human health are expected.[71] Reducing ambient ozone levels will reduce the negative health effects and perhaps concentrate those effects among subpopulations of acutely sensitive individuals, but reductions on the margins will not eliminate adverse effects on public health.[72] Any level above zero, including that produced by natural background sources, poses some risk.

The "intelligible principle" here is constraining on not the scope or degree of discretion the EPA exercises so much as *how* the agency goes about exercising that discretion. In requiring the EPA to focus on the public health consequences of different NAAQS levels, the CAA (as interpreted by the Court) provides a useful metric for hard look review, in that it identifies the particular concerns necessary for the agency to address in articulating the basis for choosing one air quality standard for another.[73] If the EPA fails to address potential health consequences of different ambient pollution levels, it can expect judicial skepticism of the resulting rule.[74]

That's not nothing and may even serve democratic values insofar as it encourages greater transparency and accountability in the rulemaking process. It may well be a sufficiently determinate test for a court to apply and could serve as a measure for judicial review of an agency's compliance with congressional instruction. Yet it is not much of a limit on delegation. If delegation is a problem, something more is required to control it.

The problem, as then-Professor Scalia noted in 1980, is that it has been difficult to identify a judicially administrable test for determining "how much delegation is too much."[75] The potential lines of inquiry that Justice Neil Gorsuch identified in his *Gundy v. United States* dissent would be a start, but they may be insufficient to yield a determinate test.[76] Allowing an agency to simply "fill in the details" may not sound like much, but in practice, the "details" are often where significant policy determinations are made. The "detail" about the precise level of air pollution that is allowed in metropolitan areas has far-reaching implications, and it's not a purely scientific determination.[77] Allowing the EPA to determine the minimum oxygen content required in gasoline may sound like a small detail to be filled in, but a slight change in the standard determines which substances may be used and which interest groups are satisfied.[78] When it comes to policymaking in complex, technical areas, the devil really is in the details.

Basing a test on the distinction between rulemaking and fact-finding is equally problematic in practice. The law-fact distinction is meaningful but difficult to operationalize for this sort of test, as nondelegation doctrine proponents have acknowledged.[79] Allowing agencies to base regulatory decisions on scientific determinations does not constrain their discretion. The scientific judgments Congress tasks federal agencies to make routinely involve normative policy judgments with broad implications.[80] It is one thing to require agencies to be transparent and explicit about their assumptions and judgments. It is quite another to pretend as if confining agencies to fact-finding is sufficient to constrain the sort of policymaking discretion about which the nondelegation doctrine is concerned. For these reasons, it is understandable (if still regrettable) that the Court has fallen back on the intelligible-principle test, even if that test does not constrain delegation to any meaningful degree.

It might be possible to supplement the "intelligible principle" inquiry with a temporal component, but the underlying line-drawing problem would remain. Just as it is difficult to determine when Congress has delegated too much power or too much policy discretion, how would a court determine whether a past delegation of power is too old or too stale? Congress has the authority to sunset agency authority by writing such provisions into federal statutes—and perhaps it should do so more often.[81] Regular reauthorization of legislative enactments would largely address the temporal component of delegation's democratic deficit. But it is not clear how courts could play this role, at least not by adopting a particular rule on the timeliness of constitutional delegations.

Any judicially imposed time limit or temporality requirement would be wholly arbitrary and lack any meaningful connection to the Constitution's text or structure. The appropriate time limit in one context may be wholly inappropriate in another, and there is no ready formula for sufficiently temporal lawmaking to be found. Is there an alternative?

From Nondelegation to Major Questions

Even though it may be difficult to identify the precise point at which a delegation becomes too broad or a principle becomes insufficiently intelligible, it does not mean such a line does not exist, nor does it suggest that the effort is not worth undertaking. It may, however, complicate the task of identifying a judicially administrable test. After all, as Justice Scalia observed, "A doctrine so vague . . . is no doctrine at all."[82]

Constitutional avoidance is one mechanism courts use to reaffirm the existence of a constitutional problem without a clear doctrinal demarcation of the line between what is constitutionally permissible and what is not. A long series of precedents hold that courts should avoid interpreting statutes in a manner that raises difficult constitutional questions.[83] In the federalism context, for example, the Court often reaffirms and reinforces the textual and structural limitations on Congress' power under Article I, Section 8, by construing statutes in ways that avoid the risk that Congress has exceeded such limits.[84] Thus, the Court has construed the scope of federal regulatory jurisdiction under the Clean Water Act narrowly to ensure the statute operates within the bounds of Congress' regulatory power under the commerce clause.[85]

This approach has been seen in the context of nondelegation.[86] In lieu of enforcing a more aggressive nondelegation doctrine, the Court has embraced several substantive canons of construction that channel nondelegation concerns through statutory interpretation.[87] As Justice Gorsuch explained in his *Gundy* dissent:

> When one legal doctrine becomes unavailable to do its intended work, the hydraulic pressures of our constitutional system sometimes shift the responsibility to different doctrines. And that's exactly what's happened here. We still regularly rein in Congress's efforts to delegate legislative power; we just call what we're doing by different names.[88]

The Court has adopted various "nondelegation canons" that reinforce nondelegation values by construing potential delegations narrowly.[89] Even some "federalism" canons can be understood as reinforcing nondelegation concerns in that they encourage courts to presume Congress has not attempted to delegate power beyond constitutional limits. By requiring a clear statement of congressional intent in the relevant statutory text, the Court avoids concluding that Congress has delegated power that might raise constitutional concerns.

The invocation of constitutional avoidance, while evading the need to render a constitutional judgment, reaffirms constitutional limits. After all, if there were no constitutional limits that could be exceeded, there would be nothing to avoid. Holdings based on constitutional avoidance further help crystallize the contours of the underlying constitutional limits and may lay the groundwork for future constitutional holdings.[90]

Insofar as the "major questions" doctrine presumes that Congress will not delegate authority to resolve questions of major economic or political significance to regulatory agencies without a clear statement, it embodies nondelegation values. As Justice Gorsuch explained in *Gundy*, "Although it is nominally a canon of statutory construction, we apply the major questions doctrine in service of the constitutional rule that Congress may not divest itself of its legislative power by transferring that power to an executive agency."[91] Not only does the Court presume Congress would not have delegated questions of major economic and political significance to federal agencies, but also some such delegations could themselves be unconstitutional, and avoidance serves a prophylactic role. Assuming the extent of permissible delegation has some outward limit, the major questions doctrine helps the Court avoid confronting (and either endorsing or deflating) the intelligible-principle tests as an outside limit on Congress' authority.

While the major questions doctrine divests agencies of the power to decide whether to embark on broad new regulatory adventures, it is not used consistently to deny agencies regulatory authority. It is cited most often to narrow agency authority or deny agencies the authority to make such choices through *Chevron* deference. The doctrine was relied on to deny the Food and Drug Administration (FDA) the authority to regulate cigarettes and other tobacco products[92] and to prevent the FCC from relaxing regulation of rival long-distance telephone carriers in *MCI Telecommunications Corp. v. AT&T*.[93] Likewise, the Court's invocation of the major questions doctrine to deny *Chevron* deference to the IRS in *King v. Burwell* was merely a prelude to the Court endorsing the IRS's position that tax credits were available for purchasing health insurance in exchanges established by the federal government.[94] And although it did not expressly rely on the major questions doctrine in *Massachusetts v. EPA*, the Supreme Court would not consider the EPA's opinion on whether the CAA actually authorized the regulation of greenhouse gases.[95] Leaving to a federal agency the authority to decide whether it should have the power to regulate greenhouse gases would have been quite the delegation of power.

The major questions doctrine may have been influenced, or even inspired, by nondelegation concerns. Nevertheless, as currently formulated, it is inadequate to address the democratic deficit caused by delegation, even setting aside the compounding of such deficits by time. The doctrine's focus on the scope of authority does not address time concerns at all, nor is it a meaningful proxy for democratic accountability concerns.

While serving as a judge on the DC Circuit, Brett Kavanaugh articulated a version of the major questions doctrine, what he termed the "major rules doctrine," which appears more sensitive to the underlying question of delegation than the "major questions" variant evident in cases such as *FDA v. Brown & Williamson Tobacco Corp.* and *Massachusetts v. EPA*.[96] Writing in *US Telecom Association v. FCC*, the "net neutrality" case, Judge Kavanaugh explained that agency authority to initiate expansive regulation of large sectors of the economy could not be presumed. In arguing the FCC lacked the authority to adopt its 2015 net neutrality rule, he stressed that "Congress did not clearly authorize the FCC to issue the net neutrality rule" and that this "lack of clear congressional authorization matters."[97] As Judge Kavanaugh emphasized, "*clear* congressional authorization" should be required; mere ambiguity is insufficient.[98] After all,

> The Executive Branch does not possess a general, free-standing authority to issue binding legal rules. The Executive may issue rules only pursuant to and consistent with a grant of authority from Congress (or a grant of authority directly from the Constitution).[99]

This approach, Judge Kavanaugh explained, "helps preserve the separation of powers and operates as a vital check on expansive and aggressive assertions of executive authority."[100] It is grounded on two related, but distinct, propositions that embody delegation concerns. First, there should be a general presumption against the delegation of "major lawmaking authority from Congress to the Executive Branch."[101] Any such delegation represents a substantial shift of power and must therefore be substantiated. Second, there should be a presumption that "Congress intends to make major policy decisions itself" rather than leave those decisions to administrative agencies.[102]

What Judge Kavanaugh did not say, but could have added, is that these presumptions are stronger when one also considers time. When Congress enacted the alleged source of authority, it could not be said Congress knew to delegate authority to address "net neutrality." Indeed, Congress did not even know the question existed.

What distinguishes Judge Kavanaugh's "major rules doctrine" from the major questions doctrine is the incorporation of a nondelegation baseline. The major questions doctrine focuses on the magnitude of the agency action in question. However, the major rules doctrine focuses on the fact that, absent legislative authorization, agencies lack the authority to adopt regulations that bind private conduct, and if we start from a baseline of no delegation—the initial allocation of power under the Constitution—the burden is on the agency to show a delegation exists.

Another advantage of the major rules doctrine, over major questions, is that it reinforces basic notions of due process. Under long-standing notions of due process, the government may constrain private conduct and punish the failure to abide by such rules only pursuant to validly enacted laws.[103] As Michael McConnell and Nathan Chapman note, "Fundamentally, 'due process' meant that the government may not interfere with established rights without legal authorization and according to law."[104] Under the due process clauses of the Fifth and 14th Amendments, "the executive could not deprive anyone of a right except as authorized by law, and that to be legitimate, a deprivation of rights had to be preceded by certain procedural protections characteristic of judicial process."[105]

From this standpoint, any ultra vires agency action not only is unauthorized but also fails to comply with due process. Depriving any person of liberty or property for violating a regulation that was not properly authorized by the legislature is thus contrary to principles of due process, whether or not courts would so hold under existing doctrine.[106]

The Nondelegation Baseline

If the aim is to operationalize the nondelegation doctrine through a canon of construction, so as to adequately address concerns about the democratic legitimacy of administrative power, something more than greater reliance on existing interpretive canons is required. A true nondelegation canon has to incorporate the separation-of-powers baseline embodied in the Constitution itself.

All legislative powers are vested in Congress. Whether or not such powers may be delegated to the executive branch, there is no question where such powers begin. Put another way, the constitutional allocation of powers embodies a nondelegation baseline: Absent legislative action, all legislative power is in the legislature's hands, and none is in the hands of any administrative agency or part of the executive branch.

In the domestic sphere, at least, administrative agencies have no inherent powers but only those powers that have been delegated to them. As the Supreme Court has noted repeatedly, "An agency literally has no power to act . . . unless and until Congress confers power upon it."[107] This means that a delegation of power is necessary for administrative agencies to act. Delegating power of any sort to an administrative agency requires an affirmative act. Congress must enact legislation that satisfies the requirements of bicameralism and presentment. Without any such act, no delegation of authority has occurred. This means that every exercise of regulatory authority by an administrative agency must be grounded in a delegation of power from the legislature. Absent a prior authorization, there can be no regulation, and absent delegation, there can be no violation of the nondelegation doctrine.

Operationalizing this baseline entails making the requirement explicit and placing the burden squarely on federal agencies to demonstrate that they have been delegated the authority they seek to exercise. The existence of such delegated power cannot be presumed; it must be shown. Further, not just any delegation of power will do. Agencies should be required to demonstrate that they have been delegated the precise sort of authority they wish to exercise, especially if they wish to act with the force of law.

Just as the Court requires a clear statement that Congress intends to intrude on state prerogatives or press the outer limits of its enumerated powers, the Court could require clear evidence that Congress delegated the power to address a particular sort of mischief in a particular way at the time of enactment. If, as the Court has counseled, statutes are to mean what they meant "at the time Congress enacted the statute,"[108] then a statute should not be interpreted to delegate power or address concerns that the enacting legislature could not have understood, let alone meant or intended.

Where the delegation of power is clear and explicit, such as with the EPA's authority to adopt standards for the emission of traditional air pollutants from various source categories that affect ambient air quality, there is no problem. When, however, the agency wants to apply this language to regulate emissions of globally dispersed compounds that do not directly affect ambient air quality and cannot be adequately or effectively controlled with the agency's traditional regulatory authorities and to revise explicit statutory emission thresholds, there is a problem. Thus, in *Utility Air Regulatory Group v. EPA*, the Supreme Court rejected the EPA's assertion of a "newfound authority to regulate millions of small sources" while retaining the unconstrained authority to determine "how many of those sources to regulate."[109] To accept this assertion of authority would have been to bless the EPA's endeavor to assume for itself the power to rewrite the CAA as it deemed necessary to effectuate its new regulatory program, a clear assumption of legislative power. "We are not willing to stand on the dock and wave goodbye as EPA embarks on this multiyear voyage of discovery," wrote Justice Scalia for the Court.[110]

A threshold inquiry into whether Congress actually delegated the power at issue—a delegation "step zero" inquiry—is in line with inquiries courts routinely undertake, although it would require courts to engage the question with more consistency and rigor. This shift to demanding evidence of an intended delegation is visible in some of the Court's *Chevron* jurisprudence. While *Chevron* itself declared that silence or ambiguity in a statute could indicate an implicit delegation of interpretive and policymaking authority to an administrative agency,[111] under *United States v. Mead Corp.*, the mere existence of a statutory ambiguity is not sufficient, by itself, to trigger *Chevron* deference.[112] A series of cases in the US Court of Appeals stress that federal agencies cannot simply presume regulatory authority.[113] Further, drawing on the Supreme Court's post-*Mead Chevron* jurisprudence, the DC Circuit has recognized that "mere ambiguity in a statute is not evidence of congressional delegation of authority."[114] Ambiguity is necessary but not sufficient. That said, there are cases, such as *City of Arlington v. FCC*, in which a majority of the Court seemed skeptical of this sort of approach to agency authority.[115]

The specific inquiry contemplated here would consider several factors, all of which center on whether a prior delegation authorizes the agency action in question. As a threshold matter, the delegation of authority must be explicit in the plain language of the authorizing statute, as it would have been understood at the time of enactment. It must be plausible that the delegation of power is supported by the statute's original public meaning. In addition, the agency must be able to demonstrate that the problem it seeks to address is that which the legislature had in mind when the authority was delegated—or was at least of the sort that the legislative enactment was designed to address. That a contemporary reading of previously enacted statutory language would seem to encompass a previously unknown problem would not be sufficient. Relatedly, insofar as the authorizing legislation embodies an "intelligible principle," this principle should be understood as it would have been at the time of enactment. Accordingly, any such delegation must be understood to address then-contemporary problems and not as an open-ended grant of future authority to be deployed in unforeseen circumstances to address unanticipated problems.

The weight of evidence necessary to support an asserted delegation should be proportional to the breadth and scope of the delegated power claimed. For the same reasons that the Court has been reluctant to assume that Congress has delegated the authority to resolve questions of great economic or political importance without a clear statement to that effect, courts should presume that Congress will be more explicit the greater the amount of power asserted. In all cases, however, the lack of evidence of a delegation should be understood to indicate no delegation occurred.

The greater the power asserted, the greater the burden on the agency to demonstrate that the power has been delegated. This would entail, among other things, that agencies would have to show not merely that they have been empowered to act in a given area but that they have specifically been delegated the power to act with the force of law before issuing orders or promulgating rules that bind private conduct.

As the Court first held in *Interstate Commerce Commission v. Cincinnati, New Orleans & Texas Pacific Railway Co.*, known as the Queen and Crescent Case, in 1897, the power to issue rules mandating or prohibiting private conduct (in this case, rates for rail transport) "is not to be presumed or implied from any doubtful and uncertain language."[116] As the Court further explained in *Chrysler Corp. v. Brown*:

> The legislative power of the United States is vested in the Congress, and the exercise of quasi-legislative authority by governmental departments and agencies must be rooted in a grant of such power by the Congress and subject to limitations which that body imposes.[117]

Merely recommitting to the enforcement of this principle—and dispensing with the notion that the authority to act or issue rules necessarily entails the authority to issue legislative rules with the force of law—would dramatically reduce potentially overbroad assertions of delegated power. As Thomas Merrill observed, "Agencies can be given authority to study, investigate, or issue advisory opinions in an area, without being given power to issue regulations and/or adjudicatory decisions that have the force of law."[118]

In applying the major questions doctrine in *King v. Burwell*, Chief Justice John Roberts noted that it would have been incongruous for Congress to delegate a major health insurance policy question to the IRS, as opposed to the Department of Health and Human Services.[119] Thus it is also appropriate for the Court to ask whether the agency is claiming delegated authority in an area within its expertise and the expertise it had at the time of the enactment. Ambiguous language and the passage of time should not present an opportunity for agencies to bootstrap authority over previously unregulated concerns.[120]

How Congress has acted since the enactment of the alleged source of delegated authority is also relevant. As the Court noted in *FDA v. Brown & Williamson*, it was implausible that Congress had delegated to the FDA the authority to regulate (and the potential obligation to prohibit) cigarettes.[121] In the years since, Congress had continued to enact legislation premised on the continued marketing and sale of cigarettes and other tobacco products. In effect, Congress created an alternative tobacco regulatory regime (albeit one less prescriptive than that the FDA sought to create).[122] If a prior Congress did, in fact, delegate authority to an agency to address a problem, one would expect subsequent Congresses to act accordingly.

The agency's behavior is relevant to the inquiry as well. An unbroken practice of interpreting and applying a delegation of authority in a particular fashion should not be disregarded.[123] As Justice Felix Frankfurter counseled, "systematic, unbroken, executive practice" suggests executive authority. At the same time, courts should be particularly skeptical when agencies (or outside litigants) purport to identify previously undiscovered and unused authority to address emergent mischief. Agency departures from past practice or prior understandings of their own authority should be particularly suspect. Indeed, where an agency seeks to enter into a new field or exercise long dormant powers, this should create a presumption against the existence of a delegation.

The Supreme Court's decision in *FDA v. Brown & Williamson* embodied the approach outlined here.[124] On the surface, the delegation of authority to the FDA to regulate nicotine was plausible. The Food, Drug, and Cosmetic Act (FDCA) authorizes the FDA to regulate "drugs" and "devices." The FDCA defines "drug" to include "articles (other than food) intended to affect the structure or any function of the body."[125] For decades, the FDA disclaimed any authority to regulate tobacco products under this provision, but the revelation of tobacco industry documents revealing the industry's awareness and use of nicotine's pharmacological effects, combined with more anti-smoking leadership in the agency, led the FDA to conclude that nicotine is a "drug" and that tobacco products are delivery "devices."

In rejecting the FDA's assertion of authority, the Court noted that it would have been remarkable for Congress to have delegated such authority to the FDA without anyone noticing. Whatever superficial plausibility the FDA's textual arguments had was outweighed by the wealth of evidence in the statute's history and structure, including the contemporaneous understanding of what it authorized, that Congress never delegated such far-reaching authority to the FDA. "There may be reason to hesitate before concluding that Congress has intended such an implicit delegation," Justice Sandra Day O'Connor wrote with some understatement.[126] Perhaps the proper way to formulate the question is whether there was any reason to conclude Congress delegated such power in the first place.

Conclusion: Delegation Step Zero

The "nondelegation inquiry always begins (and often almost ends) with statutory interpretation," wrote Justice Elena Kagan in *Gundy*.[127] True enough. But what may be missing from this statutory interpretation inquiry is the threshold question of whether Congress can be said to have delegated power in the first place. Much as the Court has learned to ask whether Congress delegated interpretive power to agencies in *Chevron* cases before granting any form of deference, perhaps the Court should learn to ask what power has been delegated at all before worrying whether there is an "intelligible principle" to guide the exercise of that delegated power. Without a delegation, agencies lack the power to command private actors or develop rules of conduct. Without a delegation of authority, there can be no violation of the nondelegation doctrine.

If the proper scope of constitutionally permissible delegations does not produce a sufficiently determinate test, perhaps the Court can safeguard delegation values by adopting a more rigorous threshold inquiry into whether there was a delegation to address the matter at hand at all. It would also help identify the boundaries of the doctrine and reaffirm the existence of a constitutional limit until there is a five-justice majority willing to enforce the nondelegation doctrine directly. This would do more to address not only the democratic deficit caused by broad and deep delegations but also those exacerbated by time. Whatever course the Court chooses, it is about time it considered the problem of time when considering delegation, and a step zero inquiry could be the first step along this path.

Acknowledgments

Portions of this chapter draw on research conducted with Professor Christopher J. Walker of Ohio State University. Reagan Joy provided research assistance. Thanks to Kristin Hickman, Min Soo Kim, Peter Wallison, Christopher J. Walker, and John Yoo for comments on prior drafts. Any errors, omissions, inadequacies, or inanities are solely the fault of the author.

Notes

1. See *Panama Refining Company v. Ryan*, 293 US 388 (1935); and *A. L. A. Schechter Poultry Corp. v. United States*, 295 US 495 (1935).

2. Gary Lawson, "'I'm Leavin' It (All) Up to You': Gundy and the (Sort-of) Resurrection of the Subdelegation Doctrine," *Cato Supreme Court Review* (2018–19): 33, https://www.cato.org/sites/cato.org/files/2019-09/cato-supreme-court-2019-4.pdf. "*Gundy* [*v. United States*] is the first time since 1935 that more than two justices in a case have expressed interest in reviving some substantive principle against subdelegation of legislative authority."

3. See *Gundy v. United States*, 139 S. Ct. 2116, 2139 (2019) (Gorsuch, J., dissenting) (joined by C. J. Roberts and Justice Thomas); *Gundy*, 139 S. Ct. 2116, 2131 (2019) (Alito, J., concurring in judgment) ("If a majority of this Court were willing to reconsider the approach we have taken for the past 84 years, I would support that effort."); and *Paul v. United States*, 140 S. Ct. 342, 342 (2019) (Kavanaugh, J., respecting the denial of certiorari) ("Justice Gorsuch's scholarly analysis of the Constitution's nondelegation doctrine in his *Gundy* dissent may warrant further consideration in future cases."). Additionally, in June 2020, Justice Clarence Thomas, joined by Justices Samuel Alito and Neil Gorsuch, said statutory authorization of the Deferred Action for Childhood Arrivals program would constitute "an impermissible delegation of legislative power." See *Department of Homeland Security v. Regents of the University of California*, 140 S. Ct. 1891, 1929 n13 (2020) (Thomas, J., concurring in the judgment in part and dissenting in part).

4. See *Industrial Union Department, AFL-CIO v. American Petroleum Institute*, 448 US 607, 685–86 (1980) (Rehnquist, J., concurring in the judgment).

5. Antonin Scalia, "A Note on the Benzene Case," *Regulation* (July/August 1980): 27, https://www.cato.org/sites/cato.org/files/serials/files/regulation/1980/7/v4n4-5.pdf.

6. *Whitman v. American Trucking Associations*, 531 US 457 (2001). See also Lisa Schultz Bressman, "Disciplining Delegation After *Whitman v. American Trucking Ass'ns*," *Cornell Law Review* 87, no. 2 (January 2002): 453. Schultz Bressman observes, "*American Trucking* brings the unanswered question to center stage: Should courts use constitutional law or administrative law for requiring administrative standards?"

7. Scalia, "A Note on the Benzene Case," 28.

8. *Whitman*, 531 US at 474. "The scope of discretion § 109(b)(1) allows is well within the outer limits of the Court's nondelegation precedents."

9. Scalia, "A Note on the Benzene Case," 27.

10. *Whitman*, 531 US at 474–75 (quoting *Mistretta v. United States*, 488 US 361, 416 (1989) (Scalia, J., dissenting)).

11. See *Federalist*, no. 37 (James Madison). "No skill in the science of government has yet been able to discriminate and define, with sufficient certainty, its three great provinces—the legislative, executive, and judiciary."

12. See *Gundy*, 139 S. Ct. at 2135 (Gorsuch, J., dissenting). Some proponents of the nondelegation doctrine dispute the need for a clear, rule-like test. See, for example, Lawson, "'I'm Leavin' It (All) Up to You,'" 63. "If the Constitution gives you a vague and mushy standard, a constitutionalist will do his or her best to apply the vague and mushy

standard." It does not appear that five justices yet embrace this view.

13. See, for example, *Whitman*, 531 US at 472. "Article I, § 1, of the Constitution vests '[a]ll legislative Powers herein granted . . . in a Congress of the United States.' This text permits no delegation of those powers." (Alteration in original.) See also *Gundy*, 139 S. Ct. at 2121. "The nondelegation doctrine bars Congress from transferring its legislative power to another branch of Government."

14. See *Gundy*, 139 S. Ct. at 2141 (Gorsuch, J., dissenting) ("We still regularly rein in Congress's efforts to delegate legislative power; we just call what we're doing by different names."); and Cass R. Sunstein, "Nondelegation Canons," *University of Chicago Law Review* 67, no. 2 (2000): 315, https://chicagounbound.uchicago.edu/uclrev/vol67/iss2/1/.

15. David Schoenbrod, "Delegation and Democracy: A Reply to My Critics," *Cardozo Law Review* 20 (1998–99): 732, https://digitalcommons.nyls.edu/cgi/viewcontent.cgi?article=1231&context=fac_articles_chapters. In *A. L. A. Schechter Poultry Corp. v. United States*, Justice Benjamin Cardozo characterized the National Industrial Recovery Act as "delegation running riot." *A. L. A. Schechter Poultry Corp.*, 295 US at 553 (Cardozo, J., concurring).

16. See Jonathan H. Adler and Christopher J. Walker, "Delegation and Time," *Iowa Law Review* 105 (2020): 1931, https://ilr.law.uiowa.edu/print/volume-105-issue-5/delegation-and-time/.

17. See Richard A. Epstein, *The Dubious Morality of Modern Administrative Law* (Lanham, MD: Rowman & Littlefield, 2020), 37. "Delegation poses the risk that the party to whom the powers are delegated, if left free of supervision, may deviate sharply from the original statutory plan."

18. Should an agency exceed the scope of delegated authority or exercise authority that was not delegated, such action would be ultra vires and unlawful, but not a violation of the nondelegation doctrine.

19. See Thomas W. Merrill and Kristin E. Hickman, "*Chevron*'s Domain," *Georgetown Law Journal* 89 (2001): 873 (outlining a "step zero" inquiry for *Chevron*).

20. US Const. art. I, §1.

21. Lawson, "'I'm Leavin' It (All) Up to You,'" 44. "The Congress is vested with all legislative powers herein granted, meaning that We the People have entrusted or delegated that particular power to specific institutional actors." David Schoenbrod, *Power Without Responsibility: How Congress Abuses the People Through Delegation* (New Haven, CT: Yale University Press, 1993), 99. "The Constitution gives the people control over the laws that govern them by requiring that statutes be affirmed personally by legislators and a president whom the people have elected."

22. US Const. art. I, §7.

23. Schoenbrod, "Delegation and Democracy," 731.

24. See US Const. art. I, §5, cl. 3.

25. Schoenbrod, "Delegation and Democracy," 731.

26. *Loving v. United States*, 517 US 748, 757–58 (1996).

27. Schoenbrod, "Delegation and Democracy," 740.

28. John Hart Ely, *Democracy and Distrust: A Theory of Judicial Review* (Cambridge, MA: Harvard University Press, 1980), 132.

29. Ely, *Democracy and Distrust*, 131.

30. Schoenbrod, *Power Without Responsibility*, 104. "Delegation lets legislators change their roles from actors who make hard choices on the record in dramatic confrontations to service providers who do favors for individual constituents in private, where they can take whatever stance happens to please that constituent."

31. Schoenbrod, "Delegation and Democracy," 747.

32. Neomi Rao, "Administrative Collusion: How Delegation Diminishes the Collective Congress," *New York University Law Review* 90, no. 5 (November 2015): 1463, https://www.nyulawreview.org/issues/volume-90-number-5/administrative-collusion/.

33. Rao, "Administrative Collusion."

34. Rao, "Administrative Collusion," 1504. "By fracturing the collective Congress and empowering individual members, delegation also promotes collusion between members of Congress and administrative agencies." See also Christopher J. Walker, "Legislating in the Shadows," *University of Pennsylvania Law Review* 165, no. 6 (2017): 1407–19, https://scholarship.law.upenn.edu/penn_law_review/vol165/iss6/3/. Walker notes that administrative agencies often assist legislative staff in drafting statutes, creating opportunities for collusion.

35. A separate question is whether a nondelegation doctrine is required by the original public meaning or original understanding of the Constitution's text. This is a question of ongoing debate. Recent works claiming that the original understanding of Article I does not prohibit delegation include Julian Davis Mortenson and Nicholas Bagley, "Delegation at the Founding," *Columbia Law Review* 121, no. 2 (March 2021), https://columbialawreview.org/content/delegation-at-the-founding/; Christine Kexel Chabot, "The Lost History of Delegation at the Founding," *Georgia Law Review* (July 17, 2020), https://papers.ssrn.com/sol3/papers.cfm?abstract_id=3654564; and Nicholas R. Parrillo, "A Critical Assessment of the Originalist Case Against Administrative Regulatory Power: New Evidence from the Federal Tax on Private Real Estate in the 1790s," *Yale Law Journal* 130, no. 6 (2021): 1288–455, https://papers.ssrn.com/sol3/papers.cfm?abstract_id=3696860. Responses to these arguments include Ilan Wurman, "Nondelegation at the Founding," *Yale Law Journal* 130, no. 6 (April 2021), https://www.yalelawjournal.org/feature/nondelegation-at-the-founding; Aaron Gordon, "Nondelegation," *New York University Journal of Law & Liberty* 12, no. 3 (2019): 718, https://www.nyujll.com/volume-12/blog-post-title-four-9shdf-gytxr-zg887-xh48y-7e77n; and Jennifer Mascott, "Early Customs Laws and Delegation," *George Washington Law Review* 87, no. 6 (May 2020): 1388, https://www.gwlr.org/early-customs-laws-and-delegation/.

36. See Epstein, *The Dubious Morality of Modern Administrative Law*, 34. "Delegation is a necessary part of the tool kit of any complex organization."

37. Epstein, *The Dubious Morality of Modern Administrative Law*, 34. "The attention span of any legislative body for a given task is limited, and its ability to fine-tune any scheme of legislation is cabined by its hazy information about the complications likely to arise down the road and the difficulties of staffing up for the administrative chores of sustained action."

38. Epstein, *The Dubious Morality of Modern Administrative Law*, 34.

39. See Christopher DeMuth, "The Regulatory State," *National Affairs* (Summer 2012), 72, https://www.nationalaffairs.com/publications/detail/the-regulatory-state. "A hierarchy can make decisions with much greater dispatch than a committee can."

40. See generally Daniel A. Farber, "Exceptional Circumstances: Immigration, Imports and Climate Change," *Hastings Law Journal* 71, no. 5 (2020): 1143–76, https://www.hastingslawjournal.org/exceptional-circumstances-immigration-imports-the-coronavirus-and-climate-change-as-emergencies/.

41. This argument is fleshed out in Adler and Walker, "Delegation and Time."

42. In theory, agency authorizations are often time limited, and the expiration of such authority should prevent the continued appropriation for expired programs, but this rule is rarely, if ever, enforced in Congress. See Adler and Walker, "Delegation and Time," 1967.

43. While some statutes impose sunsets or other limits on the delegation of power, at the federal level, such statutes are the exception, not the rule. See Adler and Walker, "Delegation and Time," 1960–64. This is even true of delegations of emergency powers, which tend to remain on the books long after such emergencies have passed. See generally Farber, "Exceptional Circumstances."

44. See Michael S. Greve and Ashley C. Parrish, "Administrative Law Without Congress," *George Mason Law Review* 22, no. 3 (2015): 502, https://papers.ssrn.com/sol3/papers.cfm?abstract_id=2514484. Greve and Parrish note Congress "consistently fails to update or revise old statutes even when those enactments are manifestly outdated or, as actually administered, have assumed contours that the original Congress never contemplated and the current Congress would not countenance." Jody Freeman and David B. Spence, "Old Statutes, New Problems," *University of Pennsylvania Law Review* 163, no. 1 (December 2014): 1, https://scholarship.law.upenn.edu/penn_law_review/vol163/iss1/1/. Freeman and Spence note the "reduced probability that Congress will update regulatory legislation in response to significant new economic, scientific, or technological developments."

45. Judge Henry Friendly lamented legislative inaction in the 1960s. See Henry J. Friendly, "The Gap in Lawmaking—Judges Who Can't and Legislators Who Won't," *Columbia Law Review* 63, no. 5 (May 1963): 792, https://www.jstor.org/stable/1120530?seq=1.

46. Indeed, the fact that the executive branch may have a reserve of delegated authority that could be plausibly used to break legislative stalemates may actually impede subsequent lawmaking insofar as it reduces political pressure to negotiate solutions to pressing problems. See Adam J. White, "Democracy, Delegation, and Distrust," *Defining Ideas*, March 12, 2019, https://www.hoover.org/research/democracy-delegation-and-distrust.

47. See generally Abbe R. Gluck, Anne Joseph O'Connell, and Rosa Po, "Unorthodox Lawmaking, Unorthodox Rulemaking," *Columbia Law Review* 115, no. 7 (2015): 1789, https://columbialawreview.org/content/unorthodox-lawmaking-unorthodox-rulemaking/.

48. See *Federalist*, no. 62 (James Madison). Madison notes the Constitution's structure created a "complicated check on legislation" that "may in some instances be injurious as well as beneficial."

49. See Phillip Wallach, "Congress Indispensable," *National Affairs* (Winter 2018), https://www.nationalaffairs.com/publications/detail/congress-indispensable. "Congress is a mess. It seems incapable of passing major legislation."

50. Note that the question of what constitutes an "automated telephone dialing system" has split the circuit courts and, at the time of this writing, is due to be considered by the Supreme Court. See *Duguid v. Facebook*, 926 F.3d 1146 (9th Cir. 2019) cert. granted, 2020 WL 3865252 (July 9, 2020). See also *ACA International v. FCC*, 885 F.3d 687 (DC Cir. 2016); *Dominguez v. Yahoo*, 894 F.3d 116 (3rd Cir. 2017); and *Allan v. Pennsylvania Higher Education Assistance Agency*, 2020 WL 4345341 (6th Cir. July 29, 2020).

51. Whether the application of older statutory text to newer technologies produces undesirable or unforeseen consequences is separate from the question of whether courts should alter the meaning of statutory language in light of such effects.

52. For a discussion of the obsolete nature of most federal environmental statutes, see David Schoenbrod, Richard B. Stewart, and Katrina Wyman, *Breaking the Logjam: Environmental Protection That Will Work* (New Haven, CT: Yale University Press, 2010). See also Freeman and Spence, "Old Statutes, New Problems," 17. "Time, science, and experience have revealed many deficiencies in this suite of laws."

53. See Schoenbrod, Stewart, and Wyman, *Breaking the Logjam*, 24. At the same time, some environmental statutes were based on incomplete or inaccurate understandings of environmental conditions and trends. For a discussion of common misunderstandings related to the 1969 Cuyahoga River fire and what preceded it, see Jonathan H. Adler, "Fables of the Cuyahoga: Reconstructing a History of Environmental Protection," *Fordham Environmental Law Journal* 14, no. 1 (2002): 89, https://ir.lawnet.fordham.edu/elr/vol14/iss1/3/.

54. See Craig Anthony Arnold and Lance H. Gunderson, "Adaptive Law and Resilience," *Environmental Law Reporter* 43, no. 5 (2013): 10436. "The foundational assumptions of U.S. environmental law are questionable."

55. Schoenbrod, Stewart, and Wyman, *Breaking the Logjam*, 23.

56. A. Dan Tarlock notes how much environmental law was based on an equilibrium paradigm that scientists no longer accept. See A. Dan Tarlock, "The Nonequilibrium Paradigm in Ecology and the Partial Unraveling of Environmental Law," *Loyola of Los Angeles Law Review* 27 (1994): 1122–23, https://digitalcommons.lmu.edu/cgi/viewcontent.cgi?referer=https://www.google.com/&httpsredir=1&article=1855&context=llr. For a discussion of the implications dynamic change has for environmental law in particular, see Jonathan H. Adler, "Dynamic Environmentalism and Adaptive Management: Legal Obstacles and Opportunities," *Journal of Law, Economics & Policy* 11, no. 2 (2015): 133, http://jlep.net/home/wp-content/uploads/2016/02/JLEP-11.2.pdf.

57. See Carol A. Casazza Herman et al., "Breaking the Logjam: Environmental Reform for the New Congress and Administration," *NYU Environmental Law Journal* 17 (2008): 1, https://digitalcommons.nyls.edu/cgi/viewcontent.cgi?article=1230&context=fac_articles_chapters. "For almost 20 years, political polarization and a lack of leadership have left environmental protection in the United States burdened with obsolescent statutes and regulatory strategies." See also Freeman and Spence, "Old Statutes, New Problems," 5. "Congress has not passed a major environmental statute in nearly a quarter-century."

58. See Freeman and Spence, "Old Statutes, New Problems," 5. "Typical statutory obsolescence made worse by atypical congressional dysfunction puts tremendous pressure on agencies to do *something* to address new problems."

59. See Richard Lazarus, "Environmental Law Without Congress," *Journal of Land Use & Environmental Law* 30, no. 1 (Fall 2014): 15–34, https://www.jstor.org/stable/43741156?seq=1. "Climate change is perhaps the quintessential example of a new environmental problem that the Clean Air Act did not contemplate."

60. See Arnold W. Reitze Jr., "Federal Control of Carbon Dioxide Emissions: What Are the Options?," *Boston College Environmental Affairs Law Review* 36, no. 1 (January 2009), https://lawdigitalcommons.bc.edu/cgi/viewcontent.cgi?article=1000&context=ealr. "From 1999 to [2007], more than 200 bills were introduced in Congress to regulate [greenhouse gases], but none were enacted."

61. See *Massachusetts v. EPA*, 549 US 497 (2007). For a critique of this decision, see Jonathan H. Adler, "Warming Up to Climate Change Litigation," *Virginia Law Review in Brief* 93 (May 2007): 61, https://www.virginialawreview.org/wp-content/uploads/2020/12/adler.pdf. For a history of the legal strategy that made the decision possible, see Richard J. Lazarus, *The Rule of Five: Climate History at the Supreme Court* (Cambridge, MA: Belknap Press, 2020).

62. To take one example, the numerical emission thresholds that trigger specific regulatory requirements were set at levels that make sense for traditional air pollutants, such as sulfur dioxide or particulates. When those same thresholds are applied to emissions of greenhouse gases, and carbon dioxide in particular, the number of regulated firms that must seek permits increases exponentially, overwhelming the capacity of administrative agencies. See Prevention of Significant Deterioration and Title V Greenhouse Gas Tailoring Rule, 74 Fed. Reg. 55,292, 55,302 (Oct. 27, 2009), noting application of the numerical emission thresholds to carbon dioxide would produce a "massive influx" of six million newly required permits under Title V, which "would overwhelm permitting authorities' administrative resources." See also Jonathan H. Adler, "Heat Expands All Things: The Proliferation of Greenhouse Gas Regulation Under the Obama Administration," *Harvard Journal of Law and Public Policy* 34 (2011): 432–35. The Supreme Court addressed the implications of these problems in *Utility Air Regulatory Group v. EPA*, 134 S. Ct. 2427 (2014).

63. See, for example, Roberta Romano, "Regulating in the Dark," in *Regulatory Breakdown: The Crisis of Confidence in U.S. Regulation*, ed. Cary Coglianese (Philadelphia, PN: University of Pennsylvania Press, 2012), 87. "Congress tends not to move nimbly to rework financial legislation when it becomes widely acknowledged as flawed or seriously deficient." See also Freeman and Spence, "Old Statutes, New Problems," 5–6, noting Congress' failure to update statutes authorizing regulation of energy, telecommunications, and drugs.

64. See Randolph J. May, "Why Stovepipe Regulation No Longer Works: An Essay on the Need for a New Market-Oriented Communications Policy," *Federal Communications Law Journal* 58 (2006): 103.

65. Seen in this light, the purported delegation of authority to the FCC would seem to be similar to that which the Court invalidated in *A. L. A. Schechter Poultry Corp.*, 295 US at 495.

66. And such regulation is worthwhile. See Jonathan H. Adler, "Without Constraint," *Times Literary Supplement*, November 13, 2015, https://www.the-tls.co.uk/articles/without-constraint/.

67. See, for example, Cary Coglianese, "Dimensions of Delegation," *University of Pennsylvania Law Review* 167 (2019): 1851, https://scholarship.law.upenn.edu/cgi/viewcontent.cgi?article=3116&context=faculty_scholarship. Coglianese notes, "The nondelegation doctrine, properly understood, concerns both the degree of *discretion* afforded to the holder of lawmaking power and the extent of the underlying *power* itself." Coglianese identifies six dimensions of delegated authority that are potentially relevant to the nondelegation inquiry. Time is not one of them.

68. As Justice Gorsuch notes in *Gundy*, what the Court now applies may be best understood as a "mutated version" of the test the Court first articulated in *J. W. Hampton Jr. & Co. v. United States*. See *Gundy*, 139 S. Ct. at 2139 (Gorsuch, J., dissenting). See also Larry Alexander and Saikrishna Prakash, "Delegation Really Running Riot," *Virginia Law Review* 93, no. 4 (2007): 1038, https://www.virginialawreview.org/articles/delegation-really-running-riot/. Alexander and Prakash characterize the current "intelligible principle" test as applied by the Court as a "'wink and nod' approach" that is "hollow and insincere."

69. 42 USC §7409(b)(1).

70. However, as the Court concluded, this language does preclude the EPA from considering cost and therefore deprives the EPA of the authority to base the NAAQS on the results of a cost-benefit analysis. *Whitman*, 531 US at 461.

71. See *American Trucking Associations v. EPA*, 175 F.3d 1027, 1034 (DC Cir. 1999). "The only concentration for ozone and PM that is utterly risk-free, in the sense of direct health impacts, is zero."

72. *American Trucking Associations*, 175 F.3d at 1035. "EPA's explanations for its decisions amount to assertions that a less stringent standard would allow the relevant pollutant to inflict a greater quantum of harm on public health, and that a more stringent standard would result in less harm."

73. This is, in effect, what the DC Circuit required of the EPA on remand. See *American Trucking Associations*, 283 F.3d at 369, 379. Among other things, the court rejected any claim that the EPA was required to "identify perfectly safe levels of pollutants, to rely on specific risk estimates, or to specify threshold amounts of scientific information." It was enough that in setting the relevant standards, the EPA acknowledged that more serious adverse health effects of air pollution are "less certain" at lower ambient concentrations.

74. See, for example, *American Lung Association v. EPA*, 134 F.3d 388 (DC Cir. 1998) (remanding EPA decision not to revise primary sulfur dioxide NAAQS for failure to adequately address relevant scientific questions).

75. Scalia, "A Note on the Benzene Case," 28.

76. See *Gundy*, 139 S. Ct. at 2135–37 (Gorsuch, J., dissenting).

77. See generally *Whitman*, 531 US at 457.

78. See Jonathan H. Adler, "Clean Fuels, Dirty Air," in *Environmental Politics: Public Costs, Private Rewards*, ed. M. Greve and F. Smith (New York: Praeger, 1992).

79. See Lawson, "'I'm Leavin' It (All) Up to You,'" 67. "The bottom line is that there is a distinction to be drawn between law and fact . . . but that there is no clear principle that can be used to draw it."

80. See generally Jonathan H. Adler, "The Science Charade in Species Conservation,"

Supreme Court Economic Review 24 (2016): 109, https://www.journals.uchicago.edu/doi/full/10.1086/695562; and Wendy E. Wagner, "The Science Charade in Toxic Risk Regulation," *Columbia Law Review* 95 (November 1995): 1613, https://www.law.uh.edu/faculty/jmantel/health-regulatory-process/2014/Wagner95ColumlRev1613.pdf.

81. See Adler and Walker, "Delegation and Time."

82. Scalia, "A Note on the Benzene Case," 28. See also Elena Kagan, "Presidential Administration," *Harvard Law Review* 114 (2001): 2364, https://harvardlawreview.org/wp-content/uploads/pdfs/vol114_kagan.pdf. "It is, after all, a commonplace that the nondelegation doctrine is no doctrine at all."

83. See, for example, *Edward J. DeBartolo Corporation v. Florida Gulf Coast Building & Construction Trades Council*, 485 US 568, 575 (1988). "Where an otherwise acceptable construction of a statute would raise serious constitutional problems, the Court will construe the statute to avoid such problems unless such construction is plainly contrary to the intent of Congress." See also Antonin Scalia and Bryan A. Garner, *Reading Law: The Interpretation of Legal Texts* (Eagan, MN: West, 2012), 247. "A statute should be interpreted in a way that avoids placing its constitutionality in doubt."

84. See, for example, *Jones v. United States*, 529 US 848 (2000) (adopting a narrowed construction of the federal arson statute to avoid exceeding the scope of Congress' commerce clause power). According to the unanimous Court in *Jones*, "where a statute is susceptible of two constructions, by one of which grave and doubtful constitutional questions arise and by the other of which such questions are avoided," a court's "duty is to adopt the latter."

85. See *Solid Waste Agency of Northern Cook County v. US Army Corps of Engineers*, 531 US 159, 172 (2001). "Where an administrative interpretation of a statute invokes the outer limits of Congress' power, we expect a clear indication that Congress intended that result." See also *Rapanos v. United States*, 547 US 715, 738 (2006).

86. See *Mistretta*, 488 US at 373 n.7. "In recent years, our application of the nondelegation doctrine principally has been limited to the interpretation of statutory texts, and, more particularly, to giving narrow constructions to statutory delegations that might otherwise be thought to be unconstitutional." See also C. Boyden Gray, "The Nondelegation Canon's Neglected History and Underestimated Legacy," *George Mason Law Review* 22 (2015): 623, http://masonlec.org/site/rte_uploads/files/Manne/Readings/Administraiton%20Unbound/Gray_Second%20Round.pdf. Gray notes the Court's repeated use of nondelegation principle as a canon of construction. The first example of the Court construing a statute narrowly to avoid an unconstitutional delegation of power appears to be *National Cable Television Association v. United States*, 415 US 336 (1974), construing a statute to authorize the imposition of a fee, instead of a tax, to avoid unconstitutional delegation of taxing power.

87. See Sunstein, "Nondelegation Canons," 322. Sunstein notes the nondelegation doctrine is "alive and well" and has been "relocated" in various canons of construction. See also John F. Manning, "The Nondelegation Doctrine as a Canon of Avoidance," *Supreme Court Review* 2000 (2000): 223, https://www.jstor.org/stable/3109680?seq=1; and Cass R. Sunstein, "The American Nondelegation Doctrine," *George Washington Law Review* 86, no. 5 (2018): 1181, https://www.gwlr.org/wp-content/uploads/2018/10/86-Geo.-Wash.-L.-Rev.-1181.pdf.

88. *Gundy*, 139 S. Ct. at 2141 (Gorsuch, J., dissenting) (footnote omitted).

89. See Sunstein, "Nondelegation Canons."

90. For example, the Supreme Court's constitutional avoidance holding in *Northwest Austin Municipal Utility District No. 1 v. Holder*, 557 US 193 (2009) laid the groundwork for ultimately concluding that portions of the Voting Rights Act were unconstitutional in *Shelby County v. Holder*, 570 US 529 (2013).

91. *Gundy*, 139 S. Ct. at 2142 (Gorsuch, J., dissenting). Then-Judge Stephen Breyer made a similar observation in 1986, when he noted that it may well be that Congress will have granted an agency authority to resolve "interstitial matters" that did not command the legislature's attention, but less likely that the legislature can be presumed to have delegated "major questions" that the legislature can be presumed to have "focused upon" during its deliberations. Stephen Breyer, "Judicial Review of Questions of Law and Policy," *Administrative Law Review* 38 (1986): 370.

92. See *FDA v. Brown & Williamson Tobacco Corp.*, 529 US 120 (2000).

93. See *MCI Telecommunications Corp. v. AT&T*, 512 US 218 (1994).

94. See *King v. Burwell*, 135 S. Ct. 2480 (2015).

95. See *Massachusetts v. EPA*, 549 US 497 (2007).

96. See Michael Sebring, "The Major Rules Doctrine: How Justice Brett Kavanaugh's Novel Doctrine Can Bridge the Gap Between the Chevron and Nondelegation Doctrines," *New York University Journal of Law & Liberty* 12, no. 1 (2018): 189, https://www.nyujll.com/volume-12/blog-post-title-four-9shdf-gytxr-zg887-xh48y-7e77n-rl53b-kmme3-w2ese-y34rx-4ga79-3p7dk-gkyf7-98yyj.

97. *US Telecom Association v. FCC*, 855 F.3d 381, 417 (DC Cir. 2017) (Kavanaugh, J., dissenting from the denial of rehearing en banc).

98. *US Telecom Association*, 855 F.3d at 421.

99. *US Telecom Association*, 855 F.3d at 419.

100. *US Telecom Association*, 855 F.3d at 417.

101. *US Telecom Association*, 855 F.3d at 419.

102. *US Telecom Association*, 855 F.3d at 419.

103. For instance, the Magna Carta guaranteed that "no free man" would be "imprisoned or disseised or outlawed or exiled or in any way ruined . . . except by the lawful judgment of his peers or by the law of the land." Magna Carta, art. 39.

104. Nathan S. Chapman and Michael W. McConnell, "Due Process as Separation of Powers," *Yale Law Journal* 121 (2012): 1679, https://www.yalelawjournal.org/pdf/1080_y4sioof3.pdf. See also Bernard H. Siegan, *Property Rights: From Magna Carta to the Fourteenth Amendment* (London: Routledge, 2001), 16–17 (noting due process traditionally required, among other things, that the reason for a deprivation be found in a "legitimately enacted law").

105. See Chapman and McConnell, "Due Process as Separation of Powers," 1679.

106. For one possible application of this approach, see Jonathan H. Adler, "Wetlands, Property Rights, and the Due Process Deficit in Environmental Law," *Cato Supreme Court Review* 12 (2012): 139, https://www.cato.org/sites/cato.org/files/serials/files/supreme-court-review/2012/9/scr-2012-adler.pdf.

107. *Louisiana Public Service Commission v. FCC*, 476 US 355, 374 (1986). See also *Bowen v. Georgetown University Hospital*, 488 US 204, 208 (1988) ("It is axiomatic that

an administrative agency's power to promulgate legislative regulations is limited to the authority delegated by Congress."); *James B. Beam Distilling Co. v. Georgia*, 501 US 529, 549 (1991) (Scalia, J., concurring) ("The Executive . . . has no power to bind private conduct in areas not specifically committed to his control by Constitution or statute."); I Richard J. Pierce, Jr. Administrative Law Treatise §6.2, at 408 (5th ed. 2010) ("An agency has the power to issue a legislative rule only if and to the extent that Congress has granted it the power to do so."); and Henry Paul Monaghan, "*Marbury* and the Administrative State," *Columbia Law Review* 83 (1983): 14, https://scholarship.law.columbia.edu/cgi/viewcontent.cgi?article=1154&context=faculty_scholarship ("The universe of each agency is limited by the legislative specifications contained in its organic act.").

108. See *New Prime v. Oliveira*, 139 S. Ct. 532, 539 (2019) (cleaned up).

109. See *Utility Air Regulatory Group v. EPA*, 573 US 302, 328 (2014).

110. *Utility Air Regulatory Group*, 573 US at 328. See also Gray, "The Nondelegation Canon's Neglected History and Underestimated Legacy," 645. "Nondelegation themes echoed throughout the Court's opinion."

111. See *Chevron U.S.A. v. Natural Resources Defense Council*, 467 US 837, 843 (1984).

112. See *United States v. Mead Corp.*, 533 US 218, 226–27 (2001). See also *City of Arlington v. FCC*, 133 S. Ct. 1863, 1875 (2013) (Breyer, J., concurring). "The existence of statutory ambiguity is sometimes not enough to warrant the conclusion that Congress has left a deference-warranting gap for the agency to fill because our cases make clear that other, sometimes context-specific, factors will on occasion prove relevant."

113. See, for example, *Atlantic City Electric Co. v. FERC*, 295 F.3d 1 (DC Cir. 2002) ("Agency authority may not be lightly presumed. 'Were courts to presume a delegation of power absent an express withholding of such power, agencies would enjoy virtually limitless hegemony.'" (cleaned up)); *American Bus Association v. Slater*, 231 F.3d 1, 9 (DC Cir. 2000) (Sentelle, J., concurring) ("Agencies have no inherent powers. They . . . are creatures of statute . . . [that] may act only because, and only to the extent that, Congress affirmatively has delegated them the power to act."); and *Railway Labor Executives' Association v. National Mediation Board*, 29 F.3d 55 (DC Cir. 1994) ("The Board would have us *presume* a delegation of power from Congress absent an express *withholding* of such power.").

114. *American Bar Association v. FTC*, 430 F.3d 457 (DC Cir. 2005).

115. See *City of Arlington*, 569 US at 290. For my views of the issues underlying that case, see Nathan Alexander Sales and Jonathan H. Adler, "The Rest Is Silence: *Chevron* Deference, Agency Jurisdiction, and Statutory Silences," *University of Illinois Law Review* 2009, no. 5 (2009): 1497, https://www.illinoislawreview.org/wp-content/ilr-content/articles/2009/5/Adler.pdf.

116. See *Interstate Commerce Commission v. Cincinnati, New Orleans & Texas Pacific Railway Co.*, 167 US 497, 505 (1897). The case is referred to as the "Queen and Crescent" case because the rail line went between the Queen City (Cincinnati) and the Crescent City (New Orleans).

117. 441 US 281, 302 (1979).

118. Thomas W. Merrill, "Rethinking Article I, Section 1: From Nondelegation to Exclusive Delegation," *Columbia Law Review* 104, no. 8 (December 2004): 2169, https://www.jstor.org/stable/4099357?seq=1.

119. See *King*, 135 S. Ct. at 2489. "It is especially unlikely that Congress would have delegated this decision to the *IRS*, which has no expertise in crafting health insurance policy of this sort." See also *Gonzales v. Oregon*, 546 US 243, 266–67 (2006).

120. See *Adams Fruit Co. v. Barrett*, 494 US 638, 650 (1990). "It is fundamental 'that an agency may not bootstrap itself into an area in which it has no jurisdiction.'" (Citation omitted.)

121. *FDA v. Brown & Williamson*, 529 US at 141.

122. *FDA v. Brown & Williamson*, 529 US at 144, noting subsequent statutes had "created a distinct regulatory scheme to address the problem of tobacco and health."

123. See *Youngstown Sheet & Tube Co. v. Sawyer*, 343 US 579, 610 (1952).

124. See Manning, "The Nondelegation Doctrine as a Canon of Avoidance," 227. "The Court's narrow construction of the FDCA reflected an evident desire to avoid otherwise serious nondelegation concerns."

125. 21 USC § 321(g)(1)(C) (2006).

126. *FDA v. Brown & Williamson*, 529 US at 159.

127. *Gundy*, 588 US at 2119.

A Two-Tiered and Categorical Approach to the Nondelegation Doctrine

MICHAEL B. RAPPAPORT

Since the 1940s, the Supreme Court has applied a lenient version of the nondelegation doctrine.[1] Under this approach, the Court has permitted extraordinary grants of policymaking discretion to the executive. But this lenient version of the doctrine has been criticized by commentators who advocate a stricter view.

This chapter offers a new approach to the strict view of the nondelegation doctrine—one rooted in the original meaning of the Constitution. Under this approach, the nondelegation doctrine has two tiers—a strict tier and a lenient tier. In some areas, the Constitution leniently allows the delegation of significant policymaking discretion to the executive, while in other areas it imposes a strict categorical prohibition on delegations. Significantly, this approach would provide a relatively determinate way to decide whether Congress has delegated legislative power to the executive.

By contrast, the leading existing approach to a strict nondelegation doctrine suffers from a serious problem of indeterminacy. This approach distinguishes between "important subjects" and "matters of less interest."[2] Congress must decide the important subjects on its own, but on "matters of less interest," such as filling in the details of a statutory scheme, it may assign decisions to the executive. Unfortunately, this distinction is quite vague.[3]

My approach would replace this nondelegation test with a two-step inquiry. The first step classifies governmental activities into one of two categories—either a lenient tier or a strict tier. In my view, the Constitution allows for significant delegation of policymaking discretion in a variety of traditional areas of executive responsibility, such as foreign and military affairs, spending, and the management of government property. In these areas, the Constitution imposes a lenient test as to delegation—one that places either no limits or weaker limits on the delegation of policymaking discretion. By contrast, in other areas—which can be roughly summarized as rules that regulate the private rights of individuals in the domestic sphere—the Constitution imposes a strict prohibition on delegation. Thus, it is only for this second class of activities that the Constitution tightly restricts the delegation of policymaking discretion.

If an activity involves matters covered by the strict tier, then one moves to the second step of the inquiry by applying the strict prohibition on delegation. Under this prohibition, the executive is categorically forbidden from exercising *any* policymaking discretion. A law confers policymaking discretion when it allows the executive to make a decision based on what the agency considers good policy. Among the tasks that do not involve policymaking discretion are interpreting the law, making a factual determination, and applying the law to the facts.

This test for whether the executive has been provided any policymaking discretion is more determinate than the test that distinguishes between important subjects and matters of less interest. Under my proposed test for the strict tier, the main questions are whether the action involves determining the content of a legal directive and whether the action involves a factual determination. While these issues can raise questions at the margin, they are similar to traditional legal issues and are more determinate than the important-subjects test, which requires judges to determine whether a decision involves a sufficiently important subject.

This chapter, it should be noted, is more of an exploration of a position than a fully developed argument in favor of it. A fully developed argument would require far more space than I have here and more research into the relevant issues. Yet, I believe the approach here is interesting enough to justify this preliminary exploration. This exploration, if promising, may hopefully serve as a guide to further work in the area.

While this chapter explores the Constitution's original meaning, it does not attempt to derive its conclusion by fully canvassing originalist source materials. Instead, it is based largely on existing originalist scholarship on the delegation prohibition, including my own prior work on the subject, that I believe offers a significant view of the original meaning.[4]

Nor in this chapter do I argue that this approach would be normatively desirable. But I do believe the delegation prohibition would significantly restrict delegation to the executive branch and therefore would serve the goals that the nondelegation doctrine is normally thought to serve. If one believes the nondelegation doctrine is normatively desirable, then one should also believe this approach is normatively desirable.

The chapter proceeds as follows. The first part describes the two-tiered approach to the nondelegation doctrine. It explains why there are two tiers, how those tiers derive from the constitutional text, and how one assigns subjects to the different tiers. The second part explores the strict tier of the nondelegation doctrine. It explains how that tier imposes a categorical test of delegation by distinguishing between law interpretation and fact-finding on the one hand from policymaking on the other. It then applies this test to various Supreme Court cases. The third part then addresses an important matter that has a significant effect on the categorical test—the judicial reviewability of executive branch determinations.

A Two-Tiered Approach to the Nondelegation Doctrine

There are two basic approaches to the constitutional issue of delegation. Under the strict approach, Congress must fully set the policy in the statute, and the executive may only enforce that policy. Under the lenient approach, Congress either sets the policy in the statute or confers significant authority on the executive to set policy. There is no requirement that Congress make all the policy decisions.[5]

Under the strict approach, legislative and executive power have narrow meanings. Legislative power is the power to determine the policy that governs an area. Executive power in this context is the power to implement the policy established by the legislature in the statute. If the legislature does not fully establish the policy in a statute, then it will not be exercising the full legislative power but will have unconstitutionally sought to transfer that legislative power to the executive. Correspondingly, if the executive has been given authority to make a policy determination, it will not be exercising executive power, because that power does not allow it to make policy determinations. The executive will be exercising legislative power.

Under the lenient approach to the nondelegation doctrine, legislative and executive power have broader meanings. The legislative power is the power to fully set the policy or to set some of the policy and confer significant policymaking authority on the executive. The executive power in this context is the power to implement a statute either by following the legislature's directions without exercising any policy discretion or by following the policy in the statute and making the policy decisions that the statute authorizes the executive to make.[6]

Both interpretations of legislative and executive power are plausible. Thus, the constitutional language on this issue appears to be ambiguous.[7] While one might see the choice between these two interpretations as a global one—with the Constitution adopting the narrow or broad interpretation in all areas—this is not true. In my view, the correct approach is that the narrow meaning applies in some areas while the broad meaning applies in others. Under that interpretation, there is a two-tiered nondelegation doctrine, with a strict prohibition on delegation in some areas and a lenient one in other areas.

This two-tiered approach can be derived from the language of the Constitution. While the ordinary-language meaning of legislative and executive power might include either the narrow or broad meanings, one might understand the legal meaning of these terms as reflecting the legal practice at the time of the Constitution. If it turned out that, under the late 18th-century Anglo-American legal regime, the legislature conferred significant policymaking discretion on the executive in certain areas and did not do so in other areas, then the correct meaning of legislative and executive power might be thought to reflect this pattern.[8] The meaning of legislative and executive power might be based on how the legal institutions to which they referred exercised their powers. Thus, this pattern—allowing the executive to be given significant policymaking discretion in some areas but not others—might be incorporated into the Constitution.

This pattern of discretion might be reinforced by considerations of structure and purpose, such as the values that appear to have motivated the relevant provisions that govern legislative and executive power.[9] If the areas where policymaking discretion was allowed to the executive were generally supported by structure and purpose, that might lend greater confidence to the view that the Constitution adopted this pattern. Where the historical evidence is unclear or mixed, one might also resolve this uncertainty by reference to structure and purpose.

In an earlier article, I developed this approach and argued that the lenient tier of the nondelegation doctrine applied to appropriation laws.[10] I also argued that the lenient tier might extend to various areas, including foreign and military affairs, foreign commerce, the management of government property, internal administration of government agencies and the courts, and prosecutorial discretion.

To illustrate the nature of the argument, consider the case for permitting discretion to be conferred under appropriation laws. It turns out there is a long history of the executive under English and American appropriation laws receiving broad discretion to determine the extent and direction of spending.[11] Appropriation laws were often lump sum and permissive.[12] To take just a single example, the first appropriation law for the entire federal government under the United States Constitution divided the authorized spending into four broad categories and limited the executive merely to not exceeding the amount in each category.[13]

Moreover, structure and purpose support allowing this discretion. It would have been extremely difficult for Congress to specify in detail, each year, how the mass of federal spending was supposed to be spent. Moreover, it was less necessary for Congress to legislate specifically in this area, because most appropriation laws were for one year. Thus, if the president were to abuse his discretion, the legislature could alter the appropriation laws to fix the problem in the next year.[14]

Another structural reason for placing appropriation laws under the lenient tier involves federalism. One reason for the strict nondelegation doctrine is that it protects federalism. If federal rules can be enacted only through bicameralism and presentment, then they will be harder to enact, and fewer of them will displace state law. But this protection of state law is less necessary in areas where the states lack authority or are not well equipped to act.[15] Thus, in areas such as federal appropriation laws, where the states lack authority, structure supports applying the lenient tier.

A second area where the lenient tier applies is foreign and military affairs. In these areas, the executive historically was allowed more discretion than it enjoyed under ordinary domestic laws.[16] In part, this was due to traditional beliefs about the advantages of executive action in these areas. While some of this discretion may have been the result of the president being able to exercise power without statutory authorization, not all of it can be explained on that basis and therefore represents an important historical basis for treating such matters under the lenient tier.[17] The Constitution's federal structure also supports placing foreign and military affairs in the lenient tier, because states are normally thought to have limited authority and ability as to foreign and military affairs.

A third area where the lenient tier applies is legislation in the territories. Both before and after the United States Constitution was enacted, Congress delegated policymaking discretion to territorial governments. This structure represented a partial continuation of the structure of American colonial governments, which were largely operated by the king and local legislatures rather than Parliament.[18] Given the great value that the American colonists placed on their colonial legislatures, it would have been odd for them to have outlawed arrangements that permitted significant local decision-making.

These delegations also gain support from other structural arguments. Treating legislation in the territories under the lenient tier derives support from the structure of federalism, because the states do not have authority to legislate in the territories, and from the treatment of foreign affairs (and foreign commerce), because the territories in some ways were similar to foreign nations, as they were outside the core of the United States.[19]

My previous article did not attempt to make a comprehensive list of the areas where the lenient tier might apply. The most important addition I would make to the areas covered by the lenient tier involves the distinction between private and public rights. While the strict tier applies to the regulation of private rights, the lenient tier extends to public rights.[20]

The distinction between private and public rights was significant in early American law. In an important article, Caleb Nelson uses this distinction to argue for a two-tiered approach to judicial power.[21] In Nelson's view, while public rights can be adjudicated finally by administrative agencies, private rights can be adjudicated only by independent courts. In my view, the same structure applies to the exercise of policymaking discretion. While the legislature can delegate significant policymaking discretion to the executive for public rights, it cannot do so for private rights.

In the early years of the republic, private rights were understood to include the rights of personal security (life, body, and reputation), personal liberty (freedom from imprisonment), and private property (free use, enjoyment, and disposal of one's acquisitions).[22] By contrast, public rights were legal interests that belonged to the public as a whole. These public rights included:

> (1) proprietary rights held by government on behalf of the people, such as the title to public lands or the ownership of funds in the public treasury; (2) servitudes that every member of the body politic could use but that the law treated as being collectively held, such as rights to sail on public waters or to use public roads; and (3) less tangible rights to compliance with the laws established by public authority "for the government and tranquillity of the whole."[23]

Two important matters that fall under public rights are government spending programs and government employment.[24]

Nelson's judicial power argument has strong similarities to the two-tier argument I make about the nondelegation doctrine. He relies on a historical pattern of behavior near the time of the Constitution's enactment that assigned private rights to courts but public rights to executive agencies.

He also provides a strong argument based on structure and purpose. Private rights were thought to be the most important rights that people enjoyed. The protection of these Lockean or natural rights was the primary reason government was established.[25] These rights belonged to the individual, and therefore the government was supposed to use an impartial judiciary to protect them.

By contrast, public rights involved the interests of the overall public. The government was thought to have special responsibilities for protecting and managing these interests. The government could therefore decide to employ either the political branches or the judiciary as it judged best.[26]

This two-tiered approach to judicial power has obvious similarities with the two-tiered approach to prohibiting the delegation of legislative power—similarities that suggest that the distinction between private and public rights might also extend to the latter issue. First, the two approaches involve directly analogous issues: the delegation of judicial power to the executive and the delegation of legislative power to the executive. Second, these two approaches both extend a strict separation of powers to a subset of cases, with the two-tiered approach to judicial power requiring private rights to be adjudicated by independent courts and the two-tiered non-delegation doctrine requiring matters in the strict tier to follow a strong separation of powers that permits only Congress to make policy.

Structure and purpose arguments also support extending the distinction between private and public rights to the two-tiered approach to delegation of legislative power. Since private rights are more important to individuals, these rights justify the greater protections that a strict delegation prohibition imposes. These restrictions ensure that policy decisions are made by democratically accountable legislatures and are subjected to a bicameral process that provides additional protection. By contrast, public rights were not thought to require as strong protection as private rights. Moreover, since private rights do not impose as strong management responsibilities on government as public rights do, the greater restrictions on legislating regulations of private rights are not as burdensome.[27]

While these purpose and structure arguments are suggestive, correctly placing public rights into the lenient tier ultimately depends on the pattern of behavior at the time of the Constitution's enactment. If such rights were regularly subjected to rules involving significant policymaking discretion by the executive, then that would be strong evidence, when combined with the purpose and structure arguments, for concluding that public rights are subject to the lenient tier. Although I do not review the evidence here, there is significant evidence that public rights were subject to the lenient tier.[28]

For my purposes here, it is neither necessary nor possible to attempt to resolve these questions. Instead, I will assume that the strict delegation prohibition applies only to the regulation of private rights in the domestic sphere. By contrast, the lenient tier covers a variety of areas, including public rights, such as spending programs, and the other areas I mention here, including appropriation laws, foreign and military affairs, and territorial legislation.

The two-tiered approach is important for at least two reasons. First, it suggests that the alleged counterexamples to the existence of a strict delegation prohibition may not be real counterexamples. If these counter-examples come from the lenient tier, they would not constitute counter-examples for the two-tiered view. Kenneth Culp Davis as well as Nicholas Bagley and Julian Davis Mortenson have argued against the strict nondel-egation doctrine on the ground that early congressional statutes delegated significant discretion.[29] But my earlier article and other works have argued that many of these delegations can be justified as falling within the lenient tier of the delegation prohibition.[30]

Second, the two-tiered approach is also important because it suggests that a categorical delegation prohibition may not be as impractical or bur-densome as such a strict prohibition is often thought to be. Most, if not all, areas where it is especially difficult for the executive to operate without policymaking discretion fall within the lenient tier.[31] By contrast, many of the areas where it is easiest to operate without policymaking discretion are covered by the strict tier.[32]

The Strict Tier of the Nondelegation Doctrine: A Categorical Prohibition

I now turn to the crucial strict tier of the nondelegation doctrine. Under this tier, there is a categorical prohibition on the delegation of legislative power—understood as policymaking discretion—to the executive. Thus, any statute involving matters in this tier that confers policymaking discre-tion on the executive will be unconstitutional.

The analysis here relies on a distinction among three types of activities: legal interpretations, factual determinations, and policy determinations. When the executive or judiciary interprets the law based on traditional statutory interpretive methods, its decision is determined entirely by the statute's meaning. Similarly, when the executive or judiciary makes a fac-tual determination, its decision is based entirely on the facts of the matter. In both cases, the decision of the executive or the judiciary is uniquely determined by the law or the facts and therefore does not involve policy-making discretion.[33] By contrast, when the executive or the judiciary takes an action pursuant to statutory authority that is not uniquely determined by the law or the facts, it is given discretion to make a policy choice.

This part is divided into several sections. First, I discuss the textual and historical basis for the categorical approach. Second, I explore the distinction between legal interpretation and policymaking, illustrating it with some examples and then applying it to some important Supreme Court cases. I then explore the distinction between fact-finding and policymaking.

The Interpretive Support for the Categorical Approach. The categorical approach to the nondelegation doctrine has significant support in the Constitution's original meaning. This support derives from text, history, structure, purpose, and early interpretations. In arguing for the categorical approach, I am largely comparing it to the leading alternative approach to a strong nondelegation doctrine—the important-subjects approach. Overall, the support for the categorical approach is stronger than that for the important-subjects approach.

It should be acknowledged at the outset that there is no explicit historical statement of the entirety of the categorical standard. But there is substantial evidence for different parts of the approach from various sources. First, the categorical prohibition represents a plausible interpretation of legislative power for a strict approach that attempts to prohibit the delegation of such power to the executive. Legislatures exercise policymaking discretion to decide what laws to enact for the polity. The categorical approach prohibits the conferral of such policymaking discretion on the executive.

By contrast, the interpretation of statutes based on traditional interpretive rules would not have been thought of as exclusive legislative power, but instead as a traditional judicial and executive power. This activity is not based on policy decisions but instead involves determining the statute's meaning. Courts and executives had long exercised this power at the time of the Constitution's enactment.

A similar argument applies to fact-finding. The finding of facts is not an exclusive activity of the legislature, but a traditional activity of courts and executives. Once again, this activity is not based on policy, but instead involves determining what the facts are. Courts and executives had long exercised this power when the Constitution was enacted.

This argument as to fact-finding also derives support from the early case of *Aurora v. United States*.[34] In that case, Congress had passed a law restricting trade with Great Britain and France but had provided that the trade prohibition should not continue in effect if the president declared by proclamation that the country had ceased to violate the neutral commerce of the United States. In response to a constitutional challenge that the statute had delegated legislative power, the Supreme Court responded in a single sentence that "we can see no sufficient reason why the legislature should not exercise its discretion in reviving the Act . . . either expressly or conditionally, as its judgment should direct."[35] In other words, since the statute merely asked the president to make a factual finding as to whether a country was respecting the United States' neutral commerce, there was no delegation problem. Thus, the Court did not view executive fact-finding as the delegation of legislative power.

This understanding of exclusive legislative power also fits well with the purpose and structure of the relevant constitutional provisions. The purpose of having a strict approach to the delegation of legislative power is to protect against the conferral of lawmaking discretion on the executive.[36] It makes sense to apply this protection to policymaking discretion, since the executive can use such discretion to determine the content of the rules. By contrast, in the case of legal interpretation and fact-finding, the executive is limited by an objective standard—determining meaning or finding facts. In these cases, the executive does not enjoy discretion to determine the content of the law, and therefore it is much less necessary for the legislature to make the decision.

Finally, this standard for the delegation of legislative power is much more judicially manageable than the important-subjects standard. One of the most serious charges against a strict nondelegation doctrine is that it does not provide a judicially manageable test.[37] While judicial manageability is not a requirement of legal provisions, it is a legitimate interpretive rule to prefer judicially manageable interpretations on the ground that the constitutional enactors would have intended judicially enforced provisions to be judicially manageable.[38]

Under the important-subjects standard, interpreters face the recurring problem of determining whether the legislature answered the important questions.[39] Answering this question is problematic, because there is no clear definition of what is an important question and each statute will require addressing it in a new context. By contrast, reading the nondelegation doctrine as a bar against conferring policymaking authority greatly reduces this uncertainty. One simply asks whether the authority conferred on the executive is the power to interpret the statute or find facts. The courts regularly answer questions of this type when interpreting the Constitution.

The categorical approach to the nondelegation doctrine also draws support from James Madison. In 1800, Madison wrote during the Alien and Sedition Acts controversy that a law might confer powers on the executive that were of a legislative nature and therefore would be unconstitutional.[40] Madison explained how the Congress could avoid an unconstitutional delegation:

> *Details to a certain degree, are essential to the nature and character of a law. . . .*
>
> To determine, then, whether the appropriate powers of the distinct departments are united by the act authorising the executive to remove aliens, it must be enquired whether it contains such *details, definitions, and rules, as appertain to the true character of a law; especially a law by which personal liberty is invaded, property deprived of its value to the owner, and life itself indirectly exposed to danger.*[41] (Emphasis added.)

Madison's statement shows strong support for the categorical approach over the important-subjects approach. To begin with, he makes clear that details are needed in laws. Madison's account indicates that Congress is not entitled simply to delegate details to be filled up by the executive. Instead, details will often be "essential to the nature and character of a law." What is more, Madison states that "details, definitions, and rules" are "especially" needed when the law regulates private rights.

It is true that Madison does not state that a law must explicitly address every detail. But that does not mean that Madison believed that laws could leave to the executive policymaking discretion to address details. Instead, Madison's statement is best understood as suggesting that ordinary law interpretation will often supply answers to details that the law does not specifically address. While some details need to be mentioned, others do not have to be addressed because "the details, definitions, and rules" supplied by the law allow interpreters using the traditional interpretive rules to answer those matters without making policy.

These various arguments—based on an extremely plausible understanding of the text, purpose and structure, early statements, early cases, and judicial manageability—provide a strong case for the categorical approach to the delegation prohibition.

The strongest argument against the categorical approach derives from Chief Justice John Marshall's *Wayman v. Southard* opinion, which is the basis for the important-subjects approach. In that opinion, Chief Justice Marshall wrote,

> The line has not been exactly drawn which separates those important subjects which must be entirely regulated by the legislature itself from those of less interest in which a general provision may be made and power given to those who are to act under such general provisions to fill up the details.[42]

Advocates of the important-subjects approach read this to mean that important subjects must be legislated but less important subjects or details can be left to the executive. But despite my high opinion of Chief Justice Marshall and the advocates of the important-subjects approach, I question whether this view is correct.

First, this opinion was written in 1825 and therefore was issued 37 years after the Constitution was written. It cannot be viewed as a contemporary exposition of the Constitution.

Second, since the case was decided on other grounds, Chief Justice Marshall's analysis here must be viewed as dicta. Such dicta has long been thought to be subject to less respect than rulings necessary to the decision.

Third, despite first appearances, Chief Justice Marshall's analysis here may actually be consistent with the categorical, two-tiered approach to the nondelegation doctrine. Marshall distinguishes between "important subjects which must be entirely regulated by the legislature" and those of "less interest," which need not be. But nothing in Marshall's opinion is clearly inconsistent with reading it as indicating that all laws that involve matters governed by the strict tier are *important subjects* that must be entirely legislated by Congress. Under that interpretation, *Wayman* would be consistent with the categorical approach to delegations as to matters covered by the strict tier.[43]

There are strong reasons why one might view laws that regulate private rights in the domestic sphere as involving important subjects that must be entirely legislated by Congress. Most significantly, private rights were deemed to be the most important rights when the Constitution was enacted, and therefore their regulation might have involved the most important subjects. While Marshall does discuss various examples of rules that the judiciary can be authorized to enact, these rules may fall under the lenient tier, depending on the view of the two tiers that one takes.[44]

Distinguishing Between Law Interpretation and Policymaking. Under the categorical approach, the executive cannot engage in any policymaking. But it can engage in law interpretation and fact-finding. This section explores the distinction between law interpretation and policymaking.

Under law interpretation, the executive merely determines the meaning of the law, doing so by reference to the traditional interpretive rules that do not involve policymaking. These interpretive rules focused mainly on determining the meaning of the law enactors' intent, as expressed in the statute's language.[45] While some of the interpretive rules did protect certain values, such as the rule of lenity, these values were established by prior law and did not involve policymaking by the judges when they interpreted the statute.[46] The main values that the interpretive rules followed were the values that the law enactors were perceived as furthering, such as the purposes of the statute or the values widely held when the statute was enacted.[47]

While modern administrative law employs the *Chevron* doctrine, which confers deference on an agency's interpretation of the statutes it administers, law interpretation does not allow *Chevron* deference. First, the traditional interpretive rules did not include *Chevron* deference.[48] Second, *Chevron* deference is commonly understood as a delegation of policymaking authority to the executive. But such delegations are unconstitutional under the categorical approach. Thus, if the strict approach to the nondelegation doctrine is adopted by the Court, the *Chevron* doctrine will have to be abandoned.

Finally, it is sometimes thought, based on legal realism, that executive or judicial interpretation inevitably involves policymaking. But an exploration of the original meaning does not appropriately rely on a jurisprudence that developed more than a century after the Constitution's enactment. Traditional legal interpretation was not supposed to follow the judge's values, and such interpretation was not thought to involve judicial policymaking.[49]

This section first illustrates legal interpretation with some examples and then applies the analysis to some important nondelegation cases.

Some Initial Examples. Consider first a statute that Congress enacts to authorize a rule governing the sale of motor vehicles. Congress provides that the Department of Transportation shall pass a rule requiring each motor vehicle sold to have a motor vehicle safety feature if that feature would reduce the lives lost from motor vehicle accidents by 2 percent and has a cost of not more than the average cost of motor vehicle safety features that are presently required.

Viewing the matter loosely, it might seem as if the statute delegates legislative power to the agency. But that is not true. Given the interpretive principles discussed above and putting to the side for the moment the factual findings required to implement this rule, there is no delegation of policymaking discretion to the executive.

The agency here merely engages in law interpretation. When implementing the statutory provision, the agency might have to make various decisions about the provision's meaning. But those decisions would merely apply the traditional statutory interpretive rules, which do not require policymaking.

For example, when interpreting the statute, the agency and then the court might have to decide a range of legal questions, including what is a motor vehicle (Does a Vespa count?), what is a motor vehicle safety feature (Do side cameras count?), what is a motor vehicle accident (Do accidents to pedestrians count?), and the average cost of existing motor vehicle safety features (Does this refer to the average cost to the seller or the buyers?). But so long as these questions are decided using traditional interpretive rules, which seek Congress' intent as expressed in the statute's text, there is no policymaking discretion.

Admittedly, some of these interpretations may involve close cases. These cases will require the agency and the reviewing court to consider matters such as the statute's purpose and structure and to make judgment calls as to which is the stronger interpretation. But so long as the decision is made based on legal, rather than policy, considerations, the decision will not involve policymaking discretion.[50]

Now consider a different statute. Under this statute, the Department of Transportation is given the authority to adopt motor vehicle safety features that are in the public interest. It is hard to argue that this statute does anything other than delegate policymaking discretion to the agency. It is, after all, not clear what "the public interest" means.

Consequently, such standards have historically been interpreted as delegations to the agency to determine what it thought the public interest was. An agency could argue for a notion of the public interest that involved cost-benefit analysis, the pursuit of the common good, or various other goals. Congress would have done little to have indicated which of these notions of the public interest had been adopted.

It is true that under a legal regime in which delegation was unconstitutional, the agency and the reviewing court, applying the avoidance canon, should seek an interpretation that would avoid a delegation of policymaking. But in the normal situation involving a public interest standard, that goal would be a bridge too far. In special circumstances, however, it might be possible to give a public interest standard a more determinate meaning. For example, if a specific area of the law had explicitly followed a dominant principle, such as cost-benefit analysis, then a court might understand Congress' reference to the public interest as adopting cost-benefit analysis.[51] But absent such special circumstances, the best interpretation of public interest would be that Congress had unconstitutionally delegated policymaking discretion.

Finally, consider an example adapted from *Motor Vehicles Manufacturers Association v. State Farm Mutual Automobile Insurance Co.*[52] Under this statute, Congress authorizes the Department of Transportation to adopt motor vehicle safety standards that promote the needs of vehicle safety. Like the hypothetical statute previously discussed involving motor vehicle safety features that are in the public interest, the most straightforward interpretation of this statute is to confer policymaking discretion on the agency (as the *State Farm* Court held). After all, it is not clear how much of a reduction in accidents, at what cost, is necessary to promote the needs of vehicle safety.

Yet, this statutory standard is somewhat more constrained than the public interest standard.[53] Assuming that the statute was enacted under a regime that categorically prohibited delegation and that applied a canon that required avoiding unconstitutional interpretations, a court might interpret this language to avoid delegating discretion to the executive. A court could interpret "the needs of motor vehicle safety" to require the adoption of all safety features that reduce automobile accidents per mile driven.

Statutes like this can raise difficult questions for courts. A court must decide whether a statute that does not have an obvious constitutional meaning should be given a constitutional interpretation or should be held to be unconstitutional. In this situation, the court will have to weigh the evidence in favor of each possibility. On the one hand, the court must decide how far it must stray from the most likely meaning to reach a constitutional interpretation. On the other hand, the court must decide how strong the canon that requires avoiding an unconstitutional interpretation is.

In the case of the statute that authorized the agency "to adopt motor vehicle safety features that are in the public interest," I concluded that a constitutional interpretation of this statutory language likely requires too great a departure from the language's ordinary meaning. By contrast, in the case of the statute that authorized the agency "to adopt motor vehicle safety standards that promote the needs of vehicle safety," I concluded that the constitutional interpretation might be sufficiently close to the language's obvious meaning that it could be found to have that constitutional meaning.

While there may be some close questions for the categorical approach, it will clearly be more determinate than the alternative important-subjects approach. Under the categorical approach, a court must engage in the ordinary judicial task of weighing which of two interpretations is the stronger based on the statute's language and traditional interpretive methods. By contrast, the important-subjects approach would require the courts to decide whether a question constituted, under the particular statute, an important subject. But it is difficult to identify how important a subject needs to be in order to be deemed an important subject, especially because the term "important subject" seems vague. Thus, the important-subjects test is significantly less determinate than asking which of two interpretations is the stronger one.

Some Real Cases. I now apply this approach to some real-world cases. Here I apply my approach to four cases since the New Deal—*Panama Refining Company v. Ryan; Industrial Union Department, AFL-CIO v. American Petroleum Institute; Whitman v. American Trucking Associations;* and *Gundy v. United States.*[54] This discussion clarifies the differences between my theory and the Supreme Court's approach.

In analyzing the constitutionality of these statutory conferrals of authority to the executive, one should engage in a series of steps. First, one interprets the statute using the traditional methods of legal interpretation to determine the authority that it confers on the executive. If the authority that is conferred is merely the power to interpret the law or find facts, then the statute is constitutional. But if the statute confers policymaking discretion, then the law unconstitutionally delegates legislative power to the executive.[55]

Panama Refining Company v. Ryan.

The first case to be discussed, *Panama Refining*, is an easy case for concluding that the statutory authority conferred was unconstitutional. In *Panama Refining*, Section 9(c) of the National Industrial Recovery Act authorized the president to prohibit the transportation in interstate and foreign commerce of petroleum and petroleum products "in excess of the amount permitted to be produced or withdrawn from storage by any State law."[56] While the act appeared to limit the president's authority to a single decision—whether to prohibit transportation of these products in excess of the amount permitted by state law—it did not establish any statutory standard to govern how the president should make this decision. Thus, the act appeared to provide the president with policymaking discretion to decide whether to impose this prohibition.

The main question under my approach is whether, despite the statute's language, one can properly interpret the statute to deny the president this discretion. But that is difficult because of the absence of any statutory language that governs the president's authority as to this decision. While the Supreme Court reviewed other provisions of the act, including the declaration of policy, none of these provisions could be reasonably interpreted to eliminate the president's policymaking discretion. Thus, the act conferred an unconstitutional delegation of legislative power.[57]

Industrial Union Department, AFL-CIO v. American Petroleum Institute. In *Industrial Union Department*, the Supreme Court reviewed a portion of the Occupational Safety and Health Act that governed exposure of workers to toxic materials. While the plurality opinion for the Court concluded that the act required certain agency findings before it could impose a standard governing toxic materials,[58] Justice William Rehnquist argued that the statute constituted an unconstitutional delegation of legislative power because it did not decide the basic question of how strictly to protect safety when there was no clear indication that the substance was dangerous.[59] In my view, however, one could properly read the statute to eliminate the policymaking discretion identified by Justice Rehnquist and therefore to be constitutional.

In *Industrial Union Department*, the statute at issue provided:

> The Secretary, in promulgating standards dealing with toxic materials or harmful physical agents under this subsection, shall set the standard which most adequately assures, to the extent feasible, on the basis of the best available evidence, that no employee will suffer material impairment of health or functional capacity even if such employee has regular exposure to the hazard dealt with by such standard for the period of his working life.[60]

Rehnquist was troubled by this provision on the ground that it was "completely precatory, admonishing the Secretary to adopt the most protective standard if he can, but excusing him from that duty if he cannot."[61] Rehnquist wrote, "In the case of a hazardous substance for which a 'safe' level is either unknown or impractical," the statute "gives the Secretary absolutely no indication where on the continuum of relative safety he should draw his line."[62] He concluded: "There is certainly nothing to indicate that these words . . . are limited to technological and [business] feasibility."[63]

But Rehnquist seems mistaken here. Under the statutory provision, once the agency concludes that a toxic health standard must be issued, it is required to engage in a two-step inquiry. First, it must identify the most protective standard it can adopt in terms of avoiding material impairments of health. But then it must impose only a standard that is feasible.

Justice Rehnquist is certainly correct that the term "feasible" has a number of meanings. Did the statute mean technologically feasible so that an employer would only be obligated to avoid exposure to the extent that a technology allowed it to prevent exposure? Did it mean business feasibility so that an employer would only be obligated to avoid exposure to the extent that it could do so without incurring bankruptcy or a decision to close down that portion of its production facilities? Or did it include economic feasibility, where the employer is not required to take an action that would have social costs exceeding social benefits?

But while Rehnquist believed the statute did not indicate which of these definitions was employed, traditional interpretive methods provide an answer. The toxic materials provision is clearly designed to protect workers even if there are substantial costs to doing so. Given the statute's purpose, the feasibility requirement should not be read to mean economic feasibility (such as cost-benefit analysis). That definition would mistakenly place the costs to the economy or business on a par with the protection of workers. By contrast, reading "feasibility" to mean technological or business feasibility prioritizes the protection of workers. It allows exposure only if there is no technological way of protecting workers or if the costs of protecting them would cause the industry to close down and eliminate the workers' jobs.

Industrial Union Department illustrates that traditional interpretive methods sometimes can discern a meaning that eliminates policymaking discretion.[64]

Whitman v. American Trucking Associations. In *Whitman*, the Supreme Court reviewed the constitutionality of a Clean Air Act provision that required the Environmental Protection Agency (EPA) to set National Ambient Air Quality Standards "'the attainment and maintenance of which ... are requisite to protect the public health' with 'an adequate margin of safety.'"[65] To determine whether this statute is constitutional, one must begin by interpreting its provisions and then by asking whether the statute confers only legal interpretive and fact-finding responsibilities or allows the executive policymaking discretion.

In reviewing the statute, the first question is what constitutes "the public health." In exploring this question, the Court initially considered whether the statute allowed the EPA to consider costs when determining the level of air quality standards. The Court, in my view correctly, held that the EPA could not consider costs, but only the effect of the standards on public health.[66]

But while this aspect of the decision was correct, it still leaves the question of what the meaning of public health is and whether the standards confer policymaking discretion on the agency. If the term "public health" had a precise meaning, then the EPA's responsibility to set air quality standards requisite to protect health would appear not to provide any policymaking discretion. Instead, the standards would have to be set based entirely on factual findings about health at different levels of air pollution.

But there does not appear to be a sufficiently clear meaning to public health in this context. There is no cutoff as to how many people need to be harmed by polluted air for it to create a public health problem. Or to examine the issue in a more sophisticated way, the term does not indicate the expected harm necessary for there to be a public health problem, which would take into account both the expected number of cases of illness and the severity of those illnesses. Thus, the EPA is given what appears to be policymaking discretion to determine what is a public health problem and would thus violate the strict tier of the nondelegation doctrine.

Of course, even if the term had an unclear meaning, the legal interpretive rules might still discern a determinate meaning for it that eliminated agency policymaking discretion. But whether such a meaning was available is questionable.

Gundy v. United States. The most recent case involving delegation is *Gundy*. That case concerned the Sex Offender Registration and Notification Act (SORNA), which had delegated to the attorney general authority to determine whether sex offenders convicted before the enactment of the statute imposing registration requirements were also required to register. The Court split on the delegation question. Four justices interpreted the statute to place limits on the attorney general's discretion and then concluded that the resulting discretion was consistent with the Constitution's (in their view) lenient nondelegation requirement.[67] Three justices interpreted the statute to provide substantial discretion to the attorney general and then concluded that the delegation was unconstitutional under their interpretation of the statute.[68] One justice concurred in the judgment of the four members who concluded SORNA was constitutional but indicated his sympathy with the position adopted by the other three justices, if the issue arose in an appropriate case.[69]

The correct analysis of the delegation in this case turns on the usual steps. First, one interprets the statute using traditional methods of legal interpretation to determine the authority that it confers on the attorney general. If the authority that is conferred is merely the power to interpret the law or find facts, then there is no delegation of legislative power. If there is a delegation of policymaking discretion, then the law is unconstitutional.

While the Court disagreed about the proper interpretation of the statute, Justice Neil Gorsuch's dissenting opinion had the better of the argument. The statute provided that the attorney general "shall have the authority to specify the applicability of the requirements of this subchapter to sex offenders convicted before the enactment of this chapter . . . and to prescribe rules for the registration of any such sex offenders."[70]

Under this statute, the attorney general appeared to have broad policymaking discretion to determine whether the reporting requirements applied to sex offenders convicted before SORNA's enactment. In addition, he had similar authority to set the rules for registration by such offenders. Clearly, this is an unconstitutional delegation of legislative power under my strict tier test, which prohibits any delegation of policymaking discretion.

While the Court might have attempted to interpret the statute to be constitutional based on the avoidance canon, this approach cannot work here to cure the delegation problem. While the plurality interprets the provision to narrow its discretion, this appears to rewrite the statute. But even if one accepts the plurality's rewriting, its claim that the statute requires the attorney general to register pre-act offenders "to the maximum extent feasible" still allows significant policymaking discretion. Under this standard, the attorney general is permitted to determine the type of feasibility that it must consider, such as technological, economic, administrative, or even political feasibility. Such authority to decide based on not law but discretion is impermissible policymaking discretion.[71]

Distinguishing Between Fact-Finding and Policymaking. Under the strict tier, another area where the delegation of policymaking discretion might be involved are decisions that are based on fact-finding by agencies and courts. Under my approach, if an agency is required to make a decision genuinely based on facts, then that decision does not involve policymaking discretion. But this approach requires that one draw a line between fact-finding and policymaking. This section explains how the distinction should be drawn.

Consider the statute discussed above that requires the Department of Transportation to pass a regulation requiring motor vehicle safety features that would reduce the lives lost from motor vehicle accidents by 2 percent and have a cost of not more than the average cost of existing motor vehicle safety features that are presently required. Under this statute, the department would be required to show, by a preponderance of the evidence, that the safety feature it promulgated would satisfy these requirements.

To promulgate a regulation, the agency would need to make certain factual findings. It would need to find the number of lives lost at present from motor vehicle accidents and predict the number of lives saved by the new safety feature. It would also need to find the costs of all motor vehicle safety features that are presently required and the cost of the new safety feature.

In making these findings, the agency would have to rely on theories or methodologies for estimating these future benefits and costs. In selecting a theory, the agency would need to make the decision, perhaps based on expert evidence, of the correct approach. In making this decision, the agency would not be making the decision based on policy. Rather, the question would be whether the theory was based on science and whether it accurately predicted the future in cases of this type.

While the above examples distinguish between fact-finding and policymaking, there are other situations in which drawing the distinction is more difficult. There can be situations—involving what are known as judgmental facts—where what seems like a factual question actually functions like a policy judgment.[72]

For example, a substance may be dangerous to humans at high exposure levels, but there may be no evidence whether the substance is dangerous at low exposure levels. Under these assumptions, whether the substance is dangerous would theoretically be a factual question but one that cannot be answered as a fact based on current knowledge. Thus, the agency's decision whether to prohibit the substance at low exposure levels can only be made on a policy basis. Therefore, the categorical approach would prohibit the agency from making this seemingly fact-based decision.

But this prohibition on judgmental facts does not mean that Congress cannot prohibit substances for which there is not at present evidence indicating that the substance is more likely than not to cause harm. Congress has various methods it could use to regulate such substances that do not violate the delegation prohibition. For example, assume that Congress seeks to prohibit substances for which there is some evidence—say a 30 percent probability—that these substances can cause death or serious illness. If Congress enacted a statute imposing this prohibition, the agency would be required to ban substances for which the requisite evidence existed. There would be no policymaking discretion conferred on the agency. It is true that determining whether a substance has a 30 percent probability of causing harm is different from determining whether it has a 51 percent probability, but in both cases the task involves fact-finding rather than policymaking.

Congress might even go further and attempt to ban substances based on a sliding scale of severity and probability of harm. For example, Congress might seek to prohibit either a moderate amount of harm that was more likely than not to occur or a more severe degree of harm that had a lower probability of occurring. The basic principle would be that a certain level of expected harm would be needed before the prohibition could be imposed. The level of expected harm could then be produced by either a higher probability of a lower severity of harm or a lower probability of a higher harm severity. This standard would be less clear than the previous ones I discussed, but that uncertainty might not be fatal if it could be resolved using the traditional interpretive rules. It would seem that traditional interpretive rules could address this situation, since a sliding scale as to probability and severity of harm has long been employed to determine whether an injunction should be issued.

Implications of the Strict Approach. The strict tier of the nondelegation doctrine employs a categorical prohibition on policymaking discretion. Under this categorical approach, agencies can engage in legal interpretation and fact-finding. In each of these cases, the agency will not have any policymaking discretion. Instead, the legal interpretation and fact-finding will be determined by the law and the facts. For each type of decision, the agency's action will be subject to a nondiscretionary duty.

Under this approach, agencies will be able to conduct a variety of activities that involve the regulation of private rights covered by the strict tier. In particular, they will be able to promulgate legislative regulations, adjudicate cases, and implement programs so long as those regulations, adjudications, and implementations are determined solely based on the law and facts.

A Complication: Reviewability

This part discusses a complication of the categorical approach. How does the extent to which legal and factual determinations are reviewable by courts affect the analysis?

In discussing law interpretation and fact-finding, I have mainly focused on the task that the executive is required to undertake. If the executive is engaged in genuine legal interpretation under the traditional interpretive rules or genuine fact-finding, then it has no policymaking discretion and therefore its actions are constitutional.

But it might be objected that even if the executive is required to engage in genuine legal interpretation or fact-finding, it might instead exercise policymaking discretion under the guise of these other tasks. As a result, the objection continues, my analysis would only be persuasive if the executive were subject to de novo judicial review, which does not occur under existing law.

This objection, however, is mistaken. There is an important distinction between a constitutional requirement and the practical effect of that requirement. As a matter of constitutional requirements, when the executive engages in law interpretation or fact-finding, it is not engaging in policymaking discretion. If the executive does not actually engage in law interpretation or fact-finding, but instead decides these matters based on its policy views, that would be unconstitutional, because the executive is not allowed to exercise such authority.

The practical effect of this legal obligation will depend on whether and, if so, the extent to which the executive's actions are reviewable by the courts.

If there is no judicial review, then the executive may be able to get away with illegal actions unless congressional oversight or impeachment were to operate as an effective deterrent.[73] But this result does not mean that the distinction between policymaking discretion on the one hand and law interpretation and fact-finding on the other is not the correct one under the original meaning. Some constitutional obligations are not as enforceable as one might hope they would be.

But even though there is only deferential judicial review under existing law for cases covered by the strict tier, that does not mean the practical effect of the nondelegation requirement can easily be ignored. Even under the existing law of reviewability, the practical limits of the categorical approach on the executive would be stricter than under the existing law's lenient nondelegation doctrine.

Under existing law, fact questions are reviewed under a deferential arbitrary-and-capricious or substantial evidence standard. Legal questions are reviewed under the reasonability standard associated with *Chevron*.[74] This deference would allow the executive some opportunity to pursue policy under the guise of making legal interpretations or finding facts. But the categorical approach would still require that the executive appear as if it is not acting based on any policy considerations. Thus, agencies could pursue policy concerns surreptitiously but could only do so to the extent that their interpretations or findings did not appear unreasonable to the courts. This involves less policymaking than under existing law, under which agencies can openly engage in policymaking.

Finally, while the existing law does allow the executive some ability to circumvent delegation limits, in my view the Constitution's original meaning as to reviewability would greatly limit the executive's power to circumvent the Constitution. It is my tentative belief that, under the original meaning, most, if not all, government acts covered by the strict tier must be reviewed de novo by the courts. As I argued above, the scope of the strict tier substantially overlaps with the scope of matters that Caleb Nelson maintains require full court review.[75] Thus, the Constitution's original meaning integrates reviewability and the delegation prohibition.[76]

Conclusion

I have argued that the Constitution's original meaning imposes a regime that differs from both the leading version of a strict nondelegation doctrine and the lenient nondelegation doctrine followed by the Supreme Court. My approach would establish a two-tiered doctrine that would permit broader delegations in certain areas but strictly prohibit actions covered by the strict tier. Under the strict tier, the Court would enforce a categorical prohibition on delegations of policymaking discretion. By contrast, the leading version of the strict nondelegation doctrine would prohibit delegations to the executive only for decisions as to important subjects under a statute.[77]

My approach also differs significantly from the lenient Supreme Court case law that currently enforces the nondelegation doctrine.[78] The differences between the original meaning and the existing law raise serious questions about the extent to which original meaning should be applied. Applying the original meaning in every case might involve an extreme disruption of a large number of government programs.

Such a disruption should be considered under the Court's precedent doctrine. For example, my own work with John McGinnis argues that non-originalist precedents should not be overturned if it would lead to enormous costs.[79] The Court might therefore introduce the original meaning by applying it to future statutes that delegate and using a more lenient approach for existing statutes.

Ultimately, the appropriate way for the Supreme Court to apply the nondelegation doctrine will depend on two main questions—the Constitution's original meaning and the applicable precedent rules. But before one addresses how to apply the original meaning under the appropriate precedent rules, one must first determine what that meaning is. This chapter has attempted to make progress on that essential task.

Acknowledgments

I would like to thank Aaron Gordon, John McGinnis, Michael Ramsey, Ilan Wurman, and the editors of this volume for helpful comments.

Notes

1. See, for example, *Sunshine Anthracite Coal Co. v. Adkins*, 310 US 381, 398 (1940).

2. *Wayman v. Southard*, 23 US (10 Wheat.) 1, 43 (1825); and Gary Lawson, "Delegation and Original Meaning," *University of Virginia Law Review* 88, no. 2 (April 2002): 327, 373–74.

3. To be clear, I do not reject the important-subjects approach because it is indeterminate. An originalist must take the original meaning as he or she finds it. See generally Steven G. Calabresi and Gary Lawson, "The Rule of Law as a the Law of Law," *Notre Dame Law Review* 90, no. 2 (2014): 483, https://scholarship.law.nd.edu/ndlr/vol90/iss2/1/. Rather, I believe that the categorical approach is a superior account of the original meaning.

4. Michael B. Rappaport, "The Selective Nondelegation Doctrine and the Line Item Veto: A New Approach to the Nondelegation Doctrine and Its Implications for Clinton v. City of New York," *Tulane Law Review* 76, no. 2 (2001): 265, https://www.tulanelawreview.org/pub/volume76/issue2/the-selective-nondelegation-doctrine-and-the-line-item-veto; Lawson, "Delegation and Original Meaning"; Phillip Hamburger, *Is Administrative Law Unlawful?* (Chicago: University of Chicago Press, 2014); Ilan Wurman, "Nondelegation at the Founding," *Yale Law Journal* 130, no. 6 (April 2021): 1288–651, https://www.yalelawjournal.org/feature/nondelegation-at-the-founding; Aaron Gordon, "Nondelegation," *New York University Journal of Law & Liberty* 12, no. 3 (2020): 718, https://static1.squarespace.com/static/5f6103f36b5eee6bf0ab2c1d/t/5f62b9f0191e4255845e5fe2/1600305650318/FINAL%2BFINALwEdits%2B-%2BGordon%2B718-827.pdf; and Caleb Nelson, "Adjudication in the Political Branches," *Columbia Law Review* 107, no. 3 (April 2007): 559–627, https://www.law.virginia.edu/system/files/faculty/hein/nelson/107colum_l_rev559_2007.pdf.

5. My formulation here of the lenient approach is intentionally vague ("confers *significant authority* on the executive to set policy") to cover different versions of the lenient approach. The lenient approach includes both a version that would allow unlimited delegation and a version that would allow substantial but not unlimited delegation of policymaking authority. I do not attempt here to answer which of the different versions of the lenient approach is correctly applied to the lenient tier.

By contrast, my formulation here of the strict approach is more restrictive. My formulation covers only the categorical prohibition on delegation. Thus, it excludes Lawson's important-subjects approach, which allows Congress to delegate policymaking details to the executive. See Lawson, "Delegation and Original Meaning," 402–3 (allowing "executive officials to exercise discretion with respect to minor or ancillary matters in the implementation of statutes"). For those who adopt the important-subjects approach, it is easy to reformulate the meaning of these terms to reflect that approach.

6. The meaning of legislative and executive power under the lenient approach will turn on the version of the lenient approach that is adopted. These terms will have one meaning if the lenient approach allows the legislature to confer unlimited discretion on the executive. By contrast, these terms will have a different meaning if the lenient approach merely allows the legislature to confer a limited amount of policymaking

discretion on the executive. As noted in note 5, I do not address here how much policy-making discretion the lenient approach allows Congress to confer on the executive.

7. The constitutional language that generates the nondelegation doctrine is primarily contained in the two vesting clauses. See US Const. art. I, § 1; and US Const. art. II, § 1.

8. John O. McGinnis and Michael B. Rappaport, "The Constitution and the Language of the Law," *William & Mary Law Review* 59, no. 4 (2018): 1321, 1342–43, https://scholarship.law.wm.edu/wmlr/vol59/iss4/4/.

9. John O. McGinnis and Michael B. Rappaport, "The Power of Interpretation: Minimizing the Construction Zone," *Notre Dame Law Review* 96, no. 3 (2021): 919–72, https://scholarship.law.nd.edu/ndlr/vol96/iss3/1/.

10. Rappaport, "The Selective Nondelegation Doctrine and the Line Item Veto," 303–44.

11. Rappaport, "The Selective Nondelegation Doctrine and the Line Item Veto," 320–40.

12. Lump-sum appropriation laws authorize the executive to spend a sum on various purposes at its discretion; itemized appropriations, by contrast, require the executive to spend a sum on a specific purpose. Permissive appropriation laws authorize the executive to spend up to a specific amount but allow the executive to spend a lower amount at its discretion. Mandatory appropriations, by contrast, require the executive to spend the entire appropriated amount. Rappaport, "The Selective Nondelegation Doctrine and the Line Item Veto," 317–18.

13. Act of Sept. 29, 1789, ch. 23, sec. 1, 1 Stat. 95, 95 (expired).

14. Rappaport, "The Selective Nondelegation Doctrine and the Line Item Veto," 343.

15. Rappaport, "The Selective Nondelegation Doctrine and the Line Item Veto," 344.

16. Rappaport, "The Selective Nondelegation Doctrine and the Line Item Veto," 353–54.

17. See, for example, Gordon, "Nondelegation," 782–86.

18. Robert Middlekauff, *The Glorious Cause: The American Revolution, 1763–1789* (Oxford, UK: Oxford University Press, 2005), 28.

19. Other areas fall under the lenient tier, but I do not develop them here. One area involves rules that govern the internal administration of the executive and the courts. There is a significant amount of evidence that agencies and courts exercised discretion in this area. Rappaport, "The Selective Nondelegation Doctrine and the Line Item Veto," 354–55. And there is substantial support based on structure and purpose for placing it under the lenient tier. For example, allowing delegation of policymaking discretion as to the internal administration of federal agencies and courts is consistent with the constitutional structure of federalism, since states are not equipped to pass laws in these areas. See also Gordon, "Nondelegation," 782.

Another area covered by the lenient tier involves foreign commerce, especially laws regulating actions taken outside the United States. See Nelson, "Adjudication in the Political Branches," 580 ("Federal statutes permitting the importation of goods from abroad were thought to create mere privileges rather than core private rights; so long as property remained outside the United States, no one had a vested right to import it."); Rappaport, "The Selective Nondelegation Doctrine and the Line Item Veto," 353–54; and

Hamburger, *Is Administrative Law Unlawful?*, 88. This exception is also supported by the fact that states were not thought to be well equipped to act as to foreign commerce and the fact that such regulations generally applied to foreigners outside the United States.

Yet another area covered by the lenient tier involves the treatment of government property. Access to such property is not a right, but it falls under the disposal of government resources. See Nelson, "Adjudication in the Political Branches," 577; Aditya Bamzai, "Delegation and Interpretive Discretion: *Gundy, Kisor*, and the Formation and Future of Administrative Law," *Harvard Law Review* 133 (November 2019): 164, 181, https://harvardlawreview.org/2019/11/delegation-and-interpretive-discretion-gundy-kisor-and-the-formation-and-future-of-administrative-law/; Rappaport, "The Selective Nondelegation Doctrine and the Line Item Veto," 354; and Gary Lawson, "Who Legislates?," *Public Interest Law Review* (1995): 147, 154–55.

20. It is sometimes argued that the English practice is not relevant to interpreting the Constitution, because the Constitution adopted a different system than the English one. See Rappaport, "The Selective Nondelegation Doctrine and the Line Item Veto," 321–22, n. 178 (discussing Justice Clarence Thomas' view). I disagree with such a wholesale rejection of English practice. The Constitution adopted many features of the English system. And even when the framers chose to depart from the English system, they often used English concepts to describe how they were departing from the English system. See Saikrishna B. Prakash and Michael D. Ramsey, "The Executive Power over Foreign Affairs," *Yale Law Journal* 111, no. 2 (November 2001): 231, 252–62, https://www.yalelawjournal.org/article/the-executive-power-over-foreign-affairs. (The framers used the term "executive power" as it was understood in 18th-century England and Europe, even though they transferred some of these executive powers to the Congress.)

One area where I believe English law remained relevant to the United States Constitution, despite differences between the two systems, involves the delegation of policymaking discretion. In my view, when deciding whether Congress can delegate discretion under the Constitution, it is relevant to consider English law (and the law in the American colonies and the independent states). Such English practice is relevant to executive discretion as to spending, regulation of foreign commerce, and foreign and military affairs, to mention just a few areas.

It is sometimes argued that the constitutional text rejects the English practice. For example, while the king of England may have enjoyed some independent authority to regulate foreign commerce (without receiving a delegation of statutory authority from Parliament), the Constitution transferred that regulatory authority to Congress. And therefore, it is argued, the president cannot be delegated discretion as to foreign commerce. But see note 19 (arguing that the regulation of foreign commerce falls under the lenient tier). Similar arguments are made regarding discretion as to spending and foreign and military affairs.

But these arguments do not necessarily hold. That the Constitution transferred to Congress the king's power to regulate foreign commerce *based on his own authority* does not necessarily mean that it eliminated the president's ability to *receive a delegation of policymaking discretion* as to foreign commerce. The traditional discretion of the executive to exercise discretion in this area might have been continued under the Constitution. Put differently, transferring the power to regulate foreign commerce to the legislature did not necessarily cause the Constitution to adopt the narrow understanding of executive and legislative power as to foreign commerce.

To determine whether the narrow or broad interpretation was adopted in this context, one would look to both structure and purpose arguments, as well as early practice under the Constitution. Structure and purpose might be thought to support executive discretion as to foreign commerce if it was generally believed that it was especially difficult for the legislature to govern the area of foreign commerce without conferring discretion on the executive. See also note 19 (arguing that discretion as to foreign commerce is supported by federalism since foreign commerce is not a core function of states). Early historical practice, through congressional enactments delegating discretion as to foreign commerce, might also point in the same direction. If structure and purpose and early historical practice point in the same direction, that supplies a strong argument that Congress can delegate policymaking discretion to the executive as to foreign commerce, even though the Constitution gave the independent power to regulate foreign commerce solely to the Congress.

21. Nelson, "Adjudication in the Political Branches," 561–90.

22. Nelson describes private rights as follows:

> As elaborated by William Blackstone, whose *Commentaries* grounded the legal education of Founding-era Americans and remained enormously important throughout the nineteenth century, the foundational documents of British law recognized three major groupings of core private rights: (1) the "right of personal security," which encompassed "a person's legal and uninterrupted enjoyment of his life, his limbs, his body, his health, and his reputation"; (2) the "right of personal liberty," which entailed freedom from "imprisonment or restraint, unless by due course of law"; and (3) the "right of private property," which involved "the free use, enjoyment, and disposal of all [one's] acquisitions, without any control or diminution, save only by the laws of the land."

Nelson, "Adjudication in the Political Branches," 567 (footnotes omitted).

23. See Nelson, "Adjudication in the Political Branches," 566.

24. See Nelson, "Adjudication in the Political Branches," 609.

25. See Nelson, "Adjudication in the Political Branches," 622.

26. Nelson's article is clearer about the requirement of judicial decision as to facts than as to law, raising the possibility that Nelson believes his argument applies only to the fact question. Nelson, "Adjudication in the Political Branches," 563. In my view, there is for the most part a single approach for judicial resolution of facts and law questions as to private rights. If the courts are required to decide fact questions de novo, it is not clear why they should not also be required to decide law questions de novo.

One possible response to my approach is that legal questions can be given to agencies as a delegation of legislative power but factual questions cannot. But, for my purposes, this answer begs the question. If one believed there was a lenient nondelegation doctrine, then one might distinguish between fact-finding and law interpretation as to what issues had to be decided by courts. But if one did not have strong evidence that the nondelegation doctrine was lenient as to private rights, then it is not clear why one would draw that distinction. Instead, one would treat the two issues that courts traditionally decided—interpretation of law and findings of fact—in the same manner.

27. Early interpretations of the Constitution also support the two-tiered approach and the application of the strict tier to private rights. In criticizing the Aliens Act in 1800, James Madison wrote that the delegation prohibition applied *"especially* [to] a law by which personal liberty is invaded, property deprived of its value to the owner, and life itself indirectly exposed to danger."* James Madison, "Madison's Report on the Virginia Resolution (Report of 1800)," in *The Debates in the Several State Conventions on the Adoption of the Federal Constitution*, 2nd ed., ed. Jonathan Elliot (1836), 559–60. (Emphasis added.)

28. For early examples of delegation as to public rights, see Act of Sept. 29, 1789, ch. 24 §1, 1 Stat. 95 (delegating policymaking authority concerning military pensions); Act of Apr. 30, 1790, ch. 10, §§11–16, 1 Stat. 119, 121 (delegating policymaking authority concerning military disability benefits); Act of July 22, 1790, ch. 33, §1, 1 Stat. 137, 137 (delegating policymaking authority concerning trade with the Indians, which falls under the public rights category of foreign commerce and foreign affairs); Act of Aug. 4, 1790, ch. 34, §2, 1 Stat. 138, 139 (authorizing the president to borrow $12 million to pay off foreign debt, leaving him discretion as to prioritization among lenders); Act of Aug. 12, 1790, ch. 47 1 Stat. 186, 186–87 (authorizing commission to exercise discretion to purchase domestic debt back from the public); and Act of Apr. 10, 1790, ch. 7, § 1, 1 Stat. 109, 109–10 (delegating discretion to the executive as to the granting of patents). While Justice Thomas treats patents as public rights under the category of franchises, Justice Gorsuch maintains they are private rights. Compare *Oil States Energy Services v. Greene's Energy Group*, 138 S. Ct. 1365, 1373–75 (2018); and *Oil States* at 1382–85 (Gorsuch, J., dissenting). Although I focus in this note on the pattern of behavior after the Constitution's enactment, the pattern before its enactment, in England and America, is also relevant.

29. See generally Kenneth Culp Davis, *Discretionary Justice: A Preliminary Inquiry*, 5th ed. (Westport, CT: Praeger, 1976); and Julian Davis Mortenson and Nicholas Bagley, "Delegation at the Founding," *Columbia Law Review* 121, no. 2 (2021), https://columbialawreview.org/content/delegation-at-the-founding/.

30. See Rappaport, "The Selective Nondelegation Doctrine and the Line Item Veto," 310 (arguing that six early delegations cited by Kenneth Culp Davis were largely explained away by the two-tiered approach); and Gordon, "Nondelegation," 779–81. Nicholas Parrillo has plausibly argued that an early example of a direct tax involved the delegation of policymaking discretion to federal officials. Nicholas R. Parrillo, "A Critical Assessment of the Originalist Case Against Administrative Regulatory Power: New Evidence from the Federal Tax on Private Real Estate in the 1790s," *Yale Law Journal* 130, no. 6 (April 2021): 1288–651, https://www.yalelawjournal.org/article/a-critical-assessment. But his argument is far from a conclusive counterexample to the strict view for a variety of reasons. First, it is not clear that the authority conferred on the executive actually provided policymaking discretion rather than a combination of fact-finding and legal interpretation. Second, it is possible that taxation was a historical area where executives had exercised discretion and therefore not under the strict tier. Of course, even if Parrillo has identified a counterexample, one such example is hardly dispositive.

31. Many of the areas in the lenient tier involve the management of government

resources, such as the operation of government agencies and management of government property. Making the large number of managerial decisions in this area requires far more discretion than legislating regulations that govern private rights. See Friedrich A. Hayek, *Law, Legislation, and Liberty: Rules and Order* (Chicago: University of Chicago Press, 1973), 1:125–26.

32. While it is not often presented this way, the two-tiered theory may be the leading view among academic defenders of a strict nondelegation doctrine. Different versions of the two-tiered theory appear to be accepted by various advocates of a strict nondelegation doctrine. See Hamburger, *Is Administrative Law Unlawful?*, 527–29; David Schoenbrod, *Power Without Responsibility: How Congress Abuses the People Through Delegation* (New Haven, CT: Yale University Press, 1993), 186; Ronald A. Cass, "Delegation Reconsidered: A Delegation Doctrine for the Modern Administrative State," *Harvard Journal of Law & Public Policy* 40 (2017): 147, 186–87, http://www.harvard-jlpp.com/wp-content/uploads/sites/21/2017/03/Cass_FINAL.pdf; Gordon, "Nondelegation," 780–81; Bamzai, "Delegation and Interpretive Discretion," 178; and Wurman, "Nondelegation at the Founding," 4.

33. When the executive applies law to the facts, its decisions also do not involve policymaking discretion. After all, if neither questions of law definition nor questions of fact determination involve policymaking discretion, then questions of law application, which merely involve a mixture of these two types of questions, also do not involve policymaking discretion. Consequently, I largely ignore these questions for the remainder of the chapter.

34. *Aurora v. United States*, 11 US (7 Cranch) 382 (1813).

35. *Aurora*, 11 US at 388.

36. See the earlier text and accompanying notes. (The narrow understanding of the executive power and legislative power vesting clauses limits the conferral of lawmaking discretion on the executive.)

37. See *Mistretta v. United States*, 488 US 361, 415 (1989) (Scalia, dissenting).

38. See McGinnis and Rappaport, "The Power of Interpretation" (discussing a judicial manageability interpretive rule at the time of the Constitution).

39. The indeterminate character of the important-subjects test is acknowledged by one of its leading defenders:

> We end up with a test for delegations that says, in essence, "Congress must make whatever decisions are important enough to the statutory scheme in question so that Congress must make them."
>
> As constitutional tests go, this one certainly sounds pretty lame—not to mention absurdly self-referential. It is no surprise that a rule-of-law devotee like Justice Scalia flees from it as a vampire flees garlic.

Lawson, "Delegation and Original Meaning," 361.

40. Madison, "Madison's Report on the Virginia Resolution (Report of 1800)."

41. Madison, "Madison's Report on the Virginia Resolution (Report of 1800)."

42. *Wayman*, 23 US at 43.

43. Under this interpretation of Marshall's statement, the courts would still have to determine, for laws that do not regulate private rights, whether Congress had legislated

as to the important subjects, leaving to the executive or judiciary only the filling in of the details.

44. In the opinion, Marshall discusses a variety of subjects concerning "the regulation of the conduct of the officer of the court in giving effect to its judgments." *Wayman*, 23 US at 45. He writes, "It is undoubtedly proper for the legislature to prescribe the manner in which these ministerial offices shall be performed," but he then notes "that there is some difficulty in discerning the exact limits within which the legislature" may rely on the courts to determine the rules governing this behavior. *Wayman*, 23 US at 45–46. These tasks of "giving effect to [the court's] judgments" would mainly, if not entirely, fall under the lenient tier under an approach like mine that treats regulation of the procedure or internal operations of the courts as falling under the lenient tier. See also Gordon, "Nondelegation," 782. Another way to classify these subjects under the lenient tier is to view them as inherent aspects of the judicial power. See Robert J. Pushaw Jr., "The Inherent Powers of Federal Courts and the Structural Constitution," *Iowa Law Review* 86, no. 3 (March 2001): 735, 798.

45. While I assert that interpretation of statutes based on the traditional interpretive rules would be constitutional, I do not mean to suggest that it would always be unconstitutional for Congress or the courts to change the interpretive rules governing statutes. My reference to the traditional interpretive rules is meant to indicate the type of interpretive rules that can pass muster under the nondelegation doctrine. The traditional interpretive rules are likely to pass muster because they would have been accepted as legal interpretation at the time of the Constitution's enactment. Those rules also provide a basis for determining the scope of policymaking discretion that can be conferred on judges and executive officials. In my view, the traditional interpretive rules denied judges all policymaking discretion (and if not all such discretion, then all but a minimal amount). While the rules did require judges to consider a statute's purpose, those were the purposes attributed to the law enactors, not the judges' values. Thus, so long as the new interpretive rules do not provide policymaking discretion to judges (or provide it only in the minimal amount that judges may have possessed traditionally), those interpretive rules will be constitutional. But if the new interpretive rules provide additional discretion, then they will be unconstitutional.

46. Applying the rule of lenity no more involves policymaking than does interpreting the Judiciary Act of 1789, which also served certain values. In both cases, the values were established by the law. It is true that the statutory interpretive rules were largely common-law rules, but that does not make the following of such established law an instance of policymaking.

47. This chapter does not offer an extended description of the traditional interpretive rules. See McGinnis and Rappaport, "The Constitution and the Language of the Law," 1369; and John O. McGinnis and Michael B. Rappaport, "Unifying Original Intent and Original Public Meaning," *Northwestern University Law Review* 113, no. 6 (April 2019): 1371, 1386–88, https://scholarlycommons.law.northwestern.edu/nulr/vol113/iss6/4/. Those rules generally sought the intent of the law enactors, not through legislative history, but through the meaning of the statutory language in context, and sought to resolve uncertainties through a variety of factors such as purpose, structure, the more common meaning, and other canons, such as the rule of lenity, the rule against

implied repeals, and the absurdity rule. These rules did not permit the judge to consider his or her own policy views. Instead, to the extent it looked to values, it did so to further the intent of the law enactors by considering the purpose of the law and the societal values at the time of the enactment.

48. See Aditya Bamzai, "The Origins of Judicial Deference to Executive Interpretation," *Yale Law Journal* 126 (2017): 908, 918, 987.

49. My argument that the executive can be given the task of genuine legal interpretation of statutes does not mean the executive can be given all tasks that judges historically exercised in areas covered by the strict tier. For example, although I do not address it here, I am extremely skeptical that the executive could be given the task of articulating or developing the traditional common law (as opposed to enforcing the traditional common law that had already been articulated by the courts). Although the judicial task of articulating the traditional common law was much less policy oriented than that of articulating the modern common law, still the executive did not appear to exercise this task historically. See Caleb Nelson, "A Critical Guide to Erie Railroad Co. v. Tompkins," *William & Mary Law Review* 54 (2013): 921, 931–935 (discussing the traditional common law). It would be all the less likely to be constitutional to assign to the executive the task of articulating the modern common law.

50. See McGinnis and Rappaport, "The Constitution and the Language of the Law," 1343–44.

51. Terms that seem abstract can often, when examined in context, turn out to have a more specific meaning. See, for example, Laura K. Donohue, "The Original Fourth Amendment," *University of Chicago Law Review* 83, no. 3 (2016): 1181, 1191–92 (arguing that "unreasonable searches and seizures" in the Fourth Amendment referred to the reason of the common law and therefore to the common-law rules governing searches and seizures).

52. *Motor Vehicle Manufacturers Association v. State Farm Mutual Automobile Insurance Co.*, 463 US 29 (1983).

53. The main difference between this statute and the previous public interest statute is that this statute appears to be directed solely at automobile safety, whereas the previous one is focused on the broader concept of the public interest. While the costs of automobile safety would not appear to be relevant (except as they affect automobile safety) for this statute, they would appear to be relevant for the previous statute. See *Whitman v. American Trucking Associations*, 531 US 457 (2001).

54. *Gundy v. United States*, 139 S. Ct. 2116 (2019); *Whitman*, 531 US at 457; *Industrial Union Department, AFL-CIO v. American Petroleum Institute*, 448 US 607 (1980); and *Panama Refining Company v. Ryan*, 293 US 388 (1935).

55. The laws reviewed in the four cases discussed in this section all appear to be covered by the strict tier of the nondelegation doctrine, since those laws all involved the regulation of private rights in the domestic sphere. See *Panama Refining*, 293 US at 405 (law restricting the right to transport petroleum in interstate commerce); *Industrial Union Department*, 448 US at 611 (law regulating workplace conditions provided by private employers to private employees); *Whitman*, 531 US at 457 (law restricting private citizens from polluting the air); and *Gundy*, 139 S. Ct. at 2121–22 (law requiring convicted sex offenders to register with the government). The least certain case here is

Whitman, since air pollution arguably implicates "propriety rights held by government on behalf of the people," such as public land. See Nelson, "Adjudication in the Political Branches," 571. In *Panama Refining*, while the law unconstitutionally conferred discretion as to interstate commerce, it also extended to foreign commerce, which might have been a public right covered by the lenient tier.

56. *Panama Refining*, 293 US at 406.

57. While I do not discuss the other National Industrial Recovery Act case, *A. L. A. Schechter Poultry*, Justice Benjamin Cardozo's description of it as "delegation running riot" was apt, and it surely delegated enormous policymaking discretion and therefore was unconstitutional under my standard. See *A. L. A. Schechter Poultry Corp. v. United States*, 295 US 495, 553 (1935) (Cardozo, J., concurring).

58. *Industrial Union Department*, 448 US at 642–43 (plurality op.).

59. *Industrial Union Department*, 448 US at 675–76, 687–88 (Rehnquist, J., concurring).

60. *Industrial Union Department*, 448 US at 612 (plurality op.) (quoting Occupational Safety and Health Act, 29 USC § 655(b)(5) (1970)).

61. *Industrial Union Department*, 448 US at 675.

62. *Industrial Union Department*, 448 US at 675.

63. *Industrial Union Department*, 448 US at 682.

64. There are other questions of legal interpretation that a court would have to interpret in *Industrial Union Department*, such as defining what constitutes a "material impairment of health or functional capacity" or whether the burden of proof of showing that a toxic substance is not safe at existing levels of exposure is on the agency or the industry. But, once again, these matters can likely be addressed using traditional methods of statutory interpretation.

65. *Whitman*, 531 US at 465 (quoting Clean Air Act, 42 USC § 7409(b)(1) (1970)).

66. See *Whitman*, 531 US at 465.

67. *Gundy*, 139 S. Ct. at 2125–26, 2129–30 (plurality op.).

68. *Gundy*, 139 S. Ct. at 2143, 2146–48 (Gorsuch, J., dissenting).

69. *Gundy*, 139 S. Ct. at 2130–31 (Alito, J., concurring).

70. *Gundy*, 139 S. Ct. at 2132 (Gorsuch, J., dissenting) (quoting Sex Offender Registration and Notification Act, 34 USC § 20913(d) (2006)).

71. One question I do not address is to what extent the nondelegation doctrine applies to the courts when they interpret laws regulating private rights in the domestic sphere. I have argued that courts do not exercise policymaking discretion when they interpret laws using traditional interpretive methods. But it might be argued that statutes could be so unclear or indeterminate that they ask courts to exercise policymaking discretion when they interpret them. See the "Some Initial Examples" section, arguing that some indeterminate statutes are best understood as delegating policymaking discretion to the executive. In my view, the best way to resolve such cases is to ask whether the statute's meaning can be determined by using the traditional interpretive rules. If the meaning can so be determined, then there is no delegation since the court merely applies the law. If the meaning cannot be determined, then the statute should not be enforced, since the law cannot be applied.

72. Michael Herz, Richard Murphy, and Katherine Watts, *A Guide to Judicial and Political Review of Federal Agencies*, 2nd ed. (Chicago: American Bar Association, 2015), 192.

73. Historically, most but not all individuals harmed by federal government action could bring a tort claim against the officer in their personal capacity. See David E. Engdahl, "Immunity and Accountability for Positive Governmental Wrongs," *University of Colorado Law Review* 44, no. 1 (August 1972): 1, 39. Such tort actions were decided by courts de novo without any deference to the officer or the agency. If such tort actions existed today, there would be far less opportunity for agencies to get away with surreptitious policymaking. While I have strong doubts about the federal government's power to eliminate these tort actions without replacing them with comparable substitutes, I leave that question for another time.

74. It is important to distinguish between two aspects of *Chevron* deference: reviewability and authority. Under the reviewability aspects of *Chevron*, agency interpretations of the statutes they administer will be set aside under step two of *Chevron* only if the courts conclude these interpretations are unreasonable. Under the authority aspects of *Chevron*, agencies are allowed to choose between reasonable agency interpretations based on policy considerations. The categorical approach rejects the authority aspect of *Chevron*, because agencies are not permitted to make decisions based on policy. But the reviewability aspects of *Chevron* are not necessarily foreclosed. Under the reviewability but not the authority aspect of *Chevron*, agencies are required to select the strongest interpretation based exclusively on the statute's meaning, but courts are required to set aside that interpretation if they believe it is an unreasonable interpretation of the statute's meaning.

75. But see note 26 (noting the possibility that Nelson requires fully reviewability only for fact questions).

76. One area where I differ with Nelson is for findings of legislative facts, which he argues do not need to be decided by courts. He bases this conclusion on two rules at the time: that fact-finding by the legislature did not need to be reviewed by courts and that certain foreign affairs cases involving legislative facts were political questions that did not require full court review. Nelson, "Adjudication in the Political Branches," 591–93. But because certain legislative facts did not need to be finally decided by the courts does not mean that all legislative facts did not need to be. It is not surprising that fact-finding by legislatures did not require judicial determination. The opposite result would have been quite a departure from traditional law. Moreover, that certain foreign affairs matters were political questions is also not surprising given the predominant role of the political branches in this area. These results do not suggest that, when an agency was given legislative fact-finding as to private rights in the domestic sphere, judicial determinations were not required.

77. The leading version has taken an agnostic approach as to whether the Constitution establishes a two-tiered approach to the doctrine. See Lawson, "Delegation and Original Meaning," 394 (citing without endorsing my earlier article and stating that "there may be certain subject matter areas in which the range of discretion permitted under the executive power (or the judicial power) is larger than in other areas").

78. See *Whitman*, 531 US at 472–76 (applying a lenient intelligible-principles test).

79. John O. McGinnis and Michael B. Rappaport, *Originalism and the Good Constitution* (Cambridge, MA: Harvard University Press, 2013).

Executive Administration of the Government's Resources and the Delegation Problem

JOHN HARRISON

In his dissenting opinion in *Gundy v. United States*,[1] Justice Neil Gorsuch asks one question to identify permissible delegations to the executive: "What's the test?"[2] This chapter addresses the constitutional test for a major category of executive activity that Justice Gorsuch did not explicitly discuss: executive decisions in which officials exercise rights of the government that are the kind of rights that both private people and governments can have. Spending programs, one of the federal government's most important activities, fall into that category.

For that large and important class of government activity, I argue, the Court's current requirement of an intelligible principle to guide the executive satisfies the Constitution's structural requirements. For example, in 1789, the First Congress directed the executive to have a lighthouse built for Chesapeake Bay, leaving many decisions to the president.[3] Like a private person, the government spent its own funds to acquire property that it then used.[4] That is the kind of activity, and discretion, this chapter is about.

Executive policy discretion is a central and controversial feature of American government. This chapter addresses the constitutional rules concerning a major field in which Congress often leaves important issues for implementing officials. Whether to include that kind of executive activity within the category of delegation is a matter of nomenclature. If the defining feature of delegation is statutory authority to decide based on policy considerations, then many proprietary-type activities involve delegation. If exercising the government's own rights is not called delegation, then delegation is part of the larger category of statutory grants of policymaking authority.

This chapter focuses on programs in which the government pursues public goals by using its own resources the way a private person can.

Lighthouses are not as important as they used to be, but that kind of government program is still significant. As of this writing, similar programs are at the center of a controversy involving the executive's use of statutorily granted discretion. The secretary of education recently issued regulations governing educational institutions' response to allegations of sexual harassment.[5] Those regulations are not mandatory rules about private conduct applicable to everyone, the way the regulations at issue in *Gundy* were. They are conditions on the receipt of federal funds, the kind of condition a private foundation might impose on a grant of financial support.

When the government exercises its own private-type rights, the constitutional structure requires nothing more from the legislature than an intelligible principle. That conclusion follows from the vesting clauses of Articles I and II, understood in light of their text and the Constitution's structure and history. When the government acts as a property owner or a contracting party, executive officials act for it, and only executive officials may do so. Acting for the government in that way routinely involves making policy decisions, so making such decisions is an unproblematic use of the Article II executive power. Only Congress may legislate. Therefore, only Congress may decide to build a lighthouse and appropriate funds for it, just as only Congress may decide to make billions of dollars in grants to all levels of education. Because the programs involved are public, serving public purposes, the uniquely legislative act of creating such a program might include choosing its purpose. If only legislative power may perform that basic function, an intelligible principle identifying a purpose performs it. Nothing more is needed from Congress.[6]

Putting the government's use of its own resources in a separate category will probably strike many judges and scholars as natural. My argument in that category—that no more than an intelligible principle is required—may also seem reasonable to many. This chapter makes another claim that I expect will be more controversial. An important set of federal regulatory programs works through government control of public resources. Broadcasting licensing is an example. When a radio or television station broadcasts, it is not simply engaging in private activity. It is using public property—intangible property like a copyright—and requires the consent of the government, which administers that property. Whenever regulation works by empowering executive officials to give permission to use a public resource or benefit, the rule that applies to spending programs applies.

The first section of this chapter discusses Justice Gorsuch's analysis of the delegation problem and argues that he did not deal with the use of the government's rights. The second section considers the problem of delegation as it arises in that category of government activity. It argues that making policy choices in the administration of the government's assets is a central function of the executive power conferred by Article II. In that context, the exclusive vesting of legislative power by Article I is satisfied when Congress creates a program that will use government assets and establishes the program's basic goals. Setting out those goals in a way that complies with the Supreme Court's current requirement of an intelligible principle will satisfy Article I. I then turn to history, showing that in the early days of the Constitution, Congress often gave executive officials broad discretion in administering the government's assets. That section concludes by discussing two examples that show the importance today of this kind of government activity and the executive discretion that comes with it.

The third section moves to the probably more controversial topic of regulation through licensing and permitting. It explains how a licensing requirement puts the government in the position of an owner of a resource. When executive officials give licenses or permits that allow otherwise-forbidden conduct, they perform a familiar function of owners, and their activity therefore falls into the category of administration of the government's assets. I then turn to history, discussing two important early forms of regulation that have been the subject of scholarly investigation: the Indian Commerce Act and steamboat boiler safety regulation. Both involved considerable executive discretion, and both worked through licensing. As far as I know, no one at the time said that delegation was permissible in a licensing system because licensing resembles public ownership. The Supreme Court did, however, understand steamboat licensing as the administration by the government of the public right of navigation. This section concludes with a discussion of two components of current environmental law that work through permitting. Both are readily characterized as government administration of a public right—a commons—and involve the kind of executive discretion that often comes when the government holds important assets such as air and water.

Justice Gorsuch's Analysis of the Delegation Problem

The United States government has been described as a pension fund with nuclear weapons. The first part of the quip emphasizes the size of Social Security and Medicare, while the second part refers to another important category of federal spending. The pandemic of 2020–21 has called into question the viability of yet another federal function, one so old it antedates the Constitution and arguably the United States as an independent sovereign: the postal system. Neither today's enormous programs of social insurance nor the venerable postal function fits comfortably into the tripartite analysis of delegation Justice Gorsuch proposed in *Gundy*.

Justice Gorsuch's analysis is based on his definition of "legislative power." The framers, he maintains, understood legislative power to mean "the power to adopt generally applicable rules of conduct governing future actions by private persons."[7] In the first of the three categories, "As long as Congress makes the policy decisions when regulating private conduct, it may authorize another branch to 'fill up the details.'"[8] The crucial problem when that happens is finding the line between policy decisions and details. In the second category, "Once Congress prescribes the rule governing private conduct, it may make the application of that rule depend on executive fact-finding."[9] When that happens, the crucial problem is finding the line between fact-finding and policymaking.

In the third situation, Congress assigns "the executive and judicial branches certain non-legislative responsibilities."[10] Sometimes, he explains, Congress' legislative authority "overlaps with authority the Constitution separately vests in another branch."[11] Quoting Professor David Schoenbrod, Justice Gorsuch says, "When a congressional statute confers wide discretion to the executive, no separation-of-powers problem may arise if 'the discretion is to be exercised over matters already within the scope of executive power.'"[12] He gives as possible examples the executive's foreign affairs powers and the courts' authority to regulate practice before them.[13]

Paying old-age benefits or operating the postal system do not fall readily into any of those three categories. Spending programs and government services are not rules about private conduct. Executive agencies that implement such programs fill in many details, but not in rules that tell private people what they may and may not do. Programs such as Social

Security and the postal system involve rules about the use of the government's resources, including its funds and the services of people it hires to perform functions such as delivering the mail. Neither classic example of the use of the government's own resources is already within the scope of executive power, if functions already within the scope of executive power are those that require no legislation. The president may not pay benefits nor operate post offices without statutory authority.

Social Security and the Postal Service do not fit into Justice Gorsuch's categories because legislative power does not *mean* the power to adopt general and prospective rules. It *includes* that power but is not limited to it. The legislative powers granted to Congress in Article I include its postal powers and its general spending power if Article I confers that authority. Those legislative powers also include some that do involve making general and prospective rules, such as the intellectual property powers.

Justice Gorsuch's neglect of this aspect of the federal government, which derives from his more limited definition of legislative power, is not surprising. Judicial opinions are written in the context of specific disputes. Judges often make seemingly general statements that are more limited than their literal meaning suggests. *Gundy* involved a general and prospective rule, a criminal law. In that context, referring only to one important part of the legislative power as if it were the whole is unsurprising.

More is at work here, though, than just a standard point about how opinions are written and should be read. Making general and prospective rules for conduct is not just a familiar exercise of legislative power. It is in a sense the core of legislative power, because it is a distinctively sovereign function. Private people cannot do that, and if Congress authorizes one private person to make rules for the conduct of others, the problem of delegation to private actors arises.[14]

Federal legislative power is not limited to that central use of it. It is often used to create a program in which the government does nothing that a private person may not do. The Postal Service delivers letters and parcels. So do FedEx and United Parcel Service. Medicare provides health insurance. So do many private firms. The National Parks Service operates campgrounds on federal land, and many private people operate campgrounds on private land.

Justice Gorsuch may not have thought about the government's use of its own resources at all, given that *Gundy* was not about that kind of federal activity. He may have thought that grants of discretion in such programs are not properly called delegation of legislative power, precisely because programs like that do not involve changing legal rules the way only a government may. Or perhaps he thought they raise delegation problems that are sufficiently distinct from those with which he was primarily concerned that he chose not to address them.

Justice Gorsuch took the seat of Justice Antonin Scalia, one of whose many memorable turns of phrase is that Congress does not hide elephants in mouseholes.[15] As the witticism with which this section began shows, any receptacle large enough to hold federal spending and similar government activities is no mousehole. It is big enough to hold some much larger beast, perhaps even an elephant.

The Problem of Delegation as It Arises in Government Activity

This section begins by explaining why acting for the government with respect to the government's own rights is within the core of the executive power. Also within that core is exercising any statutorily granted discretion as to the government's rights. I also explain how that aspect of executive power is consistent with Congress' exclusive possession of legislative power. To show that this understanding of the text and structure is firmly historically grounded, this section gives a few early republic examples of statutes that allowed executive officers to make policy choices in administering the government's rights. The section concludes by discussing two current examples of important government functions that fall into this category, in which delegation is largely unproblematic.[16]

The Core of the Executive Power. The executive power conferred by Article III includes the authority to act for the government with respect to the government's rights that are like those of private people and to exercise statutorily granted discretion in doing so.

That conclusion follows readily from the text of Article II, which conveys "executive power." Executive officials administer the government:

They conduct its operations. Legislatures make rules, but executive officials act pursuant to those rules. They make contracts, conduct criminal investigations and prosecutions, and take money from the Treasury and pay it according to law.[17]

Administering the government, which is the core of the executive power, consists largely of using the government's own assets, material and juridical, to achieve the goals of the law. Paying funds from the Treasury uses the government's assets. Suing on behalf of the United States uses its capacity as a juridical entity and its right to sue.

Just as using the government's assets is within the core of the executive power, so is exercising discretion in doing so. In purchasing goods and services for the government's use and in dispensing benefits, for example, executive officials routinely make choices based on their own policy judgments. They have done so for centuries and did so at the time of the framing. In deciding which criminal prosecutions to bring, executive officials similarly make decisions based on policy choices. For example, prosecutors may decide that a new form of fraud has become widespread and devote more of their limited time to prosecuting it to reinforce deterrence by the criminal law.

The executive's role regarding the criminal law is a central example of the concept of law execution and hence executive power. It illustrates how acting for the government, and making policy choices in doing so, are leading parts of the executive function. To execute, carry out, or implement a plan is to take concrete steps designed to bring the world into accord with the plan. Without concrete action, a plan is just an abstraction. The executor of an estate takes steps that turn the testator's instructions into reality. Administering an estate, and thereby executing a will, often involves making discretionary choices, notably with respect to the estate's assets. For example, an executor charged with realizing as much as possible from valuable artwork in the estate must make judgments about how best to do so. An auction, consignment to a dealer, and sale by the executor with no intermediary are all possibilities. Implementing the testator's plan to maximize the value of the estate entails making discretionary judgments.

That aspect of execution follows from the practical relationship between plans and the actions that implement them. For a great many plans, the planner can give meaningful guidance, often by stating a goal, but has good reason not to specify fully how to make the plan into reality. Planners' reasons for incomplete specification include the impossibility of complete specification in many situations and the high cost of foreseeing contingencies and prescribing responses when doing so is possible. An implementer, like the executor of an estate or a government official, need deal only with the contingencies that actually arise.

A description of the Constitution's executive power should make sense internally—containing a natural understanding of the concept considered in isolation—and externally—describing executive power in a way that fits into the three-power structure created by the vesting clauses of Articles I, II, and III. The description of executive power I suggest, according to which making discretionary choices in administering the government's rights is within the core of that power, makes sense in both ways. As just noted, taking a plan and making further choices to implement it are part of carrying it out or executing it. That characterization of executive power also meshes with the larger system the text creates.

The three vesting clauses sketch a structure involving three powers that are mutually exclusive and collectively exhaustive of what government can do. Those three powers also work together to perform the functions of government. Mutual exclusivity follows from separate vesting. If the powers were not distinct, not much would be accomplished by allocating different powers to institutions with different features, such as their selection and tenure. Mutual exclusivity is of course a premise of the anti-delegation principle. The presence of only three grants of the basic powers indicates that they are collectively exhaustive. If they were not, the United States would not have a complete government. To make a complete government, the powers should complement one another by working together.

The feature of executive power I stress matches the principle that the three powers are mutually exclusive, because it assumes an exclusive role for legislative power. Within the core of legislative power is the creation of legal rules where none existed before.[18] That aspect of legislative power complements well-known features of the other two powers. Executive officials need law to carry out, and courts need law to apply. Neither can supply that law for itself, but the legislature can create new law. When executive officials exercise the government's own rights, they act based on existing law and do not make new law.

Congress created the Postal Service. The conception of executive power that includes administering rights that Congress creates is thus consistent with the legislature's exclusive authority to make law. It fits the structure in which the powers are mutually exclusive. Executive administration of the government's rights fits the principle that the three powers are collectively exhaustive, because it performs a function that any government must. It fits the principle that the powers work together, because it is part of how the executive turns the legislature's abstract plans into concrete action.

A crucial question concerning delegation is whether the legislature's exclusive possession of legislative power means that it must provide basic guiding principles whenever it gives the executive power. The principle that the legislature must act before the executive may does not by itself answer this question. Executive power requires some legal support, but the legal support might be purely empowering, with no guidance as to how to use the power. For example, the president might be authorized to spend $1,000,000, with no further specification of the goal to be pursued. Executive officials must point to a legislation that authorizes what they do, such as rules that authorize them to spend public funds. Legislation that confers unfettered discretion does provide authorization, even if it includes no intelligible principle that instructs the executive.

Congress' exclusive possession of legislative power, combined with the content of its enumerated powers, likely entails that when it creates a program involving the use of the government's own assets, it must provide basic principles governing the purpose to which those assets should be put. If it does not do so, Congress does not provide adequate legislative support for an exercise of executive power. I reach that conclusion with some doubt. The analogy between proprietary-type rights held by the government and those held by private people may point against such a requirement. In the intellectual property statutes, Congress enables private people to hold property rights without giving them any instructions about how they should be used.

Despite their important similarity, rights held by private people and similar rights held by the government are not the same in all respects. Executive officials do not themselves own the public rights they administer. The government owns or administers on behalf of the public. Executive officials are agents, like the executors of estates, who do not themselves own the assets they administer. Without some indication of the goal to be pursued, an agent cannot act. The congressional powers that enable Congress to authorize executive officials to administer the government's resources thus have an important feature: They are powers to make the executive an agent of the government in managing its assets. Agents need instructions, so Congress' exercises of those powers must include instructions for the executive. Otherwise, Congress is not doing what the Constitution enables it to do—make the executive an agent of the government as to the government's rights.

Congress' Article IV power over federal territory and other property shows that executive officials are agents of the government as owner, not owners themselves. The property of the United States, real and personal, is property of the United States, not its executive officials. Congress' power to make rules about that property includes the authority to constitute the executive as agent of the owner, not to make the executive the owner. To exercise that power, Congress must put the executive in the position of an agent, who acts on behalf of a principal. Agents, as such, need some guidance.

Article IV exemplifies the point, because it is specifically about property. But any time Congress exercises its other powers to put the government in the position of an owner, any authority it gives the executive will be as an agent. In administering the public airwaves, the Federal Communications Commission (FCC) acts on behalf of the public. In disbursing Treasury funds (which may also be property of the United States within the meaning of Article IV), executive officials do so on behalf of the funds' owner, the United States. In all such programs, the source of Congress' ability to confer discretion on executive officials is its power to constitute them to act on behalf of an owner. To exercise that power, Congress must provide the kind of guidance required for one person to act for another. When it creates a program based on the use of a government asset, such as a spending program, Congress has not properly exercised its power, has not done what only it can do, until it has chosen the goal to be pursued. Pursuing that goal by administering the government's resources is part of the executive function.

Executive officials' need for a goal probably imposes constraints on Congress, but the constraints that result from the need for a goal are loose. Goals can be quite general and implicit. Telling the executive to have a lighthouse built brings with it the common purposes of lighthouses. Under current Supreme Court cases, Congress may give executive officials authority to act, provided that it supplies them with an intelligible principle to guide their action.[19] An intelligible principle that guides the use of the government's own assets will tell executive officials what purpose they are to pursue and so will be consistent with the exclusive vesting in Congress of the legislative power.[20]

Giving basic guidance is not the same as leaving only the details to the executive. Justice Gorsuch in *Gundy* apparently regarded the distinction between policy decisions and details as substantially constraining delegation. In the context he was discussing, substantial constraint and a narrow conception of details are natural. If making general and prospective rules for private conduct is defined as part of legislative power, any executive involvement in prescribing the content of those rules is problematic. Any solution to that problem must preserve the main role for the legislature. Filling in details may qualify as carrying out the policy the legislature has adopted, but details cannot be of great importance lest the executive usurp the legislature's role.

Adumbrating the concept of legislative power in the context of creating public rights, and understanding the content of Congress' enumerated powers when they are used to create public rights, calls for different principles. Many laws about private conduct require no executive implementation at all. *Gundy* is an unusual case in which the criminal law involved further specification by an executive official. Most criminal statutes provide a rule of conduct. The executive enforces those rules by bringing prosecutions; it does not add to their content with regulations. The courts decide cases the executive brings, interpreting the statute when necessary.

When Congress provides for the kind of function that has the executive administering public rights, by contrast, it is routinely in no position fully to specify what should be done. The legislative task is to choose a goal, create institutions, and provide resources. As I argued above, implementing such programs often involves making important decisions. Executive officials that do so operate within the law. Hence, in that context there is no reason to treat executive decision-making grudgingly, as

Justice Gorsuch's reference to filling in details suggests it is appropriate when private conduct is regulated.

The Supreme Court reasoned along the lines I suggest in an important case in 1911 involving federal lands, *United States v. Grimaud*.[21] In 1897, Congress had given the secretary of the interior authority to "make rules and regulations" concerning forest reservations on federal land to "insure the objects of such reservations," including authority "to regulate their occupancy and use."[22] The act further provided for criminal punishment of violations of forest reserve regulations.[23] The regulations forbade grazing sheep on forest reservations without permission, and Pierre Grimaud was prosecuted for doing so.[24] Grimaud argued that the statute impermissibly delegated legislative power to the secretary.[25]

The Court rejected the nondelegation argument. It found that "the authority to make administrative rules is not a delegation of legislative power, nor are such rules raised from an administrative to a legislative character because the violation thereof is punished as a public offense."[26] Readers in the 21st century, used to calling federal regulatory bodies administrative agencies, may wonder what distinction Justice Rucker Lamar had in mind. Most likely, he meant "administrative" in the sense of administering the government's own resources. "The implied license under which the United States had suffered its public domain to be used as a pasture for sheep and cattle" had been "curtailed and qualified by Congress to the extent that such privilege should not be exercised in contravention of the rules and regulations."[27] When "the defendants drove and grazed their sheep upon the reserve in violation of the regulations, they were making an unlawful use of the government's property."[28] An open-ended authorization of the executive to make rules about private use of public lands was not a delegation of legislative power.[29]

Executive discretion in the exercise of the government's rights, pursuant to an intelligible principle, is consistent with the separate vesting of legislative and executive power.

Early Congressional Grants of Discretion to Executive Officials. Early Congresses regularly gave executive officers substantial discretion in using the government's own proprietary-type rights. I will mention just a few examples, mainly involving federal contracting. Congress frequently gave executive officials wide latitude in choosing the government's contracting partners and in devising the terms of their contracts, including employment contracts. That practice is unsurprising, because Congress of course could not make those decisions itself, and the sheer ordinariness of the practice emphasizes that such operational decisions are at the core of the executive power.

The First Congress alone provided numerous examples. As mentioned above, Congress directed the president to choose a location for a lighthouse at the entrance to Chesapeake Bay, itself an exercise of discretion, and charged the secretary of the Treasury with entering into contracts for the lighthouse's construction and operation.[30] Other than stating the general goal, Congress gave no guidance about the choice of contractors or their specific duties. The lighthouse statute probably would fail Justice Gorsuch's test in *Gundy*. The decision to build a lighthouse is certainly more fundamental than the decision of where to put it, but the latter is not a minor detail. Once the government has decided to construct some public work, the question of its location is often important and controversial.

Similarly broad but more generic authority was given to all heads of department, to hire such clerks as they thought necessary and to pay them up to $500 per year.[31] The secretary of state was instructed to provide for publication of federal laws "in at least three of the public newspapers published within the United States" and was left to choose the newspapers and any number of them more than two.[32] United States marshals were put in charge of the first census and given authority to choose the number of assistants they would hire to carry out the enumeration and to assign each assistant to a territory defined by the marshal.[33] The president was given wide latitude in setting the compensation of the officials who enforced the excise on distilled spirits.[34] The commissioner of the General Land Office was empowered to choose the duties of his principal subordinate, the chief clerk.[35]

Perhaps the most sweeping contracting authority the First Congress granted concerned the post office. Congress' first move in that regard was to maintain the existing postal system temporarily while giving the president authority to direct the postmaster general "in performing the duties of his office, and in forming contracts for the transportation of the mail."[36] Not until the Second Congress was comprehensive legislation governing the post office adopted.[37] That statute gave the postmaster general some direction concerning contracts to carry the mail but left many decisions up to him, including the choice of contractors and their specific duties.[38] He was also charged with setting the opening hours of post offices and left to decide what hours would be appropriate.[39]

As these examples show, often Congress did not provide explicit criteria to guide the discretion it conferred. Implicit criteria could be found in the goals of the program. Lighthouses are built to assist navigation, and the postal system is organized to carry the mail. In choosing a site for a lighthouse, the president properly could have looked at other considerations besides the needs of shipping—and probably did so. Having a lighthouse for a neighbor can interfere with sleep, and the ideal lighthouse site from the standpoint of navigation may well not have been the ideal site as far as the neighbors were concerned. In deciding where to put the lighthouse, the president had to engage in the trade-offs that are familiar in policymaking. Under the statute, he did so without any indication from Congress of the factors he was to consider or the weight to be assigned to them.

Current Examples of Executive Discretion in the Conduct of the Government's Operations. This section offers two important current examples of government activities that involve use of the government's own rights and substantial executive discretion. They are offered to illustrate the point that control of the government's rights is a major tool of policy and that policymaking by the executive in administering them is familiar.

Control of the Government's Rights. The United States is a corporate entity, with the ability to both have legal interests and sue and be sued (with its consent) to vindicate those interests. When the government litigates, it does what any private party can do. Discretionary decisions in litigation thus are within executive power.

One especially important example is criminal prosecution. When the attorney general decides to allocate enforcement resources toward one set of offenses and away from others, the decision has practical importance for private conduct. If the government has a policy of prosecuting only clear violations of some statute, some private parties likely will feel safer in taking acts that fall into gray zones under it. Encouraging conduct in the gray zone may be the reason for a prosecutorial policy: High-level executive officials may have concluded that the possibility of vigorous prosecution produces over-deterrence, with lawful and beneficial conduct avoided because of fear of grave consequences.

Prosecution is just one leading example of the broader principle that policy concerning enforcement litigation can have major practical results. Much tax litigation is noncriminal, and the government's litigating policy is of considerable interest to taxpayers. Settlements in litigation can involve billions of dollars in both directions: The government sometimes collects such amounts and sometimes pays them. Consent decrees in cases with the government as defendant often rest on controversial policy choices. Controversies over lawsuits of that kind have given rise to a heightened judicial willingness to reconsider them at the behest of new administrations—that is, new executive administrations.[40]

Executive Policymaking in Distributing the Government's Resources. Even before the federal government's taxing and borrowing capacity were as vast as they are today, Congress disposed of federal assets to further its policy goals. Higher education was an early and leading beneficiary: Many prominent state universities were fostered with federal land grants.[41] Now that the federal government has cash in abundance, it distributes enormous amounts of it in support of activities Congress specifies. Higher education continues to be one of those activities.[42]

As noted above, as of this writing, the federal executive has recently used delegated power about support of education to address an issue of serious controversy. The secretary of education recently issued regulations about educational institutions' proper handling of sexual harassment claims.[43] The secretary relied on a broad statutory delegation. The substantive statutory provision provides that "no person in the United States shall, on the basis of sex, be excluded from participation in, be denied the benefits of, or be subjected to discrimination under any education program or activity receiving Federal financial assistance," with stated exceptions.[44] The statute further provides that agencies giving financial assistance are

> authorized and directed to effectuate the provisions of section 1681 of this title with respect to such program or activity

by issuing rules, regulations, or orders of general applicability
which shall be consistent with achievement of the objectives of
the statute authorizing the financial assistance in connection
with which the action is taken.[45]

The new regulations about sexual harassment deal specifically with
schools' procedures for adjudicating claims of harassment by employees and students.[46] Designing a system of adjudication requires weighing
strong and competing considerations. The most fundamental considerations are also probably the most familiar: The guilty should be sanctioned, and the innocent should not be. Inevitable human error means that
to some extent those goals compete with one another. A system designed
to minimize sanctions on the innocent almost certainly will miss many of
the guilty. That trade-off underlies a central feature of any adjudicatory
system, the burden of persuasion. An especially controversial aspect of the
new regulations concerns that issue.[47] Congress provided no guidance on
that topic other than the general goal of preventing discrimination based
on sex. Title IX provides an intelligible principle, and the Constitution
requires no more in a program that distributes government funds.

Regulation Through Licensing and Permitting

Federal spending is a flash point of current political debate in many ways,
and when executive officials make important policy decisions about
spending, they often raise controversy. Those controversies are usually
distinct from the debate over delegation, however. Spending the government's money is important, and exercising the government's other rights
is important. Executive policymaking about those activities is a legitimate
exercise of executive power as a constitutional matter and is generally
treated as such.

This section will venture into more controversial territory. I argue
that a familiar form of regulation, licensing and permitting, also involves
the executive administering the government's own proprietary-type
rights. For that reason, executive policymaking in licensing systems is
subject to the same constitutional requirements as other exercises of

the government's rights. In licensing as in spending, the Court's current intelligible-principle test is adequate to protect the separate vesting of legislative and executive power.

This section first explains the constitutional logic underlying that conclusion, showing how licensing rests on the government's possession of rights and the dispensation of related benefits to private people. It then turns to history, discussing two early systems of federal regulation that have received much attention in the scholarship on delegation. Both worked through licensing, and both involved substantial discretion by the executive. I show how they fit the structure of public rights. One of them, antebellum regulation of steamboat safety, rested on licenses to use a resource that the Supreme Court at the time understood to be managed by the government on behalf of the public: navigation of interstate waterways.

Executive Discretion in Administering Public Rights. An unproblematic example of executive discretion in administering public rights involves access to public buildings. Even today, some public records exist only as physical documents housed in government facilities. Congress may provide that those documents shall be accessible to interested members of the public at reasonable times, with the specific times to be chosen by an executive official who administers the building. If the building is in Washington, DC, and the official decides to close early during August because few people want to transact business in that city at that time of year, no private rights are impaired by closing at 4:00 p.m. rather than 5:30 p.m. The government may decide about access to its buildings as a private owner may. In general, people are allowed to enter one another's premises only with permission.

Permission has a name well-known in the law of property: a license. Homeowners who allow repair technicians into their homes give a license to enter the premises. Licenses may be conditional and revoked. They are not limited to tangible property. Patent holders license their inventions, and copyright holders license their works. Absent a license, entry on someone else's premises is trespass; absent a license, copying someone else's copyrighted work is infringement. Licensing does not necessarily involve any physical object. It does involve some category of conduct that may not be engaged in without permission.

Licenses thus arise from two of the standard sticks in the bundle of ownership. Owners have a right against some kind of conduct, which correlates with the duty to avoid that conduct.[48] Owners have a power to permit otherwise-forbidden conduct and thereby give a license.[49]

Licensing is a standard form of regulation and has that name because it has that structure: a prohibition on some kind of conduct and terms on which that prohibition is relaxed. Practicing law or medicine is forbidden without a license. During wartime, trading with the enemy is forbidden, except with a license.[50] Broadcasting over the electromagnetic spectrum is forbidden without a license.[51] Another common piece of terminology reflects the same thinking. Some conduct requires a permit from the government and thus the government's permission. Important forms of environmental regulation today work through permit requirements.

When Congress uses its enumerated powers to establish a general prohibition on some kind of conduct and to permit licensed departures from it, it uses legislative power to create two assets of the government that are like those of a private owner: the right against the forbidden conduct and the power to give the license. Exercising discretion with respect to those government assets is within the core of the executive power. As to private people who are affected, giving permission to use a government asset is distributing a benefit. Programs organized around giving that kind of permission are like spending programs.[52]

Broadcasting is a useful example. It is not only regulated through a licensing system but also routinely discussed in terms of ownership of an asset. When Congress debated radio regulation in the first decades of the 20th century, a central question was whether the airwaves should be privately or publicly owned.[53] Courts had begun to apply standard principles about the acquisition of property to broadcasting and may have been in the process of extending principles that govern whales and foxes to the operation of radio stations.[54] Congress cut that process short—and did so quite deliberately. It concluded that the government would own the airwaves.[55]

When it created a licensing system, Congress provided that the license would not create private property.[56] Perhaps some members of Congress had not heard of Albert Michelson, Thomas Morley, Albert Einstein, and the rest and thought that the luminiferous ether was a physical object.[57] Those who were more current and believed there was no ether may also have known enough about intellectual property to realize that ownership can extend beyond physical objects. Ownership is about being able to not only insist that someone else not engage in some kind of conduct but also allow that conduct.[58]

Congress' decision that the public would own the airwaves and broadcast licenses would not be private property put licenses into the category of public benefits, not private rights. The Court's recent cases have recognized the importance of the distinction between public and private rights for separation of powers.[59] In *Oil States Energy Services v. Greene's Energy Group*,[60] the justices agreed that Congress could assign adjudication concerning public rights to a non–Article III tribunal. Those who thought only public rights could be so assigned disagreed as to the proper classification of patents.[61] The majority concluded that a patent is a public right in that the government could continue to modify it and approved a system of administrative adjudication.[62] Justice Gorsuch concluded that patents are private rights and dissented.[63]

The justices in *Oil States* did not delve deeply into the reason public rights are subject to executive adjudication even if private rights are not. Executive adjudication concerning public rights, and the private non-right interests they affect, is permissible because executive power may exercise public rights. Adjudication by the executive is the mirror image of delegation. When they adjudicate, executive officials follow rules prescribed by the legislature, exercising public rights and affecting private interests that are not rights. They do so by applying the law, just as courts decide according to law. In performing that function, executive officials act much as courts do while nevertheless exercising executive power.[64] When they make policy in the administration of public rights, executive officials perform a function similar to that of legislatures. In both situations, the functional similarity is consistent with separation of powers because executive power can be used to administer public rights.[65]

Executive officials may be given discretion, or instructed to administer public rights according to law, only if Congress has power to establish the system of public rights the executive is to administer. Whether Congress may create such a licensing scheme, based on public ownership of some tangible or intangible asset, depends on the reach of its enumerated powers.

To those familiar with the long-standing debate about delegation, the argument I just made may seem like sleight of hand. Can that whole problem be avoided simply by casting regulation in the form of licensing? One response to that question is that this argument is formalistic: It works with the concepts of legislative and executive power, not with the possible reasons for separating them.

A second response, which might better satisfy both formalists and non-formalists, is that a constitutional issue as fundamental as separation of powers is crucial here. The conception of executive power I urge allows substantial executive discretion in the exercise of public rights, which affect private interests in receiving public benefits. Systems of public rights and private benefits must originate in statutes enacted by Congress in the exercise of its enumerated powers.

That principle limits the executive. The executive cannot rely on a claim of so-called inherent executive power, the kind of executive power that needs no statutory support, in this connection. Public rights and private benefits are created by legal rules that create property-type relations. At the federal level, those rules must come from Congress. It then can confer discretion on executive officials, provided it supplies an intelligible principle, but it must act first. Congress can also legislate with respect to property-type rights of the federal government created by nonfederal law. Congress does so when it exercises its power under Article IV concerning federal property. In both situations—when Congress creates the law that creates property-type rights and when the federal government has property-type rights under another body of law—Congress must act before the executive can.

Just as important by way of limitation is that Congress may act only within its enumerated powers, here as elsewhere. Only when it has a power that enables it to create the structure of public rights and benefits to private people can it confer discretion on executive officials in administering public rights. Congress can give the FCC discretion in licensing only if it can set up what amounts to public ownership. To establish public ownership, Congress must have the power to forbid private people from broadcasting without the government's permission. Perhaps Congress has no authority to regulate broadcasting at all. Perhaps any power it does have is not broad enough to justify a complete ban except with government permission. Only if Congress can put the government in the position of an owner can it take advantage of this aspect of executive power: the ability of executive officials to exercise policy discretion in administering public resources and assets pursuant to statute. When Congress does have the power to put the government in the position of an owner and uses that power, executive policymaking in the administration of the government's assets is unsurprising.[66]

Governmental ownership is a substitute for heavy regulation, or perhaps it would be better to say that heavy regulation is a substitute for government ownership. Many of the classic regulated industries in the United States are publicly owned in other countries. Public ownership of railroads has been common from the 19th century. Similarly, some countries responded to the advent of broadcasting by simply nationalizing it, establishing government monopolies in radio and then television.[67]

When Congress fully nationalizes a business, executive officials run it and make specific decisions the way managers of private businesses do. The postal system has been administered that way from its incorporation into the government set up by the Constitution. Had Congress decided to operate a national telegraph system, that system would have been managed by the executive. At the least, it would have been managed by the executive had Congress had the power to establish a telegraph system. Whether the federal postal power is sufficiently open-textured to extend to the dramatically new but functionally similar technology of the electric telegraph is one of the more interesting constitutional questions the Supreme Court never had to face.

Banking provides another illustration of the strong similarity between substantial regulation and outright public ownership. The First and Second Banks of the United States were designed as private entities that performed many functions the government could have performed itself. As fiscal agents of the federal government, they held its deposits and transferred its funds.[68] After the Jacksonians successfully resisted extending the Second Bank's charter, they had to devise a way for the government to do that itself. So close was the connection between the government and the Second Bank that its status as a private entity was debated. According to some critics, it was performing an inherently governmental function, so it was not a private body at all, but a government entity with unconstitutional features.[69]

A third response also looks to purpose and not just form. Regulation through licensing rests on a kind of public ownership. Regulation that takes that form, and is understood to do so, can be consistent with the purpose of separation of powers on which Justice Gorsuch relied in *Gundy*. That purpose is accountability. A standard concern about delegation is that it makes legislators less accountable. They can obscure what they have done. They can deliver benefits to some constituents through decisions of agencies while denouncing those same agencies to other constituents.[70] A standard response to that criticism is that voters can hold legislators accountable for buck-passing, backroom deals, influence peddling, deceit, and similar vices for which American politicians are regularly criticized and perhaps held accountable.

Buck-passing is a second-order problem; politicians can pass the buck in pursuit of any policy goal. A first-order criticism is that a politician supports socialized medicine, a government takeover of health care, public ownership of railroads, or some other program that puts the government into the position of an owner. The choice between public and private is of great importance, and Americans regularly treat it as such. Seeing regulation through licensing as based on public ownership focuses debate on that fundamental issue. It therefore can facilitate, and not retard, debate and accountability. Proponents of radio licensing in the 1920s put their position in terms of public ownership. The airwaves, they said, were a public resource that should not be handed to private people as private property.[71]

Government ownership of a resource, or provision of a service such as mail delivery or health care, is controversial partly because it brings executive discretion with it. Anyone who cared about radio regulation in the 1920s knew that public ownership would mean a substantial role for the executive. The Navy and the Department of Commerce already were making important decisions about the allocation of the spectrum.[72] The close connection between public ownership and executive discretion thus naturally figures in debates about whether some resource should be owned, or some activity managed, by the government.

That connection also appears when the policy question is a move in the opposite direction, from public ownership to privatization. Because public ownership and management mean executive policymaking, suspicion of the executive is a standard argument for privatization. For much of

American history, the postal system was a leading source of patronage.[73] Postmasters general were often the president's close political allies who kept the machine of politics well-oiled.[74] One impetus behind the Postal Reorganization Act of 1970, which was designed to make the Postal Service more like a profit-seeking corporation, was a desire to eliminate patronage and the corruption and inefficiency that come with it.[75] Privatization and semi-privatization entail less executive discretion because public ownership and management entail more.

Perhaps many voters do not understand that statutes regulating private conduct often include broad delegations to the executive. Most almost certainly understand that if the government owns a resource or provides a service, executive officials will manage its activities and make important decisions in doing so. Regulation through licensing, when seen as such, lays bare the fundamental choice between public and private and the executive authority that comes with the choice of public ownership and management. It can promote accountability as to both substance and structure.

History. Justice Gorsuch's opinion in *Gundy* draws heavily on understandings from the time of the Constitution's framing.[76] History is important in American constitutional law, and its importance is not tied exclusively to the claim that the content of the Constitution is found in its original meaning. For the past several decades, the academic debate about delegation has had an important historical component. Central to that component have been two early federal regulatory schemes, one from the 1790s and one from the first half of the 19th century. One is the Indian Commerce Act of 1790, the other the congressional program of steamboat safety regulation adopted in 1838. Both involved substantial grants of discretion to the executive.

This section adds to the debate an important feature of those programs: They operated through licensing and fit the pattern of public rights on which licensing is based. Especially important is that one of those programs, steamboat safety regulation, rested on federal control of a resource that the Supreme Court characterized as public and not private: navigation of interstate waterways. I do not assert that anyone at the time saw a connection between public ownership and executive discretion, but I do assert that steamboat safety licensing worked by controlling access to a resource that was understood to be public and administered by the government.[77]

Indian Commerce Act of 1790. Licensing systems consist of a prohibition on specified conduct and limited permissions to engage in that conduct, permissions often called a license. The First Congress created such a system with respect to the Indian trade, used the word "license" to refer to permissions to engage in the trade, and gave the chief executive broad discretion in granting licenses and deciding on their terms. Trade and intercourse with the Indian tribes without a license were forbidden.[78] Licenses were to be granted to any "proper" persons, who were required to comply with regulations concerning the Indian trade that the president might issue.[79] The statute supplied no criteria regarding those rules and regulations. It also gave the president authority to make orders permitting unlicensed trade with "tribes surrounded in their settlements by the citizens of the United States."[80] Unlicensed traders were subject to forfeiture of their merchandise.[81]

The Indian Commerce Act fit the structure in which executive discretion operates in the exercise of a public right, with effects on a private interest in a government benefit. Congress' general ban on Indian trade created a public right similar to a patent holder's right. The president was given an owner's power to give licenses. The act also shows how licensing has a characteristic policy rationale and can be related to congressional power. General prohibition of the trade, combined with limited permissions, was a reasonable policy that was connected to the purposes of the Indian Commerce Power. Trade with the Indian tribes was a source of friction to the point of warfare, with both the tribes and European powers.[82]

As such, the trade was a candidate for complete prohibition. Substantial benefits for both sides were available, however, so carefully limited permission was also sound policy. Because the traffic so easily could lead to war, prior scrutiny of the American citizens who wanted to engage in it was also justified. Allowing trade by an American who was secretly in the pay of Britain could be disastrous.[83]

To my knowledge, no one at the time rested the grant of complete discretion on the rights-privilege theory. Because it included such a sweeping delegation, the Indian Commerce Act has received attention from scholars, and as far as I know, no one has found a well-thought-out contemporaneous explanation of its constitutionality. It may be that executive discretion on such sensitive matters seemed like such an obviously good idea that no one gave the delegation problem much thought.

Steamboat Safety Regulation. In much of the antebellum period, anyone who boarded a riverboat in this country was gambling with death. Like railroads, steam-powered riverboats were a transformative technology that brought with it vast new possibilities and substantial danger.[84] In response to that danger, Congress in 1838 created the first major federal system of safety regulation.[85] That system rested on the interstate commerce power, which was exercised through licensing of vessels. That licensing system left important implementing choices to be made by executive officials, so it was a model for modern health and safety regulation. Not only did the system work through licensing, but the license requirement rested on control of access to an interest that was seen as a public right: navigation of interstate waterways.

Steamboat boiler regulation worked by adding an additional requirement in an existing licensing system. Congress began to regulate trading vessels in 1789, when it created a program of registration that would identify ships entitled to the benefits of American nationality.[86] A few years later it took an important step in defining those benefits, limiting the coasting trade and fisheries to properly registered and licensed vessels.[87] The requirements for engaging in the trade and fisheries were undemanding, mainly being limited to American ownership. In *Gibbons v. Ogden*,[88] the Supreme Court found another benefit for licensed vessels, one that members of Congress may not have had in mind: exemption from state limitations on interstate navigation.

As steamboat traffic increased dramatically, extensive loss of life from boiler accidents made boiler safety a major policy concern. In the 1838 statute, Congress used the existing licensing requirement as the vehicle for regulation of boiler safety. Compliance with safety standards became one of the requirements for a license.[89] Although the statute was not very rigorous, it did require certification based on an inspection conducted by inspectors appointed by a federal district judge.[90] That form of selection, which is consistent with the appointments clause if so-called cross-branch appointments are generally permissible, strongly suggests that the inspectors were executive officials even though they did not work for the government full-time. The act's requirement that boilers be "sound and fit for use" gave the inspectors substantial latitude in choosing, for example, acceptable levels of risk, as even a well-designed steam engine posed some danger. Substantial executive discretion was thus a feature of the regulatory program.

Whether the 1838 statute accomplished much is doubtful.[91] In response to concerns that steamboats were still unreasonably dangerous, Congress in 1852 adopted a system that more closely resembles today's regulatory programs.[92] The new statute was much more detailed and substantially more demanding than its predecessor was.[93] While it dealt with many particulars, the 1852 act still authorized inspectors to make important choices that bore on regulated parties.[94] The act directed the president to appoint, with the advice and consent of the Senate, nine supervising inspectors, who may have constituted the first federal regulatory board.[95] Local inspectors were subject to the rules and regulations adopted by the supervising inspectors, so the substantial discretion conferred by the statute was in effect exercised by the presidentially appointed supervisors, whose decisions the local inspectors were to implement.[96] Acting through general directives to be implemented in the field, the supervising inspectors had what amounted to the power to adopt regulations with legal force.[97] That force came from the need for a license, so it operated by conditioning access to a public right.

Congress' regulation of steamboat safety included executive discretion in the grant of licenses to engage in interstate navigation by steam. In two leading antebellum cases involving interstate navigation, the Supreme Court regarded private use of interstate waterways as a private benefit that was not a right, a benefit derived from the public's right of navigation that was under Congress' control through the commerce power.

The licensing system into which Congress inserted steamboat safety in 1838 is perhaps best known today from its appearance in *Gibbons*.[98] Licenses figured centrally in that case. The New York legislature had created a steamboat monopoly for the state's waters, banning steam navigation by anyone who did not have a license and granting the exclusive franchise to travel by steam to Livingston and Fulton. They in turn licensed Aaron Ogden, who carried on a passenger trade from New York to New Jersey. Thomas Gibbons held the federal license needed to engage in the coasting trade. He operated a steamboat service between New York and New Jersey that competed with Ogden's. Ogden sought an injunction in New York court that would enforce the state monopoly by forbidding Gibbons from continuing his business. The New York courts granted the injunction, and Gibbons took the case to the Supreme Court of the United States.[99]

The Court concluded that Gibbons' federal license gave him a permission good against New York law and not only against the federal ban on unlicensed navigation. Chief Justice John Marshall described Congress in a way appropriate to a property holder that had granted an interest in an asset. The relevant property right was participation in the coasting trade. The right to engage in interstate navigation, the chief justice explained, predated the Constitution, but Congress had been given control over it through the commerce power.[100] Using that power, Congress had "attache[d] certain privileges and exemptions to the exercise of a right over which its control is absolute."[101] The privilege Congress conferred regarding the right it controlled was to carry on the coasting trade.[102] The Court characterized a license as a permission given by the holder of an interest with respect to that interest.

> The word "license" means permission or authority, and a license to do any particular thing is a permission or authority to do that thing, and if granted by a person having power to grant it, transfers to the grantee the right to do whatever it purports to authorize. It certainly transfers to him all the right which the grantor can transfer, to do what is within the terms of the license.[103]

Congress, in the position of an owner due to its control over commerce, granted a license.[104]

A few decades after *Gibbons*, the Court concluded that the right of interstate navigation was held by the public and controlled on its behalf by Congress, which could allow private people to participate in the public right as the legislature thought best. The Court came to that understanding in its second decision in a case in its original jurisdiction concerning the Wheeling Bridge, which spanned the Ohio River from Wheeling, then in Virginia, to Ohio. The case began when the Commonwealth of Pennsylvania, claiming an economic interest in free navigation of the Ohio, sought an injunction. Pennsylvania argued that the bridge was so low that many steamships' smokestacks could not fit under it, that it was therefore an obstruction to interstate commerce and a nuisance, and that the Court would issue an injunction requiring that the bridge be either raised or removed.[105] The Court agreed that the bridge was a nuisance.[106]

Congress then passed a statute providing that the bridge was a lawful structure and not an obstruction to interstate commerce.[107] The case returned to the Supreme Court in *Pennsylvania v. Wheeling & Belmont Bridge Co.* (*Wheeling Bridge II*).[108] The Court in *Wheeling Bridge II* found that under the statute the bridge was now a lawful structure, so the injunction it had granted should be dissolved.[109] Injunctions governing future conduct should reflect the law, including any changes in the law, so because the bridge had ceased to be an unlawful obstruction, the injunction was no longer appropriate.

Wheeling Bridge II also reached an important conclusion regarding the right of navigation. The Court upheld the act legalizing the Wheeling Bridge against the objection that it interfered with a vested private right of navigation on interstate waterways. The statute did not abrogate any private right, the Court reasoned, because navigation is a public right under the control of the relevant legislature.[110] For interstate rivers such as the Ohio River, which the Wheeling Bridge spanned, the relevant legislature was Congress. On behalf of the public, it could make rules about private access to the public right of navigation. Changes in the use of a public resource affected private interests, but they were not rights. The Court's reasoning is especially instructive as to licensing systems, because it recognized the right of navigation as an intangible. The public did not own the water or the riverbed, but it did have a right to navigate the river.[111]

With the commerce power, Congress created an intangible right in the public to navigate interstate waterways. Congress allowed private people to participate in that public right without creating a private right. The connection between licensing and executive discretion is not discussed in the cases about navigation. All the other building blocks of the theory of regulation through licensing presented here were in place by the 1850s.

Environmental Regulation. Licensing is an important component of regulation today. Earlier in this chapter, I used broadcasting as an example of regulation through public ownership and executive discretion in allowing private people to use the public resource. It is a useful example because of the economic importance of broadcasting and because it has been seen from the beginning as posing a choice between public and private ownership. I also mentioned federal banking regulation. National bank charters, membership in the Federal Reserve System, and coverage by the Federal Deposit Insurance Corporation are all benefits the government bestows on private people who have no right to the benefit absent Congress' decision to provide it. The substantial discretion of the federal banking agencies is often exercised in the provision of public benefits and thus in the administration of the government's resources.

Health and safety regulations are frequently thought to raise a serious delegation problem. A classic exchange about delegation appeared in *Industrial Union Department, AFL-CIO v. American Petroleum Institute*.[112] The case involved regulation of benzene levels in workplaces. The levels of allowable exposure to benzene had been chosen by the secretary of labor pursuant to a statutory delegation. In a concurring opinion, then-Justice William Rehnquist maintained that the statute failed the Court's nondelegation test: It gave the secretary "absolutely no indication where on the continuum of relative safety he should draw his line."[113] According to Justice Rehnquist's reading of the legislative history, Congress had failed to come to any conclusion about a crucial issue: To what extent should the secretary consider cost in setting acceptable levels of exposure to benzene?[114] Instead, it had left the question to the secretary, with no guidance.

Justice Gorsuch in *Gundy* pointed to just such buck-passing as a pathology the nondelegation principle is designed to avoid. When making policy involves hard trade-offs between health and other important considerations, the temptation to pass the buck can be strong. Health and safety regulation, notably environmental regulation, demands such trade-offs. Moreover, the costs of compliance with federal environmental laws is high, so any issue that affects them is of great practical importance.

Regulation through licensing is a prominent part of Congress' two main environmental statutes, the Clean Air Act and the Clean Water Act.[115] Permitting under the Clean Air Act is well-known to scholars of administrative law, because it was the subject of *Chevron U.S.A. v. Natural Resources Defense Council*.[116] The case involved regulations that defined a "major stationary source" of air pollution.[117] Major stationary sources of air pollution were subject to a permitting requirement: They were not allowed to operate without government permission.[118] As *Chevron* shows, much of the content of the permits was determined by regulations, not directly by statute. That part of the Clean Air Act had, and still has today, the structure of the Indian Commerce Act. Congress imposed a general prohibition and authorized the executive to give limited permission to depart from the prohibition by giving permits.[119]

The structure of licensing, in which a category of conduct is generally forbidden and then allowed only with permission, is also clearly on display in the Clean Water Act. Central to that statute is the National Pollutant Discharge Elimination System. That system's premise is a prohibition. "Except as in compliance with" specified sections of the statute, "the discharge of any pollutant by any person shall be unlawful."[120] Those other sections provide for permits issued by state and federal agencies.[121] The EPA has substantial authority to set the requirements of permits and must make many controversial policy choices in doing so.[122]

The permitting systems of those statutes illustrate the importance of licensing to today's body of federal regulatory law. They also show that classifying licensing as public ownership is not just an analogy that may have constitutional implications. It captures the essence of much regulation, including especially environmental regulation.

A fundamental question in environmental policy is whether to choose public ownership of resources. Without some form of ownership, air and moving water are open-access commons for the discharge of pollutants. Those discharges impose negative externalities on other users of the air and water. A standard solution to commons problems is ownership, private or public. The Clean Air Act and the Clean Water Act put the federal government in the position of owner of air and water or of administrator of those resources on behalf of the public. Public ownership of air and water is even closer to the core of ownership than is the public's ownership of the airwaves; air and water are material resources, not abstractions defined by a form of conduct the way the airwaves are. Environmental regulation through permitting is properly understood as government administration of a public asset. Government administration of a public asset brings with it executive discretion.

As suggested above, understanding environmental regulation through permitting can serve the goal of accountability. The choice between public and private is fundamental in pollution control. Moreover, public ownership entails that permission for polluters to use air and water is a benefit given by the government, not a right. The claim that private people have no right to pollute the commons is an important normative claim that goes to the heart of the policy choices involved. And it should be no surprise that a program of public management of a commons may bring with it substantial policymaking by executive officials. Public rights are regularly administered through discretionary choices by executive officials. When a legislature chooses public control, the people know whom to blame or praise.

Much environmental regulation consists of administering a commons on behalf of the public. That feature of environmental regulation has important consequences for policy. It also has important implications for the possible sources of federal power to adopt statutes such as the Clean Air Act and the Clean Water Act. Insofar as Congress is empowered to act for the public with respect to national-level commons such as interstate rivers, it has a source of power that aligns well with basic features of environmental regulation. Congress has claimed a similar power as the basis of its regulation of broadcasting.

This chapter argues that when Congress holds that kind of authority—when it is authorized to act for the public in administering a commons—it may grant substantial policy discretion to executive officials. How best to understand the nature of congressional authority to regulate is thus an issue of fundamental importance. It has implications for the proper formulation of policy questions, the constitutional source of Congress' substantive authority, and the separation-of-powers question of delegation.

Conclusion

Executive officials administer the government. Doing so involves exercising the government's rights, and executive power includes making discretionary policy choices about public rights, when authorized by law. That is a central executive function, not a form of quasi-legislation to be kept in line. When Congress provides for executive implementation of a statute involving public rights and provides an intelligible principle to guide the executive, it has done its job as a legislature. Whether its job as the legislature in a national government of enumerated legislative power encompasses creating a system of public rights is not a question of separation of powers.

Notes

1. *Gundy v. United States*, 139 S. Ct. 2116 (2019).
2. *Gundy*, 139 S. Ct. at 2135 (Gorsuch, J., dissenting).
3. See "Congress' Exclusive Possession of Legislative Power" section in this report.
4. As Ronald Coase pointed out, private bodies can build and operate lighthouses and have done so. R. H. Coase, "The Lighthouse in Economics," *Journal of Law and Economics* 17, no. 2 (October 1974): 357.
5. See "Policymaking by the Executive" section in this report.
6. Whether anything from Congress less than an intelligible principle would satisfy the Constitution is a question I do not undertake to resolve. This chapter thus proposes a safe harbor, a set of sufficient conditions for lawfulness. For programs in which the government acts as proprietor, an intelligible principle from Congress always satisfies the Constitution's structural requirements. I do not say whether an intelligible principle is a necessary condition for constitutionality, nor do I discuss other kinds of government programs, like the criminal statute at issue in *Gundy*. The safe harbor I identify remains safe under the most demanding version of the nondelegation principle that is part of today's debate. According to Professor Phillip Hamburger, executive officials are categorically barred from binding individuals subject to the domestic law of the United States as to their rights. Professor Hamburger's claim about executive power does not look to matters of degree. It does not allow executive officials to fill in details in laws that affect private rights. My claim about executive power is consistent with Professor Hamburger's. When the executive uses the government's own proprietary rights—for example, when it decides whether to enter into a lease of federal mineral lands—the private interests that it affects are not themselves rights as Professor Hamburger defines them. If Congress gives the Bureau of Land Management discretion in giving out mineral leases, no private person has a right to a lease. (A lease, once made, will create private rights.) In older terminology, the private interests that are affected by the government's exercise of its own rights are privileges. Philip Hamburger, *Is Administrative Law Unlawful?* (Chicago: University of Chicago Press, 2014), 3.
7. *Gundy*, 139 S. Ct. at 2133.

8. *Gundy*, 139 S. Ct. at 2136.

9. *Gundy*, 139 S. Ct. at 2136.

10. *Gundy*, 139 S. Ct. at 2137.

11. *Gundy*, 139 S. Ct. at 2137.

12. *Gundy*, 139 S. Ct. at 2137 (quoting David Schoenbrod, "The Delegation Doctrine: Could the Court Give It Substance?," *Michigan Law Review* 83 (1985): 1260).

13. *Gundy*, 139 S. Ct. at 2137.

14. Justice Samuel Alito recently maintained that delegations of government power to private people are unconstitutional per se. *Department of Transportation v. Association of American Railroads*, 135 S. Ct. 1225, 1237 (2015) (Alito, J., concurring). "When it comes to private entities, however, there is not even a fig leaf of constitutional justification [for a grant of authority by Congress]." I think the Court's cases support Justice Alito, although the Court's most recent opinion on the topic is from the 1930s. *Currin v. Wallace*, 306 US 1 (1939). Statutory requirement of consent by regulated parties was not a delegation of Congress' legislative power to private parties and so was not unconstitutional as such a delegation.

15. "Congress, we have held, does not alter the fundamental details of a regulatory scheme in vague terms or ancillary provisions—it does not, one might say, hide elephants in mouseholes." *Whitman v. American Trucking Associations*, 531 US 457, 468 (2001) (Scalia, J.) (citations omitted).

16. The category is usefully called public rights: legal advantages of the government that are of the same kind as those held by private people. Public rights include the government's tangible assets, such as buildings, national parks, and aircraft carriers. They also include its intangible assets, such as its corporate capacity to make contracts and its funds. Although I will not explore the point in any depth, the sovereignty of the United States under international law brings with it the capacity to conduct relations with other sovereigns. It also brings with it the United States' various rights and obligations on the international plane. Public rights can be exercised in ways that affect private interests, just as private rights can be exercised in ways that affect private interests. When one private person decides whether to contract with another, the former's decision affects the latter's interest. Those effects can be negative without being unlawful, because private people may use their own rights as they wish, as long as they respect the rights of others. Similarly, the exercise of public rights can have adverse effects on private interests without violating private rights. When Congress decides to reduce funding for some kind of scientific research, for example, its decision hurts people who benefit from research programs. Deciding not to give a benefit of that kind is generally lawful. In older terminology, the private interest in receiving a benefit is called a privilege, in contrast with a right. The interest in receiving a federal research grant is a privilege and not a right.

17. As noted, while this chapter is focused mainly on domestic government, I think that the same executive power is used in the conduct of foreign relations. In the international sphere, the executive alone acts for the United States as sovereign. When the US permanent representative to the United Nations votes in the Security Council, sometimes binding the United States under international law in the process, the executive is acting. Whether executive officials' ability to act for the United States on

the international plane derives from the power to carry out the law, or from a separate foreign relations power that is included in the executive power even though is not within the core of carrying out the law and administering the government, is a matter of controversy.

18. Professor Thomas Merrill endorses the view that only the legislative power may create law where none existed before. He calls that the exclusive delegation postulate, as opposed to the nondelegation postulate, which he rejects. Thomas W. Merrill, "Rethinking Article I, Section 1: From Nondelegation to Exclusive Delegation," *Columbia Law Review* 104, no. 8 (December 2004): 2098–99, 2101. According to that postulate, "Executive and judicial officers have no inherent authority to act with the force of law, but must trace any such authority to some provision of enacted law." That distinction between legislative power and the other two—one is self-starting, as it were, while the others are not—is basic to the three concepts and any system of government built on them. (If Professor Merrill means to rule out judicial decision according to unwritten law by his reference to enacted law, I would disagree with him. I agree that federal courts have jurisdiction only from enacted law but believe that the American legal system contains binding principles that are not found in any enactment and are not created by courts the way statutes are created by legislatures.)

19. A leading case using that phrase is *J. W. Hampton Jr. & Co. v. United States*, 276 US 394, 409 (1928).

20. One reason I propose the intelligible-principle standard as a safe harbor, a sufficient condition for a valid grant of power, is that I am not entirely sure even that is required. I think it is, and in any event, it is the most the Constitution calls for.

21. *United States v. Grimaud*, 220 US 506 (1911).

22. Act of June 4, 1897, 30 Stat. 10, 35.

23. Act of June 4, 1897, 30 Stat. 10, 35.

24. *Grimaud*, 220 US at 514.

25. *Grimaud*, 220 US at 514. By the time of *Grimaud*, administration of national forest reserves had been transferred from the Department of the Interior to the Department of Agriculture. See Act of Feb. 1, 1905, ch. 288, 33 Stat. 628.

26. *Grimaud*, 220 US at 521.

27. *Grimaud*, 220 US at 521.

28. *Grimaud*, 220 US at 521.

29. Professor Logan Sawyer shows that the United States' theory of *Grimaud* was developed by Department of Agriculture lawyers, working for Forest Service Chief Gifford Pinchot, who argued that Congress had placed the Forest Service in a position similar to that of an agent of a private landowner, with broad power to manage the landowner's property. Logan Sawyer, "Grazing, *Grimaud*, and Gifford Pinchot," *Journal of Law & Politics* 24 (2008): 192–93. As Professor Sawyer explains, their argument turned on concepts that were at that point central to American legal thought: The government was a property owner, and therefore private people's interest in using its property was a privilege and not a right. Executive discretion in exercising the government's own rights was quite familiar in the early 20th century, formative days of the administrative state. When Congress enacted the Hepburn Act in 1906, substantially increasing the authority of the Interstate Commerce Commission (ICC), a hotly debated question

was whether the ICC's new powers were an impermissible delegation of legislative power. Sen. Joseph Foraker of Ohio argued that they were. Foraker responded to the bill's advocates' reliance on "the statutes under which the Postmaster-General and the Secretary of the Interior are invested with authority to decide various questions arising in their respective Departments, according to their judgment and discretion." Those statutes, he replied, "have no application whatever to the question under consideration, for the obvious reason that in all those instances the Government is dealing with its own and has a right to do so on its own terms and conditions." 40 Cong. Rec. 3109 (1906).

30. Act of Aug. 7, 1789, ch. 9, 1 Stat. 53; Act of Aug. 7, 1789, ch. 9, § 2, 1 Stat. 54; and Act of Aug. 7, 1789, ch. 9, § 3, 1 Stat. 54. Section 2 of the statute instructed the president to choose a site for the Chesapeake Bay lighthouse. Section 3 told the secretary, with the president's approval, to enter into contracts "for building a lighthouse near the entrance to Chesapeake Bay, and for rebuilding when necessary, and keeping in good repair, the lighthouses, beacons, buoys, and public piers in the several States, and for furnishing the same with all necessary supplies; and also to agree for the salaries, wages, or hire of the person or persons appointed by the President, for the superintendence and care of the same."

31. Act of Sept. 11, 1789, ch. 13, § 2, 1 Stat. 67, 68.

32. Act of Sept. 15, 1789, ch. 14, § 2, 1 Stat. 68.

33. Act of Mar. 1, 1790, ch. 2, § 1, 1 Stat. 101.

34. Act of Mar. 3, 1791, c. 15, § 58, 1 Stat. 199, 213. The president authorized, up to stated limits, "to make such allowances to the said supervisors, inspectors, and to the deputies and officers by them to be appointed, and employed for their respective services in the execution of this act, to be paid out of the product of the said duties, as he shall deem reasonable and proper."

35. Act of Apr. 25, 1812, ch. 68, § 2, 2 Stat. 716.

36. Act of Sept. 22, 1789, ch. 16, § 1, 1 Stat. 70.

37. Act of Feb. 20, 1792, ch. 7, 1 Stat. 232.

38. The postmaster general "shall provide for carrying the mail of the United States, by stage carriages or horses, as he may judge most expedient." Congress required the postmaster general to publish notice of proposed contracts to carry the mail but did not give him instructions concerning the ultimate choice of contractors. Act of Feb. 20, 1792, ch. 7, § 3, 1 Stat. 234; and Act of Feb. 20, 1792, ch. 7, § 4, 1 Stat. 234.

39. Act of Feb. 20, 1792, ch. 7, § 7, 1 Stat. 234–35.

40. See *Horne v. Flores*, 557 US 433, 449 (2009) (citation omitted). Injunctions in institutional reform cases present special problems because they "bind state and local officials to the policy preferences of their predecessors" and may thereby deprive future officials of their legislative and executive powers.

41. See Morrill Act, Pub. L. No. 37-108, 12 Stat. 503. This provided for distribution to the states of land and land scrip to be sold, with the proceeds used for the endowment, support, and maintenance of colleges whose leading object was to teach areas of learning related to agriculture and the mechanic arts.

42. The foundational statute for current programs of federal assistance to higher education is the Higher Education Act of 1965, 79 Stat. 1219 (Nov. 8, 1965). Grant

authority is codified at Fund for the Improvement of Postsecondary Education, 20 USC § 1138. This gives the secretary of education authority to make grants to institutions of higher education to improve postsecondary educational opportunities.

43. US Department of Education, "Nondiscrimination on the Basis of Sex in Education Programs or Activities Receiving Federal Financial Assistance," *Federal Register* 85, no. 97 (May 19, 2020): 30026, https://www.federalregister.gov/documents/2020/05/19/2020-10512/nondiscrimination-on-the-basis-of-sex-in-education-programs-or-activities-receiving-federal.

44. 20 USC § 1680.

45. 20 USC § 1681.

46. See US Department of Education, "Nondiscrimination on the Basis of Sex in Education Programs or Activities Receiving Federal Financial Assistance," 30030. The regulations establish procedural protections that must be incorporated in recipients' grievance procedures.

47. US Department of Education, "Nondiscrimination on the Basis of Sex in Education Programs or Activities Receiving Federal Financial Assistance," 30053. Evidentiary standard for imposing sanctions in a grievance procedure must be either preponderance of the evidence or clear and convincing evidence.

48. Restatement of Property 1 (1936). The owner generally has right that nonowners not enter on real estate.

49. A license gives "permission to do an act which, without such permission, would amount to a trespass." *Clifford v. O'Neill*, 12 App. Div. 17, 20, 42 N.Y. Supp. 407, 409 (1896).

50. 50 USC § 4303(a). This prohibits trading with the enemy without license from the president.

51. 47 USC § 301. This bans unlicensed broadcasting.

52. Executive discretion in dispensing benefits, including permission to use government assets, is consistent with the most stringent understanding of executive power. When the government decides whom to benefit with resources it manages, the private interests it affects are not private rights in the sense relevant to that understanding of executive power. In Justice Neil Gorsuch's typology in *Gundy*, licensing and permitting are based on regulation of private conduct that do not include any delegation to the executive to fill in the details. The prohibition on which licensing is based is a regulation of private conduct. Congress enacts it. Grants of permission are not regulations of private conduct, but decisions concerning the use of public rights by private people.

53. In 1917 and 1918, Congress considered legislation that would have put control over broadcasting in the Navy's hands. (Radio was especially important for ship-to-shore communication, for which the telegraph was not useful.) The secretary of the Navy testified that such an arrangement would give the Navy Department "'the ownership, the exclusive ownership, of all wireless communication for commercial purposes.'" R. H. Coase, "The Federal Communications Commission," *Journal of Law and Economics* 2 (1959): 3–4 (quoting Secretary of the Navy Josephus Daniels). Secretary Daniels testified that ownership of the airwaves would have to be in the hands of either the government or a single private corporation with a monopoly, because radio interference required sole ownership one way or another.

54. For a description of cases finding property-type protection for broadcasters based on the equivalent of first possession, and opposition to private property rights by proponents of government control through public ownership, see Coase, "The Federal Communications Commission," 30–32.

55. For a description of a Senate resolution declaring use of the airwaves to be the "'inalienable possession'" of the United States, see Coase, "The Federal Communications Commission," 33.

56. Broadcast licensing is based on the distribution of a benefit. In the face of a congressional prohibition on broadcasting, private people have no right to broadcast. Their interest in being given a license is no more a right than is their interest in being allowed on someone else's land. In older terminology, that interest is a privilege, not a right.

57. Secretary Daniels may have contributed to that way of thinking in his testimony. Asked whether sole ownership was required because of interference in the ether, he replied that there is a certain amount of ether, which cannot be divided up. Coase, "The Federal Communications Commission," 3.

58. "All property rights interfere with the ability of people to use resources." Coase, "The Federal Communications Commission," 27.

59. A better formulation would distinguish between private rights and other kinds of private interests, including the interest in receiving a benefit. Public rights do indeed figure in arrangements such as licensing, and they correlate with private benefits that are not rights: The latter is the kind of private interest that is affected by the exercise of a public right. When the focus is on the private person and not the government, the contrast is between two different kinds of private interests, only one of which is a right. The use of "public rights" has become common in cases about administrative adjudication under Article III. See, for example, *Crowell v. Benson*, 285 US 22, 50 (1932). Executive officials may be assigned adjudicatory-type functions in some cases involving public rights, however, so I will use terminology that comes from the public side of the relationship. That will also enable me, as it enables the justices, to avoid referring too often to private privileges as opposed to private rights.

60. *Oil States Energy Services v. Greene's Energy Group*, 138 S. Ct. 1365 (2018).

61. Justice Stephen Breyer took the position that the presence of a public right is a sufficient but not a necessary condition for non–Article III adjudication. *Oil States*, 138 S. Ct. at 1379 (Breyer, J., concurring).

62. *Oil States*, 138 S. Ct. at 1373–76 (Thomas, J.).

63. *Oil States*, 138 S. Ct. at 1380 (Gorsuch, J., dissenting).

64. For an explanation on how executive adjudication concerning public rights and correlative private privileges is an exercise of executive power with respect to public rights, see John Harrison, "Public Rights, Private Privileges, and Article III," *Georgia Law Review* 54, no. 1 (2020): 143.

65. The private interests at stake when public rights are exercised, like the private interest in receiving a broadcast license, are not rights. For that reason, they are consistent with the most restrictive conception of executive power, which Professor Hamburger supports. For an argument for why executive power may not bind subjects as to rights, see Hamburger, *Is Administrative Law Unlawful?*

66. Whether one of Congress' powers can be used to create a system of public rights

does not depend on whether it is specifically designed to do so. Congress does have powers that are oriented toward the creation or exercise of property-type rights. The copyright and patent clause is designed to enable creation of intellectual property, and Article IV gives Congress power to legislate concerning the territory and other property of the United States. Congress established what amounts to federal ownership of the spectrum through a regulation of conduct adopted pursuant to the commerce clause; it put the federal government into the position of an owner with respect to navigation with the same power. Power to regulate conduct, like the commerce power, can be power to create property-type rights, because property rights rest fundamentally on rules about conduct. The property owner's right to exclude correlates with nonowners' duty not to enter. Whether Congress has put the government into the position of an owner does not depend on whether statutes use that terminology. The content of the law matters, not the terms in which it is described.

67. As Coase pointed out, in 1912, one bill was introduced in Congress that provided for government ownership of wireless communications, another that gave regulatory authority to the ICC. Coase, "The Federal Communications Commission," 3.

68. See Aditya Bamzai, "Tenure of Office and the Treasury: The Constitution and Control over National Financial Policy, 1787 to 1867," *George Washington Law Review* 87 (2020): 147. Instead of chartering a private entity to perform the banks' functions, Congress could have created a bank department.

69. For a discussion on President Andrew Jackson's argument that the Second Bank of the United States, a private entity, illicitly exercised power over the currency that only the sovereign held, see Bamzai, "Tenure of Office and the Treasury," 157. Banking is especially noteworthy in this connection because a bank charter is a benefit conferred by the government. The interest in receiving such a charter is not a right; whether to grant one is up to the government. Absent a contractual undertaking to the contrary, the government may freely revoke or modify a corporate charter. Giving the power to revoke or modify to an executive official would present no problem of delegation.

70. *Gundy*, 139 S. Ct. at 2134–35 (Gorsuch, J., dissenting). Delegation can defeat accountability.

71. See Coase, "The Federal Communications Commission," 6. The Senate declared the airwaves to be the inalienable possession of the people. For many Americans in the mid-1920s, private ownership of resources such as the airwaves no doubt evoked corrupt giveaways to robber barons.

72. See Coase, "The Federal Communications Commission," 4–5. He describes major roles played by the Navy Department and the secretary of commerce in controlling broadcasting rights in the late 1920s and early 1930s.

73. Part of the struggle between President Andrew Johnson and the Republicans in Congress during Reconstruction was a contest over patronage, notably patronage through the postal system. Johnson sought to "use his formidable patronage power against his political enemies," including through a "wholesale purge" conducted by Johnson's postmaster general. Eric Foner, *Reconstruction: America's Unfinished Revolution, 1863–1877* (New York: Harper, 1988), 265, 266.

74. A classic example is James A. Farley of New York, who served as postmaster general under President Franklin Roosevelt and was chairman of the Democratic National

Committee and the New York State Democratic Committee. See *New York Times*, "James A. Farley, 88, Dies; Ran Roosevelt Campaigns," June 10, 1976, 77.

75. See US Postal Service, Office of the Inspector General, "Governance of the U.S. Postal Service," November 10, 2016, 4, https://www.uspsoig.gov/sites/default/files/document-library-files/2016/RARC-WP-17-002.pdf. The Postal Reorganization Act of 1970 was designed to ensure that the Postal Service would operate in a "less politicized, more businesslike manner."

76. For a discussion on thinking about legislative power at the time of the framing, see *Gundy*, 139 S. Ct. at 2133–35.

77. The character of those regulatory programs as licensing is a blade that cuts both ways in the debate over delegation. On one hand, it means they are examples of regulation through control of a public right, and not of regulation of purely private conduct. Their character as licensing thus undercuts the claim that delegation of the power to prescribe rules for private conduct was accepted. On the other hand, they did involve significant executive discretion in the administration of the public resource involved. For that reason, they support the claim that discretion in the control of public rights was accepted and that regulation through licensing of public rights could involve executive policymaking.

78. Act of July 22, 1790, ch. 33, § 1, 1 Stat. 137.

79. Act of July 22, 1790, ch. 33, § 1, 1 Stat. 137.

80. Act of July 22, 1790, ch. 33, § 1, 1 Stat. 137.

81. Act of July 22, 1790, ch. 33, § 3, 1 Stat. 137–38.

82. See *Federalist*, no. 24 (Alexander Hamilton). Indian tribes are natural allies of European powers with territory in North America.

83. For a discussion on the dangers of hostilities with the Indian tribes fomented by Spain or Britain, see *Federalist*, no. 25 (Alexander Hamilton).

84. For a description of loss of life from boiler explosion and calls for federal action, including by Presidents Jackson and Martin van Buren, see Jerry L. Mashaw, *Creating the Administrative Constitution: The Lost One Hundred Years of American Administrative Law* (New Haven, CT: Yale University Press, 2012), 188–89. One might say that steamboat traffic exploded in this period.

85. Act of July 7, 1838, ch. 191, 4 Stat. 304.

86. Act of Sept. 1, 1789, ch. 11, 1 Stat. 55.

87. Act of Feb. 18, 1793, ch. 8, 1 Stat. 305.

88. *Gibbons v. Ogden*, 22 US (9 Wheat.) 1, 196 (1824).

89. The statute required that all owners of steamboats and vessels propelled by steam obtain a new license from the federal licensing official for their port of enrollment. Unlicensed vessels were forbidden to "transport any goods, wares, and merchandise, or passengers, in or upon the bays, lakes, rivers or other navigable waters of the United States." Act of July 7, 1838, ch. 191, § 1, 5 Stat. 304; and Act of July 7, 1838, ch. 191, § 2, 5 Stat. 304.

90. The statute called for the district judge for the port of registration to appoint as inspectors persons skilled and competent to make such inspection and not interested in the manufacture of steam technology. The inspectors were to decide whether the vessel's boilers were "sound and fit for use." Act of July 7, 1838, ch. 191, § 1, 5 Stat. 304;

Act of July 7, 1838, ch. 191, § 3, 5 Stat. 304; and Act of July 7, 1838, ch. 191,§ 5, 5 Stat. 305.

91. See Mashaw, *Creating the Administrative Constitution*, 190. Death, injury, and property loss from exploding boilers continued despite the 1838 statute.

92. Act of Aug. 30, 1852, ch. 106, 10 Stat. 61.

93. For example, the new statute was quite specific about the precautions to be taken to keep combustible material from catching fire due to proximity to boilers. Act of Aug. 30, 1852, ch. 106, § 2, 10 Stat. 61–62.

94. The new rules about combustible materials were subject to dispensation by the inspectors, for example. When a vessel was so constructed that the statute's specific requirements could not be complied with "without serious inconvenience or sacrifice," inspectors were authorized to vary from the statute's rules, "if in their judgment it [could] be done with safety." Act of Aug. 30, 1852, ch. 106, § 2, 10 Stat. 62. Identifying serious inconvenience or sacrifice and the demands of safety required the inspectors to make important decisions concerning risk and cost, the kind of decisions that are at the heart of contemporary regulation.

95. Act of Aug. 30, 1852, ch. 106, § 18, 10 Stat. 70.

96. The supervising inspectors were to assemble at least once a year "for joint consultation and the establishment of rules and regulations for their own conduct and that of the several boards of inspectors within the districts." Act of Aug. 30, 1852, ch. 106, § 18, 10 Stat. 70.

97. In giving oversight authority to the supervising inspectors, Congress contemplated that the inspectors would promote uniformity by operating through rules rather than case by case. "They shall, as far as practicable, by their established rules, harmonize differences of opinion as they exist in different boards [of inspection at the local level]." Act of Aug. 30, 1852, ch. 106, § 21, 10 Stat. 71.

98. *Gibbons*, 22 US at 1.

99. *Gibbons*, 22 US at 1–3 (statement of the case).

100. "The Constitution found it an existing right, and gave to Congress the power to regulate it." *Gibbons*, 22 US at 211.

101. *Gibbons*, 22 US at 211–12.

102. The section of the 1793 statute giving licensed vessels the privileges of ships employed in the coasting trade, the Court reasoned, contained "a positive enactment that the vessels it describes shall be entitled to the privileges of ships or vessels employed in the coasting trade. These privileges cannot be separated from the trade and cannot be enjoyed unless the trade may be prosecuted. The grant of the privilege is an idle, empty form, conveying nothing, unless it convey the right to which the privilege is attached and in the exercise of which its whole value consists. To construe these words otherwise than as entitling the ships or vessels described to carry on the coasting trade would be, we think, to disregard the apparent intent of the act." *Gibbons*, 22 US at 212–13.

103. *Gibbons*, 22 US at 213–214.

104. The federal commerce power as described by Chief Justice John Marshall is broad, as is a property owner's. A power that broad could support the kind of general prohibition that underlies licensing, like the prohibitions Congress applied to the Indian trade and the coasting trade. The power "is complete in itself, may be exercised

to its utmost extent, and acknowledges no limitations other than are prescribed in the Constitution." It is, Chief Justice Marshall wrote, "plenary." The chief justice's descriptions likely were chosen to suggest that the power is exclusive of the states, but the legislation before the Court was a licensing requirement based on a prohibition on unlicensed activity. *Gibbons*, 22 US at 196, 197.

105. *Pennsylvania v. Wheeling & Belmont Bridge Co.*, 54 US 518, 557–58 (1851) (*Wheeling Bridge I*).

106. *Wheeling & Belmont Bridge Co.*, 54 US at 578–79.

107. Act of Aug. 31, 1852, ch. 111, §§ 6, 7, 10 Stat. 110, 112.

108. *Pennsylvania v. Wheeling & Belmont Bridge Co.*, 59 US 421 (1855) (*Wheeling Bridge II*).

109. *Wheeling & Belmont Bridge Co.*, 59 US at 430.

110. In *Wheeling Bridge II*, Pennsylvania argued that dissolving the injunction granted in *Wheeling Bridge I* would deprive it of a vested right. The Court rejected that argument, concluding that the right involved was the public's right of navigation. The ability of a private party to sue to enforce a public right, as Pennsylvania had done, did not make the right private. "But, although this right of navigation be a public right common to all, yet, a private party sustaining special damage by the obstruction may, as has been held in this case, maintain an action at law against the party creating it, to recover his damages; or, to prevent irreparable injury, file a bill in chancery for the purpose of removing the obstruction. In both cases, the private right to damages, or to the removal, arises out of the unlawful interference with the enjoyment of the public right, which, as we have seen, is under the regulation of congress." *Wheeling & Belmont Bridge Co.*, 59 US at 431.

111. The point about ownership of the water and riverbed came up in the Court's discussion of similar questions that had arisen in state cases concerning regulation by state legislatures of wholly internal streams. In those waterways, "The public right of navigation is exclusively under the control and regulation of the state legislature," and structures built pursuant to state law or under the sanction of the state legislature were not obstructions of commerce. As the Court explained, waters subject to state regulation, and the riverbeds under them, were themselves private property which the riparian owners could use for their own benefit. But if the riparian owner erected a structure that materially interfered with the public right of navigation, "The obstruction may be removed or abated as a public nuisance." A legislature did not have to own the waters to control a public right to use them. *Wheeling & Belmont Bridge Co.*, 59 US at 432.

112. *Industrial Union Department, AFL-CIO v. American Petroleum Institute*, 448 US 607 (1980).

113. *Industrial Union Department*, 448 US at 675, 676 (Rehnquist, J., concurring in the judgment). Justice William Rehnquist also called the delegation "standardless."

114. *Industrial Union Department*, 448 US at 681. The language ultimately adopted in the statute was a "legislative mirage . . . assuming any form desired by the beholder."

115. Clean Water Act is the name commonly used for the Federal Water Pollution Control Act.

116. *Chevron U.S.A. v. Natural Resources Defense Council*, 467 US 837 (1984).

117. For a description of stationary source regulations, see *Chevron*, 467 US at 840–41.

118. For a description of a permitting program, see *Chevron*, 467 US at 840. Under

the Clean Air Act's system of cooperative federalism, permits generally were issued by states, which had to comply with the Environmental Protection Agency's (EPA) regulations.

119. For a description of requirements for the permit program required by 42 USC § 7502, see 42 USC § 7503.

120. 33 USC § 1311.

121. Providing for National Pollutant Discharge Elimination System permits to be issued by the EPA administrator and the states. See, for example, 33 USC § 1342.

122. See, for example, *City of Taunton v. Environmental Protection Agency*, 895 F.3d 120 (1st Cir. 2018), *cert. denied*, *Gundy*, 139 S. Ct. 1240 (2019). This case upheld the EPA's decision to include limits on nitrogen discharges in permit for the wastewater treatment plant operated by the City of Taunton in Massachusetts.

The Sky Will Not Fall:
Managing the Transition to a Revitalized
Nondelegation Doctrine

SAIKRISHNA BANGALORE PRAKASH

The Constitution grants particular powers to specific institutions to be exercised via certain procedures. These allocations arose from deliberate choices, reflecting judgments about institutional design. Consider the pardon power. The framers vested that power in one person to facilitate its exercise.[1] Conversely, the war power's allocation reflected different concerns. In praise of the Constitution's design, Rufus King and Nathaniel Gorham observed that "as war is not to be desired and always a great calamity, by increasing the Checks [on its exercise], the measure will be difficult."[2] Those checks were bicameralism and presentment.

Readers of the Constitution readily sense that it reflects several design choices. For good reason, there is a commonsense intuition that because the Constitution empowers the House to impeach civil officers, the Congress to make federal laws, and the president to make treaties, no other entities can carry out these tasks. Hence, the Senate cannot impeach, the president cannot make laws, and the House cannot make treaties. There are exceptions to this reasonable inference, where the Constitution grants two institutions the same or similar authority, for our Constitution does hermetically seal the branches. For instance, while Congress may regulate foreign commerce via laws, the president, acting with the Senate, may regulate foreign commerce via treaties. Nonetheless, the general rule of separation (and implied exclusivity) governs more often than not.

There is an adjacent question. Namely, may federal institutions delegate their constitutional authorities to others? A common intuition is that because "We the People of the United States" assigned powers to particular institutions, those agents cannot willy-nilly transfer their powers to others.[3] The Latin maxim *delegata potestas non potest delegari* ("no one to whom power is delegated cannot himself further delegate that power"[4]) captures the principle, as further subdelegating delegated power violates an implicit constitutional rule.[5] The point of entrusting power to others is not merely to ensure the performance of tasks (lawmaking, impeaching, and so forth) but also to have certain people with particular traits carry out those responsibilities according to certain procedures. Judges should not delegate the power to make judicial judgments to law professors, presidents should not assign their pardon power to party functionaries, and Congress should not surrender its legislative powers to agencies, however expert the latter might be.

In "Delegation Really Running Riot," Larry Alexander and I observed that if Congress can delegate legislative powers, it likewise can delegate a host of powers not widely thought delegable.[6] We made two central points. First, every statutory delegation of legislative power to an independent agency not only conveys the lawmaking authority of both chambers of Congress but also negates the executive veto, for presidents cannot veto the rules of such agencies.[7] So, when Congress delegates legislative power to an independent agency, it also delegates away the president's veto authority. Two entities, the House and the Senate, basically nullify an express constitutional authority of a third institution.[8]

Second, nothing about legislative power renders it uniquely delegable.[9] Specifically, if the chambers can delegate the power to legislate by relying on the necessary and proper clause, then nothing prevents the chambers from likewise delegating their impeachment powers, their authority to punish sitting legislators, and their power to propose constitutional amendments.[10] Congress might even delegate power to *make* amendments, thereby delegating its power to propose them and, simultaneously, circumventing the role that states ordinarily play in amending the Constitution. The parallel is obvious. If Congress may nullify or bypass the president's veto power as it delegates legislative authority to others, then it can likewise nullify or bypass the role other institutions play in other processes, including the amendment process.[11]

The narrow claim that the Constitution never authorizes Congress to subdelegate lawmaking authority draws support from the writings of John Locke, debates in Congress, and early opinions of the Supreme Court. Locke said that those vested with the legislative power could not delegate that authority to others.[12] In the Second Congress, several members objected to a bill because they said it unconstitutionally delegated legislative power.[13] And in *Wayman v. Southard*, the entire Court joined Chief Justice John Marshall's opinion that insisted that legislative power was nondelegable.[14]

Some modern scholars have sought to debunk the notion that Congress cannot subdelegate its legislative powers. They argue that the Constitution permits the delegation of legislative power—that is, a conveyance of lawmaking authority, citing various broad delegations at the founding.[15] But such scholars cannot find anyone from the founding or in the early years of the republic openly averring that the Constitution authorized Congress to delegate legislative powers. Moreover, they know that many early congressmen insisted that Congress could never delegate legislative powers to others.[16] At most, these scholars reveal that early Congresses may have been insufficiently vigilant in adhering to a never-contradicted ideal. Centuries later, little has changed. Modern Congresses also violate many constitutional rules.

Other scholars have sought to divert our attention to a different principle. They argue that while Congress *can* delegate its lawmaking powers, legislators *cannot* delegate their right to vote.[17] For instance, senators cannot transfer their right to vote in the Senate. But if the Constitution permits Congress to delegate the far more significant authority to make laws, there is little reason to imagine that it limits the far less meaningful authority to cast votes on laws in Congress.[18] In any event, the implied bar on the delegation of voting authority does not undermine the more vital principle that Congress cannot delegate legislative power.

The problem with the nondelegation principle has always been a matter of implementation, of drawing lines and distinctions. The Constitution lays down many rules and standards, leaving it to the interpreters and implementers in each branch to operationalize these mandates. Legislators and executives must take hold of bare-bones provisions and give them the flesh of interpretation and practice. Subsequently, judges must examine what the other branches have wrought and decide whether these readings and customs contravene the Constitution's rules and standards. In so doing, judges create doctrines (e.g., balancing tests and tiers of scrutiny) that are meant to operationalize, albeit imperfectly, the Constitution's rules and standards.

Regarding the nondelegation principle in particular, no one denies that some discretion inevitably will remain with those who implement Congress' laws in the executive and the judicial branches. Congress will not (and cannot) specify every detail in its laws. Even a legislative command to buy pens and pencils, though narrow, will leave discretion to the executive.[19] The rub is how to distinguish permissible delegations of discretion from impermissible delegations of legislative power. Because the executive and Congress benefit from delegations, each in their own way, they are relatively unconcerned about the issue. For their part, the federal courts have long had difficulty articulating, adhering to, and enforcing this elusive but vital distinction.

That trouble has led to our modern quandary, a profound disconnect between what the courts earnestly say and what they actually do. The federal courts, from John Marshall onward, have declared that Congress cannot delegate legislative powers.[20] They have never renounced this principle. But today, Congress routinely delegates legislative powers. The last time the nondelegation doctrine had any real bite was almost a century ago.[21] Ever since, the courts have looked the other way, never striking down a law as an unconstitutional delegation of legislative power.[22] The nondelegation doctrine looks more like a nondelegation *non*-doctrine, for the courts routinely sanction truly breathtaking delegations of legislative power.[23]

That may change with four Supreme Court justices courageously calling for a course correction, a departure from the lax stance that has long sanctioned broad delegations.[24] These justices are casting about for new distinctions and frameworks. They want to breathe life into the moribund principle but are understandably wary. No justice wants judges to cherry-pick among congressional delegations, striking down only those disliked on policy grounds. And no justice favors chaos in the administrative state.

Although someone must enter this thicket and supply a manageable standard, I will not. Instead, I focus on process—judicial, agency, and congressional. In so doing, I hope to reveal how the three institutions can deftly manage the transition to a revitalized nondelegation doctrine to ensure minimal disruption. The overarching message is that the overdue reformation of the nondelegation doctrine need not be unsettling because our institutions can adroitly craft doctrine and dexterously implement it.

I first focus on the courts and consider the aftermath of a Supreme Court ruling that a federal statute unconstitutionally delegates legislative power. Although some prophesy a calamity, the Court can render these apocalyptic forecasts false. The median justices in any coalition necessary to revive the nondelegation doctrine are unlikely to adopt a severe and constraining test as a means of limiting the delegation of legislative power. Further, the lower federal courts may ameliorate any disruption to the regulatory state. They can employ their considerable discretion to ensure that Congress has ample time to codify challenged rules and, if need be, modify statutes that delegate legislative power.

I then address what agencies might do to preempt constitutional challenges. First, and perhaps most importantly, agencies can unilaterally delay the effective date of their final regulations and internal adjudications, giving Congress time to codify their rules, thereby mooting any potential challenge. Second, agencies can identify statutes that might be suspect under a reformed nondelegation doctrine because they convey too much authority. Third, they can pinpoint the existing agency rules[25] that might need congressional ratification because the underlying statutes are too broad. Finally, agencies can ask Congress to address all these problems.

Next, I consider what Congress and the president can do following a revitalized nondelegation doctrine. As David Mayhew noted decades ago, reelection is the most powerful motivation.[26] If the public desires federal regulation—safe products and clean air, for example—and only Congress can supply it under a revived nondelegation doctrine, then federal legislators will respond appropriately. After all, a failure to satisfy such demands will lead the public to "throw the bums out." Facing these incentives, a "do-nothing Congress" will adapt. Or, more precisely, knowing that a do-nothing Congress may soon be replaced by a more responsive, do-something version, with new lawmakers, incumbents will seek to satisfy the public's regulatory demands.

I also reflect on Congress' broad range of legislative options. Congress can respond, in real time, to ongoing challenges to agency rules. It can ratify or incorporate particular rules and thereby obviate constitutional challenges to them. Further, Congress can ratify the vast corpus of existing agency rules. Congress also may develop processes for ratifying rules annually. Finally, Congress can force agencies to delay the effective dates of new rules, giving Congress time to respond to new agency rules.

All in all, a revitalized nondelegation doctrine will hardly demolish the regulatory state. First, the Supreme Court is unlikely to craft a doctrinal test that renders the modern administrative state wholly unconstitutional. Second, lower courts and government agencies can give Congress time to react to any meaningful nondelegation lawsuits. In other words, they can give Congress time to adopt legislation in response to lawsuits. Lastly, Congress can adopt coping strategies. For these reasons, the courts will not be forced to strike down hundreds of statutes or rules. The regulatory state will continue, albeit under a more robust set of constraints. Congress will make more regulatory choices, as the Constitution demands.

The Courts

The judiciary can both revitalize the nondelegation doctrine and guarantee minimal disruption to the regulatory state. First, the Supreme Court can craft a new doctrine that does not necessitate invalidating hundreds of statutes. It can be minimalist even as it reinforces its nondelegation doctrine. Second, the lower courts can use their discretion to delay adjudicating nondelegation cases. This delay will give Congress time to react, to either codify challenged rules or modify the delegatory statutes.

Minimalism. Justice Stephen Breyer has sounded the alarm. He dreads that a revitalized nondelegation doctrine might jeopardize some 300,000 regulations.[27] His particular apprehension is that because agencies issued these rules pursuant to statutes that often did no more than require that agency regulations serve "the public interest," all these rules may be struck down as unconstitutional exercises of legislative power.[28] In other words, the fear is that if the Court puts some muscle into the doctrine, the lower courts will nullify all these rules.

Justice Breyer's fears are overblown, for the Supreme Court need not immediately imperil 300,000 rules. His is a worse-case scenario that the Court can ensure will never come to pass.

First, the most probable scenario is that while the Court will declare that a specific statute is unconstitutional for particular reasons, it will not articulate a definitive, pellucid test for lower courts to employ. We will know that a particular law is unconstitutional but not whether other statutes are likewise unconstitutional. Of course, Justice Breyer (and perhaps others) will insist that the decision will have catastrophic consequences for other federal laws (and the underlying rules), to which the majority will respond that the Court only decides the narrow case before it and does not rule on the fate of other statutes. We decide one case at a time, the Court will intone. This will serve to underscore the new test's uncertain consequences for other statutes.

Why will the Court pursue a minimalist approach[29] and eschew a stringent, well-defined framework that imperils many statutes? Because the chief justice (and perhaps one or more of his colleagues) will not join an opinion that portends that hundreds of federal laws constitute unconstitutional delegations of legislative power. In a recent oral argument, Justice Brett Kavanaugh referenced the "chaos principle of judging."[30] To Justice Kavanaugh, the principle counsels "that if it's a close call or a tie breaker, that we [the Court] shouldn't facilitate or create chaos."[31] He also observed that "judges are going to worry about chaos."[32] Justice Kavanaugh seems to be signaling that he is unlikely to join opinions that would generate chaos, save where the matter is not "a close call." He also might be indicating that no matter the context, judges invariably worry about issuing opinions that generate chaos. Given that there may be but five votes for a revived nondelegation doctrine, any justice who insists on a narrow nondelegation opinion will prevail on this point. Hence, there will not be a majority opinion that immediately renders hundreds of federal laws unconstitutional.

Second, whatever test the Court generates, each statute will have its own peculiar defenses against nondelegation challenges. Each federal law that allegedly delegates legislative powers will have its own historical context, its unique structure, and its distinct text. Lower courts can cite these factors to constrain a seemingly broad delegation and thus avoid a judicial conclusion that a statute is unconstitutional as a violation of the Court's revived nondelegation doctrine. In other words, lower courts may be able to distinguish the cases and statutes before them from the case in which the Court belatedly breathed some life into the nondelegation doctrine.

Third, the doctrine of constitutional avoidance will lead lower courts to read statutes narrowly to avoid finding them unconstitutional on grounds that they violate the Court's revived nondelegation doctrine. Both Cass Sunstein[33] and John Manning[34] have argued that the Court has done this from time to time, reading seemingly capacious federal laws more narrowly and thus adopting constructions that enable the Court to avoid having to decide the constitutional questions related to nondelegation. The lower courts will continue to do this, as will the Court.

In sum, ominous predictions that the sky will fall in the wake of a revived nondelegation doctrine are dubious. They perhaps reflect a desire to frighten some justices in the middle, to convince them that the consequences of a revived doctrine are too severe to contemplate. But the Court that strikes down a delegation is the same Court that will have the authority to announce a new test. The Court can simultaneously revive the nondelegation doctrine without going so far as erecting a framework that guarantees bedlam. It can announce a test laden with uncertainty and flexibility, more of a loose standard than a strict rule. The lower courts will subsequently parse the Supreme Court's ambiguous opinion and open-textured framework. As new cases slowly come before the Supreme Court, years or decades later, it will amplify and augment some aspects of its test, trim other parts, and potentially add new features. The result will be an evolving framework that cannot be read as bringing down the edifices of the administrative state in one fell swoop. Rather than triggering chaos, the first case striking down a statute on nondelegation grounds will generate trailing questions, thereby sparking a long-overdue conversation about nondelegation.

As a comparison, consider the Supreme Court's modern commerce clause cases. Despite alarm and predictions of a federalism revolution,[35] the three-part test announced in *United States v. Lopez* has not proved to be a steady, much less common, means of invalidating federal statutes on commerce clause grounds. Decades after *Lopez* struck down a law as beyond the reach of the commerce clause, the federal courts are still judiciously wrestling with the limits of Congress' commerce powers.[36] *Lopez*'s bark turned out much worse than its bite. The same would be true for a revived nondelegation doctrine. Paradoxically, prophesizing that the sky will fall will cause the Court to adopt a test that ensures the sky stays firmly in the firmament.

Delay. The courts that implement a revived nondelegation doctrine also can ameliorate its effects. First, using judicial discretion, they can deftly manage the transition from laxity to some firmness and thereby handle surprise and uncertainty. Second, the courts can provide some transition relief to Congress and the agencies in those contexts where they believe it appropriate.

When plaintiffs head to court, they typically desire a speedy resolution of their dispute. But those expectations may be dashed as the courts choose to handle other matters first. Despite a constitutional requirement to exercise their jurisdiction,[37] judges have far-reaching control over how to manage their docket. As the Supreme Court has noted,

> The power to stay proceedings is incidental to the power inherent in every court to control the disposition of the causes on its docket with economy of time and effort for itself, for counsel, and for litigants. How this can best be done calls for the exercise of judgment, which must weigh competing interests and maintain an even balance.[38]

In making these judgments, comparative hardships, matters of judicial economy, and the doctrine of constitutional avoidance must be considered. The power to stay proceedings necessarily means that a litigant "may be required to submit to delay not immoderate in extent and not oppressive in its consequences if the public welfare or convenience will thereby be promoted."[39]

The federal courts have long wielded their considerable discretion over the timing of litigation in at least two ways. They have held off adjudicating the merits, making the plaintiffs wait (an "adjudication delay"). Additionally, they have reached the merits but delayed issuing the judicial mandate, the command to comply with the court's judgment (a "judgment stay").

Consider adjudication delay. In *Brown v. Board of Education*,[40] the Supreme Court found itself divided in late 1952[41] and early 1953, after the oral argument in the case.[42] Rather than issuing a divided opinion, the Court scheduled another round of briefing and another oral argument in late 1953, with the per curiam opinion ultimately issued in May 1954.[43] This delay helped secure a consensus that had previously eluded the Court, with some justices leaving the bench and others coming around to the view that the Constitution forbade school segregation.[44] An almost two-year delay in adjudicating the merits proved extremely useful.

Sometimes the courts use adjudication delays to give Congress a chance to legislate. As discussed more fully later, the Supreme Court's purposeful delay in *Hayburn's Case* in 1792 gave the first branch time to eliminate the claimed constitutional problem, thus mooting the issue.[45] But more recent instances show courts using delay to give Congress time to enact laws. As Amanda Frost notes, *US Nuclear Regulatory Commission v. Sholly*[46] marks a more recent instance in which the Court delayed adjudicating the merits of a statutory claim.[47] After the Nuclear Regulatory Commission (NRC) lost in the court below, it petitioned the Supreme Court for review and simultaneously proposed legislation to Congress that would authorize it to take the very action the plaintiffs challenged.[48] The Court granted certiorari in 1981 "but twice postponed oral argument to give Congress the opportunity to consider the legislation."[49] In January 1983, almost two years later, Congress backed the NRC.[50] After the new legislation, the Supreme Court remanded the case to a lower court, never reaching the statutory question.[51]

District courts have also stayed adjudication to allow legislatures to pass new laws. In *Stinnie v. Holcomb*,[52] a district judge stayed proceedings relating to a constitutional challenge. The 2019 stay gave Virginia the chance to repeal or amend a law that suspends driver's licenses for nonpayment of court costs.[53] At the time of the stay, the legislature had passed a temporary halt to the rule, and it seemed possible that it might repeal the law altogether.[54] Citing *Ashwander v. Tennessee Valley Authority*[55] and the likelihood of legislative action, the court concluded that judicial economy favored staying the proceedings.[56] The stay lasted from late June 2019 until mid-March 2020 (about 8.5 months).[57]

As noted, a judgment stay is the second sort of judicial delay. It arises when a court adjudicates the merits, declaring who won or lost, but stays its judgment or mandate. The *Federal Rules of Appellate Procedure* references a particular type of stay of the mandate—namely, one designed to give parties a chance to secure Supreme Court review. The party petitioning the Court can get a 90-day delay in the effectiveness of the lower court's mandate.[58] If the Court takes the case, the stay of the mandate extends until the Court's final disposition, which can last years.[59]

But sometimes courts stay their mandates, without an express warrant in the *Federal Rules*, to give legislatures time to fix or reform a statute. In other words, courts decide the merits of a case and then stay the obligation of parties (or courts) to comply with the judgment. According to Charles Rhodes, the stays fit within

> traditional remedial discretion to account for public interests [and] . . . are typically afforded by . . . courts when the public interest is served by [allowing] . . . the legislature to address the appropriate remedy in the first instance.[60]

For instance, in *Northern Pipeline Construction Co. v. Marathon Pipe Line Co.*,[61] the Court stayed its mandate for approximately three months, saying that the "limited stay will afford Congress an opportunity to reconstitute the bankruptcy courts or to adopt other valid means of adjudication, without impairing the interim administration of the bankruptcy laws."[62]

Sometimes these stays last longer. In *Moore v. Madigan*, the Seventh Circuit held that a blanket legislative ban on possessing guns in public was unconstitutional.[63] It delayed its mandate

> for 180 days to allow the Illinois legislature to craft a new gun law that will impose reasonable limitations, consistent with the public safety and the Second Amendment as interpreted in this opinion, on the carrying of guns in public.[64]

While the mandate was stayed, the challenged law remained in effect.[65] This delay served to minimize disruption in the existing legal regime.

To be sure, the federal courts do not regularly use either adjudication delays or judgment stays.[66] Moreover, to my knowledge, neither technique has been used in a nondelegation challenge. Nonetheless, both certainly could be. After a reinvigorated nondelegation doctrine, the courts could give Congress ample time to legislate following a delegation lawsuit.

With judicial delay, Congress could moot the challenge via legislative ratification of the offending agency law or by changing the delegatory statute. Codifying agency law makes that law immune from a nondelegation challenge, even as other constitutional challenges would remain viable.[67]

Further, modifying the underlying statute to satisfy the Court's reformed nondelegation doctrine could blunt nondelegation challenges to it. Alternatively, Congress could nullify the challenged agency law, change the delegatory statute to conform to the new nondelegation test, and force the agency to start the regulatory process over.

Concretely, immediately after the Supreme Court's announcement of a revitalized nondelegation doctrine, the lower courts could supply "transition relief." In particular, lower courts could delay adjudicating the merits of nondelegation disputes for, say, 180 days. The precise time is of no moment so long as it is sufficiently lengthy. A prolonged delay, of whatever duration, would give Congress enough time to adopt legislation that would eliminate any potential problems with the challenged agency law and the underlying statute. Because the executive will be a party in almost all delegation challenges, it is well positioned to warn Congress that it ought to act in response to certain lawsuits and take immediate corrective steps.

Alternatively, in the aftermath of a reformed nondelegation doctrine, lower courts might decide the merits of nondelegation claims but then stay their mandates for 180 days only in those cases in which they conclude that some existing law violates principles of nondelegation. A judgment stay might be a better option because the plaintiff would have the satisfaction of knowing that its challenge was partly successful. Moreover, Congress would be told precisely where reforms are needed. In this scenario, the problematic regulations might continue to have force until the 180-day period expired or Congress ratified them into law.

Regarding the second option, I suggest that courts delay the issuance of their mandate for 180 days after appellate review is exhausted. If a district court concludes that a regulation is unconstitutional because it stems from a law delegating legislative power, it ought to stay its mandate until the circuit court review is complete. If a circuit court concludes that a law delegates legislative power, it ought to stay its mandate for 180 days after the Supreme Court denies review. In those rare cases in which the Supreme Court takes up a nondelegation case, it, too, ought to delay its mandate for 180 days to give Congress time to act. This sequential staying of the mandate gives Congress ample time to be informed of the situation and act at any time during the litigation. If federal legislators hope that the Supreme Court will uphold the underlying law but find out that those expectations are dashed, they still have 180 days to react and choose how best to respond.

A year or so after the Supreme Court announces its revitalized nondelegation doctrine, the lower courts will perhaps be more reluctant to grant this sort of transition relief (i.e., to regularly delay cases involving nondelegation challenges). After all, Congress would have had sufficient time to digest the reformed nondelegation doctrine and react to it. Nonetheless, there may be cases in which particular trial courts will suppose that some sort of delay is warranted. The option to implement an adjudication delay or judgment stay would remain in the trial court's hands, wielding that discretion as it judged useful and appropriate.

Would an adjudication delay or a judgment stay meant to benefit Congress be extraordinary or unfair? Not at all. The courts already grant similar succor to the executive branch. In *Clinton v. Jones*,[68] the Supreme Court denied that sitting presidents enjoyed a temporary immunity from civil damages suits. Yet it also spoke of the need for trial courts to respect the president's high office. Citing the trial court's broad scheduling discretion, the Court said:

> Although we have rejected the argument that the potential burdens on the President violate separation-of-powers principles, those burdens are appropriate matters for the District Court to evaluate in its management of the case. The high respect that is owed to the office of the Chief Executive . . . should inform the conduct of the entire proceeding, including the timing and scope of discovery.[69]

What is good for presidents is good for Congress. It too deserves "high respect"—in this case, time to respond to a revamped nondelegation doctrine.

Even though agencies have no constitutional rights, they, too, receive judicial succor. For instance, courts sometimes declare an agency rule to have been promulgated in violation of the Administrative Procedure Act (APA) but do no more than remand to the agency, thereby allowing the agency rule to continue to have force in the interim.[70] If an agency can continue to enforce an *illegal* rule because the courts have an appropriate concern for disruption and respect for the agency, the same concern and respect ought to lead courts to stay judicial proceedings and judgments in a manner that grants Congress the time to react and amend existing federal law.

Thus far, I have discussed how the federal courts might wield their discretion "to control the disposition of the causes on its docket with economy of time and effort for itself"[71] and with due regard for Congress. But if the Supreme Court wished to make the delay mandatory, it could promulgate procedural and appellate rules under the Rules Enabling Act[72] that would require lower courts to delay adjudication or stay judgments in cases involving nondelegation challenges. The Court might wish to do this if it wanted to establish a uniform system of deferral and avoid the possibility that some lower courts might fail to invoke the power to delay.

In sum, should the federal courts move to a regime more faithful to the Constitution, one marked by a more vigorous implementation of the nondelegation principle immanent in the Constitution, they can simultaneously mitigate ensuing disruptions. Federal judges need not be fearful that chaos or confusion would engulf the administrative state because they have ample tools at their disposal to ensure that Congress has sufficient time to react to the new regime and respond to new lawsuits. The courts can dexterously manage the transition to a sounder nondelegation regime and supply needful relief in particular cases.

The Agencies

Following a reformed nondelegation doctrine, federal agencies can engage in a bit of self-help. They can take measures that make it easier for Congress to enact legislation codifying agency law and thereby avert nondelegation challenges.

To see how agencies might prevent such suits, we must first recognize that nondelegation lawsuits arise in concrete situations, only after an agency exercises its delegated lawmaking authority. I am unaware of any nondelegation lawsuit brought before an agency's issuance of a regulation or an agency enforcement action. In part, such lawsuits do not arise because regulated industries typically do not have an intellectual attachment to the nondelegation doctrine. They are wholly uninterested in filing suit to vindicate a constitutional principle, no matter its importance to some scholars.

More importantly, such lawsuits do not arise because no one can march into court and demand adjudication of the unadorned claim that a federal statute violates the nondelegation doctrine. To begin with, any such lawsuit would be unripe because no party can show they will likely be injured by any eventual agency law.[73] In particular, how does any person or entity establish that a delegatory statute harms them in some way when the statute, by itself, *regulates* nothing? Such laws merely authorize the agency to regulate, via rulemaking or adjudication.

Further, no person or entity can demonstrate that an agency is likely to issue a rule (or a principle of law) that harms them. Most agency law, even as it burdens selected parties, simultaneously advantages others. Indeed, even as some companies oppose some regulation, others may favor it, believing it gives them a competitive advantage over rivals. Given this reality, no one can confidently predict whether future agency law will harm or benefit them. It follows that no one can establish that the mere passage of a federal statute that delegates lawmaking authority to agencies concretely harms them.[74] For these reasons, I rather doubt that anyone has a justiciable case immediately after the passage of a new law that delegates legislative power. Litigants will have to wait until the agency promulgates rules or adjudicates the meaning of that vague statute.

Once agencies have finalized their rules or adjudicated cases, however, particular litigants have a far better claim that their ox has been gored. It is in this more familiar context that agencies can engage in a bit of self-help. Specifically, agencies can choose to delay the effective date of their final rules or adjudications, thereby giving Congress time to intervene and sanction agency law.

Typically, statutes grant agencies discretion to make regulations, including when to promulgate them and when they will take effect. The common practice for informal rulemaking is to issue a notice of proposed rulemaking, digest public comments, and then promulgate a final rule.[75] From the publication of the final rule, the APA requires at least a 30-day delay in effectiveness, except where certain exceptions apply.[76] But the APA does not require that all rules subject to its strictures *must* take effect 30 days after publication.[77] In other words, the APA establishes a floor, but not a ceiling, for effective dates. Without rules in their organic laws that command a particular rule for effective dates, agencies can go higher than the APA floor, delaying implementation of their new rules.

Indeed, some statutes impose longer delays on rulemaking. For instance, the Congressional Review Act (CRA) imposes a minimum effective date of 60 days for so-called major rules,[78] a delay meant to give Congress the time to nullify agency rules before they take effect. For direct final and interim final rules (rules meant to be noncontroversial and hence no proposal is necessary), the effective date is sometimes 90 days.[79] Should someone object to a direct final or interim final rule, the agency withdraws the rule and uses the traditional method of proposing the rule, seeking public comment, and ultimately issuing a final rule.[80] The idea is that noncontroversial rules can take immediate effect; if a seemingly uncontentious rule proves otherwise, the agency withdraws the rule and pursues the familiar rulemaking process.

The power to delay can be extremely useful. When agencies sense that there is (or may be) a constitutional difficulty with their delegated authority, they can, nonetheless, proceed to draft agency law. Merely crafting proposed law poses no difficulty. To partially protect themselves from potential nondelegation challenges, however, agencies can choose to delay the effective date of any final rules. Although I would suggest a delay of 180 days or so, the precise period is irrelevant as long as it is sufficiently lengthy. Relatedly, when agencies promulgate their final regulations, they can notify congressional leadership, urging them to adopt legislation to sanction those rules and change problematic statutes that might be seen as delegating legislative authority. The agency might notify the party leadership in both chambers, along with the chairs and ranking members of the committees that have jurisdiction over the agency.

Agencies also can impose delays on their internal adjudications. Agencies can establish practices that stay their adjudication of the merits of a dispute or stay the judgment of an agency tribunal, again for 180 days or so. During such delays, the agency can seek either a reform of the underlying statute or, more narrowly, congressional approval of the agency law that the agency adjudicator has preliminarily sanctioned. Agencies would delay adjudications when they are particularly concerned that the agency law emerging from adjudication might be a product of an unconstitutional delegation of legislative power.

Obviously, delay of the effective date cedes Congress time to consider the agency's law and, if it wishes, to ratify it. Legislative ratification of agency law would wholly preclude a nondelegation challenge, for Congress would have chosen to adopt that law. When Congress endorses agency law, it has done all that the Constitution requires. The nondelegation principle bars the delegation of the power to *make law* and does not bar Congress from taking agency rules and incorporating them into the *United States Code*.[81]

If Congress chooses not to ratify agency law brought to its attention by an agency, representatives and senators would know a court could strike down the underlying statute and nullify any agency law issued thereunder. After all, the agency and its lawyers would have put federal legislators on notice that there may be constitutional difficulties with the delegatory statute. Where Congress has been warned that a delegation is unconstitutional and it does nothing to change the law or, equally important, fails to adopt the agency lawmaking as its own, the courts should feel little compunction about implementing a reformed nondelegation doctrine and, if need be, striking down the statute and voiding agency law.

To be clear, when implementing that doctrine, the courts should pay little heed to congressional inaction. Under any reformed nondelegation doctrine, federal legislators know full well that some agency law will be constitutional because the underlying statutes do not delegate legislative power. Given this background, legislators may have remained passive in the wake of new agency law because they may have supposed that the underlying statute does not run afoul of the revitalized nondelegation doctrine. Hence, congressional inaction should not be read as a signal, strong or weak, that legislators implicitly hope that the courts will nullify agency law.

The president can play a vital role here. Chief executives sometimes issue rules pursuant to congressional delegations, and they may delay the effective dates of their presidential rules. More than that, presidents can regulate the lawmaking of executive (and, perhaps, independent) agencies, commanding them to delay the effective dates of any rule for an extensive period. These commands would be legal, except when particular laws require rule promulgation by a date certain. For example, if a new law requires an agency, say the Environmental Protection Agency, to promulgate new rules 90 days after its enactment, the agency will be unable to delay the new rules for 180 days.

Summing up, an agency that delays the effective date of its various forms of agency law helps ensure that Congress has the time to ratify that law and amend the delegatory statute. When an agency believes congressional sanction of its rules is necessary or prudent, the agency can notify key federal legislators. Should Congress sanction that agency law, via bicameralism and presentment, that law may no longer be challenged on nondelegation ground. Contrariwise, if legislators do nothing, judges should not hesitate to apply a reformed nondelegation doctrine.

Congress and the President

As noted, it likely will take years, if not decades, of courts implementing a revised nondelegation doctrine before we have a fuller sense of which laws are unconstitutional. While uncertainty is often unwelcome, it is advantageous in this context, as the lack of clarity gives our political institutions time to react. Nondelegation cases will slowly wend their way through the district and circuit courts, with lower courts often coming to different conclusions about particular statutes and regulations. As these cases gradually progress, and as judges reach thoughtful conclusions, the political branches will have ample time to respond.

How will these two branches, the Congress and the presidency, react? Will they be paralyzed, as some might imagine? Or will they respond to the challenge, legislating in at least some of those cases in which the courts have struck down (or are likely to strike down) existing statutes? As noted, some predict that the regulatory sky will fall. This dark forecast turns crucially on Congress and the president. If the two branches respond and legislate, the prophesy will prove false. So those who foretell doom must have an unstated premise. They must suppose that the political branches cannot or will not respond, an assumption that betrays a lack of confidence.

In contrast, I (and many others) believe that Congress and the president, like the Constitution itself, can "adapt[] to the various crises of human affairs."[82] These two branches routinely rise to challenges (civil war, world wars, financial crises, economic downturns, and pandemics)— never perfectly, but typically adequately. In the past two economic crises, Congress passed truly sweeping legislation. Similarly, in the aftermath of a reformed nondelegation doctrine, the sky will not fall, and we will not suffer polluted streams, explosive toys, or poisonous medicines. Given the incentives and choices federal legislators will confront, Congress will react and adapt, taking on greater responsibility for the content of federal law. Widespread popular pressure for federal regulation will force no less from our legislators and president.

Different Incentives. Although Winston Churchill never actually said that you can count on the Americans to do the right thing after they have tried everything else,[83] one could say something similar of Congress. It will do the right thing after it has exhausted all other possibilities. In a regime in which legislators find it expedient to delegate the details to agencies and there is no meaningful bar on delegating legislative power, we should not be surprised that Congress regularly conveys legislative power.

For some, it may be rather difficult to imagine that Congress can ever do otherwise. We know that legislators favor the current regime, one in which they pass statutes with broad, popular goals (e.g., "clean the air"), leaving the nettlesome details to agency experts. When agencies generate rules that impose pains and penalties on regulated parties, members of Congress throw up their hands in faux astonishment and say, "Do not blame me. I had nothing to do with this. The agency mishandled its authority, misconstrued the statute, and abused its power."

In this regime of credit claiming and blame deflecting, members have their cake and eat it too. Regulated industries can partly see through this, because they are sophisticated enough to know that members passed the statute delegating authority, requiring the agency to fill in the details. But the blame is at least partly deflected, leaving legislators at liberty to bask in the accolades for "doing something" about clean air, shady securities offerings, and federal election campaigns.

Yet to imagine that Congress cannot or will not change is to misapprehend the incentives facing its members. Legislators will face a different array of choices in a reformed nondelegation regime. The old option—

duck and delegate—will be somewhat off the table. Two options will remain. One possibility is to do nothing, to regulate nothing, for fear of the responsibility for irksome, even awful legislative regulations. In other words, pass no laws regulating mortgages, pollution, or pharmaceuticals. The other option for legislators is to regulate more precisely to ensure responsible lending, clean air, and so forth, fully recognizing that while they will be able to claim some credit, they also will have to shoulder some blame.

I predict that Congress generally will choose legislative regulation and responsibility. Why? In many (but certainly not all) instances, legislators will conclude that it is better than doing nothing. The reason is a profound fear of the public's wrath, an anger that will cause members to lose their reelection bids. Legislators will have to conduct the following thought experiment: Will constituents be more furious with me in a world with no consumer product safety rules than one in which I enact, and must take responsibility for, such rules, both popular and unpopular? The choice is between meeting public demands versus dodging responsibility.

If, as many progressive politicians and scholars suppose (and as I believe), the American public desires some federal regulation of smog, securities, and safety, then the American people will demand that Congress supply the needful regulation. And members of Congress will accept the good (satisfying public expectations) even though it comes with some bad (accepting a measure of responsibility). Put another way, in the wake of a revitalized nondelegation doctrine, Congress will reform its ways if the American public continues to demand regulation and the assumption of responsibility for federal regulation is the only way to meet that popular expectation.

Regulated industries will certainly have a great say in the regulations Congress adopts because they donate and contribute considerable funds to election campaigns, enjoy significant expertise, and expend funds to ensure their voices are heard. Indeed, they already exercise considerable sway over agency rules, for agencies are somewhat responsive to industries.[84] What regulated industries will be unable to insist on is an end to the regulatory state. They will not be able to "purchase" a do-nothing Congress, in which legislators sit on their hands and regulate nothing.

First, incumbents know that reelection votes are paramount. They are far more important than campaign donations from industry. There is a reason candidates eschew donations from pornographers and Klansmen. In recent times, the list of unwelcome donors often includes tobacco companies and the fossil-fuel industry.[85] For many candidates, money from such groups is not worth the adverse publicity.[86]

To be sure, industry donations can help generate votes because their contributions help publicize the incumbent's virtues. But sometimes no amount of money can make a candidate viable. Modern campaigns are littered with candidates who spent far more than rivals and went nowhere. Michael Bloomberg proves the point. He spent more than $900 million running for the Democratic nomination, vastly more than the combined spending of his rivals.[87] Nonetheless, he could not win a meaningful electoral contest.[88] In the same way, campaign donations from industry groups are no substitute for actual votes. And to secure actual votes, candidates must, at some level, cater to the desires of voters over donors.

Second, many citizens favor regulation, and they donate to reelection campaigns. Hence, while a vote to regulate an industry may deter some industry donations, many individuals will choose to donate in part because the legislator favors regulation of tobacco or trade. Some individuals will even donate to incumbents who promise to limit their freedom, out of a belief that everyone in society ought to face constraints on matters such as endangered species and air pollution. The point is that favoring federal regulation will help secure some votes and individual contributions.

Third, on many (if not most) issues, some segment of regulated industry *favors* government regulation. To begin with, certain regulations may advantage a portion of an industry.[89] Sometimes a regulation imposes costs on other firms that some companies are already bearing. For instance, a nationwide regulation may impose costs that some firms already bear under state law. Such firms will favor the national rulemaking, whether it comes from Congress or an agency, precisely because its competitors will now face those costs too.[90] Other times a regulation disproportionately burdens some firms and thus essentially favors the remaining cohort.[91] For example, a regulation that regulates oil drilling may prove more burdensome for some companies given the geology of their current drilling sites. The general point is that some industry segments *favor* government regulation because they benefit from it.

Thus far, I have spoken of Congress and said little about the president and his preferences. Presidents are largely motivated by the same factors as legislators are. They desire reelection, and they want to make history, to garner a measure of fame. Although some presidents stump for deregulation, no president (or candidate) has ever endorsed a pure no-regulation platform. Rather, even de-regulatory presidents often wish to rationalize federal regulations. They seek to purge wasteful regulations and ensure that regulations do not act at cross-purposes, as when one regulation seeks to control some pollutant while another inadvertently encourages its emission.

Hence, I predict that presidents will support some legislative action in the wake of a revived nondelegation doctrine. Presidents do not want to be remembered for making it possible for manufacturers to sell exploding toys or flammable baby blankets. Federal regulation will endure, almost always with the president's signature on congressional bills. As much as libertarians might hope that a reinvigorated nondelegation doctrine will spell the death of federal regulation, Congress will not long gratify such hopes, at least not systematically.

Legislative Responses. I have argued that Congress will flex its somewhat atrophied muscles in response to the Court's revival of the nondelegation doctrine and thereby do its part to prevent disorder. It will assert itself not merely because that is good policy but because the public will demand greater congressional regulation once agency regulation declines. In this section, I offer legislative solutions and suggestions. The first branch has a host of options, from approving regulations and modifying specific statutes to fundamentally revamping its relationship with rulemaking agencies.

Legislating the Status Quo. The first legislative priority consists of responding to lawsuits, both actual and reasonably foreseeable. Private parties are certain to challenge existing regulations, and the underlying delegatory laws, on the grounds that they transgress the Court's revamped nondelegation doctrine. What can Congress do to respond to such suits or, better yet, stave them off? Congress' authority is vast and flexible. While satisfying bicameralism and presentment, Congress has a smorgasbord of policy options, from retail fixes to omnibus packages.

Retail responses. Perhaps the easiest and narrowest congressional action consists of codifying or sanctioning a particular set of rules and, if desired, narrowing the underlying delegatory statute. Although Congress is often seen as plodding, it can act with lightning speed, as its responses to various crises—war, financial, or pandemics—fairly attest. Congress can likewise legislate with alacrity in the wake of litigation challenging agency rules.

Indeed, Congress has long been capable of quickly reacting to litigation. Consider *Hayburn's Case*.[92] In 1792, the attorney general, Edmund Randolph, sought a writ of mandamus from the Supreme Court to compel a lower court to place William Hayburn on the military pension list.[93] The question was whether Congress could force federal judges to decide pension eligibility subject to administrative review by the war secretary.[94] After hearing from Randolph twice in the same day, the second time as a private lawyer, the Supreme Court held the case over until the next term.[95] According to Maeva Marcus and Robert Teir, the Court "clearly hoped that Congress would change the Invalid Pension Law before the Court" had to decide the constitutional question.[96] In 1793, a few months later, Congress gratified that hope,[97] enabling the Court to avoid a possible declaration that the 1792 Pension Act was unconstitutional. Judicial delay avoided what could have been the first instance of the Supreme Court striking down a congressional law as unconstitutional.

There is another, more infamous legislative response to litigation. Following William Marbury's December 1801 demand for a writ of mandamus against James Madison in the Supreme Court, Congress effectively canceled the Supreme Court's 1802 session (a move perhaps designed to intimidate the judiciary) regarding the Marbury petition and any potential challenge to the 1802 repeal of the 1801 Judiciary Act.[98] Congress seemed to deliver a brass-knuckled message.

As Amanda Frost notes, a swift congressional response is also possible in less fraught circumstances.[99] In *US Department of Treasury v. Galioto*, a person brought an equal protection challenge to a federal law banning gun sales to felons and the mentally ill.[100] The supposed constitutional difficulty was that while felons could apply for a waiver from the prohibition, the mentally ill could not.[101] After the Supreme Court heard oral argument, but before it issued a decision, Congress amended the federal law, extending the waiver provision to the mentally ill.[102] Less than two months had passed from the argument. That qualifies as a speedy legislative reaction. Congress knew that the new provision would moot the issue in the Supreme Court.[103]

If Congress can respond to an equal protection challenge, it likewise can react to a nondelegation lawsuit. For example, if someone challenges a civil law enforced by the Department of Justice (DOJ) on the grounds that the law effectively delegates legislative power to either the DOJ or the courts, Congress can, at the behest of the DOJ, respond in real time to narrow the statute.

Likewise, agencies facing a legal challenge to their regulations (or to any agency law that emerges from agency adjudications) can advise key legislators with committee jurisdiction of the nondelegation threat and suggest the advisability (perhaps necessity) of swift congressional action. Sympathetic legislators can then take up and enact legislation to shelter particular agency lawmaking from delegation claims.

As noted earlier, when Congress enacts an agency rule, it does not matter if the rule was originally promulgated pursuant to an unconstitutional delegation.[104] When Congress enacts a rule, either pasting it verbatim into the statutes at large or incorporating it by reference, it has done all that the Constitution requires, in terms of *Congress* exercising the legislative power. That the rule or legal standard originated in an agency, via rulemaking or adjudication, is of no moment, for Congress need not generate the texts it enacts into law via bicameralism and presentment. Again, the nondelegation doctrine regulates the delegation of the power to *make law*, not an agency's ability to *draft proposed law* that Congress thereafter makes law.

Congress also can act in a more targeted fashion. If Congress wishes to shelter particular forms of agency law from nondelegation challenges but leave open other challenges, it can specify as much. For instance, a new congressional law can shield a challenged agency rule from the nondelegation doctrine but simultaneously provide that the rule remains contestable under the APA. Regarding the actual mechanics, Congress could adopt the rule into law retroactively from the date the agency originally promulgated it and impose a condition—namely, that the rule shall have no force if the agency did not comply with the APA in promulgating it.

Essentially, Congress would be declaring that the rule will be unenforceable if the agency previously violated the APA in some way.

Federal legislators already do something similar. Congress sometimes chooses to limit judicial review to certain APA issues, thereby barring judicial consideration of other issues.[105] If it can do this in advance of litigation, it can certainly do something similar in the teeth of ongoing litigation. A new statute that effectively insulates an existing agency law from a nondelegation challenge but allows other APA claims to proceed serves as a partial codification of the agency law, one that defeats the nondelegation claim.

Congress might choose to sanction agency rules partially (rather than wholly) because a narrow legislative approval lowers the total cost of passing legislation. Because parties burdened by the rules can still raise other challenges, they have less incentive to fight the partial sanction. For their part, federal legislators may suppose that a limited sanction of rules, one that eliminates nondelegation challenges, revives the status quo ante that existed before the Supreme Court beefed up the nondelegation doctrine. After all, when legislators enacted the delegations and left them subject to APA review, they likely intended that APA review would be the principal means of invalidation and supposed that the nondelegation doctrine was a dead letter. A partial congressional sanction restores that world because it satisfies the Constitution's nondelegation principle while leaving the APA gauntlet in place.

Furthermore, Congress should consider modifying the relevant delegatory statute to conform it to the Supreme Court's revitalized doctrine. Such a reform might eliminate future nondelegation challenges to future agency lawmaking and thereby eliminate the need to respond to litigation continually. And yet, inaction on this score would not be catastrophic because Congress would have already sanctioned the far more important regulations. A failure to modify the delegatory statute would mean, at most, that future agency regulations *might* be struck down in future litigation. That is hardly a calamity. It is certainly not disruptive. After all, congressional adoption of the agency rules, paired with inaction with the statute, would leave intact the existing constellation of legal rights, responsibilities, and privileges.

A wholesale response. Recall Justice Breyer's fears about thousands of regulations on the precipice of invalidation. Congress can easily avoid any such catastrophe. If it chooses a wholesale response to a new nondelegation doctrine, Congress can enact all (or most) existing agency law. In particular, Congress could pass an Omnibus Adoption Act and thereby safe harbor the entire existing set of federal rules in the *Code of Federal Regulations* (CFR) and whatever rules are in agency adjudications. Congress could also sanction whatever judicial lawmaking arises from judicial construction of federal statutes. This would make nondelegation challenges moot because Congress would have made these regulations wholly statutory.

Needless to say, federal legislators must decide whether they wish to ratify every existing rule found in the CFR and the law that emerges from adjudications. To the extent that Congress excludes some non-congressional laws from any omnibus ratification bill, such agency law would be left vulnerable to the Court's beefed-up nondelegation doctrine. Courts might strike down some such law because the underlying statute granted too much discretion to the agencies or courts. But the federal courts likely would uphold other rules and statutes because, even after applying the Court's more stringent nondelegation test, the lower courts might conclude that the underlying statute is constitutional. As should be obvious, agency law would not be invalid under a nondelegation doctrine merely because Congress elected not to safe harbor them.

As mentioned earlier, Congress could legislatively sanction the existing slate of agency law only partially and condition its validity on a previous question—namely, whether the agency satisfied APA rulemaking requirements, such as the rule that agency action be neither arbitrary nor capricious. Again, by safe harboring most or all rules from nondelegation challenges only, Congress would not be appreciably harming plaintiffs seeking to challenge existing agency rules.

If Congress sought a faster but temporary fix, it could codify rules for six months or a year, giving itself time to react to a revived nondelegation doctrine. Congress sometimes does this with continuing resolutions and appropriations. While legislators and the president are hammering out details over final spending deals, they sometimes agree to a stopgap appropriations measure extending existing spending levels for weeks or months. This guarantees continuous funding to programs and ensures that the negotiators have breathing room to wheel and deal and reach a compromise. Something similar can be done for a legislative codification of existing rules. If legislators want some period of repose, they can enact a law that codifies existing regulations (and agency interpretations) for six months or a year. They can use that space to decide, with the president, which agency regulations to codify long term or permanently or, more likely, which administrative rules to exclude from an eventual final package.

Congress also could borrow from the past, emulating the successes of the various Base Realignment and Closure Commissions. Those commissions proposed the closure of dozens of military bases. These recommendations were sent to Congress, with each chamber voting on the proposed list using a process that barred congressional amendments.[106] Congress could not add to or subtract from the list. Similarly, Congress could create a Regulation Commission and grant it authority to come up with a legislative package of existing agency regulations that would be codified, either temporarily or permanently. The Regulation Commission's package would include some regulations and exclude others, with each chamber committing in advance to vote on the package without amendments. This would enable members of Congress to vote for a package of rules and escape some measure of censure for its contents. If this process worked to close military bases, which are far more important to legislators than the nondelegation doctrine is, it can work for regulations as well. In drawing up the package, commissioners would undoubtedly take the president's preferences into account and hence could be confident that the president would sign any regulatory package that the commission would generate.

Legislating for the Future. Thus far, the focus has been on the existing corpus of agency law and how best to legislatively adopt it. Now consider future agency law. Agencies will continue to engage in rulemaking because, again, the courts will not decree that every existing agency statute runs afoul of the Court's revitalized nondelegation doctrine. Congress could adopt strategies to deal with these new agency rules, procedures that will help insulate those new rules from the effects of the Supreme Court's new nondelegation doctrine.

Although the CRA makes it easier for Congress to overturn agency rules, the process still requires a heavy lift. The CRA imposes a 60-day delay on the effective date for "major rules."[107] During that period, both chambers must pass a disapproval resolution, albeit under rules that somewhat privilege floor consideration.[108] Any disapproval resolution is subject to a presidential veto.[109] Until recently, the possibility of congressional rejection proved something of a mirage. Before 2017, Congress had rejected only one rule.[110] In 2017, however, a Republican Congress used it many times to reject rules promulgated in the Obama administration's twilight.[111]

To soften the blow of a revived nondelegation doctrine, Congress should consider a Congressional Adoption Act. In particular, Congress can create a biannual regulation process, whereby twice a year Congress can approve all new agency rules. This would be akin to the annual appropriations process. That process has largely broken down from a practice of passing 13 separate appropriation bills to a now routine practice of using one or more continuing resolutions to appropriate funds.[112] Rather than take up regulations by category, as the appropriations process is supposed to do, a biannual omnibus ratification bill that sanctions most, if not all, new agency regulations would be more efficient.[113]

To give time for Congress to consider whether to sanction regulations, Congress can provide that an agency's final regulations will not take effect for 180 days from publication in the *Federal Register*. This would, in effect, modify grants of rulemaking authority across every agency. This delay in effective date would give Congress ample time to include the regulations in its omnibus ratification bills. If the regulation is important and time sensitive, Congress could ratify it in the next omnibus bill, one that might be taken up in a month or a few weeks. If the agency rules are relatively unimportant, they can wait until the later omnibus ratification bill.

Further, Congress could privilege the biannual ratification bills in each chamber, meaning the chambers cannot amend them. Congress also could limit debate, thereby precluding filibusters. Congress has done something similar regarding bills implementing trade agreements, using rules spelled out in statutes.[114] The reform would ensure that legislators have ample time to consider which agency rules Congress ought to ratify and further ensure that ratification bills face an up or down vote rather than the prospect of interminable amendments, poison pills, and delays.

This proposal will have its skeptics. Doubters may cite the CRA's relative nonuse and suppose that this proposal will suffer the same fate. But a revitalized nondelegation doctrine would heighten the importance of such a process. New agency rules sanctioned by Congress via lawmaking will not be subject to successful nondelegation challenges. Accordingly, every agency fearful that its new rules might be struck down, because they are a product of unconstitutional delegatory statutes, will plead for Congress to codify agency rules continually. Further, those members of Congress favoring agency rules have an incentive to act for the reasons mentioned earlier. If the public demands new regulations, they will demand that Congress act to legislate and therefore safeguard those regulations.

We should expect that Congress will adopt new agency rules when those rules are relatively uncontroversial. When legislators predictably exclude some new agency regulations from their omnibus bill, presumably because they are particularly divisive or unpopular, those rules will not automatically be invalid or unconstitutional. Rather, such uncodified agency rules would be subject to challenge under the Court's more stringent nondelegation test. Some would survive such a challenge, and others would be struck down. That is as it should be.

A Different Regulatory Sky. While the sky will not fall, it will have a different cast. To begin with, any new regulations that emerge from legislative processes will not be the ones that would have materialized from the agencies had the Supreme Court never reformed the nondelegation doctrine. None of this should be surprising. Regulations that emanate from the Federal Communications Commission reflect the commissioners' preferences, influences, constraints, and incentives. Communications regulations that would emerge from bicameralism and presentment would reflect the preferences, influences, constraints, and incentives of senators, representatives, and the president. New congressional regulations will never mimic the content of the agency regulations that would have been adopted without a reformed nondelegation doctrine.

Likewise, if Congress chooses to safeguard existing regulations, it might decide not to protect some portions of those rules. Congress is unlikely to codify the most controversial agency rules; hence, such rules would be subject to the Court's novel nondelegation test. Although this will generate dismay in some quarters, there is nothing amiss about Congress choosing to exclude some regulations from any protective shield that it chooses to erect following a revived nondelegation doctrine. In any event, unshielded regulations would not be unconstitutional merely because Congress chose not to safeguard them.

Another difference relates to the mutability of regulations. Because agency regulations can be made sometimes by one person, and oftentimes with no more than three individuals (as in the case of a five-person commission), those rules are relatively easy to modify or rescind.[115] In contrast, congressional regulation may be more durable. Generally, it is hard to change a congressional law. But Congress could adopt a familiar tactic to combat this tendency: the sunset clause. Congress could declare that all (or some portion) of its regulations will sunset after five years or so. As that period draws to a close, Congress could decide whether to renew its regulations, modify them, or allow them to expire.[116]

Perhaps the best example of sunsets comes from the Patriot Act.[117] Congress passed the act in 2001 and reauthorized it with significant changes several times.[118] Each time the reauthorization was necessary because portions of the act were set to elapse or had expired. By imposing an expiration date, members of Congress could ensure some flexibility in the contours of the Patriot Act. Congress could more easily respond to public pressure precisely because new action was required before the Patriot Act would continue as law.

Congress could do much the same with its regulations. When legislators suppose that certain congressional regulations should be reconsidered periodically, they can attach a sunset of five, seven, or 10 years to those regulations. Such an expiration would force Congress to occasionally revisit whether regulatory burdens ought to continue and, if so, in what form.

Some Disruption Is Inevitable. As noted earlier, those favoring the current regime often tend to focus on (if not exaggerate) the consequences of any departures from it. Supreme Court justices routinely do this to deter those seeking reform in doctrine. Legislators and presidents do the same when they oppose change. All these claims carry some weight because *any* reform to an existing legal framework will tend to disrupt. Again, because of their controversial nature, some agency regulations struck by the courts will never become law via bicameralism and presentment.

But we must never forget that ours is a system grounded in the rule of law. In 2020, the Supreme Court overturned an almost 50-year-old precedent that permitted nonunanimous jury verdicts in state trials. In *Ramos v. Louisiana*, the Court held that individuals could not be punished via nonunanimous verdicts.[119] In dissent, Justice Samuel Alito spoke at great length about the consequences of this holding, claiming that two states might now face a "tsunami of litigation," as hundreds of criminal defendants would inevitably challenge their convictions on direct appeal.[120] Even worse, those long incarcerated would be able to belatedly challenge their long-standing convictions on collateral review, and many of them might secure judicial relief—namely, release or a new trial.[121] Despite all this, the Court nonetheless decided that the almost half-century precedent needed to be abandoned.[122]

What is true for jury verdicts is true for legislative power. The Constitution cannot be violated merely because some find it advantageous. *Immigration and Naturalization Service v. Chadha* is apt.[123] In that case, the Court considered whether legislative vetoes (one- or two-house vetoes of administrative action) were constitutional.[124] At the time, hundreds of statutes and decades of practice were erected on the belief that legislative vetoes were constitutional.[125] Despite the credible claim that such vetoes were advantageous, the Court denied that it mattered: That

> a given law or procedure is efficient, convenient, and useful in facilitating functions of government, standing alone, will not save it if it is contrary to the Constitution. Convenience and efficiency are not the primary objectives—or the hallmarks—of democratic government.[126]

Despite the assertion that legislative vetoes were ubiquitous (by 1977 almost 300 were in congressional laws), the Court said, "Our inquiry is sharpened, rather than blunted, by the fact that congressional veto provisions are appearing with increasing frequency in statutes which delegate authority to executive and independent agencies."[127]

Similarly, that agency lawmaking is "efficient, convenient, and useful" cannot save the unconstitutional practice. The Court's concern about congressional delegation should be "sharpened, rather than blunted" by the sheer number of unbridled delegations of lawmaking authority. The ability of dozens of agencies to make law outside of bicameralism and presentment is an affront to Article I, and the perceived utility or ubiquity of agency lawmaking cannot matter. One final quote from *Chadha* is quite instructive, even illuminating. The Constitution's

> choices . . . often seem clumsy, inefficient, even unworkable, but those hard choices were consciously made by men who had lived under a form of government that permitted arbitrary governmental acts to go unchecked. There is no support in the Constitution or decisions of this Court for the proposition that the cumbersomeness and delays often encountered in complying with explicit constitutional standards may be avoided, either by the Congress or by the President. With all the obvious flaws of delay, untidiness, and potential for abuse, we have not yet found a better way to preserve freedom than by making the exercise of power subject to the carefully crafted restraints spelled out in the Constitution.[128] (Citation omitted.)

Because the Constitution never authorizes the chambers to subdelegate their legislative functions, much less negate the presidential veto, the nation will have to endure whatever "delay, untidiness, and potential for abuse" that inescapably arises from ordinary lawmaking. Bicameralism and presentment are not bugs to be ignored or circumvented, as pro-delegation proponents sometimes suggest. They are foundational features of our Constitution.

But we need not be fundamentalists. We need not declare *fiat constitutio, ruat coelum*—let the Constitution be vindicated, even if the heavens fall. We need not endorse such a maxim because the heavens will not tumble. As noted, the Supreme Court will not adopt an earth-shattering nondelegation test, one that renders much of the *US Code* and *Statutes at Large* null and void. Justice Kavanaugh and others will invoke the chaos principle and craft a test that is relatively opaque and more of an invitation for continued judicial dialogue.[129] To be sure, the heavens may shake here and there because the constellation of federal regulations will assume a different shape as cases proceed in the lower court and as statutes are slowly declared unconstitutional. And there will be those on earth who moan and faint at the prospect of enforcing the new doctrine. But the sky will not tumble.

Our Sloughing and Slippery Legislators. Legislators can adopt some or all these mechanisms and still slough off a great measure of responsibility. A more potent nondelegation doctrine will not end the evasion of accountability. There is a reason the public consistently has a low opinion of Congress as an institution even as most individuals hold their particular representative or senator in higher esteem.[130] As they do now, individual legislators can continue to finger a byzantine legislative process, a benighted and stubborn congressional leadership, a biased media, and their colleagues. Many voters will be unable to see through such obfuscation because the inner workings of Congress often seem no more decipherable than the Rosetta stone would seem to kindergarteners. Public confusion and misperception help lower the costs of codifying agency law, thereby making that option more palatable to members of Congress. No matter what Congress codifies, legislators will continue to claim credit for clean air, safe workplaces, and sound banks even as they attempt to shun at least some responsibility for job-killing regulations and outrageous restraints on the use of private property.

Conclusion

The prospect of a reinvigorated nondelegation doctrine frightens some, particularly those who favor the administrative state and its regular enactment of rules-cum-laws. If you favor more federal regulation, you may fear there will be far less once the Supreme Court identifies and applies a more potent nondelegation principle.

But the alarm is unwarranted. There are several ways for the three actors—the courts, the agencies, and Congress—to mitigate the supposedly destructive fallout of a reformed nondelegation doctrine. To begin with, the courts can stay their hand, delaying adjudication and staying mandates in a bid to give Congress time to respond to nondelegation challenges. The courts owe this deference to a coordinate branch, particularly in the aftermath of a revitalized nondelegation doctrine.[131] Further, the agencies can take modest steps to protect themselves. In a slight shift in practice, agencies can impose a greater delay in the effective date of new agency law, thereby giving Congress ample time to ratify it. Finally, Congress can respond to litigation, ratify the existing corpus of agency law, and conduct a biannual review of new regulations.

I will not falsely claim that all will be just as it is now. Sometimes, Congress will not act to protect dubious regulations or modify broad statutes. Sometimes, agencies will not give Congress sufficient warning about dubious rules and statutes. And occasionally, courts will strike down laws and void agency rules. But the existence of a constitutional doctrine fairly presupposes that courts will sometimes deploy it to invalidate some official acts. The problem with the existing nondelegation doctrine is that, though the Constitution contains a nondelegation principle, the courts have erected a mere Potemkin doctrine, creating a facade of constraint. That is why the courts must reform and revitalize the nondelegation doctrine.

Although the Constitution is not so elastic as to permit Congress to delegate legislative powers, it is supple enough to allow Congress to harness agency expertise and time and subsequently take formal responsibility for our nation's laws. We need not fear that an invigorated nondelegation doctrine will lead to a catastrophe of polluted streams, unsafe medicines, or the unregulated sale of bogus investments. Under the original Constitution, we can have regulation and responsibility.

Perhaps Chief Justice John Roberts put it best, when he said in another context: "One can have a government that functions without being ruled by functionaries, and a government that benefits from expertise without being ruled by experts."[132] It is time for another jurisprudential adjustment, one that helps ensure that Americans are not "ruled by experts." It is time for the experts and functionaries to supply their expertise and then recede into the background, thereby allowing our elected leaders to decide what rules Americans will have to obey and abide. "Our Constitution was adopted to enable the people to govern themselves"[133] through a familiar process of bicameralism and presentment. It is high time we return to that first principle.

Acknowledgments

Thanks to Francis Adams, Barrett Anderson, Eric Dement, John Harrison, Matthew Hoke, Peter Wallison, and John Yoo for comments. Gratitude to Anderson, Dement, Hoke, and Refdesk for research assistance.

Notes

1. For a discussion on why vesting pardon authority in one person facilitates its exercise and why a legislative check would prove troublesome, see *Federalist*, no. 74 (Alexander Hamilton).

2. Rufus King and Nathaniel Gorham, "Response to Elbridge Gerry's Objections," in *The Documentary History of the Ratification of the Constitution*, ed. John P. Kaminski and Gaspare J. Saladino (Madison, WI: Wisconsin Historical Society Press, 1997): 4:186, 190.

3. *Gundy v. United States*, 139 S. Ct. 2116, 2133 (2019) (Gorsuch, J., dissenting).

4. Law Times Journal, "Delgata Potestas Non Potest Delegari," October 31, 2019, https://lawtimesjournal.in/delegata-potestas-non-potest-delegari/.

5. *J. W. Hampton Jr. & Co. v. United States*, 276 US 394, 405–6 (1928). "The well known maxim '*delegata potestas non potest delegari*' . . . is well understood, and has had wider application in the construction of our federal and state constitutions than it has in private law."

6. Larry Alexander and Saikrishna Prakash, "Delegation Really Running Riot," *Virginia Law Review* 93, no. 4 (2007): 1038–39.

7. Alexander and Prakash, "Delegation Really Running Riot," 1051–54.

8. Alexander and Prakash, "Delegation Really Running Riot," 1052. Remember that if Congress can delegate lawmaking authority, it can do so over the president's veto. Hence, Congress can pass a bill delegating rulemaking authority to an independent agency—say, the Securities and Exchange Commission (SEC)—the president can veto that bill, and Congress can then override the veto and make the bill law. Hence, Congress can override a presidential veto and, in so doing, enact a law that will henceforth nullify the president's veto with respect to SEC lawmaking.

9. Alexander and Prakash, "Delegation Really Running Riot," 1054.

10. Alexander and Prakash, "Delegation Really Running Riot," 1054–55.

11. Alexander and Prakash, "Delegation Really Running Riot," 1059.

12. John Locke, "Second Treatise of Government § 141," in *Two Treatises of Government*, ed. Peter Laslett (New York: New American Library, 1963): 408–9. "The legislative cannot transfer the power of making laws to any other hands: for it being but a delegated power from the people, they who have it cannot pass it over to others."

13. Ilan Wurman, "Nondelegation at the Founding," *Yale Law Journal* 130, no. 6 (April 2021): 1506–8.

14. *Wayman v. Southard*, 23 US (10 Wheat.) 1, 42–43 (1825).

15. Julian D. Mortenson and Nicholas Bagley, "Delegation at the Founding," *Columbia Law Review* 121, no. 2 (March 2021).

16. See, for example, Rep. Thomas Hartley's statements during the Second Congress when arguing against a proposed delegation to the president to determine the routes for post office roads. "[Congress] represent[s] the people, we are constitutionally vested with the power of determining upon the establishment of post roads; and, as I understand at present, ought not to delegate the power to any other person." 3 Annals of Cong. 231 (December 1791) (statement of Hartley).

17. Eric Posner and Adrian Vermeule, "Interring the Nondelegation Doctrine," *University of Chicago Law Review* 69, no. 4 (2002): 1756. "The individual [Congress] members may no more transfer their powers to the whole Congress than they may transfer them to anyone else."

18. Larry Alexander and Saikrishna Prakash, "Reports of the Nondelegation Doctrine's Death Are Greatly Exaggerated," *University of Chicago Law Review* 70, no. 4 (2003): 1323–27.

19. Saikrishna Prakash, "Deviant Executive Lawmaking," *George Washington Law Review* 67, no. 1 (1999): 13–15.

20. See, for example, *Wayman*, 23 US at 42–43.

21. See *Panama Refining Company v. Ryan*, 293 US 388, 414–15, 433 (1935). This case declared unconstitutional a provision in the National Industrial Recovery Act permitting the president to make it illegal to ship oil that exceeded state law quotas. *A. L. A. Schechter Poultry Corp. v. United States*, 295 US 495, 521–22 (1935). This case declared unconstitutional a provision in the National Industrial Recovery Act that permitted the president "to approve 'codes of fair competition'" for slaughterhouses.

22. *Gundy*, 139 S. Ct. at 2138 (Gorsuch, J., dissenting). Under the current doctrine, Congress may delegate legislative power (what the court calls "discretion") to agencies as long as it provides "intelligible principles" to guide them. *Whitman v. American Trucking Associations*, 531 US 457, 472 (2001).

23. For recent discussions on how to better operationalize the nondelegation doctrine, see *Gundy*, 139 S. Ct. at 2136–37 (Gorsuch, J., dissenting). The justice proposed a three-part test for applying the nondelegation doctrine. For a proposal linking the nondelegation doctrine to the right-privilege distinction, see Aditya Bamzai, "Delegation and Interpretive Discretion: Gundy, Kisor, and the Formation and Future of Administrative Law," *Harvard Law Review* 133 (2019): 177–82.

24. In *Gundy*, four justices called for the Supreme Court to reconsider its current nondelegation doctrine. Justice Samuel Alito's concurrence in the case stated that he would be "willing to reconsider the [nondelegation] approach we have taken for the past 84 years." Justice Neil Gorsuch's dissent, joined by Justices John Roberts and Clarence Thomas, argued for a stricter nondelegation test that prohibited delegating the power to make generally applicable rules governing private persons except in three instances: (1) statutes that make the important policy decisions but permit other branches to "fill up the details," (2) statutes that prescribe a rule "may make the application of that rule depend on executive fact-finding," and (3) Congress may grant the other branches certain nonlegislative responsibilities for powers that the Constitution already vests in that branch. *Gundy*, 139 S. Ct. at 2131–37.

25. This chapter principally discusses how Congress ought to respond to agency rulemakings, both formal and informal. Yet nondelegation problems also can arise from adjudications. Suppose a federal statute "bars the waste of resources" and authorizes an agency, say the Resource Management Agency, to enforce that prohibition. If agency personnel or federal courts decide the meaning of this vague standard in the course of adjudications, we arguably have lawmaking occurring via adjudication. As in the agency rulemaking context, Congress will have to play some role in ratifying or sanctioning agency law generated via adjudication.

26. David Mayhew, *Congress: The Electoral Connection* (New Haven, CT: Yale University Press, 1974): 28–29.

27. Transcript of Oral Argument at 7–9, *Gundy v. United States*, 139 S. Ct. (2018) (No. 17-6086), https://www.supremecourt.gov/oral_arguments/argument_transcripts/2018/17-6086_9oli.pdf.

28. Transcript of Oral Argument at 7–9, *Gundy*, 139 S. Ct. (No. 17-6086).

29. Cass Sunstein, *One Case at a Time: Judicial Minimalism on the Supreme Court* (Cambridge, MA: Harvard University Press, 1999).

30. Transcript of Oral Argument at 33, *Chiafalo v. Washington*, 140 S. Ct. 2316 (2020) (No. 19-465), https://www.supremecourt.gov/oral_arguments/argument_transcripts/2019/19-465_l537.pdf.

31. Transcript of Oral Argument at 33, *Chiafalo*, 140 S. Ct. at 2316 (No. 19-465).

32. Transcript of Oral Argument at 33, *Chiafalo*, 140 S. Ct. at 2316 (No. 19-465).

33. Cass Sunstein, "The American Nondelegation Doctrine," *George Washington Law Review* 86, no. 5 (2018): 1192–96.

34. John Manning, "The Nondelegation Doctrine as a Canon of Avoidance," *Supreme Court Review* 2000 (2000): 242–46.

35. *United States v. Lopez*, 514 US 549, 630–31 (Breyer, J., dissenting). This dissent argued that the majority's holding would lead to legal uncertainty and the potential unconstitutionality of hundreds of statutes with similar language. Erwin Chemerinsky, "The Federalism Revolution," *New Mexico Law Review* 31, no. 1 (2001): 7; Jesse H. Choper, "Did Last Term Reveal 'a Revolutionary States' Rights Movement Within the Supreme Court'?," *Case Western Reserve Law Review* 46, no. 3 (1996): 663; and Steven G. Calabresi, "'A Government of Limited and Enumerated Powers': In Defense of *United States v. Lopez*," *Michigan Law Review* 94, no. 3 (1995): 752.

36. See, for example, *Gonzales v. Raich*, 545 US 1, 17 (2005). This case held that purely intrastate activity of cultivating cannabis fell within the scope of Congress' commerce power because it was part of a "class of activities" that substantially affected interstate commerce.

37. *Cohens v. Virginia*, 19 US (6 Wheat.) 264, 404 (1821). "We have no more right to decline the exercise of jurisdiction which is given, than to usurp that which is not given."

38. *Landis v. North American Co.*, 299 US 248, 254 (1936).

39. *Landis*, 299 US at 256.

40. *Brown v. Board of Education*, 347 US 483 (1954).

41. Michael Klarman, *Brown v. Board of Education and the Civil Rights Movement* (New York: Oxford University Press, 2007): 63–64.

42. Klarman, *Brown v. Board of Education and the Civil Rights Movement*, 66–67.

43. *Brown*, 347 US at 483 (per curiam).

44. *Brown*, 347 US at 495–96.

45. Amanda Frost, "Certifying Questions to Congress," *Northwestern University Law Review* 101, no. 1 (2007): 30–32.

46. *US Nuclear Regulatory Commission v. Sholly*, 463 US 1224 (1983).

47. Frost, "Certifying Questions to Congress," 32.

48. Frost, "Certifying Questions to Congress."

49. Frost, "Certifying Questions to Congress."

50. Nuclear Waste Policy Act, 42 USC §§ 10101-10270 (2012).

51. Frost, "Certifying Questions to Congress."

52. *Stinnie v. Holcomb*, 396 F. Supp. 3d 653 (W.D. Va. 2019).

53. *Stinnie*, 396 F. Supp. 3d at 660.

54. *Stinnie*, 396 F. Supp. 3d at 659.

55. *Ashwander v. Tennessee Valley Authority*, 297 US 288, 347 (1936) (Brandeis, J., concurring).

56. *Stinnie*, 396 F. Supp. 3d at 660.

57. *Stinnie*, 396 F. Supp. 3d at 656. The court granted a stay until the Virginia General Assembly's 2020 session.

58. Fed. R. App. P. 41(d)(2).

59. Fed. R. App. P. 41(d)(2)(B)(ii).

60. Charles W. Rhodes, "Loving Retroactivity," *Florida State University Law Review* 45, no. 2 (2018): 415.

61. *Northern Pipeline Construction Co. v. Marathon Pipe Line Co.*, 458 US 50 (1982).

62. *Northern Pipeline Construction*, 458 US at 88. See also *Buckley v. Valeo*, 424 US 1, 142–43 (1976). In *Buckley*, the Court delayed its mandate for 30 days to "afford Congress an opportunity to reconstitute the Commission by law or to adopt other valid enforcement mechanisms without interrupting enforcement of the provisions the Court sustains, allowing the present Commission in the interim to function *de facto* in accordance with the substantive provisions of the Act."

63. *Moore v. Madigan*, 702 F.3d 933, 942 (7th Cir. 2012).

64. *Moore*, 702 F.3d at 942.

65. *Moore*, 702 F.3d at 942.

66. See Aaron-Andrew P. Bruhl, "Deciding When to Decide: How Appellate Procedure Distributes the Costs of Legal Change," *Cornell Law Review* 96, no. 2 (2011): 248.

67. *A. L. A. Schechter Poultry Corp.*, 295 US at 554. The Court signaled that if Congress had adopted a chicken code, the rules would not raise nondelegation issues.

68. *Clinton v. Jones*, 520 US 681 (1997).

69. *Clinton*, 520 US at 707.

70. Kristina Daugirdas, "Evaluating Remand Without Vacatur: A New Judicial Remedy for Defective Agency Rulemakings," *New York University Law Review* 80, no. 1 (2005): 279–81.

71. *Landis*, 299 US at 254.

72. Rules Enabling Act of 1943, 28 USC § 2072(a) (1943). This act authorizes the Supreme Court to promulgate procedural rules for district and circuit courts.

73. *Abbott Laboratories v. Gardner*, 387 US 136, 148 (1967).

74. The analogy to proposed rules is instructive. A proposed rule is not "final agency action" and hence is not challengeable in court. See *Center for Auto Safety v. National Highway Traffic Safety Administration*, 710 F.2d 842, 846 (DC Cir. 1983). "The issuance of a notice of proposed rulemaking . . . often will not be ripe for review because the rule may or may not be adopted or enforced." If parties cannot attack a proposed rule, it would be odd to suppose that they can challenge a mere statute that does nothing but delegate legislative power.

75. Todd Garvey, "A Brief Overview of Rulemaking and Judicial Review," Congressional Research Service, March 27, 2017, 2–3, https://fas.org/sgp/crs/misc/R41546.pdf.

76. Administrative Procedures Act, 5 USC § 553(d).

77. Administrative Procedures Act, 5 USC § 553(d).

78. Administrative Procedures Act, 5 USC § 801(a)(3).

79. See, for example, 33 CFR § 1.05-55. This rule provides that the US Department of Homeland Security's direct final rules will be effective no earlier than 90 days after publication in the *Federal Register*. As another example, consider 49 CFR § 190.339. This rule provided that the US Department of Transportation's direct final rules related to pipelines would take affect no earlier than 90 days.

80. Ronald M. Levin, "Direct Final Rulemaking," *George Washington Law Review* 64, no. 1 (1995): 1.

81. Admittedly, the Court has held that who crafts final *executive* regulations does matter. *AT&T Corp. v. Iowa Utilities Board* vacated a Federal Communications Commission regulation because it did not contain "limiting standard[s]" and, pertinently, allowed private entities to fix the regulation's content. *AT&T Corp. v. Iowa Utilities Board*, 525 US 366, 387–89 (1999). In *A. L. A. Schechter Poultry Corp.*, the Court said that permitting private groups to draft regulations that the president then approves runs afoul of the constitutional design. "Such a delegation of legislative power is unknown to our law, and is utterly consistent with the constitutional prerogatives and duties of Congress." But the Supreme Court has signaled that congressional lawmaking is different. For instance, if Congress had adopted a chicken code, the rules clearly would not raise nondelegation issues. *A. L. A. Schechter Poultry Corp.*, 295 US at 537, 554.

82. *McCulloch v. Maryland*, 17 US (4 Wheat.) 316, 415 (1819).

83. Scott Horsley, "A Churchill 'Quote' That U.S. Politicians Will Never Surrender," National Public Radio, October 28, 2013, https://www.npr.org/sections/itsallpolitics/2013/10/28/241295755/a-churchill-quote-that-u-s-politicians-will-never-surrender.

84. See George Stigler, "The Theory of Economic Regulation," *Bell Journal of Economics and Management Science* 2, no. 1 (1971): 3.

85. Corbin Hiar and Nick Sobczyk, "Opposition to Fossil Fuel Cash Splits Democrats," E&E News, January 30, 2019, https://www.eenews.net/stories/1060118929.

86. Hiar and Sobczyk, "Opposition to Fossil Fuel Cash Splits Democrats."

87. Shane Goldmacher, "Michael Bloomberg Spent More Than $900 Million on His Failed Presidential Run," *New York Times*, March 21, 2020, https://www.nytimes.com/2020/03/20/us/politics/bloomberg-campaign-900-million.html.

88. Goldmacher, "Michael Bloomberg Spent More Than $900 Million on His Failed Presidential Run."

89. See, generally, Mancur Olson, *The Logic of Collective Action: Public Goods and the Theory of Groups, with a New Preface and Appendix* (Cambridge, MA: Harvard University Press, 1965).

90. In the recent debate concerning California's ability to regulate fuel efficiency standards, major automakers stated, "A 50-state [federal] solution has always been our preferred path forward." David Shepardson and Ben Klayman, "California, Four Automakers Defy Trump, Agree to Tighten Emissions Rules," Reuters, July 26, 2019, https://www.reuters.com/article/us-autos-emissions/california-four-automakers-defy-trump-agree-to-tighten-emissions-rules-idUSKCN1UK1OD.

91. The capture theory explains that incumbent firms seek favorable regulations that protect themselves by creating hurdles for new entrants. Olson, *The Logic of Collective Action*.

92. *Hayburn's Case*, 2 US (2 Dall.) 408 (1792).

93. *Hayburn's Case*, 2 US at 408.

94. *Hayburn's Case*, 2 US at 408.

95. *Hayburn's Case*, 2 US at 408.

96. Maeva Marcus and Robert Teir, "Hayburn's Case: A Misinterpretation of Precedent," *Wisconsin Law Review* 1988, no. 3 (1988): 539.

97. Act of Feb. 28, 1793, 1 Stat. 324 (1793).

98. Louise Weinberg, "Our Marbury," *Virginia Law Review* 89, no. 6 (2003): 1264–65.

99. Frost, "Certifying Questions to Congress," 32–33.

100. *US Department of the Treasury v. Galioto*, 477 US 556 (1986).

101. *US Department of the Treasury*, 477 US at 558–59.

102. *US Department of the Treasury*, 477 US at 559.

103. H.R. Rep. No. 99-495, at 15, 29 (1986).

104. Most agency rules affect civil liability. When an agency rule generates criminal liability or increases criminal sanctions, congressional ratification of those rules would not resolve all constitutional difficulties. Anyone charged with criminal conduct that occurred before congressional ratification could allege that the application of the rule against their prior conduct violates the nondelegation doctrine and that, given the ex post facto clause, the congressionally ratified rule cannot be applied to conduct before the congressional ratification.

105. 2 USC § 1571(a)(2).

106. 10 USC § 2687; and Kenneth Mayer, "Closing Military Bases (Finally): Solving Collective Dilemmas Through Delegation," *Legislative Studies Quarterly* 20, no. 3 (1995): 393.

107. 5 USC § 801(a)(3)(A).

108. 5 USC § 802(c).

109. 5 USC § 801(a)(3)(B).

110. Maeve P. Carey and Christopher M. Davis, "The Congressional Review Act (CRA): Frequently Asked Questions," Congressional Research Service, January 14, 2020, 6, https://crsreports.congress.gov/product/pdf/R/R43992/12.

111. Carey and Davis, "The Congressional Review Act (CRA)."

112. Kevin P. McNellis et al., "Continuing Resolutions: Overview of Components and Practices," Congressional Research Service, April 19, 2019, 9–11, https://fas.org/sgp/crs/

misc/R42647.pdf.

113. Congress could extend this ratification concept to the agency law that emerges from agency adjudications as well, thereby shielding those determinations from nondelegation attack.

114. For the provision limiting debate in the House of Representatives, see 19 USC § 2191(f)(2). For the provision limiting debate in the Senate, see 19 USC § 2191(g)(2).

115. To be sure, the agency will have to satisfy the Administrative Procedures Act as it modifies or rescinds its rules. Administrative Procedures Act, 5 USC §§ 551-59, 701-06, 3105, 3344, 5362, 7521.

116. Saikrishna Bangalore Prakash, *The Living Presidency: An Originalist Argument Against Its Ever-Expanding Powers* (Cambridge, MA: Belknap Press, 2020): 258–59.

117. USA Patriot Act, Pub. L. No. 107-56.

118. See, for example, USA Patriot Improvement and Reauthorization Act of 2005, Pub. L. No. 109-177, 120 Stat. 192 (2006); FISA Sunsets Extension Act of 2011, Pub. L. No. 112-14, 125 Stat. 216; and USA Freedom Act, Pub. L. No. 114-23, 129 Stat. 268 (2015).

119. *Ramos v. Louisiana*, 140 S. Ct. 1390 (2020).

120. *Ramos*, 140 S. Ct. at 1436 (Alito, J., dissenting).

121. *Ramos*, 140 S. Ct. at 1436–37 (Alito, J., dissenting).

122. *Ramos*, 140 S. Ct. at 1436–37 (Alito, J., dissenting).

123. *Immigration and Naturalization Service v. Chadha*, 462 US 919 (1983).

124. *Chadha*, 462 US at 955–59.

125. *Chadha*, 462 US at 959–60 (Powell, J., concurring). "Congress has included the veto in literally hundreds of statutes, dating back to the 1930's."

126. *Chadha*, 462 US at 944.

127. *Chadha*, 462 US at 944.

128. *Chadha*, 462 US at 959.

129. Transcript of Oral Argument at 33, *Chiafalo*, 140 S. Ct. at 2316 (No. 19-465).

130. Gallup, "Congress and the Public," https://news.gallup.com/poll/1600/congress-public.aspx.

131. Courts show respect to Congress in several ways. For example, such regard perhaps justifies a version of the constitutional avoidance canon, the canon to avoid actual unconstitutionality. This long-used canon provides that courts should not interpret a law in a manner that renders it unconstitutional if another permissible reading exists. See Caleb Nelson, "Avoiding Constitutional Questions Versus Avoiding Unconstitutionality," *Harvard Law Review Forum* 128, no. 8 (2015): 331.

132. *Free Enterprise Fund v. Public Company Accounting and Oversight Board*, 561 US 477, 499 (2010).

133. *Free Enterprise Fund*, 561 US at 499.

Can the Supreme Court Learn from the State Nondelegation Doctrines?

JOSEPH POSTELL

Although the nondelegation doctrine's fate at the national level is unclear, at least one recent journal article claims that it is "alive and well" at the state level.[1] As this chapter argues, this seems to overstate the case. Although state courts have invoked a nondelegation doctrine from time to time, the examples are not numerous. Nevertheless, what these cases show is that even when the nondelegation has been invoked in state-level cases, it does not appear to have unduly interfered with the administrative process.

Looking to the states is a useful exercise for several reasons. First and most important, the nondelegation doctrine is applied more frequently and more strictly at the state level than at the national level, but it has not resulted in repeated invalidation of major regulatory statutes and programs. Given the possibility that some of the justices might hesitate to reinvigorate the doctrine if it led to invalidation of most of the regulatory state, the states' experience under a more robust doctrine is significant evidence that it can be applied in a way that leaves most of the modern administrative state intact. Even in the states where several nondelegation challenges have been successful in the past few decades, there has not been an avalanche of litigation or widespread invalidation of statutes or regulations that would cripple those states' administrative capacities. While it is not clear why these states have not experienced the results that many of the nondelegation doctrine's opponents fear, this outcome is noteworthy.

Second, the states offer the closest approximations to the constitutional system and text at the national level. Rather than looking to foreign sources, examining the application of the nondelegation doctrine at the state level offers the most similar points of comparison to US constitutional law. As

Edward Stiglitz writes, "The states exist within a federal system that constrains the extent to which they may differ," and "the states further share a common history that induces a measure of homogeneity in institutions."[2] Consequently, they bear more similarity to the federal Constitution and its nondelegation doctrine than to foreign constitutions, which do not appear to impose strict nondelegation doctrines.

Admittedly, state constitutions and the US Constitution have significant differences. As this chapter discusses, some state constitutions contain more explicit prohibitions on delegation or stronger separation-of-powers language. However, scholars and jurists generally do not dispute whether the US Constitution contains a nondelegation principle; they merely disagree over how to distinguish between legitimate and illegitimate delegations of legislative power.[3] The relevant question, then, is the same at both the state and national levels: not whether the relevant constitution prohibits delegation of legislative power, but how to distinguish such a delegation when it occurs.

Third, as this chapter explains, the state nondelegation doctrines are applied differently depending on context. Some states, as described below, treat delegations of tax power, or delegations to private actors, differently than delegations of lawmaking or regulatory authority. This nuanced approach to applying the nondelegation doctrine could guide the Supreme Court as the justices consider how to apply the doctrine in a way that respects judicial restraint and stare decisis.

This chapter examines the state nondelegation doctrines, drawing from as broad an array of cases and states as space permits. After a brief treatment of more targeted applications of the nondelegation doctrine at the state level, involving private delegations, delegation of tax power, delegation by incorporation, and other contexts, it proceeds to the typical nondelegation inquiry concerning delegation of legislative or regulatory authority at both the state and federal levels. The key question is whether the states have devised any tests for applying the nondelegation doctrine to delegations of legislative or regulatory authority that might serve as a guide to the US Supreme Court. Some states, in fact, have devised more robust yet workable tests for nondelegation. Therefore, the chapter's final section considers the implications of state nondelegation doctrines for the future of the nondelegation doctrine at the national level.

Targeted Applications of the State Nondelegation Doctrines

Little has been written about the state nondelegation doctrines. Only two recent articles, both published in the 1990s, survey the nondelegation doctrines across the states.[4] These articles, however, are of questionable use in discerning the current status of the nondelegation doctrine in the states because they rely on cases that are now dated or interpret some state courts' pronouncements on the nondelegation doctrine as stronger than they actually are.[5] A chief problem with these studies is that they treat all nondelegation cases as part of a single category. If the cases are decided on delegation grounds, they are counted as typical nondelegation cases. As this section illustrates, many of the cases in which state courts have invalidated statutes use the language of nondelegation, but the cases present unique or narrow circumstances that distinguish them from typical nondelegation inquiries. Once we separate these cases from the typical cases, the state nondelegation doctrines will appear clearer.

Nondelegation as Ultra Vires. Several states have invoked the nondelegation doctrine since 1980 to invalidate agency actions for what should more accurately be described as ultra vires reasons. Most prominently, the New York Court of Appeals (New York's highest court) invalidated the New York City Department of Health and Mental Hygiene's "soda ban" under a test devised by a major 1987 case *Boreali v. Axelrod*.[6] The *Boreali* case struck regulations governing smoking in public areas because the agency had "overstepped the boundaries of its lawfully delegated authority when it promulgated a comprehensive code to govern tobacco smoking in areas that are open to the public."[7] In other words, the problem in *Boreali* and the soda ban case was that the agency assumed authority not granted in the delegation, not whether the statute lawfully delegated authority. Similar challenges have recently prevailed in other states, sometimes adopting nondelegation language.[8]

These cases offer relatively little guidance for the Supreme Court's nondelegation jurisprudence since the Court has incorporated ultra vires considerations in other doctrines. Most notably, the Court has consistently used the nondelegation doctrine as a canon of construction to limit agency actions that are based on expansive interpretations of statutory delegations. It has also incorporated these concerns into its *Chevron U.S.A. v. Natural Resources Defense Council* analysis of agency statutory interpretation.[9]

Nondelegation and Incorporation by Reference. State statutes often incorporate definitions of legal terms promulgated by other governmental bodies or agencies. In some cases at the state level, nondelegation challenges have succeeded on the grounds that such laws improperly delegate legislative authority because they enable nonlegislative actors to define the terms of statutes. These laws typically fall into one of two categories: incorporation of federal definitions or incorporation of technical terms and standards from trade organizations.

In one prominent 1978 case from Arizona, *State v. Williams*, the Arizona Supreme Court declared a welfare statute unconstitutional because it incorporated federal and state definitions of fraud contained in administrative rules that could be changed post-enactment. The court claimed that "an incorporation by state statute of rules, regulations, and statutes of federal bodies to be promulgated subsequent to the enactment of the state statute constitutes an unlawful delegation of legislative power."[10] The statute was invalidated on these grounds, with the court also invoking the US Supreme Court's "intelligible principle" test for determining whether a delegation of legislative power has occurred. Under this standard, a statutory delegation will be unlawful unless accompanied by an intelligible principle that will guide the administrative agency.

Similarly, the Oklahoma Supreme Court invalidated a law in 1995 for tying the prevailing wage rate to that of the US Department of Labor, thus authorizing a body outside the state to make the law in the state.[11] In most states, if the law incorporates a term or definition that is frozen in another state or federal statute, it is equivalent to the legislature enacting that into law and therefore raises no delegation problem. On the other hand, if another governmental body can change the incorporated standard, the legislature has effectively delegated its lawmaking power to that body, since the latter can change the law that the former enacted.[12]

Incorporating private organizations' standards, typically in cases involving occupational licensing, presents more challenging issues for state courts. This is partly due to the private nature of the delegation, which many states scrutinize more strictly than delegations to governmental bodies (as explained in the following section). In some states, these delegations have been found invalid. The Supreme Court of Kansas, for instance, invalidated a scheme for registering pharmacists that required applicants to graduate from a college accredited by a private accreditation organization.[13] This scheme, the court claimed, "has the effect of delegating to [the accreditation agency] through its accreditation process the standards of education required before registration is permitted." The court concluded that such a delegation "constitutes an unlawful delegation of legislative authority to a nongovernmental association and is constitutionally impermissible."[14] On the other hand, most states affirm the constitutionality of occupational licensing schemes when they are challenged on nondelegation grounds.[15]

Private Delegation in the States. In *Carter v. Carter Coal*, the Supreme Court found that the delegation of legislative power to private actors was "legislative delegation in its most obnoxious form."[16] Following that view, many states have imposed heightened scrutiny against delegations of power to private actors. The Supreme Court of Louisiana struck statutes in 2013 that assessed rice growers to pay for marketing for the state's rice industry, with the assessments voted on by the rice growers themselves.[17] In 1999, the Arkansas Supreme Court invalidated a similar scheme.[18] The Pennsylvania Supreme Court recently applied the nondelegation doctrine against a workers' compensation statute that required physicians to use impairment ratings from the American Medical Association.[19] In Kansas, the state's supreme court struck down a statute that set up a Workers' Compensation Board containing members selected by the Kansas Chamber of Commerce and the Kansas State AFL-CIO.[20]

The Louisiana and Pennsylvania courts held that private delegations must be treated more strictly than delegations to public agencies. Louisiana's court invoked the Supreme Court's statement from *Carter Coal* regarding private delegation and indicated that the rice marketing assessment was unconstitutional because "the Legislature cannot delegate to private citizens the power to create or repeal laws."[21] The Pennsylvania Supreme Court opined that in giving the American Medical Association's impairment ratings legal authority, the General Assembly delegated authority to a private entity, not to a government agency or body. Conceptually, this fact poses unique concerns that are absent when the General Assembly ... vests an executive-branch agency with the discretion to administer the law.[22]

The most prominent instance of a state crafting a private delegation doctrine, however, comes from Texas. In *Texas Boll Weevil Eradication Foundation v. Lewellen*, the Texas Supreme Court struck down a 1993 statute similar to the rice marketing scheme struck by Louisiana's court two decades later.[23] The law authorized cotton growers to propose geographic eradication zones and impose assessments for cotton growers to pay for boll weevil eradication. The court argued it was "axiomatic that courts should subject private delegations to a more searching scrutiny than their public counterparts."[24] To apply this principle, the court constructed an eight-factor balancing test to evaluate the constitutionality of such delegations. According to this test, the following factors must be considered.

- Are the private delegate's actions subject to meaningful review by a state agency or other branch of state government?

- Are the persons affected by the private delegate's actions adequately represented in the decision-making process?

- Is the private delegate's power limited to making rules, or does the delegate also apply the law to particular individuals?

- Does the private delegate have a pecuniary or other personal interest that may conflict with its public function?

- Is the private delegate empowered to define criminal acts or impose criminal sanctions?

- Is the delegation narrow in duration, extent, and subject matter?

- Does the private delegate possess special qualifications or training for the task delegated to it?

- Has the legislature provided sufficient guidelines to guide the private delegate in its work?[25]

The Texas Supreme Court, in *Boll Weevil* and subsequent cases, indicated that "the importance of each factor will necessarily differ in each case."[26] It went on to use *Boll Weevil*'s multifactor test in some important cases, including a decision regarding the validity of water quality zones that were created by homeowners in Houston.[27] In *Boll Weevil*, the court made clear that this heightened scrutiny applied "only to private delegations, not to the usual delegations by the Legislature to an agency or another department of government."[28]

Delegation and the Tax Power. Delegation of the tax power to private entities is especially vulnerable to judicial scrutiny in several states. In many cases, private delegation and the delegation of tax power are intermingled, making it difficult to discern whether these cases constitute a separate category or a subset of the private delegation cases.

In Virginia, a statute delegating taxing power to the Northern Virginia Transportation Authority (NVTA), a political subdivision of Virginia that encompasses several Northern Virginia counties, was held unlawful on nondelegation grounds.[29] The Supreme Court of Virginia concluded that the state's general assembly left NVTA with "the sole discretion to impose the regional taxes and fees." Because the state's bill of rights enshrined in Article I of its constitution mandated that taxes could not be imposed without the consent of the people or their representatives, the court concluded that the state legislature could not delegate the tax power "to a non-elected body such as NVTA."[30] Virginia, therefore, clearly prohibits delegating the taxing power to unelected bodies.

Idaho and North Dakota have also addressed the delegation of tax power in recent cases. For instance, the Idaho Supreme Court upheld a law in 1984 authorizing the creation of auditorium districts that could impose sales taxes on hotels. The court defended the legitimacy of the delegation by focusing on provisions in the law that narrowed the scope of the delegation by defining the specific purposes for which the taxes must be used and the limit on the amount of the tax that could be imposed.[31] The following year it used the same framework to uphold a similar delegation of tax authority.[32] One justice dissented from the court's opinion in the latter case and summarized the court's approach as follows: The court will uphold delegations of tax power if the law contains

> (1) clear definitions of *who* could tax and *what* could be taxed; (2) an established *upper tax limit* by which the [agency] could not exceed [sic] in imposing a tax; (3) a *clear purpose* for which the revenues thus earned must be spent; and (4) *specific details* by which the tax would be administered and collected.[33] (Emphasis in original.)

Although this summary of the prevailing doctrine comes from a dissenting opinion, it seems to summarize accurately the factors the Idaho court uses to determine the legitimacy of previous delegations of tax power.

North Dakota takes a stronger stance against such delegations. One notable case that other state courts have extensively cited is *Scott v. Donnelly*, in which the North Dakota Supreme Court held that the state legislature could not grant the authority to set excise tax rates on potatoes to the North Dakota Potato Development Commission appointed by the governor.[34] In doing so, the court not only ruled against a delegation of the taxing power but also did so when the delegation went to a public rather than a private entity.[35]

These four contexts—ultra vires, reference by incorporation, private delegations, and delegations of tax power—present unique circumstances that many state courts treat differently than the typical nondelegation case, which focuses on the delegation of lawmaking or regulatory power to administrative agencies. Separating these cases and issues from the typical category allows us to focus more sharply on the narrow set of states and cases in which courts have created tests to apply the nondelegation doctrine in that context.

Delegation of Lawmaking or Regulatory Authority

In contrast to the issues discussed in the previous section, the central controversy over the Supreme Court's potential revival of the nondelegation doctrine is Congress' delegation of lawmaking or regulatory authority to administrative bodies. The core of the nondelegation doctrine is in its application to the delegation of legislative or regulatory power. Thus, this section provides an extended discussion of the states' doctrines as applied in that context.

Those looking to the states for robust nondelegation doctrines that limit delegations of lawmaking or regulatory authority to administrative agencies will be disappointed. While some state courts imposed strict limits on such delegations through the mid-20th century, few do so today. In the states where nondelegation challenges have been successful in recent years, the analysis does not appear different from the Supreme Court's intelligible-principle test. The difference is in how the courts apply the test. In these few states, the test is whether there are adequate standards and procedural safeguards to ensure proper judicial review of administrative rules and provide accountability to the public.

The highest courts of a few states, however, have applied a more workable and specific test to determine whether a statute violates the nondelegation doctrine. In these cases, courts ask whether statutes adequately define an agency's scope of authority by examining whether the persons subject to the agency's authority are carefully identified in the statute. Illinois and Florida, in particular, have constructed such tests in recent years.

Also recently, other states have invalidated statutes on nondelegation grounds, but the statutes seem to have been carelessly crafted and have contained no limits on agency discretion. They simply authorized an administrative officer or body to exercise authority without any guidance as to the ends to be pursued. This is the case with decisions from Alaska, Montana, New Hampshire, Oklahoma, and Vermont, as discussed below.

This section begins by briefly describing the prevailing lax approach to nondelegation the vast majority of states have taken. It then focuses on the states where the nondelegation doctrine is applied with some rigor and quotes extensively from the cases to illustrate the approach state courts take in these cases.

The Majority of States: Nondelegation Is Weak. Most states apply a weak nondelegation doctrine, similar to that of the US Supreme Court, which simply looks to statutes for vague standards or statements of policy to uphold them. While not explicitly using the intelligible-principle test, these state courts use essentially the same approach. States as varied as Arizona, Arkansas, California, Colorado, Kansas, Maryland, Massachusetts, Michigan, Mississippi, New York, Ohio, and Utah have all followed this approach since the middle of the 20th century.[36] In many of these states, courts also focus on the procedural safeguards that accompany the delegation in determining whether a statute is constitutional.[37] Some combination of broad standards and procedural safeguards is sufficient to survive nondelegation challenges. In all these states, though, the approach mirrors the US Supreme Court's traditional approach, applying the intelligible-principle test to regulatory statutes.

The Ohio case *Redman v. Ohio Department of Industrial Relations* is representative.[38] In that case, an oil company challenged a law that declared that "no person shall drill a new well . . . without having a permit to do so issued by the chief of the [Ohio] Division of Oil and Gas [ODOG]." If a proposed well was to be located in a coal-bearing township, the law required the ODOG chief to transmit copies of the permit application to the Ohio Division of Mines (ODM) chief. The ODM chief was required by law to notify the owner (or lessee) of any "affected mine" of the application and, if that owner (or lessee) objects, to disapprove the application "if in the opinion of the chief [of ODM] the objection is well-founded."[39] In short, the statute required the ODM chief to determine whether there were any "affected mines" and to disapprove applications if their objections were "well-founded."

Redman Oil Company alleged that these phrases constituted unlawful delegations of legislative power to the ODM chief. After acknowledging the importance and long history of the nondelegation doctrine in Ohio, the Supreme Court of Ohio argued that "a rigid application of the nondelegation doctrine would unduly hamstring the administration of the laws." Therefore, the court concluded, citing a previous case,

> A statute does not unconstitutionally delegate legislative power
> if it establishes, through legislative policy and such standards

as are practical, an intelligible principle to which the administrative officer or body must conform and further establishes a
procedure whereby exercise of the discretion can be reviewed
effectively.[40]

After quoting from some general policy statements set forth at the
beginning of the statute, the Supreme Court of Ohio easily concluded,
"These policy statements establish intelligible principles: the safety of persons; the conservation of property; the maximum utilization, development,
and production of coal in an environmentally and economically proficient
manner; and the prevention of physical and economic waste."[41] In sum,
the Supreme Court of Ohio determined that vague statutory goals such as
"safety of persons" and "prevention of physical and economic waste" were
sufficient to establish that a statute contained intelligible principles and
would survive nondelegation challenges.

Ohio's application of the nondelegation doctrine in *Redman* illustrates
the kind of weak nondelegation doctrine that most states apply to delegations of lawmaking authority to administrative agencies. The remainder of
this section discusses the few states that enforce a more robust nondelegation doctrine.

Illinois Creates and Abandons a Nondelegation Test. One state is
worth close attention despite the decline of its nondelegation doctrine
into obsolescence. Until approximately 40 years ago, the Supreme Court
of Illinois was notorious for striking statutes on nondelegation grounds.[42]
The court's nondelegation test, established in the 1977 case *Stofer v. Motor
Vehicle Casualty Co.*, contained three requirements for any statute facing
a nondelegation challenge.[43] To be held valid, statutes had to identify
"(1) the persons and activities potentially subject to regulation; (2) the
harm sought to be prevented; and (3) the general means intended to be
available to the administrator to prevent the identified harm."[44]

The court also identified principles that should guide the judicial inquiry
at each prong of the test. As the court explained,

(1) The legislature must do all that is practical to define the
scope of the legislation, i.e., the persons and activities which

may be subject to the administrator's authority. . . . (2) With regard to identifying the harm sought to be prevented, the legislature may use somewhat broader, more generic language than in the first element. It is sufficient if, from the language of the statute, it is apparent what types of evil the statute is intended to prevent. . . . (3) Finally, with regard to the means intended to be available, the legislature must specifically enumerate the administrative tools (e.g., regulations, licenses, enforcement proceedings) and the particular sanctions, if any, intended to be available.[45]

Applying the test to the facts in *Stofer*, the court upheld an insurance statute from the 1930s that authorized the state's director of insurance to promulgate rules to promote uniformity in all basic fire and lightning insurance policies. Two years later, however, in *Thygesen v. Callahan*, the court used the *Stofer* test to invalidate a statute that authorized a director of financial institutions to promulgate maximum rates for check cashing and writing of money orders.[46] The court found that the first prong of the *Stofer* test was satisfied because the statute identified the persons and activities subject to regulation—namely, currency exchanges. The statute failed the second part of the test, however, because it did not identify the harm to be prevented. Instead, the statute merely authorized the director to promulgate "reasonable" rates.

In the same year, the court applied the *Stofer* test in another case, this one involving allocations for municipalities to divert water from Lake Michigan under a rationing system.[47] The court applied the three-part test from *Stofer* and found that the law establishing the rationing system clearly identified the persons subject to regulation, the harm sought to be prevented, and the primary means to be employed.[48] It therefore upheld the allocations against nondelegation challenges from several municipalities.

For reasons that have, to this author's knowledge, never been fully explained by scholars, the Supreme Court of Illinois retreated to a more permissive test in the years following *Stofer* and *Thygesen*. That test was a generalized "intelligible standards" test that resembles the permissive intelligible-principle test used in many states and by the US Supreme Court. The intelligible-standards test, from the 1966 case *Hill v. Relyea*, merely requires "that intelligible standards be set to guide the agency charged with enforcement, and the precision of the permissible standard must necessarily vary according to the nature of the ultimate objective and the problems involved."[49] This test was used to uphold statutes authorizing regulation subject to a vague "public interest" requirement in the 1982 case *People v. Carter*, without any mention of the *Stofer* precedent or test.[50] *Stofer* seems to have disappeared as an authority in Illinois delegation cases, and the state now applies a looser requirement. Although Illinois can no longer be categorized as a strict nondelegation state, it is nonetheless noteworthy that until recently it had devised and applied a workable, multipronged nondelegation test that policed the outer boundaries of legislative delegations to administrative bodies.

Nine States Where Nondelegation Is Still Robust. Unlike Illinois, several states continue to enforce a relatively vigorous nondelegation doctrine in the regulatory context. In these states, the nondelegation analysis asks whether statutes contain standards or guidelines that serve to limit agency discretion. Even in these states, however, it is difficult to determine whether the courts have applied the nondelegation doctrine consistently.

Alaska, for instance, applies a "sufficient standards" test that requires a statute to contain sufficient standards to withstand scrutiny.[51] In *State v. Fairbanks North Star Borough*, the Alaska Supreme Court invalidated a gubernatorial impoundment of funds from the legislature's appropriation.[52] The decision was authorized by the state's Executive Budget Act, which enabled the governor to withhold appropriations in the face of a looming budget deficit. The Alaska Supreme Court invalidated the statute as "an unconstitutional delegation of legislative power."[53]

The court distinguished the broad discretion given to the governor from recent cases in which delegations were upheld.[54] This case was unique, the court claimed, because it was "a delegation of authority over the entire budget"; it "articulated no principles, intelligible or otherwise, to guide the executive"; and it provided "no policy guidance as to how the cuts should be distributed."[55] In short, the Alaska Supreme Court held the law invalid only because it dealt with budgetary authority rather than regulatory authority and contained no guidance or intelligible principles. In Alaska, most delegations are upheld as long as the law does not grant authority over major policies with little to no guidance. Cases subsequent to *Fairbanks North Star Borough* have upheld delegations as long as the court can find some statement of purpose or policy in the law.[56] There has not been a wave of litigation on the nondelegation doctrine in Alaska due to the court's decision in *Fairbanks North Star Borough*.

Eight states in addition to Alaska—Florida, Kentucky, Montana, New Hampshire, Oklahoma, Pennsylvania, Vermont, and West Virginia—have followed this same trend: Statutes sometimes ran afoul of the nondelegation doctrine, but these cases were rare, the circumstances were often extraordinary, and the invalidated statutes were typically crafted in extraordinarily vague terms. In Florida, the leading case is *Askew v. Cross Key Waterways*, which invalidated a provision of the state's Environmental Land and Water Management Act that empowered an agency to designate areas of "critical state concern" for environmental protection.[57] Although the statute at issue more closely resembled an ordinary delegation of regulatory power than those analyzed in the other cases in this subsection, the Florida Supreme Court's analysis found the statute devoid of standards.

The court's opinion suggested that one specific feature of the law resulted in its invalidation: "the absence of legislative delineation of priorities among competing areas and resources which require protection."[58] The decision noted similar legislation in other states, but with one key difference: Whereas the other states' statutes defined the geographic areas to be protected in the law, the Florida statute left the scope of the law to administrative definition.[59] A connection might be drawn between the court's reasoning in *Askew* and the first prong of the Supreme Court of Illinois' test in *Stofer*.[60] In both cases, the law left the agency to determine the scope of the authority granted to it. This resembles delegations of authority to federal agencies, such as the US Fish and Wildlife Service's authority to define the extent of protected "critical habitat" in the Endangered Species Act. When an agency receives the power to determine the scope of its own authority, these tests suggest that the nondelegation doctrine is especially implicated.

The Florida Supreme Court's reasoning in *Askew* also cited the lack of statutory standards as a reason for striking the statute. As the court concluded,

> When legislation is so lacking in guidelines that neither the
> agency nor the courts can determine whether the agency is car-
> rying out the intent of the legislature in its conduct, then, in
> fact, the agency becomes the lawgiver rather than the adminis-
> trator of the law.[61]

This more conventional nondelegation analysis was employed to invalidate another Florida statute in the high-profile case of Terri Schiavo.
In that case, the Florida Supreme Court invalidated "Terri's law," which
authorized the governor to issue a stay to prevent withholding nutrition
and hydration from patients under certain circumstances, on the grounds
that the law failed to provide any standards or purposes to guide the governor's discretion.[62] In another Florida case, *Chiles v. Children A, B, C, D,
E, and F*, decided in 1991, the state's supreme court invalidated a law that
authorized the governor to establish an administrative commission to
reduce state agencies' operating budgets to prevent a deficit.[63] The facts,
in other words, were similar to those in the Alaska *Fairbanks North Star
Borough* case.[64] As with *Fairbanks North Star Borough*, the Florida court
noted that the legislature's power to appropriate state funds was especially
legislative and "is to be exercised only through duly enacted statutes."[65]

As one scholar noted, many Florida laws have been challenged on nondelegation grounds since *Askew*, and some challenges have been successful.[66] At the same time, the doctrine has not led to wholesale invalidation
of major regulatory programs in the state. The Florida Supreme Court
continues to acknowledge the need for some delegation, which is possible
even in the confines of a relatively strict nondelegation doctrine.[67] In other
words, Florida's adoption of a somewhat robust nondelegation doctrine
has not led to the crippling of administrative agencies.

Kentucky employs a relatively robust nondelegation principle, even in
comparison to the other states on this list.[68] The classic nondelegation case
in Kentucky is *Flying J Travel Plaza v. Commonwealth Transportation Cabinet*,
a 1996 decision invalidating a statutory provision that authorized billboard
regulation by the Kentucky Transportation Cabinet. The provision permitted roadside advertisements presenting "public service information such
as time, date, temperature, weather, or similar information." The Supreme
Court of Kentucky deemed this provision an unconstitutional delegation of

legislative power because the legislature failed to define "public service information" and "similar information," thus granting too much discretion to the
cabinet.[69] In *Flying J*, the Supreme Court of Kentucky enforced the nondelegation doctrine even in the face of relatively specific statutory language
regarding "public service information." In fact, the legislature narrowed the
statutory term by offering a set of examples: time, date, and temperature.
Nevertheless, the court deemed the statute insufficiently specific.

Although it may take a backseat to Kentucky in terms of nondelegation's
rigor, Montana may be the state with the largest number of statutes invalidated on nondelegation grounds in the past few decades. The Montana
Supreme Court invalidated a statute in 1979 because it provided no standards for the Department of Business Regulation to apply when ruling on
merger applications by savings and loan associations.[70] The statute merely
authorized mergers "by and with the consent and approval" of the department.[71] In striking the statute, the Montana Supreme Court acknowledged
that "the trend is away from requiring that statutory standards or guides
be specified" in legislation but announced that "while this may be the
trend under federal law and in some states, it is not Montana's position."[72]
In this case, as in the *Schiavo* case in Florida or *In re Petition* in Oklahoma,[73]
the statute simply failed to specify any standards. It "provides no standards or guidelines either expressed or otherwise ascertainable," merely
requiring the agency's consent and approval.[74]

The Montana Supreme Court has invalidated several other statutes
since 1979. In 1983, the court ruled that a zoning ordinance requiring neighbors' consent to grant a variance was an unconstitutional delegation of legislative power because it contained no guidance to determine the propriety
of withholding consent.[75] Five years later the court struck down a statute
empowering a science and technology board to make public investments in
technology.[76] Although the statute contained an extensive list of criteria to
guide the board in making the investments (including "prospects for col-
laboration" between public and private sectors, "prospects for achieving
commercial success," "job creation potential," and "involvement of existing institutional research strength"), the court claimed the criteria did not
"rise to the level of the objective criteria" contained in other statutes that
were held constitutional. Rather, "They are more akin to general policy
considerations underlying the entire technology investment program."[77]

While there appeared to be standards limiting the board's discretion in making the technology investments, the court found them too subjective to serve as meaningful limits. The opinion did not elaborate on why these criteria were "policy considerations" rather than "objective criteria," though that distinction seems to have been pivotal in the statute's demise.

Finally, in the 2000 case *Hayes v. Lame Deer High School District*, the court invalidated a statute delegating authority to county school superintendents to rule on petitions to transfer territory among school districts. The law only required the superintendents to consider "the effects that the transfer would have on those residing in the territory proposed for transfer as well as those residing in the remaining territory of the high school district."[78] In the court's view, this broad standard "fails to provide any checks on the discretion of the county superintendent" and provided "no criteria for balancing the effects felt by the parties involved."[79] Montana's Supreme Court, in brief, has invalidated several statutes on nondelegation grounds over the past few decades. In doing so, it has required not only that statutes contain standards but also that those standards are sufficiently objective that they can be measured and tested to determine whether the agency is following the law. Presumably, this would render some vague statutory phrases such as a "public interest" or "public convenience or necessity" standard vulnerable to nondelegation challenges, but it does not appear that Montana's Supreme Court has invalidated those sorts of provisions.

The New Hampshire Supreme Court invalidated statutes on nondelegation grounds in two cases in the 1980s for a similar lack of sufficiently objective standards. The leading case, *Smith Insurance v. Grievance Committee*, articulated the test and held unlawful a delegation authorizing an insurance grievance committee to "order the insurance company to rescind termination" of an agency agreement between the company and an insurance agent.[80] The statute did not guide the committee's discretion. It simply established the committee and declared that it "shall hold hearings on grievances brought by insurance agents relating to termination of their contracts with insurance companies, and the committee may order the insurance company to rescind termination."[81] The court acknowledged the legitimacy of legislative delegations as long as they are accompanied by "a declared policy or a prescribed standard laid down by the legislature."[82]

But here the law "neither declare[d] the legislative policies which underlay the enactment of the statute nor establishe[d] standards to guide the Grievance Committee in the exercise of its power."[83] In reaching this conclusion, the court laid out a general statement to guide nondelegation inquiries: The legislature "may not create and delegate duties and powers to an administrative agency if its commands are in such broad terms as to leave the agency with unguided and unfettered discretion in the assigned field of activity."[84] (Internal citations and ellipses omitted.)

Six years later, the court invalidated another statute authorizing a director of motor vehicles to suspend or revoke any driver's license "for any cause which he may deem sufficient."[85] The court found that the statute granted this power "without *any* express or implied qualifications, and thus provides no aid for judicial construction."[86] (Emphasis in original.) But these broadly worded statutes are the exception, and most delegations are upheld under New Hampshire's relatively permissive test.[87] The court uses the doctrine to police delegations that are entirely standardless, which allows most statutes to survive scrutiny.

Like New Hampshire, Oklahoma's highest court has held laws invalid only on rare occasions when no guidance accompanies a delegation to administrative officials. In a curious case from 1982, the Oklahoma Supreme Court refused to compel the state's attorney general to implement provisions of the Oklahoma Campaign Finance Act that the attorney general deemed unconstitutional.[88] The attorney general claimed that the law's provisions enabling funding of political parties violated the state constitution's requirement that funds be spent for public purposes. The court decided that to answer this question, it had to inquire into "the policy of the law as declared by the legislature" and "the standards to be followed by an agency in carrying out the policy."[89] But the law was deemed to contain no policy or standards. Thus, "the fundamental function of policy-making has been left by the Act to unbridled agency discretion. Power so to be exercised by an agency does not rest on constitutionally firm underpinnings."[90] The court determined that the case was "not presently justiciable" because "absent a declared policy with effective agency rules fashioned pursuant to a lawfully delegated authority, the Act is unfit for implementation."[91] The court's opinion in *Democratic Party of Oklahoma v. Estep* did not clearly identify the nondelegation doctrine as the reason for invalidating the statute. Rather, it used the nondelegation doctrine to conclude that the law's purposes cannot be gleaned, making the case nonjusticiable.

The Oklahoma Supreme Court applied the nondelegation doctrine more conventionally in a 2002 case, *In re Initiative Petition No. 366*.[92] The case involved an initiative to designate English as Oklahoma's official language and require English on all state documents and in state meetings and publications. The petition contained an exception for educational institutions and granted rulemaking authority to the state's board of education and board of regents to implement that exception. The court declared the petition invalid because, inter alia, the rulemaking authority violated the nondelegation doctrine. While the petition's language authorized the rulemaking "to promote the following principles," no principles were articulated. The petition, in the court's terse analysis, "fails to provide any principles."[93] With no principle or policy to guide the state's education officials in making rules regarding the state's official language, the court concluded, the law "leaves the fundamental policy-making function to the unbridled discretion of the State Board of Education and the Board of Regents for Higher Education."[94]

The court's analysis suggests that a statute delegating authority with no statement of policy or standards whatsoever will be vulnerable to a nondelegation challenge. Statutes containing even vague policy statements or standards, however, are commonly upheld.[95] Like New Hampshire, Oklahoma's nondelegation doctrine is employed only rarely to strike statutes containing no intelligible principles at all.

Similarly, the Supreme Court of Pennsylvania has articulated a standard for nondelegation cases that looks for adequate standards to guide agency discretion.

> While the General Assembly may, with adequate standards and guidelines, constitutionally delegate the power and authority to execute or administer a law, the prohibition against delegation of "legislative power" requires that the basic policy choices be made by the General Assembly.[96]

In one case from 1989, *Blackwell v. Commonwealth State Ethics Commission*, the court invalidated a state law sunsetting the state's ethics commission.[97] The law established a leadership committee (composed of members of the general assembly) and authorized it to postpone the sunsetting of any agency "if necessary."[98] Because the sunset law did not contain "adequate standards and guidelines" directing the leadership committee's discretion, it was "pure and simple, an unconstitutional exercise of the legislative power to make and enact laws."[99] Language authorizing an administrative body to do something "if necessary" did not have the effect of making the policy choice. It did, however, fail to provide a standard, thereby leaving the administrators to make the policy choices.

In 2005, the Supreme Court of Pennsylvania invalidated a law that established the Pennsylvania Gaming Control Board but did not provide any standards to guide the use of its discretion.[100] The board was authorized to preempt local zoning regulations, but it could "in its discretion consider such local zoning ordinances when considering an application for a slot machine license." It was required to notify localities about applications, provide a 60-day comment period, and consider "recommendations" from the locality regarding "impact on the local community" and "land use and transportation impact."[101] Quoting *Blackwell*, the court granted that the state legislature could legally

> delegate authority and discretion in connection with the execution and administration of a law; it may establish primary standards and impose upon others the duty to carry out the declared legislative policy in accordance with the general provisions of the enabling legislation.[102]

The court also cited numerous instances of delegations that were upheld under this standard. In this case, however, the law "allows the Board in its discretion to consider local zoning ordinances," but "the Board is not given any guidance as to the import" of those ordinances. The law did not tell the board what to do with the input that it received from local authorities or even what general policy priorities to weigh in the consideration. The provision was therefore held invalid as a standardless delegation.

Most recently, in 2016 the Supreme Court of Pennsylvania held that a provision of the state's public school code that authorized a five-member School Reform Commission, appointed by the state's governor, to oversee school districts that are in financial distress violated the nondelegation doctrine.[103] The provision authorized the commission to suspend regulations of the Pennsylvania Board of Education and the school code.[104] A charter school that was hurt by the commission's policies challenged the provision on the grounds that it gave the commission unlimited power to suspend the school code without any standards guiding the use of the power. The court agreed, noting that "there are few, if any, concrete measures embodied in the Distress Law to effectively channel the [Commission's] discretion . . . *and* there is no requirement that the [Commission] hold hearings or explain the grounds for its suspension decisions."[105] (Emphasis added.) In this case, the court therefore suggested that it was the combination of the lack of standards to guide discretion and the absence of procedural safeguards that rendered the law unconstitutional.

West Virginia invalidated several laws over the past few decades on nondelegation grounds, but most of the cases came with a twist: They gave power to the judiciary, not to an administrative agency. For example, in 1995 the Supreme Court of Appeals of West Virginia invalidated a law that authorized state circuit courts to issue concealed carry permits, citing several previous cases also involving delegations to the judiciary. "In view of these holdings," the court declared, there was a well-settled "policy of strong adherence to the several constitutional provisions relating to the separation of powers . . . and particularly as to the jurisdiction of courts."[106] The court was concerned not to delegate the ministerial task of issuing permits to the judiciary. As it explained, the law provides "nothing more than a judicial endorsement of a license application." It "eviscerate[s] any judicial discretion when it compels the granting of the license if all qualifiers on the application are satisfied."[107] The court did not object to the lack of intelligible principles or standards in the legislation but to the fact that the power given to the judiciary was not judicial in character.

In 1982, West Virginia's highest court struck down a law that granted the state's Public Service Commission the power of contempt.[108] But in doing so, the court emphasized the narrowness of its holding, stating,

> We recognize that the Legislature may create an administrative agency and give it quasi-judicial powers to conduct hearings and make findings of fact without violating the separation of powers

doctrine.... [In previous cases] we recognized that from a practical standpoint, it was often impossible to maintain a complete
separation between the three branches of government.[109]

The court distinguished the contempt power from other powers that
may be lawfully delegated to administrative bodies. But transferring the
contempt power, the court reasoned, was "a direct and fundamental
encroachment by one branch of government into the traditional powers
of another."[110] In effect, the nondelegation doctrine is imposed with some
frequency to invalidate statutes in West Virginia, but only in relatively narrow circumstances that are not typical of delegations of regulatory power
to administrative agencies.

Vermont presents the most curious case of the eight (by this chapter's
count) states in which the nondelegation doctrine is still relevant in the
lawmaking or regulatory context. Before 2000, Vermont could rightfully be
classified as a weak nondelegation state. In 2000, the Vermont Supreme
Court decided *In re Handy*, which invalidated a law that forbade town
administrators from issuing permits during a "pendency period" between
the date of public notice of proposed amended zoning bylaws and their date
of effect, without the written consent of the town's legislative body.[111] The
court claimed that the law gave "town selectboards unbridled discretion to
decide whether to review applications under the old or new zoning bylaws,
with no standards to limit the exercise of that discretion."[112] *In re Handy*,
however, does not appear to portend a resurgence of the nondelegation doctrine in Vermont and was most likely attributable to unique circumstances.

The State of the States' Nondelegation Doctrines. To summarize: Eight
or nine states (Alaska, Florida, Kentucky, Montana, New Hampshire, Oklahoma, Pennsylvania, West Virginia, and perhaps Vermont) have enforced
the nondelegation doctrine against legislative or regulatory delegations in
a relatively robust manner in the past several decades (since 1980). Except
for the Florida Supreme Court's decision in *Askew*, however, the cases
in these states do not devise elaborate tests to distinguish permissible
and impermissible delegations. Rather, they approach the doctrine similarly to the Supreme Court's opinion in *A. L. A. Schechter Poultry v. United
States*. They look to see if statutes provide adequate standards and policy

guidance, so that the policy is made by the legislature and the administrative agency is simply tasked with implementing that policy. This is still the reigning approach at the national level, but these state courts put teeth into the test, striking statutes on the outer edges, where the law provides no standards or guidelines whatsoever.

These examples indicate three important points. First, they suggest that the Supreme Court does not need to construct an elaborate new test to apply the nondelegation doctrine. Rather, the Supreme Court could put teeth into the nondelegation doctrine by better applying its existing precedents. For example, in *A. L. A. Schechter Poultry*, the Supreme Court simply asked whether Congress' statute "has itself established the standards of legal obligation, thus performing its essential legislative function" or whether it has failed "to enact such standards" and "attempted to transfer that function to others."[113] The Supreme Court could follow its leading precedent, ignoring the intelligible-principle test altogether and simply focusing on whether the relevant statute provides any guidance or standards to the agency. This would mimic the inquiry adopted in states such as Florida, Kentucky, Montana, Oklahoma, Pennsylvania, and Vermont.

Second, these states suggest that reinvigorating the nondelegation doctrine would not lead to apocalyptic results. None of the states discussed in this section have crippled their governments by applying the doctrine more vigorously. The doctrine has been used to strike the most egregious statutes rather than invalidate most of their regulatory programs. One recent empirical study finds little correlation between robust nondelegation doctrines and legislative drafting in the states.[114] Even in those states where the nondelegation doctrine has been used to strike statutes on multiple occasions over the past few decades, the state legislatures have not adjusted their behavior significantly.

Third, there does not seem to be an "ideological" nature to nondelegation challenges at the state level. The states where nondelegation challenges are successful in the lawmaking or regulatory context are not predominantly rural or urban, nor predominantly Democratic or Republican. Although legal scholars commonly claim that the use of the nondelegation doctrine is "all so transparently partisan" and that "by design [it] will frustrate Democratic efforts to govern," the history of the doctrine at the state level supplies evidence to refute such claims.[115] One study finds no relationship between such factors as the size of a state's economy or population size and the robustness of its nondelegation doctrine and a minor, statistically insignificant correlation between a state's political leaning and its nondelegation doctrine: "The same nondelegation regime, weak or strong, exists in roughly the same measure in different types of states, rich or poor, liberal or conservative, large or small."[116]

Most nondelegation challenges at the national level involve the delegation of lawmaking or regulatory authority to administrative agencies. In these cases at the state level, the nondelegation doctrine appears in most cases not "alive and well"[117] but dead or on life support. The analysis in these states—all but eight, in this chapter's analysis—tends to follow the same path as the Supreme Court's intelligible-principle test: If the statutory provision at issue contains even vague standards or guidelines (or, in many cases, procedural safeguards) to constrain the agency's discretion, it will be upheld.

That is not to say that the state nondelegation doctrines afford no guidance to the Supreme Court justices. For one, they illustrate that a test that requires statutory standards does not have to be a dead letter. As explained above, some states have put teeth into the test and have struck statutes that provide no guidance to administrative agencies.[118] In addition, those states where the nondelegation doctrine continues to be enforced have not experienced incapable or inefficient government. If anything, the application of the nondelegation doctrine at the state level should reassure those who are afraid that, in Justice Elena Kagan's words, a revived doctrine means that "most of Government is unconstitutional."[119]

Implications for the Court's Jurisprudence

The cases cited in the previous two sections address both the delegation of lawmaking power and other, more specific aspects of delegation such as private delegations and the delegation of tax power. The complete picture presents a few possible avenues for the Supreme Court as it shapes the future of its nondelegation doctrine.

In the first and most obvious set of delegation cases, in which the power to make law through binding rules and regulations is concerned, states generally adopt the same intelligible principle–type test that the Supreme Court has used for the past several decades. But a significant number of states apply it with actual teeth, periodically finding statutes devoid of such principles and therefore constitutionally invalid. The Supreme Court could note these cases as grounds for its own, more rigorous application of the intelligible-principle test, emphasizing that the state-level cases have not significantly disrupted the functioning of those governments. Alternatively, the Supreme Court could consider crafting a more specific test, perhaps with multiple factors, that examines specific aspects of a delegation to determine whether it runs afoul of the Constitution, as the Illinois court did in *Stofer* and the Florida court did in *Askew*.

The more specific applications of the nondelegation doctrine are also instructive. Delegations to private actors have been subjected to greater scrutiny, and Texas evaluates multiple factors in private delegation cases. Such examples give weight to contemporary calls for a stricter nondelegation principle in cases involving private delegation.[120] Of course, such multifactor tests are notoriously unpredictable and imprecise. But given the heightened scrutiny given to such delegations, future litigants should identify areas in which Congress has delegated authority to private actors and challenge such schemes.[121]

Furthermore, the state-level doctrines on the delegation of tax power may provide support for reconsidering the Supreme Court's conclusion in *Skinner v. Mid-American Pipeline Co.* that the Constitution does not "require the application of a different and stricter nondelegation doctrine in cases where Congress delegates discretionary authority to the Executive under its taxing power."[122] That pronouncement seems to fly squarely in the face of several state-level applications of the nondelegation doctrine.

Although the state nondelegation doctrines are not as robust as some scholars claim, the doctrine is not moribund at the state level. State courts have extensive experience with nondelegation challenges and have crafted more sophisticated and specific tests than the US Supreme Court has for distinguishing between lawful and unlawful delegations. If the majority of justices on the US Supreme Court decide to breathe new life into the nondelegation doctrine, it is worth consulting the states to examine the tests that have emerged and alleviate concerns about the practical implications of reviving the nondelegation doctrine.

Notes

1. Jason Iuliano and Keith E. Whittington, "The Nondelegation Doctrine: Alive and Well," *Notre Dame Law Review* 93 (2017): 619.

2. Edward Stiglitz, "The Limits of Judicial Control and the Nondelegation Doctrine," *Journal of Law, Economics, and Organization* 34 (2018): 27, 29–30.

3. For instance, even Eric Posner and Adrian Vermule acknowledge, in an article dedicated to "lay[ing] the [nondelegation] doctrine to rest once and for all, in an unmarked grave," that they "agree that the Constitution bars the 'delegation of legislative power.'" Eric Posner and Adrian Vermeule, "Interring the Nondelegation Doctrine," *University of Chicago Law Review* 69 (2002): 1723. All the Supreme Court's major decisions applying the nondelegation doctrine have accepted that Article I, Section 1 of the US Constitution implies a nondelegation principle. One important recent exception to this consensus is Julian Davis Mortenson and Nicholas Bagley, "Delegation at the Founding," *Columbia Law Review* 121 (2021): 277. As of this writing, it remains to be seen whether the Mortensen and Bagley article will lead the Court to reconsider whether the Constitution contains a nondelegation principle.

4. See Gary Greco, "Standards or Safeguards: A Survey of the Delegation Doctrine in the States," *Administrative Law Journal of American University* 8 (1994): 567; and Jim Rossi, "Institutional Design and the Lingering Legacy of Antifederalist Separation of Powers Ideals in the States," *Vanderbilt Law Review* 52 (1999): 1167. A third, more recent article by Jason Iuliano and Keith Whittington provides an empirical view of the state nondelegation doctrines without discussing the holdings in the cases or the types of issues that were raised in the cases. Iuliano and Whittington, "The Nondelegation Doctrine," 619.

5. A full discussion of the places where this chapter differs from the assessments offered by Gary Greco and Jim Rossi is beyond the scope of the chapter. For a thorough discussion of the existing scholarship on the state nondelegation doctrines and the limitations of those articles, see Joseph Postell, "The Myth of the State Nondelegation Doctrines" (unpublished). In this section, I use only recent cases (those decided in the past 40 years) as indicative of the state courts' application of the nondelegation doctrine in these narrow categories of cases.

6. *New York Statewide Coalition of Hispanic Chambers of Commerce v. New York City Department of Health and Mental Hygiene*, 16 N.E.3d 538 (N.Y. 2014); and *Boreali v. Axelrod*, 71 N.Y.2d 1 (N.Y. 1987).

7. *Boreali*, 71 N.Y.2d at 7.

8. In Arkansas: *McLane Co. v. Davis*, 110 S.W.3d 251 (Ark. 2003); and *Williform v. Arkansas Department of Human Services*, 2018 Ark. App. 314 (Ark. App. 2018). In Michigan: *Belanger v. Department of State*, 438 N.W.2d 885 (Mich. Ct. App. 1989). In some states, the controversy has centered on whether agencies can claim sovereign immunity to avoid ultra vires challenges. In Arkansas, the state court affirmed that ultra vires challenges could be brought against agencies. See *Monsanto Co. v. Arkansas State Plant Board*, 2019 Ark. 194 (Ark. 2019). However, in Texas, courts have ruled that state agencies are immune from such challenges. See *City of El Paso v. Heinrich*, 284 S.W.3d 366 (Tex. 2009).

9. *Chevron U.S.A. v. Natural Resources Defense Council*, 467 US 837 (1984). For examples of how the Court has used nondelegation-type considerations in the interpretation of statutes, see, for example, *Industrial Union Department, AFL-CIO v. American Petroleum Institute*, 448 US 607 (1980); *FDA v. Brown & Williamson Tobacco Corp.*, 529 US 120 (2000); and *King v. Burwell*, 576 US 988 (2015).

10. *State v. Williams*, 199 Ariz. 585, 598–99 (Ariz. 1978).

11. *City of Oklahoma City v. State ex rel. Oklahoma Department of Labor*, 918 P.2d 26 (Okla. 1995).

12. F. Scott Boyd presents cases from many states following this approach. See F. Scott Boyd, "Looking Glass Law: Legislation by Reference in the States," *Louisiana Law Review* 68 (2007): 1254–57.

13. *Gumbhir v. Kansas State Board of Pharmacy*, 228 Kan. 579 (Kan. 1980).

14. *Gumbhir*, 228 Kan. at 587.

15. See Iuliano and Whittington, "The Nondelegation Doctrine," 643.

16. *Carter v. Carter Coal Co.*, 298 US 238, 311 (1936).

17. *Krielow v. Louisiana Department of Agriculture and Forestry*, 125 So.3d 384 (La. 2013).

18. *Leathers v. Gulf Rice Arkansas* (Ark. 1999).

19. *Protz v. Workers' Compensation Appeals Board*, 161 A.3d 827 (Pa. 2017). *Protz* illustrates how these nondelegation issues overlap. The case raised both private delegation and incorporation concerns, since the law authorized the incorporation of AMA guidelines governing impairment ratings. The court dealt with the incorporation concern by distinguishing between enacting existing definitions and agreeing to adopt subsequent changes to those definitions: "The non-delegation doctrine does not prevent the General Assembly from adopting as its own a particular set of standards which already are in existence at the time of adoption. However, . . . the non-delegation doctrine prohibits the General Assembly from incorporating, sight unseen, subsequent modifications to such standards." *Protz*, 161 A.3d at 838–39.

20. *Sedlak v. Dick*, 887 P.2d 1119 (Kan. 1995).

21. *Krielow*, 125 So.3d at 389.

22. *Protz*, 161 A.3d at 837. The Supreme Court of Pennsylvania was not willing to say "unequivocally . . . that the General Assembly cannot, under any set of circumstances, delegate authority to a private person or entity." But it noted that "hostility toward delegations of governmental authority to private actors" is increased compared to delegations to administrative agencies.

23. *Texas Boll Weevil Eradication Foundation v. Lewellen*, 952 S.W.2d 454 (Tex. 1997).

24. *Boll Weevil*, 952 S.W.2d at 469.

25. *Boll Weevil*, 952 S.W.2d at 472.

26. *FM Properties Operating Co. v. City of Austin*, 22 S.W.3d 868, 875 (Tex. 2000).

27. *FM Properties*, 22 S.W.3d at 875.

28. *Boll Weevil*, 952 S.W.2d at 472.

29. *Marshall v. Northern Virginia Transportation Authority*, 657 S.E.2d 71 (Va. 2008).

30. *Marshall*, 657 S.E.2d at 79–80.

31. *Greater Boise Auditorium District v. Royal Inn of Boise*, 684 P.2d 286 (Idaho 1984).

32. *Sun Valley Co. v. City of Sun Valley*, 708 P.2d 147 (Idaho 1985).

33. *Sun Valley Co.*, 708 P.2d at 158.

34. *Scott v. Donnelly*, 133 N.W.2d 418 (N.D. 1965).

35. South Carolina has also addressed the delegation of tax power. See *Crow v. McAlpine*, 277 S.C. 240, 244 (S.C. 1981), finding "an implied limitation [in the state's constitution] upon the power of the General Assembly to delegate the taxing power. Where the power is delegated to a body composed of persons not assented to by the people . . . this constitutional restriction is violated."

36. This list is not meant to be comprehensive. For cases, see *State v. Williams*, 119 Ariz. at 595; *McQuay v. Arkansas State Board of Architects*, 337 Ark. 339 (Ark. 1999); *People v. Wright*, 30 Cal.3d 705 (Cal. 1982); *Monsanto v. California Office of Environmental Health Hazard Assessment* (Cal. 5th Circuit, 2018); *Redman v. Ohio Department of Industrial Relations*, 75 Ohio St. 3d 399 (Ohio 1996); *Capital Care Network of Toledo v. Ohio Department of Health*, 153 Ohio St.3d 362 (Ohio 2018); *Lussier v. Maryland Racing Commission*, 343 Md. 681 (Md. 1996); *Blank v. Department of Corrections*, 462 Mich. 103 (Mich. 2000); *Oshtemo Township v. Kalamazoo Company Road Commission*, 302 Mich. App. 574 (Mich. App. 2013); *City of Belmont v. Mississippi State Tax Commission*, 860 So.2d 289 (Miss. 2003); *Citizens for Orderly Energy Policy v. Cuomo*, 78 N.Y.2d 398 (N.Y. 1991); *Salt Lake City v. Ohms*, 881 P.2d 844 (Utah 1994); and *Robinson v. State*, 20 P.3d 396 (Utah 2001). While *State v. Williams* involved a successful nondelegation challenge, as discussed above, the court objected because the law at issue in that case adopted US Department of Agriculture regulations defining welfare fraud by incorporation. The Arizona Supreme Court insisted that in most other contexts the approach to the nondelegation doctrine would be permissive of delegations to administrative bodies.

37. See, for instance, *People v. Lowrie*, 761 P.2d 778 (Colo. 1988); *Christ v. Maryland Department of Natural Resources*, 335 Md. 427 (Md. 1994); *Powers v. Secretary of Administration*, 412 Mass. 119 (Mass. 1992); *Department of Environmental Services v. Marino*, 928 A.2d 818 (N.H. 2007); *In re Blizzard*, 163 N.H. 326 (N.H. 2012); and *Panzer v. Doyle*, 2004 WI 52 (Wis. 2004).

38. *Redman*, 75 Ohio St. 3d at 399.

39. *Redman*, 75 Ohio St. 3d at 399.

40. Quoting *Blue Cross of Northeast Ohio v. Ratchford*, 64 Ohio St. 2d 256, 256 (Ohio 1980).

41. *Redman*, 75 Ohio St. 3d at 399.

42. Louis Jaffe wrote that the Supreme Court of Illinois was "a veritable graveyard of delegation" during the New Deal period. Louis L. Jaffe, "An Essay on Delegation of Legislative Power: II," *Columbia Law Review* 47 (1947): 561, 564. For a useful summary of the approach in Illinois up to the 1970s, see George Bunn et al., "No Regulation Without Representation: Would Judicial Enforcement of a Stricter Nondelegation Doctrine Limit Administrative Lawmaking?," *Wisconsin Law Review* (1983): 341, 348–51.

43. *Stofer v. Motor Vehicle Casualty Co.*, 369 N.E.2d 875 (Ill. 1977).

44. *Stofer*, 369 N.E.2d at 879.

45. *Stofer*, 369 N.E.2d at 879.

46. *Thygesen v. Callahan*, 385 N.E.2d 699 (Ill. 1979).

47. *Village of Riverwoods v. Department of Transportation*, 77 Ill. 2d 130 (Ill. 1979).

48. *Village of Riverwoods*, 77 Ill. 2d at 142.

49. *Hill v. Relyea*, 216 N.E.2d 795, 797 (Ill. 1966).

50. *People v. Carter*, 454 N.E.2d 189 (Ill. 1982).

51. *Anchorage v. Police Department*, 839 P.2d 1080, 1085 (Alaska 1992). "A significant component of our analysis of the delegation issue . . . centers on the question whether sufficient standards exist to guide the arbitrator's exercise of the authority delegated by the Assembly."

52. *State v. Fairbanks North Star Borough*, 736 P.2d 1140 (Alaska 1987).

53. *Fairbanks North Star Borough*, 736 P.2d at 1143.

54. *Fairbanks North Star Borough*, 736 P.2d at 1143.

55. *Fairbanks North Star Borough*, 736 P.2d. at 1143.

56. See, for example, *Anchorage*, 839 P.2d. at 1085.

57. *Askew v. Cross Key Waterways*, 372 So. 2d. 913 (Fla. 1978).

58. *Askew*, 372 So. 2d. at 919.

59. See *Askew*, 372 So. 2d. at 921–22. The Florida Supreme Court contrasted the statute in *Askew* with statutes from California, Rhode Island, and New Jersey.

60. See *Askew*, 372 So. 2d. at 921–22. See text in endnote 59.

61. *Askew*, 372 So. 2d. at 918–19.

62. *Bush v. Schiavo*, 885 So. 2d 321 (Fla. 2004).

63. *Chiles v. Children A, B, C, D, E, and F*, 589 So. 2d 260 (Fla. 1991).

64. *Chiles*, 589 So. 2d at 260.

65. *Chiles*, 589 So. 2d at 265.

66. See John E. Fennelly, "Non-Delegation Doctrine and the Florida Supreme Court: What You See Is Not What You Get," *St. Thomas Law Review* 7 (1995): 247.

67. For other relevant cases, see Fennelly, "Non-Delegation Doctrine and the Florida Supreme Court," 256–61.

68. As one writer notes, the Supreme Court of Kentucky "boasted that, 'in the area of nondelegation, Kentucky may be unsurpassed by any state in the Union.'" Benjamin Silver, "Nondelegation in the States" (unpublished manuscript), on file with author, quoting *Board of Trustees of Judicial Reform Retirement System v. Attorney General of Com.*, 132 S.W.3d 770, 782 (Ky. 2003).

69. *Flying J Travel Plaza v. Commonwealth Transportation Cabinet*, 928 S.W.2d 344, 350 (Ky. 1996).

70. *In re Gate City S&L Association*, 182 Mont. 361 (Mont. 1979).

71. *In re Gate City S&L Association*, 182 Mont. at 363.

72. *In re Gate City S&L Association*, 182 Mont. at 369.

73. *In re Gate City S&L Association*, 182 Mont. at 370

74. *In re Gate City S&L Association*, 182 Mont. at 370.

75. *Shannon v. City of Forsyth*, 205 Mont. 111, 114 (Mont. 1983).

76. *White v. State*, 233 Mont. 81 (Mont. 1988).

77. *White*, 233 Mont. at 90.

78. *Hayes v. Lame Deer High School District*, 303 Mont. 204 (Mont. 2000).

79. *Hayes*, 303 Mont. at 210.

80. *Smith Insurance v. Grievance Committee*, 120 N.H. 856, 424 A.2d 816 (N.H. 1980).

81. *Smith Insurance*, 120 N.H. at 860, 424 A.2d at 816.

82. *Smith Insurance*, 120 N.H. at 862, 424 A.2d at 816.

83. *Smith Insurance*, 120 N.H. at 862, 424 A.2d at 816.

84. *Smith Insurance*, 120 N.H. at 861, 424 A.2d at 816.

85. *Guillou v. State of New Hampshire*, 127 N.H. 579 (N.H. 1986).

86. *Guillou*, 127 N.H. at 581.

87. See, for example, *New Hampshire Department of Environmental Services*, 928 A.2d; and *In re Blizzard*, 42 A.3d 791 (N.H. 2012).

88. *Democratic Party of Oklahoma v. Estep*, 652 P.2d 271 (Okla. 1982).

89. *Democratic Party of Oklahoma*, 652 P.2d at 276.

90. *Democratic Party of Oklahoma*, 652 P.2d at 276.

91. *Democratic Party of Oklahoma*, 652 P.2d at 276.

92. *In re Initiative Petition No. 366*, 46 P.3d 123 (Okla. 2002).

93. *In re Initiative Petition No. 366*, 46 P.3d at 128. The court appears to have been correct on this point. The grant of rulemaking authority "to promote the following principles" is the end of the section. A preamble to the first section of the petition does announce a policy "to encourage every citizen of this state to become more proficient in the English language, thereby facilitating participation in the economic, political, and cultural activities of this state and of the United States," but that language did not "follow" the grant of rulemaking authority so is likely not among the "following principles" referred to in the section granting the authority.

94. *In re Initiative Petition No. 366*, 46 P.3d at 129.

95. See, for example, *Nelson v. Nelson*, 954 P.2d 1219 (Okla. 1998); and *Tulsa County F.O.P., Lodge 188 v. Board of County Commissioners of Tulsa County*, 995 P.2d 1124 (Okla. 2000).

96. *Blackwell v. Commonwealth State Ethics Commission*, 523 Pa. 347, 360, 567 A.2d 630 (Pa. 1989).

97. *Blackwell*, 523 Pa. at 360, 567 A.2d.

98. *Blackwell*, 523 Pa. at 356, 567 A.2d at 356.

99. *Blackwell*, 523 Pa. at 361, 567 A.2d at 361.

100. *Pennsylvanians Against Gambling Expansion Fund v. Commonwealth*, 877 A.2d. 383 (Pa. 2005).

101. *Pennsylvanians Against Gambling Expansion Fund*, 877 A.2d.

102. *Pennsylvanians Against Gambling Expansion Fund*, 877 A.2d., quoting *Blackwell*, 523 Pa. at 360, 567 A.2d.

103. *West Philadelphia Achievement Charter Elementary School v. School District of Philadelphia*, 132 A.3d 957 (Pa. 2016).

104. *West Philadelphia Achievement Charter Elementary School*, 132 A.3d at 959.

105. *West Philadelphia Achievement Charter Elementary School*, 132 A.3d at 967.

106. *In re Dailey*, 195 W. Va. 330 (W. Va. 1995).

107. *In re Dailey*, 195 W. Va. at 338.

108. *Appalachian Power Co. v. Public Service Commission*, 296 S.E.2d 887 (W. Va. 1982).

109. *Appalachian Power Co.*, 296 S.E.2d at 889.

110. *Appalachian Power Co.*, 296 S.E.2d at 889.

111. *In re Handy*, 171 Vt. 336 (Vt. 2000).

112. *In re Handy*, 171 Vt. at 336.

113. *A. L. A. Schechter Poultry Corp. v. United States*, 295 US 495, 530 (1935).

114. Stiglitz, "The Limits of Judicial Control and the Nondelegation Doctrine," 27, 29–30.

115. Nicholas Bagley, "A Warning from Michigan," *Atlantic*, October 7, 2020, https://www.theatlantic.com/ideas/archive/2020/10/america-will-be-michigan-soon/616635/.

116. Stiglitz, "The Limits of Judicial Control and the Nondelegation Doctrine," 34.

117. Iuliano and Whittington, "The Nondelegation Doctrine," 643.

118. As Rossi explains, "Despite the doctrinal similarities" between the state and federal tests, many "state courts are much more likely to strike down statutes as unconstitutional than their federal counterparts." Rossi, "Institutional Design and the Lingering Legacy of Antifederalist Separation of Powers Ideals in the States," 1200. In other words, the doctrines are the same but are applied more strictly by the states.

119. *Gundy v. United States*, 139 S. Ct. 2116 (2019).

120. See, for instance, James Rice, "The Private Nondelegation Doctrine: Preventing the Delegation of Regulatory Authority to Private Parties and International Organizations," *California Law Review* 105 (2017): 539.

121. The crafting of agricultural marketing orders by growers is one possibility that comes to mind. For another possibility, see Frank David Ditta, "Leading the Way in Unconstitutional Delegations of Legislative Power: Statutory Incorporation of the LEED Rating System," *Hofstra Law Review* 39 (2010): 369.

122. *Skinner v. Mid-American Pipeline Co.*, 490 US 212, 222–23 (1989).

A Judicially Manageable Test to Restore Accountability

DAVID SCHOENBROD

The Declaration of Independence states that governments derive "their just powers from the consent of the governed."[1] To establish a government whose powers are derived from such consent, Article I of the Constitution vested the power to make rules of private conduct—that is, the laws that govern the people—and other basic powers in the branch of government most accountable to the people: Congress.[2] To make its members personally responsible to the people for controversial exercises of these powers, Article I also requires that how these legislators vote—"yea" or "nay"—be published when requested by one-fifth of those present.[3] Article I was understood to bar them from delegating these powers and thereby dodging responsibility.[4]

Nonetheless, the modern Supreme Court has allowed members of Congress to delegate to agencies the power to make rules of private conduct so long as the statute states something, no matter how vacuous, about the goals the agency should pursue. As Justice Elena Kagan summarized this so-called intelligible-principle test in her opinion for the Court in *Gundy v. United States*, "We have over and over upheld even very broad delegations" including "to regulate in the 'public interest.'"[5] Such delegations allow Congress to blame agencies for promised benefits not delivered and burdens imposed. That guts consent of the governed.[6]

The Court did not set out to mangle democracy, but rather to authorize a system in which Congress would make the policy and experts insulated from politics would rely on scientific methods to translate that policy into rules of private conduct. That, however, is not the system we now have. In the wake of recent elections, presidents have unilaterally decreed radical changes in regulation, tariff, immigration, and other policy.[7] These abrupt changes suggest that Congress has often left much of the policymaking to presidents and their political appointees rather than to experts.

The governed have not consented to this arrangement. Polls show that the public wants Congress to shoulder responsibility.[8] Perceiving public support for Congress making the hard choices, incumbents make a pretense of doing so.[9] Members of Congress claim a desire to shoulder responsibility but coyly avoid turning such claims into actual responsibility. At a recent House Committee on Rules hearing, Rep. Tom Cole (R-OK) explained, "I have a lot of colleagues on both sides that like to rail against the administrative state, but they certainly wouldn't want to have to vote on all those rules and regulations, because they are high risk votes."[10]

The breakdown in consent of the governed is thus plain to see. In February 2020, 70 former senators, including 47 Democrats, 19 Republicans, and four independents, stated in an open letter to current members of the Senate: "Congress is not fulfilling its constitutional duties. . . . To the extent that Congress doesn't function as the Framers intended, policymaking is left to the less democratic executive and judicial branches."[11] Congress' abdication, the letter continues, allows "the executive branch to effectively 'legislate' on its own terms through executive order and administrative regulation."[12]

In a dissent in *Gundy*, Justice Neil Gorsuch, joined by Chief Justice John Roberts and Justice Clarence Thomas, called for the Court to limit Congress' delegation of legislative powers. In other opinions, Justices Samuel Alito and Brett Kavanaugh have signaled the possibility of joining in and thus producing a majority.[13]

In his *Gundy* opinion, Justice Gorsuch asked the key question: "What's the test?"[14] His answer: "As long as Congress makes the policy decisions when regulating private conduct, it may authorize another branch to 'fill up the details.'"[15] In other words, Congress may delegate the power to make such rules so long as the enabling statute speaks to such "important subjects" as the limits on an agency's jurisdiction and how it should address the important policy choices to be encountered in writing the rules.[16] This test, like the intelligible-principle test, speaks to how Congress may delegate the power to make law.

I argue that, whether the Court adopts Justice Gorsuch's test or sticks with its current one, the Court should adopt an additional test that directly enforces the Constitution's bar on the lawmakers delegating the power to make law. Given the constraints on full judicial enforcement, this test could be applied to only a limited, but highly important, set of new rules of private conduct: those imposed in a regulatory action found "significant" under a long-standing executive order and promulgated after the Court adopts this test. Under this test, a court would invalidate such a rule if it had not yet been approved through the legislative process.[17] This additional test would increase Congress' accountability more than Justice Gorsuch's test by itself—or the Court's current test—and thereby better enforce the Constitution's meaning.

In this chapter, I first argue that the Constitution means that Congress must itself make the federal rules of private conduct. Next, I show that Supreme Court justices from across the ideological spectrum have long adopted tests for judicial enforcement of the Constitution that under-enforce constitutional meaning, when full judicial enforcement would run up against constraints on the exercise of judicial power. I then identify the constraints on judicial enforcement pertinent to delegation that led to the Court's current test, which grossly under-enforces the Constitution's state-the-rule meaning. I then argue that, when constraints ebb or new ways around them appear, the Court has and should change its tests to enforce the Constitution's meaning more fully. I suggest a test for delegation that bars making new rules of private conduct found significant under the executive order unless they are voted into effect through the Article I legislative process, and I show that this test would not run afoul of the constraints on judicial enforcement. In particular, I argue that this test would itself be judicially manageable and would reduce concerns about the judicial manageability of any additional test focused on how Congress delegates. I conclude by arguing that the justices are duty bound to adopt a test that better protects consent of the governed.

Overall, my objective is to propose a judicially manageable way for the courts to better enforce the Constitution's bar on Congress delegating the power to make rules of private conduct.

Congress Must Take Responsibility for the Law

To impose consent of the governed, Article I of the Constitution vests "all legislative Powers herein granted" in a Congress legislating in tandem with a president.[18] The legislators' personal responsibility for the use of these powers was central to the compact that the framers of the Constitution offered to the people. As James Madison wrote in *Federalist* 51, "A dependence on the people is, no doubt, the primary control on the government."[19]

Responsibility would fall on these members even though voters may pay little attention until an exercise of legislative power directly affects them. As Justice Kagan, quoting Madison, wrote:

> To retain an "intimate sympathy with the people," [members of Congress] must be "compelled to anticipate the moment" when their "exercise of [power] is to be reviewed." Election day—next year, and two years later, and two years after that— is what links the people to their representatives, and gives the people their sovereign power. That day is the foundation of democratic governance.[20]

Delegation of legislative power undercuts such responsibility. Indeed, debate at the Constitutional Convention proceeded on the premise that Congress had to make the laws that govern the people itself rather than delegate that job to others.[21] John Locke, who influenced many of the framers, thought a people's grant of legislative power was "only to make *laws*, and not to make legislators."[22] Making regulatory law meant not just passing statutes but passing statutes that state the rules of private conduct.[23] Alexander Hamilton wrote in *Federalist* 75 that "the essence of the legislative authority is to enact laws, or, in other words, to prescribe rules for the regulation of the society."[24] He added in *Federalist* 78 that the legislative authority includes prescribing "the rules by which the duties and rights of every citizen are to be regulated."[25]

In *Fletcher v. Peck*, decided in 1810, the Supreme Court wrote, "It is the peculiar province of the legislature to prescribe general rules for the government of society; the application of those rules to individuals in society would seem to be the duty of other departments."[26] In *Gibbons v. Ogden*, decided in 1824, the Court wrote that the power to regulate commerce, which Article I includes in the legislative power, is "to prescribe the rule by which commerce is to be governed."[27]

In *Aurora v. United States*, decided in 1813, the Court recognized in dicta that Congress may not delegate the power to make the rules of private conduct.[28] For many decades after the adoption of the Constitution, the lawmakers in Congress tried to do their lawmaking duty.[29]

I argue that Article I requires Congress itself to make the federal rules of private conduct.[30] An example of such a rule would be a limit on pollution from designated factories.

In contrast, a statute like the modern Clean Air Act that tells an agency to make rules to achieve some pleasing goal such as "protect the public health" with "an adequate margin of safety" states a goal rather than a rule.[31] Stating goals is insufficient because Congress can state goals in ways that allow it to sidestep responsibility. When inserting "protect the public health" in the Clean Air Act in 1970,[32] Congress sidestepped the choices it knew would have to be made about how completely to protect health and apportioning the cleanup burden on pollution sources.[33] So, the legislators had plausible deniability for almost any unpopular consequences of the rules announced on agency letterhead—whether to impose some burden or allow some harm to health to continue—yet an almost unanimous Congress still claimed credit for protecting health.[34]

A statute that takes the form of a rule but fails to state a rule of conduct in understandable terms—such as one that bars large factories from emitting "unreasonable" pollution—also conflicts with the Constitution's meaning. What was unreasonable may have been understandable when early courts instructed juries in tort actions that the standard of reasonable care was how people in their community customarily behave, but it would not be understandable in modern air pollution regulation.[35] Custom is hardly a guide to the meaning of "unreasonable" when a statute is supposed to respond to newly understood threats and newly invented means to deal with them. Such a statute fails to achieve Article I's objective: to make the elected lawmakers responsible for the politically salient choices.

Of course, even a forthright rule will require interpretation in some cases.[36] Yet, interpreting the law is distinct from policymaking.[37]

Interpretation calls for an inquiry into how the enacting legislature would have clarified the law's ambiguities; policymaking calls for an inquiry into what makes sense to the policymaker. In deciding how the Congress that passed the statute would have resolved an ambiguity, a judge can get information from all the standard tools of statutory interpretation.[38] For example, by indicating outcomes in most cases, the rule reveals the relative weight the legislature gave to conflicting policy goals, such as enhancing regulatory protection versus avoiding regulatory burdens.

The Court Bases Constitutional Tests on Both Meaning and Constraints

Earlier I discussed constitutional meaning, but the Court can establish tests for judicial enforcement that under-enforce constitutional meaning. Professor Lawrence Lessig shows why in a recent book that explains the work of justices from across the ideological spectrum from the early years to modern times.[39] His model of judicial behavior has two parts: "fidelity to meaning," referring to the meaning of the Constitution, and "fidelity to role," referring to the constraints on judicial enforcement of meaning imposed by the Court's role in a republic.[40] Lessig writes that decisions prompted by constraints "are instances of *infidelity* (to meaning) in order to preserve or enable the capacity of the judicial institution more generally."[41]

For an example of the distinction between constitutional meaning and constitutional test, consider "one person, one vote." Legislative districts equal in population is what the Constitution means, but a constraint in enforcing that meaning is the state's legitimate interest in matters other than complete equality—such as legislative district boundaries corresponding to municipal boundaries. So, the Court's test presumes that the districting is constitutional if the deviations among the populations of districts do not exceed 10 percent.[42]

In an earlier article, Professor Lawrence Sager demonstrated that constraints can lead to constitutional tests that under-enforce constitutional meaning.[43] The Equal Protection Clause, he writes, means that "a state may treat people differently only when it is fair to do so,"[44] but full enforcement of that meaning runs up against the constraint that federal courts should not second-guess policy decisions the Constitution leaves to states.[45] So, to reduce trespasses on state power in cases that do not involve dubious classifications such as race, federal courts use a test that permits inequality if it bears a "rational relationship" to the government's justification for it.[46] This test ends up crediting some pretextual justifications, thus underenforcing constitutional meaning.

That a constraint results in a test that under-enforces the Constitution's meaning does not, however, change its meaning.[47] Sager argues that constitutional norms (i.e., meanings)

> which are underenforced by the federal judiciary should be understood to be legally valid to their full conceptual limits, and federal judicial decisions which stop short of these limits should be understood as delineating only the boundaries of the federal courts' role in enforcing the norm.[48]

So officials remain duty bound to strive to adhere fully to the Constitution's meaning even if courts are unable to fully enforce it.

Neither Lessig nor Sager apply their explanations of why courts under-enforce constitutional meaning to delegation of lawmaking power.[49] I will.

Constraints on Courts' Stopping Unconstitutional Delegation

Four constraints have led the Court to adopt the intelligible-principle test, which prevents courts generally from enforcing the Constitution's state-the-rule meaning: (1) infeasibility of Congress enacting all the federal rules of private conduct, (2) lack of a judicially manageable test, (3) fierce political opposition, and (4) the public's reliance on delegation. Yet, as I discuss later, the Court now under-enforces the constitutional meaning to a far greater extent than these constraints require.

Infeasibility of Congress Making All the Rules. For the Court to require the impossible would jeopardize its authority.[50] The Court concluded in deciding *Mistretta v. United States* in 1989 that "in our increasingly complex society, replete with ever-changing and more technical problems, Congress simply cannot do its job absent an ability to delegate power under broad general directives."[51]

Even earlier, however, in deciding *Wayman v. Southard* in 1825, the Court recognized the burden on Congress of making every rule.[52] A statute instructed federal district courts to adopt rules of procedure that track state court procedural rules but authorized "alterations and additions."[53] *Wayman* saw no obstacle to Congress delegating the making of rules of *official* conduct, but the case dealt with a rule that "extended beyond the mere regulation of practice in the court"[54] and thus regulated *private* conduct. Unless the Court cut Congress some slack, producing federal court rules that correspond to the extent practical with state court rules would require Congress to evaluate each procedural rule of every state and then subsequent amendments to them. Instead of imposing this burden on Congress, Chief Justice John Marshall's opinion for the Court stated:

> The line has not been exactly drawn which separates those important subjects which must be entirely regulated by the legislature itself from those of less interest in which a general provision may be made and power given to those who are to act under such general provisions to fill up the details.[55]

Thus, the Court adopted the following test: On "subjects . . . of less interest," but not on "important subjects," Congress could enact "general provisions" to authorize a delegate to "vary minor regulations."[56] That test under-enforces the Constitution's state-the-rule meaning. Yet, by requiring Congress itself to enact the rules on important subjects, and thus presumably the more politically salient ones, the Wayman test would largely preserve "consent of the governed."

Professor Gary Lawson explains that Chief Justice Marshall enforced the people's delegation of legislative powers to Congress in much the same way that common-law courts had long enforced private people's delegations of power to agents. It would often be infeasible for a private agent to do everything required by a delegation. For example, an agent with the delegated power to take goods abroad to sell them need not personally steer the ship or stand guard over them day and night. At common law, the agent could subdelegate matters of less interest, but not important matters—and so too with Congress.[57] Chief Justice Marshall's test of delegation could be read as combining the state-the-rule meaning of the Constitution and the constraint on its enforcement based on infeasibility.

The Lack of a Judicially Manageable Test. Lessig states the Court bows out when it lacks a judicially manageable test—that is, a test that guides judges in deciding the issue—because otherwise the Court would seem to be acting politically and thereby jeopardize its credibility as a judicial institution.[58]

The Court has, however, adopted a test of delegation that is entirely unmanageable. A century after *Wayman*, in *J. W. Hampton Jr. & Co. v. United States*,[59] the Court stated, "If Congress shall lay down by legislative act an intelligible principle to which the person or body authorized to fix such rates is directed to conform, such legislative action is not a forbidden delegation of legislative power."[60] Whatever that meant,[61] within a generation, intelligible principle came to represent a test at odds with *Wayman*. It allows Congress to delegate making rules on unquestionably "important subjects" so long as the statute states goals and boundaries to guide the agency's rulemaking.[62] The theory is that, when so guided, the agency is not exercising legislative powers in making rules of private conduct.

This test, taken at face value, raises two difficult questions. First, how much guidance is sufficient? Because transforming goals into rules of conduct typically requires policy choices, sufficiency is a matter of degree.[63] Given the different topics of regulation such as protecting health, stopping unfair trade practices, and preventing discrimination, rank ordering how much guidance the goals of various statutes provide would be difficult, to say the least.[64]

Second, how confining must the boundaries on the agency's authority be? The concept of boundaries is clear, but any statute other than one delegating Congress' entire Article I authority will impose some boundary on the agency's authority. So, a boundary-based test must ride on the tightness of the statutory boundaries. As with goals, rank ordering the tightness of the boundaries in statutes would be difficult.

In two cases in which the Court struck a statute for delegating legislative power, the Court found the statute failed to provide an intelligible principle without defining how intelligible the principle must be. *Panama Refining*

Company v. Ryan found that the delegation gave the president unfettered discretion.[65] *A. L. A. Schechter Poultry Corp. v. United States* found that the delegation gave the president vast authority.[66] As Justice Benjamin Cardozo stated in concurring in *A. L. A. Schechter Poultry*, the statute meant "anything that Congress may do within the limits of the commerce clause for the betterment of business may be done by the President. . . . This is delegation running riot."[67]

So, except in extreme cases like *Panama Refining* and *A. L. A. Schechter Poultry*, the intelligible-principle test as it now stands is mush and therefore judicially unmanageable and unenforceable. The problem is with this test for judicial enforcement of the constitutional norm rather than the constitutional norm itself—that Congress enact the laws—which is itself clear. As this chapter will show, the Court could craft a test for judicial enforcement of this norm that is entirely judicially manageable. By failing to do so, however, the Court has relieved itself of responsibility. So, the Court lets Congress outsource responsibility for the laws by giving lip service to the vaguest of goals.[68]

Ironically, the judicially manageability constraint itself also rides on a question of degree: Do the courts have a test definite enough to save them from appearing to act politically? How definite the test must be depends in part on the fierceness of the political opposition that a decision employing the test is likely to evoke.

Fierce Political Opposition. Fierce political opposition is another constraint, according to Lessig.[69] That the Court would back down in the face of political opposition may seem strange, given that the Constitution is supposedly counter-majoritarian. That is why Lessig notes, "It is in [the nature of this constraint] that its nature cannot be announced."[70]

Jurists should not, of course, base decisions on what will bring them popularity or save them from criticism, but it is quite another matter when political opposition grows so fierce as to imperil the Court's independence—as happened partly in response to the Court's decisions on delegation.

The year after the two famous delegation decisions of 1935—*Panama Refining* and *A. L. A. Schechter Poultry*—the Court in *Carter v. Carter Coal Co.* struck down another New Deal statute partly because it delegated rulemaking power to private parties.[71] The three decisions denied President Franklin D. Roosevelt powers he claimed he needed to deal with a national calamity: the Great Depression. With the Court defying him on multiple issues including delegation, the president stated, "The Court has been acting not as a judicial body, but as a policy-making body" by overriding "the judgment of the Congress on legislative policy." Moreover, the justices were poor legislators because, being old men, they were out of touch with "facts and circumstances under which average men have to live and work."[72]

After a landslide reelection victory in 1936, President Roosevelt famously proposed a statute authorizing him to appoint additional justices.[73] This court-packing plan would have robbed the Court of its independence. The plan almost passed but did not.[74] Even before the court-packing plan was announced, however, the Court had begun to go easier on New Deal legislation.[75] Justices acknowledged that they sought to insulate the Court from political turmoil.[76] In this endeavor, the unmanageability of the intelligible-principle test helped the Court sidestep a divisive issue. The Court struck down no statute on delegation grounds during the balance of the New Deal, despite many statutes broadly delegating legislative power.[77]

The Public's Reliance on Delegation. Congress has passed many statutes in the belief that the courts will permit delegation to agencies. Many, if not most, of the regulatory statutes in the *United States Code* and the rules in the *Code of Federal Regulations* conflict with the requirement that Congress itself state the rules of private conduct.[78] Businesses, state and local governments, nonprofit institutions, and individuals have structured their operations in reliance on these rules. The public relies on the protection these rules provide. To impose a tough new test for delegation, the Court would need some way to deal with the public's reliance on existing rules.

The Court Is Obligated to Search for a Test That Better Protects Accountability

Lessig argues that the Court should search for tests that better enforce the Constitution's meaning.[79] As he states, "What a court needs when it recognizes failure is the freedom to try again: 'Our aim is to preserve X. We have tried techniques A and B; they've proven too costly. We'll now try C.'"[80] He gives this example: When under-enforcement occurred because political opposition was, in his words, "a kind of *force majeure*, then it follows that when the force is removed, the obligation to return to the Constitution's . . . meaning returns as well."[81]

It so happens that, because of political opposition and other constraints, the Court's current test grossly fails to protect the people's right to a Congress that is accountable for rules of private conduct. Yet, public opinion now calls for the "lawmakers" in Congress to take responsibility. The public opinion supposedly in favor of delegation during the New Deal[82] no longer persists. According to Professor David Mayhew, in polls conducted by different polling organizations in 1958, 1977, and 2004–05, by a margin of three to one, voters prefer Congress rather than the president to "make policies."[83] Mayhew, a widely honored scholar of Congress,[84] finds that voters overwhelmingly want Congress to take responsibility despite appreciating its gridlock and partisan divisions, because "the public sees constitutional checks and balances as a good thing."[85] The icing on the cake is the open letter from 70 former senators to current members of the Senate urging Congress to shoulder responsibility.[86]

Congress' continued shirking of its constitutional responsibility gives the people less regulatory protection at greater expense, as I have shown in detail elsewhere.[87]

A Test That Better Protects Accountability

Justice Gorsuch's dissent in *Gundy* states that "as long as Congress makes the policy decisions when regulating private conduct, it may authorize another branch to 'fill up the details.'"[88] In other words, Congress may delegate the power to impose the rules of private conduct, so long as the statute speaks to such major policy decisions as the scope of the agency's power and the goals it should pursue in writing the rules.

Whether the Court adopts this test or sticks with the existing one, the Court should adopt an additional test that enforces the actual meaning of the Constitution—but only to the extent permitted by the constraints on judicial enforcement. That meaning, as shown earlier, bars the imposition of rules of private conduct unless approved through the Article I legislative process. Given those constraints, as will be shown in this section, courts could apply this meaning to an important set of new rules.

How important something must be to be deemed important is a question of degree and therefore challenging to define. In the case of new rules, however, the courts can get help from a surprising source: the president. Recent presidents have employed a system to identify important regulatory actions. An executive order requires the administrator of the Office of Information and Regulatory Affairs (OIRA) in the Executive Office of the President to identify "significant regulatory actions." The definition of that term was inserted in the order issued by President Bill Clinton over a quarter century ago and has remained unchanged under Presidents George W. Bush, Barack Obama, Donald Trump, and Joe Biden.[89]

Under the test that this chapter proposes, a court would invalidate a new rule imposed by a regulatory action found significant under the executive order if it has not yet been approved through the legislative process. The rule would be invalidated on statutory grounds, if available, but otherwise on constitutional grounds.[90] The rule rather than the statute would be struck.

The Court could adopt this test by invalidating such a rule that the legislative process has not approved. The decision would invalidate that rule but make it clear that, otherwise, the test will be applied only to rules subsequently promulgated. Alternatively, the Court could give forewarning of the test in explaining why the Court is not applying it to an old rule or a new rule that does not qualify as significant under the executive order.[91]

Still another alternative would be for the Court, the first time it applies the test, to delay invalidating the rule in that case for a limited time to give Congress a chance to approve it. This would be analogous to what courts have done after finding that a legislative districting violates the one-person, one-vote norm. As the Court stated in *Reynolds v. Sims*, "Judicial relief becomes appropriate only when a legislature fails to reapportion according to federal constitutional requisites in a timely fashion after having had an adequate opportunity to do so."[92]

This additional test would make the legislators more accountable than they would be even if they responded to Justice Gorsuch's test by doing their best to embed the major policy choices in instructions to agencies for writing the rules. Giving precise instructions for doing even commonplace tasks can be difficult, as we acknowledge when we are sometimes tempted to say, "It would be simpler to do it myself." Giving instructions for writing regulatory rules would be much more difficult. The legislators cannot know the facts that the agency will encounter when it goes to make the rules, often years or even decades later. So, the instructions in the statute will likely be somewhat abstract. That abstraction would give legislators leeway to blame the unpopular consequences of the rule on the agency's rulemaking. Moreover, the legislators who voted for the instructions may well not be in office when the agency issues the rule. The legislators' accountability would be at its maximum when they declare "yea" or "nay" on the rules of private conduct as the Constitution intended.

The test this chapter proposes differs from the one I proposed in a recent article—that a new regulation requires approval through the legislative process if it meets the first part of the executive order's definition of "significance"—that it would have "an annual effect on the economy of $100 million or more."[93] The other parts of the definition, such as "adversely affect in a material way the economy, a sector of the economy, productivity, competition, jobs, the environment, public health or safety, or State, local, or tribal governments or communities" seemed too vague to be judicially manageable. Meanwhile, Professor Susan E. Dudley, a former administrator of OIRA, had assured me that that the $100 million threshold could be met by either compliance costs or regulatory benefits such as improved public health or improved air quality and that it could be met by decreases in compliance costs from deregulation, as my article stated.[94] I now propose a simpler, more deferential, and potentially more inclusive test: that new regulations require approval through the legislative process if OIRA finds them significant. The remainder of this section shows that this test is consistent with the constraints on judicial enforcement and then addresses the concern that some truly important rules may not be found significant under the executive order.

Judicially Manageability. The executive order's gauge of importance has key advantages. The definition of significance was designed to identify those agency actions with which it was particularly crucial to deal responsibly rather than to evade responsibility. It has been in force under administrations of both parties, applies to rules that either regulate or deregulate, is triggered because of either their benefits or their costs, and includes rules of private conduct that are not regulatory such as tax rules. Finally, courts could readily tell from the administrator's decision whether the rule should be treated as important.[95]

The executive order would not, however, work as well for old rules. Its system for identifying significant regulatory actions was not in effect before 1994. Besides, defining important old regulatory actions would require deciding which provisions of *Code of Federal Regulations* constitute a regulatory action. Some of its sections have been modified by many separate promulgations, and some of the promulgations have changed many sections. Thus, it would be difficult to construct a judicially manageable way to define important old regulatory actions. That is one reason I conclude the test should not apply to old rules.

The significant new rule test would not only be judicially manageable itself but also reduce somewhat the concerns about judicial manageability of a test that addresses how Congress delegates the power to make law. If a rule flunks the significant new rule test and Congress fails to enact the rule, the case would become moot. If the rule flunks the significant new rule test but then its promulgation is approved through the Article I process, the elected lawmakers would have taken responsibility for the rule. Thus, the courts would need to apply a test geared to how Congress delegates only to rules that do not qualify as new and significant and thus tend to be less controversial.

Infeasibility of Congress Making All the Rules. A court would not be acting like a court if it required a legislature to do the infeasible. So, the justices will ask themselves: Could Congress cope with the new test?

The answer is plainly "yes" for regulatory actions taken after the Court announces the proposed test. Congress could cope by establishing a fast-track process that would require prompt, up-or-down votes on whether to approve or disapprove rules identified as significant under the executive order. Congress has passed statutes mandating such a process for military base closings and other matters.[96] A fast-track statute for important new regulatory actions could set deadlines by which the House and Senate must vote, limit debate, and bar amendments and filibusters on such bills. It could also provide that a bill of approval that gained majorities in both houses would be presented to the president for signature, thus avoiding the objection that doomed the legislative veto in *Immigration and Naturalization Service v. Chadha*.[97]

Congress has the time to have fast-track votes on all the new "significant regulatory actions" as defined under the executive order. The number of votes required each year would be about the same as the current votes on symbolic public laws such as those naming federal buildings.[98] Voting on significant regulations would require legislators to shoulder more responsibility than naming buildings, but the Constitution includes voting on rules of private conduct in Congress' job description, not naming buildings. Moreover, members would have at their disposal the agency's recent statement of reasons for promulgating the rule.

It would, however, not be feasible for Congress to vote on all the regulatory actions that OIRA has designated as significant from 1994 to the present. That would entail voting on all such actions promulgated for over a quarter of a century. Not only would there have to be an impossibly large number of votes, but Congress could not rely on the agencies' statements of reason, which generally would now be outdated. Therefore, the Court should state that the lower courts would apply the new test only to regulatory actions promulgated after the test is announced.

The Court could avoid applying the new test to old regulations despite the statement in *Harper v. Virginia Department of Taxation* that

> when this Court applies a rule of federal law to the parties before it, that rule is the controlling interpretation of federal law and must be given full retroactive effect in all cases still open on direct review and as to all events, regardless of whether such events predate or postdate our announcement of the rule. . . . We now prohibit the erection of selective temporal barriers to the application of federal law in noncriminal cases.[99]

Yet, *Harper* itself brought a new judicially created rule—one involving retroactivity—and what the Court did there in one direction, it can do again in another direction on another distinct issue. The issue here is distinct because the usual reason given for denying retroactive effect is fairness to those who relied on the old rule. The reasons advanced here are lack of a judicially manageable standards and infeasibility.

Moreover, the reasons the Court gave for the rule in *Harper* either do not apply here or do so weakly. One reason offered in Justice Thomas' opinion for the Court is that the judicial function "strips us of the quintessentially 'legislat[ive]' prerogative to make rules of law retroactive or prospective as we see fit."[100] This point is too broad because, as Justice Antonin Scalia recognized, "A certain degree of discretion, and thus of lawmaking, *inheres* in most executive or judicial action."[101]

Another reason Justice Thomas offered is that "selective application of new rules violates the principle of treating similarly situated [parties] the same."[102] That, in effect, begs the question of whether applying the consent-of-the-governed norm to new regulations but not old ones would readily allow courts to treat all similarly situated persons the same way: All those similarly involved with old regulations would be treated one way, and all those similarly involved with new ones another way. Besides, as previously described, applying a new and stronger test of the consent-of-the-governed norm to old regulations would cause widespread pain given the ensuing doubt about the validity of the huge volume of old regulations. Given the uncertainty and upset, it would cause harm to just about everyone.

Finally, Justice Scalia's concurring opinion in *Harper* helps distinguish the delegation context. In support of the anti-prospectivity rule that *Harper* adopts, he wrote, "Prospective decisionmaking is the handmaid of judicial activism."[103] Yet, the Court's past evisceration of the consent-of-the-governed norm constituted massive judicial activism that the Court would be fully entitled—indeed, obliged—to reverse as much as possible. In sum, a strong case can be made that the rule in *Harper* should not bar refraining from applying the new consent-of-the-governed test to old regulations.

It could not be argued that a fast-track statute for new regulatory actions is infeasible because it would block judicial review of administrative action. Congress could, if it wished, provide in the statute that Congress votes to approve the agency's promulgation of a rule rather than to enact the rule.[104] That way, the rule, once approved, would still be subject to judicial review on, say, whether the agency acted within its statutory authority.[105] Congress approving the promulgation of a rule rather than enacting it would also allow the agency to amend the rule without action of Congress unless the amendment was, itself, a significant regulatory action.

It might seem strange that a rule reviewed by both houses of Congress and the president could be reviewed again by a court or amended by an agency. Surely, however, Congress can approve the promulgation of a single, known rule when it now has on the books statutes that approve in advance and wholesale the promulgation of future, and thus unknown, rules. The former, by making Congress accountable, serves the purpose of the Constitution.

Moreover, Congress is within its power to approve an action for one purpose but leave it to the courts to decide its legality for other purposes. For example, *Tennessee Valley Authority v. Hill* rejected the Tennessee Valley Authority's argument that Congress' appropriation of money to build a project insulated it from challenge under an environmental statute.[106]

It could not be objected that this way of compliance is unworkable because, as the COVID-19 pandemic warns us, emergencies sometimes require rules to go into effect faster than the deadline a fast-track statute might set. Equitable discretion would give courts leeway to refrain from nullifying an unapproved rule immediately to avoid harm to the public disproportionate to the harm that the plaintiff would suffer if the illegality were not stopped immediately, especially when Congress strives to end such illegality expeditiously by having in place a statute that requires votes by a deadline.[107] Congress could, if it wished, make it easier for courts to grant such leeway by including in its statute a provision allowing a new regulation to have immediate effect if the president certifies the need but would cease to have effect unless the promulgation is approved within the statutory deadline.

The Public's Reliance on Delegation. Because it would be judicially unmanageable and infeasible to apply the new test to old rules, the proposed test poses no threat to the reliance on old rules.

Fierce Political Opposition. The Court enforcing the Constitution's consent-of-the-governed norm will, of course, upset both Democrats and Republicans in Congress because they will have to cast what Rep. Cole called "high-risk votes." Yet, these legislators and others in Washington whose power or income derives from delegation will have trouble turning the public against the Court.

What unleashed fierce political opposition during the New Deal was the Court nullifying statutes that the representatives, senators, and president whom the people elected had approved and therefore were presumably for the people's benefit. The test herein proposed would not nullify statutes. Rather, it would allow significant new regulations to go into effect if approved by the representatives, senators, and president whom the people elected. Thus, the Court would not be standing athwart what was presumably for the benefit of the governed but rather standing for the consent of the governed, which the Constitution requires and, as the polls discussed earlier show, the people want. The justices would thus not be acting as legislators but rather insisting that the legislators do their constitutional duty.

If Congress delayed in adopting a way to take responsibility, it would take most of the blame for the consequences. Congress, of course, often ends up gridlocked, but where the blame it receives is great enough, it finds a way to unlock, as illustrated by its managing in most instances to avoid impasses over appropriations shutting down the government.[108] Moreover, unlike appropriations, a statute that would provide a practical way to comply with the Court's new test need be passed only once rather than every year.

Moreover, the courts would be further shielded from fierce political opposition because they would not be seen as picking and choosing which statutes to strike down as during the New Deal. Instead, they would strike down only new rules promulgated in regulatory actions deemed significant by the administrator of OIRA that Congress has not approved.

Omissions of the Test. The executive order's definition of significance calls, of course, for line drawing so actions just below the line will not be found significant. For example, one of the criteria that the order provides for defining an action as significant is that it will have "an annual effect on the economy of $100 million or more."[109] That leaves out actions with a $99 million effect. Yet, such arbitrariness is inherent in bright-line tests that the courts adopt to make the enforcement of norms judicially manageable.[110]

The executive order's definition of significant regulatory action excludes some categories of new actions such as those promulgated by independent agencies[111] and executive order.[112] These omissions stem largely from the executive order's purpose, which is to identify and scrutinize the more important actions of the agencies that the president does control to ensure that these agencies serve the president's interests. The president is the only elected official likely to get much blame for the unpopular consequences. The president cannot, however, dictate to the independent agencies and so is less likely to get blamed for their actions.

The Executive Office of the President generally writes the executive orders, so it can look out for the president's interests directly. To correct these omissions, the president could in theory amend the executive order to include the actions from independent agencies and in executive orders in those scanned for significance but stop short of requiring OIRA to otherwise evaluate such rules.

Nonetheless, the current executive order covers "any substantive action by an agency . . . expected to lead to the promulgation of a final rule or regulation."[113] Thus, a test based on OIRA's findings of significance would go a long way to force Congress to vote on important new rules.

Constitutional tests often under-enforce constitutional meaning. The Court's current intelligible-principle test is a stunning example. So, the Court could adopt a test based on OIRA's findings of significance despite its omissions.

Other omissions could come from the executive branch trying to evade the Court's test by amending the executive order or changing how it is administered. The incentive for evasion is obvious. A president could shield some new rules from a vote in Congress.

Vulnerability to evasion has not, however, stopped the Court from adopting other constitutional tests. For example, as Sager showed, under the rationale basis test of equal protection, officials can get away with treating people unequally for illegitimate reasons by ginning up some rationale for the inequality that appears legitimate. Similarly, in one-person, one-vote cases, the courts presume legislative districting is valid if the variation in the population of districts is less than 10 percent, thus giving states more than trivial scope to give some peoples' votes more weight than others' votes.[114] Moreover, the majority in *Rucho v. Common Cause* maintained that it would continue to enforce one person, one vote even though it would not stop partisan gerrymandering, which is another way to give some people's votes more weight than others' votes.[115]

While the incentives for evasion are obvious, the disincentives are less obvious. By easing the making of favorite rules, the president would have helped a successor in office repeal those same rules. In addition, as already noted, Congress writes statutes to shift blame for unpopular consequences to the agencies, and some of that blame spills over to their boss, the president. By having OIRA designate a regulation as significant, the president could shift back to Congress much of the blame it had shifted to the executive branch. Turnabout is fair play.

Furthermore, the president could lose popularity by changing the administration of the executive order to relieve Congress from responsibility. The public supports Congress shouldering fuller responsibility. The letter from 70 former senators reflects elite concern with Congress' dereliction of duty.

Moreover, the Court would no longer be giving Congress cover for its dereliction by holding that the legislators had done their constitutional responsibility by authorizing agencies to make even the most important rules with no more than vacuous guidance. To the contrary, the Court would make it clear that Congress has the duty to vote on all the new rules even though the Court's test for judicial enforcement reaches only those in new regulatory actions deemed significant under the executive order. So, if a clearly important rule is imposed without votes in Congress, voters will know that the president and the members of Congress have failed to honor their oaths of office to enforce and support the Constitution.[116]

Finally, if OIRA changes how it decides which rules are significant to evade the Court's new constitutional test, the Court could, as Lessig argues it long has done, change its test in response to the affront to constitutional meaning.

Conclusion

The Supreme Court has no duty more supreme than judging compliance with the Constitution. None of the Constitution's objectives is more supreme than the consent of the governed. As Justice Kagan wrote, "If there is a single idea that made our Nation (and that our Nation commended to the world), it is this one: The people are sovereign."[117] She added, "The need for judicial review is at its most urgent in cases" in which "politicians' incentives conflict with voters' interests, leaving citizens without any political remedy for their constitutional harms."[118]

Yet, the sovereignty of the people somehow is forgotten when the Court deals with the legislators' duty to make themselves accountable to the governed. The justices began calling this duty the "nondelegation doctrine" in 1971; the label derives from scholarship that calls for scrapping that duty.[119] This label masks its constitutional purpose no less than would calling equal protection "nondifferentiation" or freedom of the press "nonfiltering."

The Supreme Court has allowed the elected lawmakers to defile consent of the governed by delegating responsibility for the laws. In response to assertions that Congress fails to do its duty by outsourcing responsibility to agencies, the Court outsources its own responsibility for judgment to Congress. That is poetic injustice. It should stop.

Acknowledgments

I thank Susan E. Dudley, Aaron Gordon, Marci Hamilton, Gary Lawson, Saikrishna Prakash, Edward A. Purcell Jr., Peter Wallison, and John Yoo for penetrating comments on earlier drafts of this chapter and New York Law School students Ethan Clarkson, Michael Falbo, and Chloe Van Bourgondien for assiduous research assistance.

Notes

1. Declaration of Independence para. 2 (US 1776).

2. US Const. art. I, § 8.

3. US Const. art. I, § 5, cl. 3. "Each House shall keep a Journal of its Proceedings . . . and the Yeas and Nays of the Members of either House on any question shall, at the Desire of one fifth of those Present, be entered on the Journal." The Constitution does not call for popular election of the president. See US Const. art. II, § 1, cl. 2–3. Nor did it do so for senators until the ratification of the 17th Amendment. See US Const. art. I, § 3, cl. 1. Nonetheless, even without direct elections, popular sentiment could result in either presidents or senators failing to get reelected.

4. For more information, see the section "Congress Must Take Responsibility for the Law" in this chapter.

5. *Gundy v. United States*, 139 S. Ct. 2116, 2129 (2019) (citing *National Broadcasting Co. v. United States*, 319 US 190, 216 (1943) and *New York Central Securities Corp. v. United States*, 287 US 12, 24 (1932)).

6. David Schoenbrod, "Consent of the Governed: A Constitutional Norm That the Court Should Substantially Enforce," *Harvard Journal of Law and Public Policy* 43, no. 1 (2020): 213, 274.

7. For example, a *New York Times* analysis "counts more than 70 environmental rules and regulations officially reversed, revoked or otherwise rolled back under Mr. Trump. Another 26 rollbacks are still in progress." Nadja Popovich, Livia Albeck-Ripka, and Kendra Pierre-Louis, "The Trump Administration Is Reversing Nearly 100 Environmental Rules. Here's the Full List.," *New York Times*, October 15, 2020, https://www.nytimes.com/interactive/2020/climate/trump-environment-rollbacks.html.

8. For more information, see the section "The Court Is Obligated to Search for a Test That Better Protects Accountability" in this chapter.

9. An example is the air pollution legislation passed in 1970. David Schoenbrod, *Saving Our Environment from Washington: How Congress Grabs Power, Shirks Responsibility, and Shortchanges the People* (New Haven, CT: Yale University Press, 2005), 23–38.

10. HouseRules, "Rules Committee Meeting on Article One," YouTube, March 10, 2020, https://youtu.be/2Y6MoUBJP5U?t=4596.

11. *Washington Post*, "70 Former U.S. Senators: The Senate Is Failing to Perform Its Constitutional Duties," February 25, 2020, https://www.washingtonpost.com/opinions/former-us-senators-the-senate-is-failing-to-perform-its-constitutional-duties/2020/02/25/b9bdd22a-5743-11ea-9000-f3cffee23036_story.html.

12. *Washington Post*, "70 Former U.S. Senators."

13. Justice Samuel Alito stated in his concurring opinion that "if a majority of this Court were willing to reconsider the approach we have taken for the past 84 years, I would support the effort." See *Gundy*, 139 S. Ct. at 2131 (Alito, J., concurring in the judgment). Justice Brett Kavanaugh did not participate in the decision but later praised Justice Neil Gorsuch's "scholarly analysis." See *Paul v. United States*, 140 S. Ct. 342, 342 (2019) (Kavanaugh, J., concurring in denial of certiorari).

14. *Gundy*, 139 S. Ct. at 2135.

15. *Gundy*, 139 S. Ct. at 2136 (Gorsuch, J., dissenting).

16. *Gundy*, 139 S. Ct. at 2136 (Gorsuch, J., dissenting).

17. For more information, see the section "A Test That Better Protects Accountability" in this chapter.

18. US Const. art. I, §§ 1, 2, 7–8.

19. *Federalist*, no. 51 (James Madison).

20. *Rucho v. Common Cause*, 139 S. Ct. 2484, 2512 (2019) (Kagan, J., dissenting) (citation omitted) (second alteration in original) (quoting *Federalist*, nos. 52, 57, at 124 (James Madison)).

21. John L. FitzGerald, *Congress and the Separation of Powers* (Westport, CT: Praeger, 1986), 35–39; and Joseph Postell, *Bureaucracy in America: The Administrative State's Challenge to Constitutional Government* (Columbia, MO: University of Missouri Press, 2017).

22. John Locke, *Second Treatise of Government*, ed. Richard H. Cox (1690; Wheeling, IL: Harlan Davidson Inc., 1982): 87.

23. For an argument to the contrary, see Eric A. Posner and Adrian Vermeule, "Interring the Nondelegation Doctrine," *University of Chicago Law Review* 69 (2002): 1733. I criticize their argument at Schoenbrod, "Consent of the Governed," 265–66.

24. *Federalist*, no. 75 (Alexander Hamilton).

25. *Federalist*, no. 78 (Alexander Hamilton).

26. *Fletcher v. Peck*, 10 US (6 Cranch) 87, 136 (1810); and *Gundy*, 139 S. Ct. at 2138 (Gorsuch, J., dissenting).

27. *Gibbons v. Ogden*, 22 US (9 Wheat.) 1, 196 (1824).

28. *Aurora v. United States*, 11 US (7 Cranch) 382, 388 (1813).

29. Schoenbrod, "Consent of the Governed," 266–71.

30. For a fuller discussion of why delegation may be permitted for rules regulating government property arising under Article IV, see David Schoenbrod, *Power Without Responsibility: How Congress Abuses the People Through Delegation* (New Haven, CT: Yale University Press, 1993), 186–89. For a discussion of various arguments that the Constitution means no limit on delegation, see Schoenbrod, "Consent of the Governed."

The precedents and authorities I have cited against delegation all pertain to rules of private conduct arising under Article I. Yet, federal rules of private conduct can arise under authority other than Article I. Article IV states, "The Congress shall have Power to dispose of and make all needful Rules and Regulations respecting the Territory or other Property belonging to the United States." US Const. art. 4, § 3, cl. 2. In addition, national accountability may well not be appropriate for rules applying only to territories.

31. See 42 USC § 7409(b)(1) (2012).

32. Clean Air Amendments of 1970, Pub. L. No. 91-604, § 109(b)(1), 84 Stat. 1676, 1680.

33. David Schoenbrod, *Power Without Responsibility*, 65–67. Congress knew that the Environmental Protection Agency could not protect public health completely.

34. For a fuller discussion of how Congress claimed credit and ducked blame in the Clean Air Act, see Schoenbrod, *Saving Our Environment from Washington*, 23–38.

35. See, for example, Aldred's Case 77 Eng. Rep. 816, 820–21 (K.B. 1610); and Oliver Wendell Holmes, *The Common Law*, ed. Mark DeWolfe Howe (1881; New York City: Little, Brown & Co. 1963): 87–88.

36. See, for example, Ronald M. Dworkin, "Is Law a System of Rules?," in *Essays in*

Legal Philosophy, ed. Robert S. Summers (Oxford, UK: Oxford University Press, 1968), 25, 52.

37. See, for example, Ronald Dworkin, "Hard Cases," *Harvard Law Review* 88 (1975): 1058–60.

38. William N. Eskridge, Philip P. Fricke, and Elizabeth Garrett, *Legislation and Statutory Interpretation* (St. Paul, MN: Foundation Press, 2006). Congress could call on an agency to interpret a rule stated in a statute. For example, a statute might require that, starting five years hence, no fossil-fueled power plant may emit sulfur at more than half the current average emission rate for such plants and direct the agency to issue a binding regulation stating the future limit in numerical terms. The agency would need to interpret and apply the statute, but Congress would have faced the salient policy choices. The agency would be applying a rule rather than making it.

39. Lawrence Lessig, *Fidelity & Constraint: How the Supreme Court Has Read the American Constitution* (Oxford, UK: Oxford University Press, 2019), 17.

40. Lessig, *Fidelity & Constraint*, 5.

41. Lessig, *Fidelity & Constraint*, 451 (emphasis added).

42. See *Brown v. Thomson*, 462 US 835, 842–43 (1983); *Reynolds v. Sims*, 377 US 533, 566 (1964); Sandra M. Stevenson and Wendy Van Wie, *Antieau on Local Government Law*, 2nd ed. (New York: Matthew Bender Elite Products, 2019), § 86.04(2); and John P. Ludington, Annotation, *Constitutionality of Legislative Apportionment: Supreme Court Cases*, 77 L. Ed. 2d 1496 (2012).

43. Lawrence Gene Sager, "Fair Measure: The Legal Status of Underenforced Constitutional Norms," *Harvard Law Review* 91 (1978): 1221; and US Const. amend. XIV, § 1.

44. Gene Sager, "Fair Measure," 1215, 1263–64 (internal quotation marks omitted).

45. Gene Sager, "Fair Measure," 1216.

46. Gene Sager, "Fair Measure," 1216–17.

47. Gene Sager, "Fair Measure," 1221. "The limited judicial construct which [federal tribunals] have fashioned or accepted . . . does not derive from a judgment about the scope of the constitutional concept itself."

48. Gene Sager, "Fair Measure."

49. Professor Lessig does mention *A. L. A. Schechter Poultry Corp. v. United States* and *Panama Refining Company v. Ryan* but does not use his model to analyze them. See Lessig, *Fidelity & Constraint*, 88–89, 92–93.

50. As justices sometimes state, "The Constitution . . . is not a suicide pact." *Kennedy v. Mendoza-Martinez*, 372 US 144, 160 (1963).

51. *Mistretta v. United States*, 488 US 361, 372 (1989).

52. *Wayman v. Southard*, 23 US (10 Wheat.) 1 (1825).

53. *Wayman*, 23 US at 31.

54. *Wayman*, 23 US at 42.

55. *Wayman*, 23 US at 43.

56. *Wayman*, 23 US at 45.

57. See, generally, Gary Lawson, "Mr. Gorsuch, Meet Mr. Marshall: A Private-Law Framework for the Public-Law Puzzle of Subdelegation" (working paper, Boston University School of Law and Legal Theory, Boston, MA, May 2020), https://papers.ssrn.com/sol3/papers.cfm?abstract_id=3607159.

58. See Lessig, *Fidelity & Constraint*, 42, 154–57. Thus, the Court cannot seem to be acting politically rather than judicially.

59. *J. W. Hampton Jr. & Co. v. United States*, 276 US 394 (1928).

60. *J. W. Hampton*, 276 US at 409 (internal quotations omitted).

61. *Gundy*, 139 S. Ct. at 2139 (Gorsuch, J., dissenting).

62. Schoenbrod, "Consent of the Governed."

63. David Schoenbrod, "The Delegation Doctrine: Could the Court Give It Substance?," *Michigan Law Review* 83 (1985): 1230.

64. Schoenbrod, "The Delegation Doctrine," 1231 (cited with approval in *Gundy*, 139 S. Ct. at 2140 (Gorsuch, J., dissenting)); *Department of Transportation v. Association of American Railroads*, 575 US 43, 79 (2015) (Thomas, J., concurring in the judgment); and *Printz v. United States*, 521 US 898, 927 (1997).

65. *Panama Refining Company*, 293 US at 431.

66. *A. L. A. Schechter Poultry Corp. v. United States*, 295 US 495, 529–42 (1935).

67. *A. L. A. Schechter Poultry Corp.*, 295 US at 553.

68. See, for example, *Yakus v. United States*, 321 US 414 (1944); and *Sunshine Anthracite Coal Co. v. Adkins*, 310 US 381 (1940).

69. See Lessig, *Fidelity & Constraint*, 450.

70. Lessig, *Fidelity & Constraint*, 452.

71. *Carter v. Carter Coal Co.*, 298 US 238, 310–12 (1936) (citing *A. L. A. Schechter Poultry Corp.*, 295 US at 537).

72. Franklin D. Roosevelt, "March 9, 1937: Fireside Chat 9: On 'Court-Packing,'" University of Virginia, Miller Center, March 9, 1937, https://millercenter.org/the-presidency/presidential-speeches/march-9-1937-fireside-chat-9-court-packing.

73. See James F. Simon, *FDR and Chief Justice Hughes: The President, the Supreme Court, and the Epic Battle over the New Deal* (New York City: Simon & Schuster, 2012), 312–15.

74. Simon, *FDR and Chief Justice Hughes*, 333–34.

75. One of the Court's changes of position was derisively labeled the "switch in time that saved nine," suggesting it was to stop the court-packing plan, but the evidence shows that the change was decided on before the president announced his plan, though made public afterward. Simon, *FDR and Chief Justice Hughes*, 327.

76. Chief Justice Charles Evans Hughes worked to frame decisions to minimize the likelihood of the Court's independence being crimped. See Simon, *FDR and Chief Justice Hughes*, 299–300, 302–6, 323–29, 332, 335–37, 392. For another example, see Justice Felix Frankfurter's opinion in *Colegrove v. Green*, 328 US 549, 553–54 (1946) (plurality op.).

77. A recent article claims, "There never was a time in which the courts used the nondelegation to limit legislative delegations of power." Keith E. Whittington and Jason Iuliano, "The Myth of the Nondelegation," *University of Pennsylvania Law Review* 165 (2017): 381, 384–87, 402, 429. The article does not mention *United States v. L. Cohen Grocery Company*, *Knickerbocker Ice Co. v. Stewart*, or *Washington v. Dawson* and downplays the aspects of *Panama Refining*, *A. L. A. Schechter Poultry*, and *Carter* that are unhelpful to the article's thesis.

78. See Richard B. Stewart, "Beyond Delegation Doctrine," *American University Law Review* 36 (1987): 327.

79. See Lessig, *Fidelity & Constraint*, 172, 192–94, 196–204. "If [Justice] Jackson's view was that the Court couldn't enforce the limits of the Constitution because he couldn't craft a judicially administrable rule, that left open the possibility that other, more creative, Justices could do so later."

80. Lessig, *Fidelity & Constraint*, 269.

81. Lessig, *Fidelity & Constraint*, 85–90, 357–63, 431.

82. Professor Bruce Ackerman argues there was such opposition. Bruce A. Ackerman, *We the People: Foundations* (Cambridge, MA: Belknap Press, 1991), 306–11; and Bruce A. Ackerman, "The Storrs Lectures: Discovering the Constitution," *Yale Law Journal* 93 (1984): 1013, 1053–57, 1070–71.

83. David R. Mayhew, *The Imprint of Congress* (New Haven, CT: Yale University Press, 2017), 7–8.

84. For his curriculum vitae, see David Mayhew, "David R. Mayhew, Sterling Professor of Political Science Emeritus, Yale University—February 2018," https://cpb-us-w2.wpmucdn.com/campuspress.yale.edu/dist/5/444/files/2019/01/mayhew_david-CV-short-2019-09-1wy3amj.pdf.

85. Mayhew, *The Imprint of Congress*, 8.

86. *Washington Post*, "70 Former U.S. Senators."

87. Schoenbrod, "Consent of the Governed," 248–53 (using air pollution as an example). Congress has failed to update almost all the environmental statutes for 30 years or longer, even though experience in the relatively new and rapidly evolving field of environmental protection has revealed ways to get more environmental protection bang for the buck. See David Schoenbrod, Richard B. Stewart, and Katrina M. Wyman, *Breaking the Logjam: Environmental Protection That Will Work* (New Haven, CT: Yale University Press, 2010). We propose new statutory designs based on a project involving some 50 experts from across the ideological spectrum. When Professor Richard Stewart and I went to Capitol Hill to urge Congress to update the obsolete statutes, both Democrats and Republicans told us they wished our suggestions were in the statute books but Congress would not adopt them because legislators do not want the responsibility. David Schoenbrod, *DC Confidential: Inside the Five Tricks of Washington* (New York City: Encounter Books, 2017). If, however, legislators had to vote on major regulations, they would bear responsibility for the failures to protect the environment and the unnecessary burdens, which would give them an incentive to update the obsolete statutes to allow agencies to propose regulations that would produce more bang for the buck.

88. *Gundy*, 139 S. Ct. at 2136 (Gorsuch, J., dissenting).

89. Exec. Order No. 12,866, § 3(f)(1), 3 C.F.R. 638, 641–42 (1994), reprinted as amended in 5 USC § 601 note (2012). The provision defines "significant regulatory action" to be those regulatory actions likely to result in a rule that may: "(1) Have an annual effect on the economy of $100 million or more or adversely affect in a material way the economy, a sector of the economy, productivity, competition, jobs, the environment, public health or safety, or State, local, or tribal governments or communities; (2) Create a serious inconsistency or otherwise interfere with an action taken or planned by another agency; (3) Materially alter the budgetary impact of entitlements, grants, user fees, or loan programs or the rights and obligations of recipients thereof; or (4) Raise novel legal or policy issues arising out of legal mandates, the President's

priorities, or the principles set forth in this Executive order."

90. "The Court will not pass upon a constitutional question, although properly presented by the record, if there is also present some other ground upon which the case may be disposed of." *Ashwander v. Tennessee Valley Authority*, 297 US 288, 347 (1936) (Brandeis, J., concurring). Where, however, there is no way to read the statute to narrow the agency's authority, the court can strike an agency's action on constitutional grounds. For example, see *Horne v. Department of Agriculture*, 135 S. Ct. 2419, 2428 (2015). It held that the reserve requirement imposed on growers by the Raisin Administrative Committee of the Department of Agriculture constituted "a clear physical taking." Consider the possibility that a regulatory action deemed significant imposes regulation of private conduct but fails to state the rule. Such would be the case if, for example, a significant regulatory action under the Clean Air Act forbids "unreasonable" pollution. Such a regulation fails to state the rule of conduct but rather leaves its definition to the enforcement process. In that case, Congress' approval of the promulgation of the regulation action cannot be an approval of the yet-to-be-defined rule of private conduct. Congress would not have taken responsibility for the rule.

91. An example could have been the case challenging on delegation grounds the emergency tariffs that President Donald Trump imposed on steel imports. *American Institute for International Steel v. United States*, 806 F. App'x 982, 984 (Fed. Cir. 2020), *cert denied*, 139 S. Ct. 2748 (US June 22, 2020) (No. 18-1317). The tariff rule was imposed by an executive order, and the executive order that calls for agency rules to be identified as significant does not apply to executive orders. See the section "Omissions of the Test" in this chapter.

92. *Reynolds v. Sims*, 377 US 533, 586 (1964); and Saikrishna Bangalore Prakash, "The Sky Will Not Fall: Managing the Transition to a Revitalized Nondelegation Doctrine," in *The Administrative State Before the Supreme Court: Perspectives on the Nondelegation Doctrine*, ed. Peter J. Wallison and John Yoo (Washington, DC: AEI Press, 2022).

93. Schoenbrod, "Consent of the Governed," 259–65 (explaining why this test would be manageable and citing Exec. Order No. 12,866, § 3(f)(1), 3 C.F.R. 638, 641–42 (1994), *reprinted as amended in* 5 USC § 601 note (2012)).

94. Schoenbrod, "Consent of the Governed."

95. The test also, of course, requires distinguishing the making of a rule from interpreting or applying it. That distinction rides in the first instance on a difference of kind, as discussed in the section "Congress Must Take Responsibility for the Law" of this chapter, and so is judicially manageable. Schoenbrod, "The Delegation Doctrine," 1224. Of course, the state-the-law test also requires that the rule be understandable, and understandability is a question of degree. That, however, is like a question courts do decide in void-for-vagueness cases, in which the Court is concerned with not only the failure of the legislature to do its lawmaking job but also its failure to make understandable to the public what conduct is criminal. See, for example, *United States v. L. Cohen Grocery Company*, 255 US 81 (1921); *Papachristou v. City of Jacksonville*, 405 US 156, 168–70 (1972); and *Smith v. Goguen*, 415 US 566, 575 (1974). Moreover, the issue would be the understandability of a rule of conduct, which is a much less abstract issue than the sufficiency under the intelligible-principle test of the goals and boundaries that supposedly guide an agency in making rules of conduct. The new test would be judicially manageable even under

the strict concept of manageability that *Rucho* used to find that the courts could not judge claims of unfair partisan gerrymandering. The majority found that claims of political gerrymandering "have proved far more difficult to adjudicate" than those claiming violations of the one-person, one-vote rule. "The basic reason is that, while it is illegal for a jurisdiction to depart from the one-person, one-vote rule, or to engage in racial discrimination in districting, 'a jurisdiction may engage in [some] constitutional political gerrymandering.'" *Rucho*, 139 S. Ct. at 2497, 2500–2 (quoting *Hunt v. Cromartie*, 526 US 541, 551 (1999)). In contrast, the meaning of the consent-of-the-governed norm is every bit as absolute as that of the one-person, one-vote norm. There are, however, constraints on complete judicial enforcement of both the one-person, one-vote norm, as discussed earlier, and the consent-of-the-governed norm.

96. "Fast-track" procedures for facilitating international trade negotiations originated with the Trade Act of 1974. Trade Act of 1974, 19 USC §§ 2191–94. The current iteration, Trade Promotion Authority (TPA), incorporates existing expedited procedures prescribed in the 1974 act regarding time limits on congressional consideration and an up-or-down vote with no amendments. Ian F. Ferguson and Christopher M. Davis, "Trade Promotion Authority (TPA): Frequently Asked Questions," Congressional Research Service, June 21, 2019, 22, https://fas.org/sgp/crs/misc/R43491.pdf. In the context of domestic base management, Congress, through intermittent grants of Base Closure and Realignment (BRAC) authority, has established temporary commissions capable of recommending base closures. Implementation of BRAC initiates by default unless Congress rejects the recommendations in their entirety within 45 days by enacting a joint resolution. Christopher T. Mann, "Base Closure and Realignment (BRAC): Background and Issues for Congress," Congressional Research Service, April 25, 2019, 2–3, https://fas.org/sgp/crs/natsec/R45705.pdf.

97. Stephen Breyer, "The Legislative Veto After Chadha," *Georgetown Law Journal* 72 (1984): 793.

98. Schoenbrod, "Consent of the Governed," 153.

99. *Harper v. Virginia Department of Taxation*, 509 US 86, 97 (1993).

100. *Harper*, 509 US at 95 (alteration in original) (quoting *Griffith v. Kentucky*, 479 US 314, 322 (1987)).

101. *Mistretta*, 488 US at 417 (Scalia, J., dissenting).

102. *Harper*, 509 US at 95 (alteration in original) (quoting *Griffith*, 479 US at 323) (internal quotation marks omitted).

103. *Harper*, 509 US at 105 (Scalia, J., concurring).

104. See David Schoenbrod, "Responsibility for Regulation Act," DC-Confidential. org, 2019, https://www.dc-confidential.org/responsibility-regulation-act/.

105. See 5 USC § 706(2)(C) (2018).

106. *Tennessee Valley Authority v. Hill*, 437 US 153, 172–73, 189–90 (1978). For a collection of other cases in which courts grant legislatures time to make the policy decisions needed to remedy violations, see David I. Levine et al., *Remedies: Public and Private*, 5th ed. (St. Paul, MN: West Academic Publishing, 2009), 372–76.

107. *Brown v. Board of Education*, 347 US 483 (1954); and *Rucho*, 139 S. Ct. at 2497.

108. See Congressional Research Service, "Shutdowns of the Federal Government: Causes, Processes, and Effects," December 10, 2018, 3, https://fas.org/sgp/crs/misc/RL34680.pdf.

109. Exec. Order No. 12,866, § 3(f)(1), 3 C.F.R. 638, 641–42 (1994), reprinted as amended in 5 USC § 601 note (2012).

110. Here are some examples. Faced with enforcing the constitutional provision that requires the president to get the Senate's consent for important appointments except "during the Recess of the Senate" but does not define "recess," the Court decided that Senate confirmation is presumptively needed if it is out of session for less than 10 days. US Const. art. II, § 2, cl. 3; and *National Labor Relations Board v. Noel Canning*, 573 US 513, 538 (2014). Faced with enforcing the Equal Protection Clause's requirement that both houses of the state legislature must be apportioned based on population, but acknowledging that some deviations from population equality may be necessary, the Court decided that population deviations of 10 percent or less were insufficient to make a prima facie case of invidious discrimination. US Const. amend. XIV, § 1; and *Brown v. Thomson*, 462 US 835, 842 (1983). Faced with enforcing the Sixth Amendment's right to a jury trial without defining the size of that jury, the Court decided that a jury with fewer than six members would impair the jury's purpose and function. US Const. amend. VI; and *Ballew v. Georgia*, 435 US 223, 239 (1978). Faced with enforcing the constitutional provision requiring probable cause for searches and seizures without defining a time-line for providing probable cause, the Court decided that determination of probable cause within 48 hours of arrest will generally comply with the Fourth Amendment's promptness requirement. US Const. amend. IV; and *County of Riverside v. McLaughlin*, 500 US 44, 56 (1991). The Court also deals with amorphous constitutional norms by adopting bright-line tests that are not numerical. For holding that police cannot initiate an interrogation after a defendant has requested counsel, see *Michigan v. Jackson*, 475 US 625, 636 (1986). For finding an exception to the Fourth Amendment's probable cause requirement for temporary detentions when there is a warrant to search a house for drugs, see *Michigan v. Summers*, 452 US 692, 699–701, 704–5 (1981).

111. Exec. Order No. 12,866, § 3(b), 3 CFR 638, 641–42 (1994), reprinted as amended in 5 USC § 601 (2012).

112. Exec. Order No. 12,866 at § 3(d). Also, the definition does not mention an impact on civil liberty as a reason to identify a rule as significant and in practice has not been applied to tariff rules. Bridget C. E. Dooling, "OIRA's Expanded Review of Tax Regulations and Its Surprising Implications," *Business, Entrepreneurship, and Tax Law Review* 3 (2019): 224, 230–35.

113. Exec. Order No. 12,866 at § 3(e).

114. *Reynolds v. Sims*, 377 US 533, 566 (1964).

115. *Rucho*, 139 S. Ct. at 2497.

116. US Const. art. II, § 1, cl. 8; US Const. art. VI, cl. 3; and Sager, "Fair Measure," 1227.

117. *Rucho*, 139 S. Ct. at 2511 (Kagan, J., dissenting).

118. *Rucho*, 139 S. Ct. at 2523 (quoting *Gill v. Whitford*, 138 S. Ct. 1916, 1941 (2018) (Kagan, J., concurring)) (internal quotation marks omitted).

119. The earliest use of the term "nondelegation doctrine" or "non-delegation doctrine" in a Supreme Court opinion is in a passage citing with approval Professor Kenneth Culp Davis' call to explicitly abandon the doctrine. *McGautha v. California*, 402 US 183, 274 (1971) (Brennan, J., dissenting) (citing Kenneth Culp Davis, *Administrative Law Treatise* (St. Paul, MN: West Publishing Co., 1958)).

Conclusion

JOHN YOO

The authors in this volume propose answers to the problem of the non-delegation doctrine. They all agree that the Constitution limits the authority that Congress can transfer to others. While the Supreme Court agrees, too, it has not rejected a federal law on nondelegation grounds since 1935.[1] As recently as 2001, the justices unanimously upheld one of the broadest delegations known to federal law, the Clean Air Act.[2] Nonetheless, five justices of the Roberts Court have expressed their intention to bring the nondelegation doctrine back from the dead.[3]

Identifying the right principle poses the first challenge to the nondelegation doctrine's resurrection. In *Gundy v. United States*, Justice Neil Gorsuch asked: "What's the test?"[4] That direct question is not as simple as it seems. It expresses a deeper concern about the proper role of the federal courts in our system of separated powers.

If the Court cannot develop a judicially manageable standard, to borrow a phrase from the political question doctrine, it could fall prey to its own policy preferences when it reviews the broad agency decisions. A conservative majority might limit economic regulation, as the per curiam Court recently did in blocking the Biden administration's nationwide moratorium on evictions. A liberal justice might restrict delegations in criminal law, as Justice Elena Kagan did in *Gundy* itself. Without a clear principle to guide courts in their application of the nondelegation doctrine, the judiciary might not only open itself up to criticism of an ideologically driven use of a vast power but also tempt itself into actually crossing the line from law into politics.

Concern over a politicized use of the nondelegation doctrine explains the efforts of several authors to articulate bright-line rules. Perhaps the best example is David Schoenbrod, who believes courts cannot enforce the nondelegation doctrine in its current form and wants Congress, if not the courts, to reject regulations that cause more than $100 million in impact on the economy. He says that the Office of Management and Budget has used this approach to successfully apply cost-benefit analysis to major regulations across presidential administrations of different parties.

Other authors seek clear distinctions where the nondelegation doctrine will not apply, which would narrow the area where judges might have difficulty ignoring their ideological preferences. John Harrison excludes from the nondelegation doctrine cases in which the government acts in the role of proprietor, while Michael Rappaport would apply a lenient nondelegation doctrine to other traditional areas of executive responsibility, such as military and foreign affairs and the distribution of appropriated funds.

Coming at the question from the side of the legislature, Mark Chenoweth and Richard Samp seek to identify "core" legislative powers that Congress cannot delegate: taxing, spending, criminal laws, policy disputes, and its ability to check the executive. These tests may not satisfy because they do not fully answer how to police delegations that occur outside these preserves. But courts might support a more aggressive nondelegation doctrine if they understood it would apply to a more limited range of statutes. Chenoweth and Samp encourage precisely this outcome in seeking greater application of a nondelegation doctrine in the remaining areas.

Others in this volume propose more flexible standards than hard-and-fast rules. Gary Lawson and Jonathan Adler develop their tests by looking to the past. Lawson would apply the 18th-century common law of agency, which he believes Chief Justice John Marshall had in mind when he first examined the delegation question in *Wayman v. Southard*.[5] Adler asks whether the Congress at the time it enacted legislation would have thought it had delegated powers over new subjects.

Todd Gaziano and Ethan Blevins borrow their test not from history but from other legal doctrines—in their case, the Court's void-for-vagueness test for unconstitutional criminal laws. Joseph Postell examines the record of the states to show courts developing nondelegation tests that go beyond the Supreme Court's intelligible-principle requirement. These chapters offer courts the reassurance of familiar common-law approaches, though they may well suffer from the faults of the common law in their unpredictability and their concentration of power in judges.

We can understand the approaches of these chapters as expressing a difference between rules and standards. All the chapters in this book agree that the current intelligible-principle test offers neither a test nor a standard because—as applied by the courts—it does not regulate conduct at all. But in the tests that the authors propose as replacements, we can detect a difference in emphasis between rules and standards.

Law and economics scholars have shown that these two types of norms can make an important difference in the operation of a regulatory system.[6] A typical example of a rule is a strict speed limit for driving a car, such as a ban on speeds faster than 55 miles per hour (mph) on interstate highways. Government could also regulate speed with a less precise standard, such as a law that prohibits driving unreasonably fast under the conditions.

Neither rules nor standards are perfect for every situation. Instead, they strike different trade-offs between economy and accuracy and between the timing of review and power. Rules are clear and easy to apply. Anyone who drives a car above 55 mph has violated the law regardless of the reason. This clear rule reduces the cost to the legal system of identifying violations, creates greater certainty and predictability, and demands less information to implement.

Rules have their downsides too. With bright-line rules, those who enforce the rule cannot craft an outcome that addresses the unique circumstances before them. A strict 55 mph rule prevents judges from considering the flow of traffic or the presence of an emergency, nor does it allow judges to cite a violator who drove recklessly but at 54 mph. A rule only allows the court to determine whether the police officer accurately measured the car's speed. Their absolute nature forces rules to sweep in too many or too few; they can be both underinclusive and overinclusive at the same time. Rules will experience higher rates of error because they cannot consider the totality of the circumstances.

Standards strike an opposing trade-off of accuracy versus economy. Acting reasonably under the circumstances allows decision makers who enforce the rule in the future to consider all the facts of the case before them. It will reduce error costs and increase the accuracy of a decision. After a judge takes up a case of speeding, he or she will hear all witnesses, take evidence about the conditions, and then balance these factors to determine whether the driver violated the reasonableness standard. The judge can exempt the driver, for example, who had good reasons for driving too fast or who posed no risk to anyone else on the road. An unreasonableness standard may avoid absurd or inefficient outcomes, but it also generates less predictability and more uncertainty over the line between legal and illegal conduct.

Standards have this feature because they grant future decision makers greater discretion than rules do. When a legislature adopts a rule, it keeps more authority for itself and restricts the power of those who would enforce the norm in the future. The writers of a 55 mph rule for speeding give little space for future police, prosecutors, and judges to adjust the application of the norm to the particular circumstances before them. The stricter the rule, the more cases that the past legislator has decided. The future enforcers are reaching the outcomes that the past legislator would have sought.

A standard has the opposite feature. Judges who apply a reasonableness standard have much greater discretion than under a 55 mph rule in applying the law to an individual case. They may or may not reach the outcomes the legislator would have intended. Between a standard and a rule, the former grants greater power to future enforcers, while the latter keeps power in the hands of the legislators of the past.

In choosing a standard or a rule, lawmakers are rendering a judgment about the quality of future decisions. If the legislature expects future executive and judicial officers to make more errors than acceptable, it should choose a rule that narrows their freedom. The rule will reduce mistakes by limiting the discretion of the inferior officials of the future and maintain authority in the hands of the present legislators who know their intentions best. A legislature might also choose a rule not because it believes in its own superiority, but because it has access to better information or can decide under less political, social, or economic pressure that might distort decision-making. Rule makers may worry that future enforcers might be prone to emotional appeals or have insufficient independence from the political passions of the day.

Conversely, legislators should adopt standards when the opposite conditions hold. If the legislature anticipates that future officials will be better trained and educated, it should choose a standard. If it expects that enforcers will have access to superior information or prove better insulated from popular passions that could distort decisions, it should choose a standard. If the legislature understands that it cannot anticipate future circumstances, it should adopt a standard. Indeed, delegation proceeds from the problem that legislators cannot legislate specifically for all future cases due to the unpredictability of circumstance.

We can see the factors involved in choosing between rules and standards at work in the chapters of this book. Schoenbrod would adopt a strict rule, such as the Office of Information and Regulatory Affairs' major impact rule, because he does not believe the courts can develop a judicially manageable test. Without a clear test, judges would have the discretion afforded by the intelligible-principle test to bless all transfers of power from Congress to the administrative state. Scholars might believe that today's judges cannot withstand the political pressure to uphold broad delegations. As several scholars have already pointed out, both Congress and the president benefit from a weak nondelegation doctrine. Congress can escape politically controversial choices, such as the level of pollutants or the cost of safety precautions, while the executive branch increases its control over policies that will bear on its popular support. Courts may have little stomach for disrupting agreements between the elected branches to share power within the province of the federal government alone.

We see this idea expressed by some of the authors—including coeditor Peter J. Wallison—in their call for judicial fortitude. "It would require an uncommon portion of fortitude in the judges to do their duty as faithful guardians of the Constitution," Alexander Hamilton wrote in *Federalist* 78, "where legislative invasions of it had been instigated by the major voice of the community."[7] Hamilton defended the judiciary's lifetime terms and irreducible salaries so the courts would have enough institutional independence to invalidate popular, yet unconstitutional, laws. As with other strict rules, this approach views modern decision-making as inferior to that of the past due to the susceptibility of today's judges and officials to contemporary political, economic, and social pressures.

This problem does not uniquely afflict the separation of powers. The counter-majoritarian difficulty has long challenged scholars, who have focused primarily on protecting the individual rights of the minority from the majority. Theorists of both the structural and individual rights provisions of the Constitution, however, share a desire to encourage greater judicial activity in policing legislation, even though it involves unelected judges disregarding the wishes of an elected majority.

Some of the authors in this volume support a rule because they would prefer to keep authority in the framers' hands rather than with contemporary officials and judges. Elevating the framers can result from a commitment to the original understanding: that we must interpret the Constitution based on the understanding of its terms held by those who wrote and ratified it. But originalism itself does not seem to dictate the nature of the test for many of the authors; rather, several use originalism to exclude certain types of delegation from judicial review.

Lawson is the only author who seeks to re-create the type of test that the founders themselves might have used: common-law principal-agent principles. There does not appear to be strong evidence, however, that American courts in fact used such an approach in the periods directly before or after the Constitution's ratification. Until Chief Justice Marshall's opinion in *Wayman*,[8] it does not appear that a federal court had to confront the question at all—and the Court would not overturn any federal law on any ground after *Marbury v. Madison*[9] until the infamous *Dred Scott v. Sandford*.[10] On the other hand, judges at the time of the framing need not have developed any significant test because the American political system did not engage in broad delegations until the rise of the progressive regulatory regime in the late 19th century. When Congress did delegate, courts would have applied common-law principal-agency law.

Instead, favoring a strict nondelegation doctrine test implies greater trust in yesterday's framers than today's judges. There could be several reasons for this judgment. Although engaged in the political process, the drafters and ratifiers acted at the level of high constitutional politics when they fought over our permanent form of government. They would have proceeded with less attachment to political, economic, and social interests than had the elected politicians who would serve under the Constitution itself. *Marbury* relies on this difference between the higher law that emerged from the constitution-making process (characterized by conventions the people specifically chose for that sole purpose) and the regular politics that would prevail in enacting legislation.

Scholars who favor a strict nondelegation test believe that today's legislators cannot match the founders' disinterestedness in deciding what powers should reside in Congress and which it can delegate to agencies. Today's judges may inhabit a world that discounts the founders' constitutional design in favor of a modern technocratic bureaucracy. They might experience a great deal of political and professional pressure to refrain from interfering in an administrative state constructed by the elected branches of government—with judicial concurrence—over a century. They might adopt the leading theory, prevalent for much of that century, that the judicial role should focus on protecting individual rights from majority oppression rather than policing the separation of powers and federalism.[11]

Arrayed against these concerns, however, are the factors that support the use of standards. The world before us presents economic and social complexities that the founders could not have anticipated. Technology has made possible an industrial revolution and now an information revolution that has reduced the costs of producing, transporting, and using goods and services. People, products, and capital move easily across interstate and even international borders. As the nation's economy nationalized and then globalized, the demands for government regulation followed. In a policymaking environment so radically different from that of the founding, today's officials will have superior training and better information to strike the optimal balance between legislative and executive lawmaking for a 21st-century economy and society.

While a strict test for nondelegation might find support in the logic of *Marbury*, a loose standard would draw from *McCulloch v. Maryland*. In resting the constitutionality of a national bank on the necessary and proper clause, Chief Justice Marshall observed that the "Constitution [is] intended to endure for ages to come, and consequently to be adapted to the various crises of human affairs."[12] He resisted the notion of a strict test for the necessary and proper clause: "To have prescribed the means by which Government should, in all future time, execute its powers would have been to change entirely the character of the instrument and give it the properties of a legal code."[13] Expressing the context when a standard should prevail over a rule, he observed, "It would have been an unwise attempt to provide by immutable rules for exigencies which, if foreseen at all, must have been seen dimly, and which can be best provided for as they occur."[14]

Several factors thus may influence the justices when they decide whether to adopt a rule or a standard for any resurrected nondelegation doctrine. They will balance how much power they wish to grant current decision makers or whether to privilege the framers' view. They will have to judge whether an increase in decision costs is worth the reduction in errors. They will decide whether they value predictability and certainty over flexibility. One last issue that may also influence the choice, but which does not arise as often in the common-law context, is the effect of a rule versus standard on the Court's standing in the current political context.

These are the concerns that motivate the chapters by Judge Douglas Ginsburg and Saikrishna Bangalore Prakash. Both address the transition from a toothless nondelegation doctrine to one that involves a greater judicial role in policing transfers of authority from Congress to the agencies. I believe it fair to say that they expect the Court will encounter more success with a stricter nondelegation doctrine if it does not invalidate any popular statutes that sit at the core of the power wielded by the administrative state. Invalidating a minor law that creates a sex offender list is one thing; striking down the Clean Water Act is another. Implicit in this view is that the Roberts Court—like the Hughes Court of 1936–37—could well shy away from a broader nondelegation project if it were to encounter fierce political criticism and resistance.

On this point, from an institutional perspective, a standard might prove more helpful to the Court than a rule. A standard allows judges to take all circumstances into account when arriving at an outcome. In the common law, this characteristic encompasses all the facts of the case. But in our federal system, with its separation of powers and limited judicial role, it might also include the political circumstances of the case and the Court's institutional position in relation to the elected branches.

A standard could allow the Court to moderate its revival of the nondelegation doctrine by applying it to narrower circumstances. It could find newer regulations under the Clean Air and Clean Water Acts, such as nationwide efforts to control greenhouse gases, as beyond the law's scope, without threatening older rules governing pollution from factories or cars. A standard would allow the Court to examine recent, broader rules without having to identify any single factor or authority as dispositive in a totality of the circumstances test that seeks to measure regulations against a norm of nondelegation.

Critics would attack such an approach as standardless, unpredictable, and ripe for policymaking. The Court, however, has often used balancing tests to judge important separation-of-powers disputes. In *Morrison v. Olson*, for example, the Court upheld the independent counsel law because it found that the government's need for a protected investigation into high-ranking government officials outweighed any intrusion into the president's control over law enforcement officials.[15] *Mistretta v. United States* used the same balancing test to shield the Sentencing Commission from attack as a violation of the judicial role in the separation of powers.[16] In *United States v. Nixon*, the Court held that the judiciary's need to enforce the Watergate defendants' Sixth Amendment right to exculpatory evidence outweighed the president's right to executive privilege.[17]

Justice Antonin Scalia and conservative legal scholars criticized the majorities in *Morrison* and *Mistretta* for employing standards that could allow the Court to uphold or strike down any government arrangement it pleased. In his well-known essay "The Rule of Law as a Law of Rules," Justice Scalia even charged that standards undermined the rule of law in our limited constitutional system by arrogating excessive power to the judiciary.[18] Liberal scholars and judges, however, defended these outcomes because they deferred to the political branches in their construction of the administrative state. Indeed, conservative judges cannot extinguish standards from constitutional law; they seem demanded by the Fourth Amendment's bar on unreasonable searches and seizures and the Fifth and 14th Amendments' guarantee of due process.

While standards might undermine a system of predictable constitutional rules, they might also give the Court the political leeway to advance norms that are true to the original constitutional design. Balancing tests allow the Court to take into account not just the law and facts of the disputes at hand but also the political system's response to more aggressive enforcement of the separation of powers. After each decision, it can measure whether its outcomes rest within the boundaries acceptable to the political system.

Positive political theory would observe that the Court has the freedom to enforce such a norm within the range of preferences held by a blocking minority of the Congress. In other words, a Court decision striking down a rule on nondelegation grounds will survive so long as 40 percent of the

Senate—the number necessary to mount a successful filibuster—is willing to accept judicial enforcement of the nondelegation doctrine in a particular case. A majority on the Court, however, will have difficulty, ex ante, identifying where those boundaries lie.

A gradual, common law–like process of enforcing a standards-based test in cases of extreme delegation will allow the Court to gather information on the range of preferences the system can tolerate. As it continues to expand the reach of the nondelegation doctrine, the Court could gradually transform its standard into a stricter rule that can gain the agreement of a majority of the justices, without triggering a political backlash.

This process has occurred, for example, with the conflict between the president's Article II removal power and Congress' necessary and proper clause authority to structure the government agencies. As well debated elsewhere, the president and Congress have long struggled over the president's right to control law enforcement through his or her ability to remove subordinate officials—a power that Article II does not specifically ascribe to the chief executive. Congress has sought to insulate officials, especially those of the so-called independent agencies, from presidential control for a variety of reasons, ranging from protecting technical expertise from political influence to balancing presidential control with legislative oversight.

After *Morrison* upheld the controversial independent counsel law with a balancing test, a majority of justice began to return to the stricter rule—first set out by Chief Justice William Howard Taft in *Myers v. United States*[19]—that Congress could not place conditions on the president's removal power. It began with a series of cases that addressed inconsequential laws, such as the statute governing the DC airport system,[20] and then cases in the Coast Guard Court of Criminal Appeals.[21] Only in the past decade has the Court struck down efforts to insulate important executive officials—most recently, the head of the Consumer Financial Protection Bureau in *Seila Law v. Consumer Financial Protection Bureau*.[22] The earlier cases allowed the Court to realize there would be little challenge to its steady expansion of the *Myers* approach, and indeed now the Court has limited the protection for the independent agencies blessed by *Humphrey's Executor v. United States*[23] to the facts of those cases. Three decades after *Morrison*, it appears the Court will use the strict test of *Myers* to invalidate any effort by Congress to create a new executive office outside the direct removal power of the president.

As the justices consider the tests offered by the chapters in this book, they may initially favor a standard that appears lawless, unpredictable, and open to manipulation. But a standard might allow the Court today to reach the norm, in a course of decisions, held by the founders for the proper division between congressional lawmaking and presidential execution. At first, such a test would grant significant discretion to the justices as they coalesce around the norm, even as they identify for themselves the reasons for supporting it. Some may do so because they believe it expresses the original understanding, while others may conclude that it advances contemporary values of democratic accountability.

A standard will allow the Court to slowly advance a revitalized nondelegation doctrine through minor cases at first, such as *Gundy* itself, while it gathers information on the effects of its decisions on the administrative state, the judiciary, and their relationships with the elected branches. This will call on the Supreme Court to exercise significant resources in its own decision costs and monitor the lower courts and the agencies. As it gains more experience, the Court can adjust its standard and modify balancing tests into a stricter rule that will prove more predictable and easier to administer. In the end, the nondelegation doctrine may not have to choose between standards and rules, as proposed in the chapters of this book, but instead gradually evolve from the former to the latter as the norm takes firmer root in the constitutional law of the 21st century.

Notes

1. *A. L. A. Schechter Poultry Corp. v. United States*, 295 US 495 (1935).

2. *Whitman v. American Trucking Associations*, 531 US 457 (2001).

3. *Gundy v. United States*, 139 S. Ct. 2116, 2131 (2019) (Gorsuch, J., dissenting); *Gundy*, 139 S. Ct. at 2131 (Alito, J., concurring in the judgment); and *Paul v. United States*, 140 S. Ct. 342, 342 (2019) (opinion by Kavanaugh, J.).

4. *Gundy*, 139 S. Ct. at 2135 (Gorsuch, J., dissenting).

5. *Wayman v. Southard*, 23 US (10 Wheat.) 1 (1825).

6. See, for example, Richard A. Epstein, *Simple Rules for a Complex World* (Cambridge, MA: Harvard University Press, 1995), 30–36; and Louis Kaplow, "Rules Versus

Standards: An Economic Analysis," *Duke Law Journal* 42, no. 3 (1992): 557, https://scholarship.law.duke.edu/dlj/vol42/iss3/2/.

7. *Federalist*, no. 78 (Alexander Hamilton).

8. *Wayman*, 23 US at 1.

9. *Marbury v. Madison*, 5 US (1 Cranch) 137 (1803).

10. *Dred Scott v. Sandford*, 60 US 393 (1857).

11. See, for example, John Hart Ely, *Democracy and Distrust: A Theory of Judicial Review* (Cambridge, MA: Harvard University Press, 1980); and Jesse H. Choper, *Judicial Review and the National Political Process: A Functional Reconsideration of the Role of the Supreme Court* (Chicago: University of Chicago Press, 1980).

12. *McCulloch v. Maryland*, 17 US (4 Wheat.) 316, 415 (1819).

13. *McCulloch*, 17 US at 415.

14. *McCulloch*, 17 US at 415.

15. *Morrison v. Olson*, 487 US 654 (1988).

16. *Mistretta v. United States*, 488 US 361 (1989).

17. *United States v. Nixon*, 418 US 683 (1974).

18. Antonin Scalia, "The Rule of Law as a Law of Rules," *University of Chicago Law Review* 56, no. 4 (1989): 1175, https://chicagounbound.uchicago.edu/uclrev/vol56/iss4/1/.

19. *Myers v. United States*, 272 US 52 (1926).

20. *Metropolitan Washington Airports Authority v. Citizens for the Abatement of Airport Noise*, 501 US 252 (1991).

21. *Edmond v. United States*, 520 US 651 (1997).

22. *Seila Law v. Consumer Financial Protection Bureau*, 140 S. Ct. 2183 (2020).

23. *Humphrey's Executor v. United States*, 295 US 602 (1935).

About the Authors

Jonathan H. Adler is the Johan Verheij Memorial Professor of Law and the director of Coleman P. Burke Center for Environmental Law at Case Western Reserve University School of Law.

Ethan Blevins is a litigator at Pacific Legal Foundation specializing in separation of powers and free speech matters.

Mark Chenoweth is executive director and general counsel of the New Civil Liberties Alliance. He has formed his administrative state views from perches in all four branches of the federal government—as chief of staff to a member of Congress, as legal counsel to a Consumer Product Safety commissioner, as attorney adviser in the Office of Legal Policy at the US Department of Justice, and as law clerk to Judge Danny Boggs on the US Court of Appeals for the Sixth Circuit. He is a graduate of Yale College and the University of Chicago Law School.

Todd Gaziano is chief of legal policy and strategic research and director of the Center for the Separation of Powers at the Pacific Legal Foundation. He was counsel of record for the foundation's amicus brief in *Gundy v. United States*.

Douglas H. Ginsburg is a judge on the United States Court of Appeals for the District of Columbia Circuit. After studying at Cornell University and the University of Chicago Law School, he clerked for Justice Thurgood Marshall on the United States Supreme Court. Thereafter, Judge Ginsburg was a professor at the Harvard Law School, then assistant attorney general for the Antitrust Division of the Department of Justice. He was appointed to the court in 1986, and while on the bench, he has taught at the law schools of the University of Chicago, Columbia University, and New York University. He is currently professor of law at the Antonin Scalia Law

School at George Mason University and a visiting professor at University College London, Faculty of Laws. Judge Ginsburg recently completed filming a three-part series on the Constitution—*A More or Less Perfect Union*—currently being broadcast on PBS stations and available streaming from PBS.org and the FreeToChooseNetwork.org.

John Harrison is the James Madison Distinguished Professor and Thomas F. Bergin Teaching Professor at the University of Virginia School of Law.

Gary Lawson is the Philip S. Beck Professor at Boston University School of Law.

Joseph Postell is an associate professor of politics at Hillsdale College. He is the author of *Bureaucracy in America: The Administrative State's Challenge to Constitutional Government* (University of Missouri Press, 2017).

Saikrishna Bangalore Prakash is the James Monroe Distinguished Professor of Law, the Albert Clark Tate Jr. Professor of Law, and a Miller Center senior fellow at the University of Virginia.

Michael B. Rappaport is the Hugh and Hazel Darling Foundation Professor of Law and the director of the Center for the Study of Constitutional Originalism at the University of San Diego School of Law.

Richard Samp is a senior litigation counsel at the New Civil Liberties Alliance. Throughout his 40-year career in private law practice in Washington, DC—including more than 30 years as chief counsel for the Washington Legal Foundation—Samp has specialized in appellate litigation with a focus on constitutional law. He has participated directly in more than 200 cases before the US Supreme Court. Samp is a graduate of Harvard College and the University of Michigan Law School and clerked for a federal judge in Detroit.

David Schoenbrod is Trustee Professor of Law at New York Law School and a senior fellow at the Niskanen Center.

Peter J. Wallison is a senior fellow emeritus at the American Enterprise Institute, where he studies constitutional law and the growth of the administrative state (that is, the increasing power of unelected officials of executive branch agencies).

John Yoo is a nonresident senior fellow at the American Enterprise Institute; Emanuel S. Heller Professor of Law at the University of California, Berkeley; and a visiting fellow at the Hoover Institution.